Daughters of Erebus

Daughters of Erebus

Paul Holmes

Hodder Moa

National Library of New Zealand Cataloguing-in-Publication Data
Holmes, Paul, 1950-
Daughters of Erebus / Paul Holmes.
Includes bibliographical references and index.
ISBN 978-1-86971-250-1
1. Collins family. 2. Aircraft accidents—Antarctica—Erebus, Mount.
I. Title.
363.124109989—dc 22

A Hodder Moa Book
Published in 2011 by Hachette New Zealand Ltd
4 Whetu Place, Mairangi Bay
Auckland, New Zealand
www.hachette.co.nz

Designed and produced by Hachette New Zealand Ltd

Printed by Griffin Press, Australia

MIX
Paper from responsible sources
FSC
www.fsc.org
FSC® C009448

The paper this book is printed on is certified against the Forest Stewardship Council® Standards. Griffin Press holds FSC chain of custody certification SGS-COC-005088. FSC promotes environmentally responsible, socially beneficial and economically viable management of the world's forests

For those who died and for those who struggle still.

And for my father, Henry Holmes, 2NZEF 1940–1945,
who taught me to care for the underdog.

From the masthead the mirage is continually giving us false alarms. Everything wears an aspect of unreality. Icebergs hang upside down in the sky; the land appears as layers of silvery or golden cloud. Cloud banks look like land, icebergs masquerade as islands or nunataks, and the distant barrier to the south is thrown into view, although it really is outside our range of vision. Worst of all is the deceptive appearance of open water, caused by the refraction of distant water, or by the sun shining at an angle on a field of smooth snow or the face of ice cliffs below the horizon.

— Sir Ernest Shackleton, *South*,
on the deceptions of polar light

But in this case, the palpably false sections of evidence which I heard could not have been the result of mistake, or faulty recollection. They originated, I am compelled to say, in a predetermined plan of deception. They were very clearly part of an attempt to conceal a series of disastrous administrative blunders and so, in regard to the particular items of evidence to which I have referred, I am forced reluctantly to say that I had to listen to an orchestrated litany of lies.

— Justice Peter Mahon, paragraph 377,
Aircraft Accident Report

No time was ever wasted making a really close study of something.

— Peter Mahon, writing to his son Sam, May 1980

Contents

Foreword

Paul Holmes has written the book on the Erebus scandal that has been crying out to be written ever since some members of the old Air New Zealand management got away with the greatest cover-up and wrongful passing of blame in New Zealand's history. He possesses the gift of being able to convey a complex story in a clear but gripping manner which previous writers, regrettably including myself, have lacked.

In 2010, I took a phone call. It was Paul Holmes on the line. My initial bewilderment at why the media should be contacting me quickly turned to interested anticipation when he told me he was writing a book about the disastrous crash of an Air New Zealand DC-10 on a sightseeing flight in Antarctica.

I had long respected Paul as an insightful, empathetic and fair interviewer. I considered his newspaper columns balanced and written in a way that conveyed essential points clearly and succinctly. One of these had been a column he'd written in 2009 for the anniversary of the crash which made it clear he had mastered the essentials of the story.

My interest in the case had arisen during the Christmas holidays of 1981–1982 when I read a copy of the decision of the Court of Appeal. The more I studied the material relating to the disaster, the more concerned I was. It became clear the Erebus affair was a dreadful scandal.

In the Erebus case there were many participants involved — the witnesses for Air New Zealand management, the Office of Air Accidents Investigation, the Civil Aviation Division, even the highest court of the country, the Privy Council.

Now, so long after the event, there was the prospect of Paul Holmes bringing the whole terrible truth to the general public. I hadn't the slightest doubt he would present the facts in readable form better than anyone else I could think of.

I made available to him all the Erebus research material I had. This included the evidence and submissions given to the Royal Commission together with the additional papers involved in the Court of Appeal and Privy Council cases and the Washington case — 26 volumes in all.

Paul spent over a year carrying out meticulous research. It all seemed too good to be true to read each gripping chapter. The speed at which he mastered the facts and produced chapter after riveting chapter was breathtaking. He was objectively critical about what he wrote and sent me revision after revision of the chapters.

As a friend of many of the insiders of that time, he was well placed to obtain an insight into the working of the establishment. These friends include Richard Griffin, who for five years was press secretary to former Prime Minister Jim Bolger, and who served 15 years in the Parliamentary Press Gallery. Maurice Williamson, MP, was another source. Williamson worked for the airline at the time and told Paul how he watched as documents which should have been produced in evidence were in fact being shredded.

Paul has also been able to reveal other damning evidence hitherto suppressed. All this new material has been recorded during in-depth tape-recorded interviews with, amongst others, former Air New Zealand employees, a mountaineer and two serving police inspectors.

By January 2011, a time of year when most people's thoughts are focused on relaxation, the chapters continued to arrive. I was excited at the thought of the long overdue righting of a terrible wrong. I emailed him: 'Atta Boy, take no holidays.'

Stuart Macfarlane
Retired Law Lecturer
Auckland

Acknowledgements

What happened on the northern slope of Ross Island that day 32 years ago to cause the DC-10 to collide with Mount Erebus was really very simple. Yet the reading is very complicated and much of what was understood at the time, especially regarding mindsets, polar visual deceptions and the dishonesty of the government, its agencies and the airline itself, in their various ways, was new to me. Nevertheless, everything we need to know is in the literature of the time, all there to be mined.

I could not have written this without the support of the Collins girls: Maria, Kathryn (now Kathryn Carter), Elizabeth, Philippa (whom they call Pip) and Adrienne (whom they call Didi). They are central to our story. I thank you all for your help. I hope my efforts will bring comfort to your hearts. I thank Elizabeth for generously allowing me to use her own biographical material, which she wrote some years back. Where I have used Elizabeth's material I have, of course, acknowledged it. For the chapter about Maria's parents, I am deeply indebted to Elizabeth's memoir. Thank you. To all of the Collins women, thank you for trusting me with your stories and your lives.

And to Maria, the great battler for the name of her husband, thank you for the access to your vivid memories of the time of the disaster. And to Kathryn, who carries on with determination her own battle for the good name of her father, thank you for your friendship and the warm Friday nights in your family home.

There are many people who have supported the Collins family and who have never stopped believing that Captain Jim Collins and First Officer Greg Cassin were blameless that day on the mountain, as Justice Peter Mahon so clearly and brilliantly established 30 years ago.

Retired DC-10 Captain Arthur Cooper was welcoming and generous when I went to see him. Arthur's knowledge of DC-10 flying and his verbal portraits of so many of those involved were shrewd and incisive.

Inspectors Stu Leighton and Greg Gilpin of the New Zealand Police were happy to share memories, not only of the body recovery on the mountain conducted in the extreme Antarctic conditions but also, in the case of Greg Gilpin, of the finding and subsequent mysterious story of Captain Collins's ring binder.

Sam Mahon, though we never did get to meet each other, was generous both in his encouragement and his correspondence. His mother, Mrs Margarita Mahon, was cheerful, gracious, generous and wise. She helped greatly in my understanding of Peter Mahon.

But the giant upon whose shoulders I stood and relied was retired law lecturer Stuart Macfarlane. Stuart Macfarlane is a walking authority on the Erebus disaster and his weighty tome *The Erebus Papers*, published in 1991, is nothing less than the Erebus encyclopaedia. No serious study of Erebus can be undertaken without a copy of this book at an author's side. Stuart's wife and collaborator, Alison, says that after Stuart read the Court of Appeal decision on Mahon and decided the Court was being 'silly', he didn't come home for dinner for about eight years, working, as he was, on what became his impossibly exhaustive *The Erebus Papers*. There is nothing Stuart Macfarlane does not know about the Erebus incident in terms of the accident itself and the subsequent inquiries. Stuart and Alison did their best to answer any question I may have been stuck on. It was Stuart who wrote the epilogue to Gordon Vette's book *Impact Erebus* back in the early eighties. He also wrote the scrupulously detailed and brilliantly researched 'Notes on the Text' between pages 299 and 347 of Vette's book. Stuart also constructed the book's photographic essay of the final minutes of the fatal flight using passenger photographs. Stuart held nothing back from me. Thank you, Stuart and Alison Macfarlane. Stuart was Mahon's greatest ally. I'm not sure, from what Stuart has told me about meetings with him, that Mahon ever understood that.

Thanks to Squire Speedy for his passenger's map from the first Air New Zealand Antarctic flight.

My wife Deborah endured the long months of silence as I sat hour after hour at my desk submerged in books and documents, sometimes not typing or even uttering a word for hours, trying to make sense of this whole great, heart-breaking thing. She put lunch under my nose when I completely forgot to eat and, often, dinner.

Thanks to Antarctica New Zealand, Professor Nigel Roberts, Stuart Macfarlane and Gordon Vette for the use of your photographs.

Thank you to Paul Davison QC for sharing his memories of that extraordinary Royal Commission of Inquiry at which he and other counsel worked so hard to establish the truth.

And, finally, thank you to my publisher at Hachette New Zealand, Kevin

Chapman. When I took to him the idea of a book about the Erebus disaster, much of it from the point of view of Captain Collins's wife and daughters, and done with a view to demonstrating once and for all the blamelessness of the captain, he embraced the idea immediately. He felt it was an important endeavour. His encouragement when I sent the odd chapter to him was greatly appreciated. And thanks to his long-suffering editorial director, Warren Adler, who demonstrated infinite patience with an author who likes to tinker. Right to the end.

I have done my best to eliminate mistakes or misunderstandings. The views in this book are my own — as, of course, are any errors.

Paul Holmes.
Mana Lodge, Poukawa
March 2011

The Cast

Kathryn Carter (nee Collins) **Elizabeth Collins** **Philippa (Pip) Collins** **Adrienne (Didi) Collins**	Daughters of Jim and Maria Collins. Daughters of Erebus.
Maria Collins	Wife of Captain Jim Collins and mother of their four children.
Captain Jim Collins	Commander of Flight TE901, the DC-10 that crashed on Ross Island.
Margarita Mahon	Wife of Peter Mahon.
Peter Mahon	Justice of the High Court of New Zealand and Royal Commissioner inquiring into the reason for the disaster. Resigned as a judge after being rebuked by the Court of Appeal. A man of deductive brilliance.
First Officer Greg Cassin	Co-pilot
First Officer Graham Lucas	The spare co-pilot
Gordon Brooks	Flight engineer
Nick Moloney	Flight engineer
Peter Mulgrew	Antarctic explorer and the in-flight commentator.

Ron Chippindale	Chief Inspector of Air Accidents, determined in secret why 257 people died. Reached incredible, impossible conclusions.
David Baragwanath QC	Later Justice Baragwanath, counsel assisting the Commission.
Gary Harrison	Counsel assisting the Commission, Mahon's researcher.
Paul Davison QC	Counsel representing ALPA, The Air Line Pilots' Association, and the estate of Jim Collins. He was counsel for Maria Collins. Twenty-eight years old at the time of the inquiry. Tore the navigation evidence apart.
Lloyd Brown QC	Counsel for Air New Zealand at the Royal Commission. Close friend of Peter Mahon but their friendship was torn asunder, broken forever, by the Commission of Inquiry.
Sir Robert Muldoon	Prime Minister, the only shareholder in Air New Zealand. Good friend of Morrie Davis.
Morrie Davis	Chief Executive of Air New Zealand. Convinced the crew were to blame and contemptuous of Mahon. 'I get pissed off when people lord the gentleman, who, in terms of that determination, was incompetent.' (*North and South* magazine, November 1989). The man who ordered 'surplus' documents shredded in the days after the accident.

Captain Gordon Vette	The pilot whose research into whiteout, the deceptive phenomenon of polar light, turned the inquiry on its head.
Captain Ian Gemmell	The chief pilot, actually 'Flight Manager, Technical', architect of the Antarctic flights and the man who believed the company's planning of the Antarctic flights was impeccable. Reminded Mahon of German Field Marshal Erich von Manstein. Answered the lawyers' questions 'with thinly veiled contempt'.
Captain George Oldfield	The airline's safety officer. He did not have a job description.
Captain Ross Johnson	The briefing officer for the Antarctic flights. Flight Manager, Line Operations. Swore black and blue that he briefed Captain Collins he would be flying over Mount Erebus. Had, himself, flown at 3000 feet round McMurdo Station.
Captain John Wilson	The other briefing officer. Had never been to Antarctica. Admitted eventually that DC-10s flew lower than the airline insisted they did and that pilots were permitted to descend below 6000 feet with the permission of McMurdo Air Traffic Control. A key moment at the Commission of Inquiry.
Captain Arthur Cooper	DC-10 captain, one of the transcribers of the cockpit voice recorder in Washington DC.

Captain Bruce Crosbie	The man who 'disappeared' the ring binder pages.
Keith Amies	Air New Zealand navigation systems specialist.
Brian Hewitt	Chief Navigator, the man who made the mistakes.
Captain Edgar Kippenberger	Director of Civil Aviation. The man who said that all on the flight deck must have become insane in the last minutes before impact. The court was incredulous at the foolishness of the man.
Captain Doug Keesing	Former Director of Flight Operations at Air New Zealand. Showed up at the inquiry and made it clear to Mahon he was being told nonsense.
Captain Les Simpson	Antarctic flight pilot. Attended same briefing as Collins and Cassin and made it clear they gained the impression the flights were programmed straight down McMurdo Sound, not over Erebus.
Alan Dorday	Flight despatcher, who worked out the cause before the wreckage was even found.
David Greenwood	Worked with Alan Dorday that night, told Ian Gemmell about the late navigation coordinate change on the morning after the crash.

Justice Sir Owen Woodhouse and Justice Sir Duncan McMullin	The authors of the minority judgement at the Court of Appeal.
Sam Mahon	Artist and author, son of Peter and Margarita Mahon.
Professor Nigel Roberts	Scott Base photographer, the man who took the iconic photograph of the tail fin of the crashed DC-10.
Stuart Macfarlane	Retired law lecturer, a man who spent years researching the Erebus disaster. His book *The Erebus Papers* is essential reading.

Letter to the Parliament of New Zealand

To all Members,
Respectfully.

Dear Member,

This book is a call for a parliamentary motion of exoneration for Captain Jim Collins and First Officer Greg Cassin, the pilots of the DC-10 which crashed on the side of Mount Erebus 32 years ago on 28 November 1979.

The report of the air accident investigation conducted by Ron Chippindale — in secret — blamed the pilots. A Royal Commission of Inquiry held in the open, with all evidence subject to examination and cross-examination, found the air accident inspector to have been entirely wrong. The accident was caused by the most appalling blunders at Air New Zealand's head office. The coordinates for the destination waypoint of the flight were changed in the early morning of the fatal flight without Captain Collins being told when he reported for duty. The effect was that whilst he thought he was programming his aircraft towards the safety of the flat sea ice of McMurdo Sound, the airline had programmed him to a mountain.

He, for his part, had diligently plotted the flight path upon which he had been previously briefed on his own charts at home the night before the flight. He was betrayed. The accident was caused by a cruel coincidence of an 'appalling' administrative blunder and the treachery of polar light. Mr Justice Mahon declared that the pilots were entirely and convincingly cleared of blame. He did so in his report, which was tabled in this Parliament in August 1999.

There was one other way in which both Civil Aviation and Air New Zealand failed the pilots. Both organisations knew about the perfidious nature of whiteout and sector whiteout. Both failed dismally to brief the crew. Air New Zealand decided consciously not to warn its Antarctic crews of whiteout. If not the coordinate change of which the pilots were not told, it was whiteout that caused the DC-10 to crash into the mountain.

But the pilots deserve a clearer statement, a once and for all, out in the open, parliamentary resolution that it was not their actions that caused the catastrophe on the mountain that day. Mr Justice Mahon's brilliant accident report makes it clear that they deserve it. Both Captain Jim Collins and First Officer Greg Cassin carried the unjustified blame for the deaths of 257 souls and the destruction of a public asset worth tens of millions of dollars.

The politics at that time were cruel. The families of the pilots suffered terribly, and not only through the manipulative and calculating early release of the Chippindale Report by a government determined that the pilots should be held culpable. This suffering has been unrelieved through the refusal of successive governments to recognise officially one of the greatest accident reports ever written — one that was a world leader in its time. It was a report that said there can be a muddle at the head office of an airline that can directly cause a catastrophe on a mountain 4000 kilometres away.

The Privy Council, while it held that Mr Justice Mahon exceeded his brief in claiming that he had had to listen to 'an orchestrated litany of lies', said this:

> . . . their Lordships have had occasion to read and to re-read with close attention before, during and since the hearing of the appeal all 167 printed pages of the Royal Commission Report. Having done so, they would desire to place on record their tribute to the brilliant and painstaking investigative work undertaken by the judge (with the support of counsel appointed to assist him) in the course of hearings which lasted for 75 days and other investigations that he or counsel assisting him undertook in addition to the public hearings. (Privy Council: re Erebus Royal Commission, 1983, p. 665)

The Privy Council also said:

> The Royal Commission Report convincingly clears Captain Collins and First Officer Cassin of any suggestion that negligence on their part had in any way contributed to the disaster. That is unchallenged. The judge was able to displace Mr Chippindale's attribution of the accident to pilot error . . . (Privy Council: re Erebus Royal Commission, 1983, p. 684)

In this book, I will explain how he did so.

The reputation of two fine pilots was cruelly stained by an inadequate and dishonest inquiry by the Chief Inspector of Air Accidents. For the sake of the pilots' families, the stains should, once and for all, be removed.

I urge Members to give the matter of a parliamentary motion of exoneration for Captain Jim Collins and First Officer Greg Cassin long overdue consideration.

Sincerely,
Paul Holmes, CNZM

Glossary of Terms

AINS (area inertial navigation system) — The state of the art electronic navigation system on jet airliners at the time. The route was programmed into it and the aircraft followed it over vast distances. It was legendarily accurate.

ATC (air traffic control) — Controllers who monitor any given airspace and issue orders and advise pilots about directions they should fly and altitudes they should maintain.

'Clean' flying — Flying at high altitude configuration, meaning without using lift devices like flaps for lower speed and with the undercarriage retracted. The DC-10s flew clean round McMurdo in case flaps froze and made the journey home too slow for the fuel load to get them back to Christchurch.

Coordinates — The latitude and longitude numbers of a position on a map.

CVR (cockpit voice recorder) — Recorded for 30 minutes before beginning to wipe the previous 30 minutes. The recording quality on Flight 901 was very bad and everything said, apart from that said by the two pilots, was very indistinct.

DFDR (digital flight data recorder) — The black box. Records everything technical about the aircraft for 30 minutes, including height, direction, speed and engine performance. Matched up with the time sequence of the CVR, it provides an invaluable record of the flight.

DME (distance measuring equipment) — Tells a pilot how far the aircraft is from the DME ground station. The DME at McMurdo was the TACAN (see p. 24). It does not guide the aircraft in. It simply indicates distance.

Endurance — The length of time an aircraft's fuel load will allow it to remain airborne.

Flight level (FL) — An expression of height, e.g. FL16 is 16,000 feet. FL39 is 39,000 feet. (Based on a standard altimeter setting.)

Flight plan — The route a pilot is planning to fly. In commercial aviation it would have calculated waypoints, expected winds to be encountered and expected fuel consumption.

GMT (Greenwich Mean Time) — The time used in commercial aviation, used on the CVR transcript and which was used at McMurdo. The aircraft therefore crashed at 00.49.50. Based on New Zealand Daylight Saving Time, which is the only time I have used in this book, the DC-10 collided with the mountain at 1.49.50.

Grid navigation — Navigation used in polar zones. Normal navigation becomes unreliable as longitudes close in on each other.

High frequency radio — Long distance radio. Does not need line of sight between the station transmitting and the receiver. Can play in Antarctica.

HSI (horizontal situation indicator) — A key instrument, right in front of the pilot. It shows the distance to the next waypoint in one corner, ground speed in another and tells the pilot whether the aircraft is left or right of track, or dead on track.

IFR (instrument flight rules) — Flying by instruments when the weather precludes the pilot seeing sufficiently safely.

IMC (instrument meteorological conditions) — Instrument flying weather.

MSA (minimum safe altitude) — Over high ground, for example. An altitude below which a pilot can only descend with permission from ground controllers.

Nav Track — The course the aircraft is programmed or scheduled to fly.

NDB (non-directional beacon) — A radio transmitter an aircraft can pick up and follow. A pilot can plot a heading from the signal of an NDB. An NDB can 'guide' the pilot in. Captain Collins understood that the McMurdo NDB was not working, which is why he took the opportunity of descending through a vast hole in the cloud.

NOTAM (Notice to Airmen) — Messages about changes to conditions or routes that pilots should know about.

Radar — A radio device to detect objects in the air at a distance. The DC-10 radar was used to detect cloud and rain storms ahead of the aircraft in order for the crew to avoid bad weather and keep things smooth and safe for the passengers.

RCU (Route Clearance Unit) — Where pilots were briefed on the routes they were about to fly.

TACAN (tactical air navigation aid) — A military navigation device. Of limited use to civilian aircraft.

VFR (visual flight rules) — Standard flight rules for visual flight, such as height above terrain and the distance the eye can see.

VHF (very high frequency) — A good, clean radio signal with very little interference to be encountered but has to be line of sight. Usually used around airports.

VMC (visual meteorological conditions) — Conditions in which a pilot can use visual flight rules (VFR); that is, has sufficient visibility to fly safely.

Visual approach — An approach to a point, usually an airfield, in which the pilot is flying visually.

Prologue

It is a late afternoon in early November 2010, just short of 31 years since the collision of the DC-10 with the lower slopes of Mount Erebus on Ross Island in Antarctica. I am up the road at my friend Jock's house, sitting in glorious sun on his wide old deck, looking across at a sprawling Lake Poukawa and the folding, rolling hills beyond. The sun is white fire on the water. Through a couple of the trees I watch the water form two strands of brilliant tinsel. The sun is shining through a long break in the cloud, a long strip of blue, just above the hills. Above the blue, a layer of cloud is grey black. All of the trees round us are lit golden by the late afternoon light. The hills, through the haze, are blue green and there are shadows in their folds. The world feels impossibly good.

Jock is sitting on the concrete ruin of a rumpled old tennis court talking to someone on his phone. My wife and my daughter will come up to Jock's soon and we'll all have takeaways for dinner. We'll have an evening of laughter with Jock and Kate and their two girls.

An hour ago, I took a phone call that made me realise, for the first time probably, the trouble this book could cause me. Well, so be it. I do not mean it to cause trouble, but it probably will.

I have written it in order to right an old wrong. The wrong was that the two Erebus DC-10 pilots, Captain Jim Collins and First Officer Greg Cassin, in a damning accident report, were made to take the blame for the disaster. They were accused of flying negligently, like cowboys. This impression was cultivated by the government and Civil Aviation and the Chief Inspector of Air Accidents. After Erebus, much occurred that was dishonest and wrong.

The Erebus disaster is a major chapter in the New Zealand narrative. It pained us all and shamed us all. We all own this story.

When the DC-10 smashed its belly into the gentle slope of the Antarctic mountain — gouging a 2-metre hole in the ice — and disintegrated within seconds, 257 people lost their lives. It was a disaster of the first magnitude. Hundreds of families, not only in New Zealand but round the world, lost loved ones.

This is the story of one of those families, that of the captain of the aircraft, Jim Collins. He left a wife, Maria, and four daughters, Kathryn, 15, Elizabeth, 14, Pip, 9, and Adrienne, 6. They all loved him dearly.

His daughters have become women. They are women of intelligence, courage and humour. They, and their mother, are women who endured not only the violent loss of a beloved husband and father but the abandonment of him after his death by many friends and colleagues who should have been better people. They endured his abandonment by the airline he served so faithfully and they endured too the blackening of his name by an air accident inspector determined that neither Civil Aviation nor Air New Zealand should take any serious blame for the accident — he did the job he was expected to do and his task required sustained dishonesty.

They endured the joy of the Royal Commission finding that Captain Collins and his first officer were entirely blameless for the disaster, only to see those findings rubbished and set aside, ignored by a cynical, dishonest prime minister.

I have come to know these women. They have been open with me about their lives. They are honest people. Through them, I feel as if I have come to know Jim Collins as well. One day, early on, before I had really explored the story of Erebus, before my researches had even begun to throw me so deeply into the literature for months and months, I asked Kathryn, Jim Collins's eldest daughter, 'How can you be sure your father wasn't to blame?' Her reply was heartachingly simple. 'Because I know my father. And I saw him working on his maps the night before the flight. He showed us his flight path.'

As Justice Peter Mahon, the Royal Commissioner, showed us, Jim Collins knew exactly where he was going when he took that aircraft south to Antarctica. He knew where his flight path would be and he had no reason whatsoever to doubt it. He was deceived, however, by an appalling airline blunder for which someone — probably the Chief Executive, it was so fundamentally a management error — should have gone to jail. The destination waypoint was changed in the airline's computer hours before take-off and the captain was never told. Captain Collins, at the point of impact, was certain he was entering the middle of McMurdo Sound. That was where he had been briefed to fly.

In fact, because no one thought to tell him of the change of flight path, Captain Collins was some 40 kilometres east of where he thought he was, and what Justice Mahon called 'a malevolent trick of the polar light' finished him off. Not one of the four highly trained airmen on the flight deck, in broad daylight, saw the mountain. How could that have been?

So this is the story of that flight. It is the story of Justice Mahon's inquiry. It is the story of Mahon's devoted wife, Margarita. But mostly it is the story of the Collins girls. Of who they were and who they have become, Maria, Kathryn, Elizabeth, Pip and Adrienne.

I sometimes wondered, as I spent the months researching and writing, whether I was always going to write this book. The Erebus story, I have always felt, was unfinished business.

Certainly, the wife and daughters of Captain Jim Collins feel so. They feel it painfully. When justice finally came for them, in the findings of the Royal Commission, it was cast aside, thrown away. The matter was never resolved. I have always admired Maria Collins tremendously for the way she battled on, holding her family together after the savage assault of the Erebus crash and the loss of the husband she thought the world of, with whom she had four children — the husband who received the blame for the crash.

I met Maria and the girls quite by accident after I came back from living in Vienna, Austria, in the mid-1980s to live in Wellington. It was the summer of 1985–86 and I was touring the Far North. I happened upon a perfect little coastal settlement called Matapouri Bay and decided to stay a few days. The motelier — inappropriately, probably — pointed out a woman and her young daughters on the beach and told me that they were the wife and children of the Erebus captain. Somewhere in those couple of days I started talking to Maria Collins. I felt very much for her. Someone was missing. This beach, I learnt later, was the family's place of retreat when the girls were young. I did not bring up the subject of Erebus.

Two years later I was transferred to Auckland for the great battle of the Auckland radio airwaves, and I wondered if Maria was a listener. She was not. She is firmly National Radio. Then came *HOLMES* and I wondered, sometimes, if she watched and recalled her meeting on the beach with the man from nowhere.

In November 2009, I sat down to write my column for the *Herald on Sunday*. It was the thirtieth anniversary of Erebus. There was something Kathryn had said to me years before, privately, when I got to know her slightly in the early nineties, and I wanted to use it. I tracked her down and asked her permission. The article appeared on the Sunday and Kathryn rang me late morning to thank me. Later Maria called, telling me I got only one thing wrong. I had written 'east' when I should have written 'west'.

I called Kathryn back. 'I suppose it's time for the book, isn't it, Kathryn?' She assembled her sisters at her mother's home one Sunday in February 2010. I had not met her sisters since that distant summer at Matapouri Bay. We talked about the project. What I remember most of that meeting was the laughter, and how deeply Erebus has affected them.

At the lunch table, Maria said, 'Paul, you sit there, where Jim used to sit.'

I went away and submerged myself in the literature. After about five months, I felt I understood enough to start writing. I hope I have done Maria and her daughters justice. I hope I have done justice to Peter Mahon and to Margarita. I hope I have done justice to two brave policemen, part of the team who achieved the near impossible: the task of getting the bodies off the mountain.

And I hope I have done justice to Captain Jim Collins and First Officer Greg Cassin. For there was bad injustice served out to these two fine men.

This is a sad story — and a dirty one. I shall try to keep it simple, so that we may all, at last, understand what happened. It got too complicated. It did not have to be.

There is the modern Air New Zealand, a high performance, internationally award-winning company, with a compassionate heart and admired management and Chief Executive, a company of which all New Zealanders can be proud. This is the company that laid on the inexpensive flights for people who wanted to leave Christchurch after the crippling earthquake in February 2011.

There was an old Air New Zealand of which we were all proud, too — and it was staffed by skilled and dedicated men and women who were rocked by the Erebus disaster.

But within that company were some men of profound arrogance, untruthfulness and ruthlessness. When they confronted the Royal Commission established to find out why one of the company's DC-10s crashed in clear air into the side of an Antarctic mountain, they treated the judge with contempt.

But this is not really about Air New Zealand at all. As I was drawn more deeply into the project I became appalled at the layers of dishonesty that existed amongst the powerful in New Zealand then, how the departments of state did everything to avoid blame, and how readily the poor dead pilots were held responsible. I began to realise how the establishment looked after itself then and how the Old Boys' network looked after everything. Civil

Aviation looked after Air New Zealand, Air New Zealand looked after Civil Aviation and the Chief Inspector of Air Accidents looked after all of them.

The Chief Inspector was vested with great power. He seemed to be a law unto himself, answering to no one. It seems incredible that even after his bizarre accident report, which was discredited by the Royal Commission, he continued in his job, unchecked for another couple of decades.

It still seems incredible now, 32 years on, that in New Zealand in our lifetime the management of an airline, which had just carried 257 people to their deaths, would immediately after the accident begin shredding documents.

I also saw how an unchecked, overbearing and dictatorial Prime Minister, Robert Muldoon, when he wasn't turning New Zealand into an economic ruin, made sure the airline and its senior people were protected. Except the airline's dead flight crew, of course. They were not protected. The dead could not speak. They would have to take the blame. None of the living would have to wear any responsibility for the destruction of the DC-10 and the deaths of the 257 people.

And the senior men at the airline who caused the accident would have got away with it — and Muldoon too — had it not been for one brave man of formidable, incisive and shrewd intelligence, a judge of the High Court of New Zealand, Justice Peter Mahon. His accident report, exonerating the aircrew completely, remains a brilliantly lucid document to read, a gripping journey of discovery.

The accident was a paradox, complicated, yet simple nonetheless. Mahon navigated his way through the obfuscation and untruths thrown at him and found the true reasons the disaster happened. With inexorable logic he showed how incompetent the planning for the flight had been.

As Auckland law professor Mike Taggart told Peter Mahon's wife, Margarita, years after Mahon's death, Mahon spoke truth to power. No judicial authority has ever doubted Mahon's findings as to accident causation. The Privy Council marvelled at his investigation. No one living ever took responsibility for the crash. Thanks to the Court of Appeal and the Privy Council, they never had to.

This is also the story of the last, sad days of the heroic Peter Mahon and the patient, clever and loving wife who cared for him.

As I say, I shall try to keep it simple. This I determined when I started; it is a story that belongs to all New Zealanders and all of our people have the right to understand it. It is, above all, the story of an honest pilot, the women who loved him, and the flight of a great airliner that ended in seconds as a long black smudge on the side of a faraway Antarctic mountain.

Finally, I make no apology for the emphatic views expressed in this book. I have not consulted some who for thirty years have held Mahon to be wrong and have called for the pilots to shoulder at least some of the blame for the Erebus disaster. I have not tried to contact those who for thirty years and for their own various reasons have denied the truth. Above all, the simple logic of Mahon, endorsed by the Privy Council, exonerates the aircrew.

1

28 November 1979

The enemy of the truth is very often not the lie — deliberate, contrived and dishonest — but the myth — persistent, persuasive and unrealistic.

— John F. Kennedy

Just another Wednesday morning. Dads went to work and mums got up, saw Dad off, made breakfast for the children, made the school lunches, took the kids to school and in many cases went to work themselves. Today promised to be pleasant — a rare November day in Auckland when winter might at last be over. In Auckland, November is the cruellest month.

At 7 o'clock in the morning, DC-10 Captain Jim Collins and First Officer Greg Cassin arrived together at Flight Despatch at Auckland International Airport where they received their Antarctic envelope, their briefing papers and at least two topographical charts for the flight ahead. Jim Collins, in any case, had brought at least two charts of his own, as well as his atlas. Neither Jim Collins nor Greg Cassin had flown to Antarctica before. Greg Cassin, in his morning rush, had left his briefing notes at home. This would later assume great importance.

The flight crew walked out onto the flight deck of their DC-10. They would take off that morning for a five-hour flight to the scenic wonder of the white wilderness of Antarctica before returning to New Zealand at Christchurch. At Christchurch, the crew would be relieved and become passengers on the final leg to Auckland.

In the check-in area, 237 passengers were turning up for what promised to be the excursion of their lives, a day trip to Antarctica. One hundred and eighty were New Zealand nationals, 24 were Japanese, 23 were Americans, five were Britons, two were Canadian and there was one passenger each from Australia, France and Switzerland. Together with 20 New Zealand crew members, they were to leave about 8 o'clock in the morning and get back to Auckland about 9 o'clock in the evening, having refuelled at Christchurch. Today, there would be room for three standby passengers.

The Antarctic flights were not difficult, but if you got into trouble, there wasn't a heck of a lot of help to be had. You couldn't land a DC-10 on the ice runway either — not at this time of year. A DC-10 was too heavy, the ice too thin. Not good. But the flights were simple enough. Straight down McMurdo Sound, turn left at the head of the Sound with another few miles to fly across to McMurdo Base. You circled round anywhere between 1500 feet and 3000 feet if the visibility was good — keeping a keen eye on your fuel because the DC-10, like all jets and especially the big jets, guzzled fuel at the low altitudes.

And you had to keep your airspeed up because even though you were low, you had to fly clean. That meant no flaps for extra lift at lower speeds because the flaps might freeze for the flight home, meaning you'd have to fly slowly and low and go through the gas like a packet of salts. But while you were doing that, your eyes could, nevertheless, feast on scenery described by Justice Peter Mahon, after he saw it for himself, as some of the grandest to be seen on earth, a part of the world that was also rich in heroic history.

For the crews, the flights were a wonderful day out; something different, a welcome break from the routine of the long, unchallenging hours of sitting in the sky above the oceans, seemingly never moving, sitting there for hours in the middle of the night. It was only when they made an approach and landing, greasing the huge aircraft onto the runway at Los Angeles or Honolulu or wherever their trans-oceanic roster took them, that they got to the bit that made flying the thing that the flyboys want to do.

And what's more, with the Antarctic flights, you got home that night. There were no empty hotel rooms, no overnight layovers. You went down, saw Antarctica, the passengers partied on their champagne and you brought them home safely, parked the DC-10 and got a taxi home, had dinner with the family, got the kids to bed and talked to your wife about the long day. God, the Antarctic flights made international commercial flying almost like a normal job. And Jim Collins's flight colleagues had all done the flight before completely without incident.

So the passengers partied and they took their hundreds of photographs and you spoke to them often and your in-flight commentator provided the geographic and historical knowledge as you kept an eye on your speed and hauled the aircraft round Scott's last hut, New Zealand's Scott Base and the sprawling American McMurdo complex with its runway at Williams Field — the wide and long runway nearby for whiteout landings if one of their American fellows came in through zero visibility and had to be talked right down onto the deck.

Yes, nice and easy. Keep an eye out — it's Antarctica, after all — and Bob's your uncle. None of the frenzied, rat-a-tat jabber of the Los Angeles air traffic controllers who moved millions of tons of metal and their vulnerable, trusting human cargo down through crowded airspace every day and night of the year. There would be none of that stress. Not that LAX or Heathrow or Narita were super stressful for an experienced DC-10 pilot. You just had to know what you were doing. You had to hear everything. You repeated to the air traffic controller every instruction given and you checked it all with your first officer.

You were mates in that cockpit, professionals together. And you did it right because that was what you did. That is why you were there. You were a DC-10 captain. You were trained for command. You had responsibility not only for the flight crew and the cabin staff, but you had in your hands the safety — on this day, Jim Collins's flight — of 237 passengers as well. This was big stuff. Your sacred duty was to get the passengers where they wanted to go and then to get them safely down, nice and smooth, roll them to the gate, open the doors to let the friendly staff bid them thanks for flying with us, and wish them good luck and sunshine as they walked out onto God's safe, dear ground. And you did it. You did it every day the company asked you to fly. You did it with joy because you loved to fly. Flying was flying. Flying was the true joy.

And you flew the DC-10, the most modern, the most beautiful, most majestic aeroplane of the modern era. If the Boeing 747 was the saloon, the DC-10 was the very large sports car. And they let you fly the $40 million DC-10 way beyond the seas to frantic airfields in foreign lands because they trusted you. They trusted your training, your skill, your years, your intelligence and your sanity. They trusted your judgement, your ability to react to adversity and to what was in front of you and to do it instantly and professionally. You flew in the cockpit of the DC-10 because you were the best of the best and you commanded the flight deck of the DC-10, held custody of those hundreds of lives because you were the best of the best of the best. You were no less than that.

At some stage amidst all the flight deck preparation and checks, two of the flight crew, probably First Officer Greg Cassin, or maybe Cassin along with the spare first officer, Graham 'Brick' Lucas — we will never know — programmed into their flight navigation computer the latitudinal and longitudinal coordinates, taken from the airline computer, of the route to Antarctica and back.

Flight engineers Gordon Brooks and Nick Moloney walked round the outside of the aircraft, examining some of the exterior engineering with trained and hawkish eyes. All airmen are trained to do this before engine start and take-off. It is drummed into trainee pilots. Who knows what little piece of neglect you might find that, undetected, might kill you?

These were serious pre-flight inspections. The DC-10 had been the centre of three famous incidents, the first of which, in 1972, became known famously as the Windsor Incident because it happened over the town of Windsor, Ontario.

On this occasion, a cargo door of American Airlines Flight 96 blew out, causing the decompression of the cargo hold. This caused the rear floor of the passenger cabin to collapse. As it did so it jammed the rudder cables and caused the rudder to stick hard right. The pilots still had the ailerons — the hinged flaps on the wings that allow the pilot to roll and bank — as well as the relative thrust of the two wing engines by which to control the aircraft. Somehow, they brought the aircraft into a Detroit runway at terrifyingly high speed with only a few minor injuries.

A dramatic change to the cargo door locking mechanism was suggested by the Federal Aviation Authority, but manufacturer McDonnell Douglas objected to the difficulty and the expense of the request and a compromise solution was reached.

Two years later, in early 1974, a Turkish Airlines DC-10 packed with 346 people climbed out of Paris and turned towards London. Shortly after take-off, the cargo door blew out. The sudden decompression caused the floor to collapse and cut the control columns. The pilots had nothing to work with as the DC-10 smashed into a forest and disintegrated. Such was the totality of the destruction of the airliner, emergency services found only small, isolated fires to extinguish.

Then, just months before Captain Jim Collins and his crew were running through their start-up checks on this Wednesday morning in late November 1979, fate struck American Airlines again. On a fine afternoon in May, another DC-10, with 271 people on board, lined up on Runway 32 Right at Chicago's O'Hare Airport for its regular flight to Los Angeles. Captain Wally Lux, a veteran pilot with 22,000 flying hours, was given take-off clearance, pushed his three throttle controls forward to take-off thrust, and accelerated along the runway.

Just seconds after take-off, at about 300 feet, Captain Lux's left engine snapped away from its pylon, flicked itself over the top of the wing and crashed back onto the runway. As it flipped over the leading edge of the wing, however, it tore the leading edge hydraulics to shreds. All that Captain Lux knew in those few seconds was that he had lost power in his number one engine. There was no time for discussion, no time for thought. We know that Captain Lux and his first officer, in those final seconds, flew the aircraft by the book.

Then the nightmare happened. The left wing stalled while the right wing continued to lift. Wings are wings. They can act independently. This meant the right wing went high while the stalled left wing pointed to the ground and took the nose of the aircraft with it. The aircraft crashed nose and wing first into a field by a trailer park and all were dead. A forklift, replacing that left engine after an inspection, had damaged the wing pylon. It was an ill-advised maintenance procedure but it saved American Airlines the cost of 200 man-hours.

The media, the flying public and the Federal Aviation Administration (FAA) freaked. The DC-10 had now cost the lives of 662 passengers, let alone the couple of hundred over Windsor, Ontario who would never forget their outing that day. The FAA grounded the worldwide DC-10 fleet until mid-July 1979, for about two months. The grounding cost Air New Zealand hundreds of thousands of dollars.

So when the flight engineers on Flight 901 walked round that DC-10 at Gate 2 in Auckland that November morning, checking the wings, checking the doors (which by this stage could not be closed without flight engineer supervision), their eyes were serious. Funny things could happen to the DC-10. Beautiful aircraft, but, well, funny things happened. She could bite.

With the flight engineers giving the aircraft the all clear, with the passengers settled in their seats in the clean and immaculate cabin, Jim Collins might have reminded himself about the blue cod. There was a fish shop in Christchurch, near the airport. The Air New Zealand crews knew about it. If you were an Auckland crew going through Christchurch, you brought some blue cod back.

It was such good blue cod. Maria Collins always made it her duty to see if any of her good friends wanted some. On Tuesday night, the night before the Antarctic flight, Maria phoned her friend of 20 years, Kathryn Schollum. (Jim and Maria Collins's eldest daughter is named after Kathryn Schollum.) Did she want any fish? Jim was going to Antarctica tomorrow, returning via Christchurch. In fact, Maria told her friend, Jim was on the floor now with his maps spread out going over with Kathryn and Elizabeth where he was flying to, and the route he would be taking.

Kathryn Schollum would have reason later never to forget this humdrum conversation. And yes, please, she would like some blue cod.

'Don't forget the fish.' It was the last thing Maria Collins ever said to her husband, the last words in a blissful and fulfilled married life together with their four lively, singular girls.

There is a story, told by Ken Hickson, in his 1980 book, *Flight 901 to Erebus* (an unfortunately timed piece of work as we shall see) of a woman passenger who, when the cabin door was closed and the aircraft was about to be pushed away from the gate for the engine start, began to panic and begged to be let off the aircraft. The door was opened and she was taken back into the departure lounge where staff soothed her and persuaded her she would have a great day. Much calmed, the woman agreed to give it another go and took her seat again on the aircraft.

Captain Jim Collins lined up on the runway awaiting take-off clearance. Next to him, in the right-hand seat, was 37-year-old First Officer Greg Cassin, husband of Anne and father of three young children. The spare first officer, Graham Lucas, was, like Jim Collins, air force trained and, also like Jim Collins, a trained navigator. Gordon Brooks, the experienced flight engineer, was probably seated in his position between them and a little behind, his expert eye darting over his indicators. The other flight engineer, Nick Moloney, may have been on the flight deck. Gordon Brooks was the sort to speak his mind. Gordon didn't care much about the niceties of rank if things were not right.

On the flight deck, too, might have been the Antarctic commentator for the day, Peter Mulgrew. He was filling in for Sir Edmund Hillary. Hillary had flagged the job today. Peter could do it. Behind them were 15 cabin staff and 237 passengers.

What a day it was going to be. What a great world we had become! Shackleton, Scott, Amundsen — they'd all had to sail their ships in treacherous, bitterly cold seas, risking the perfidious power of the ocean and the sea ice and the cruelty of the painful trudging across hundreds of miles of snow and ice in blizzards until, in Scott's case, it all went pear shaped. They huddled hungry and frostbitten in their tents and wrote the heroic goodbyes with frozen hands and sent their love to England and died. To hell with that. Today in 1979, we could do the whole thing in a day, in comfort, high above the ice in an air-conditioned capsule at speeds unthought of a hundred years before.

Yes, what a day, all right. Jim Collins unleashed the power of the three mighty engines and the DC-10 began its thrilling, accelerating roll to take-off speed.

But what we know now is that when he reached take-off speed, eased the yoke towards him, lifted the nose wheel off the tarmac and put his aircraft onto Nav Track, all on board were doomed. They were all, as another hero of this saga, Captain Gordon Vette, would write later, programmed to their deaths.

A last minute Head Office blunder was sending Jim Collins, his crew and his 237 passengers to their instant deaths on a mountain in the most remote and hostile place on earth — a mountain few outside the mountaineering or Antarctic communities had ever heard of, one the most active volcanoes on the planet, Mount Erebus.

They did not know this on board, of course. No one knew this. In any case, whatever happened, Jim would get them home. Don't worry about Jim! Jim Collins was the most thorough, methodical captain in the airline. Jim could drive you crazy with his checking and cross checking. As Arthur Cooper, Jim's colleague and another DC-10 captain, will tell you, Jim was almost pedantic about his preparation.

Jim Collins had got a damaged and bucking DC-10 down before, back in the early 1970s when lightning struck his aircraft and tore some panels shortly after take-off from Los Angeles. Jim Collins flew round dumping fuel, too heavy to land with full tanks. He swung the aircraft back towards LAX, lined up for an emergency landing, let his passengers know what was going on and brought the aircraft safely in.

As Jim Collins climbed the giant aircraft out of Auckland, he turned control of the aircraft over to auto-pilot and let the auto-pilot fly the aircraft on Nav Track, the area inertial navigation system or AINS which directed the aircraft on its course at every second.

About 1.30 p.m. New Zealand time, Jim Collins was working his way down from cruise altitude in great loops, through breaks in the cloud, to an altitude at which he could fly in clear air up McMurdo Sound so his passengers could get the breathtaking view they had paid for.

In his descending orbits, as they called them up the front of a DC-10, he was careful to fly no further south than when he started the orbits, until he could see the sea and the headlands each side of McMurdo Sound and continue safely south. Remember, he was one of the most cautious men in the fleet, Jim Collins. In any case, no Air New Zealand pilot took silly risks. You didn't do that. You had to be deranged to do so, or a deeply committed jihad man, but the jihad men weren't doing the suicide thing then.

There was a great, sprawling mountain in the region, an active volcano that perpetually belched steam, but they would not see that today. The mountain top was hidden in cloud. It was a pity because passengers loved taking pictures of Erebus. It was also way over to the left of the navigation track.

They had not told him much about Antarctic flying but Jim had done his own research and knew that you did not fool round down here. That was for sure. So Jim was flying the aircraft religiously on the Nav Track. Navigation Section knew what they were doing when they plotted this course. Why doubt Navigation Section? Who ever doubted Navigation Section? Navigation Section always got it right. Best in the world, the Air New Zealand Navigation Section. And this was the course all the other fellows had flown.

Jim Collins and Greg Cassin, Gordon Brooks, Nick Moloney and Peter Mulgrew all kept an eye out, looking ahead out the cockpit window. What they saw was what they expected to see. That is always a good feeling when you're flying an aircraft. It is the way it always should be when you are captain of a DC-10.

Up ahead was that entirely expected endless flat white mass with possibly a distinguishable horizon way in the distance. It was just as Jim assumed McMurdo would look as they approached that isolated, dedicated hive of human exploration and research which seemed to drive the lives of the people he might soon see waving below him and which brought them all to this surreal, spectacular and forbidding bottom of the world.

First Officer Greg Cassin had already made radio contact with McMurdo

Air Traffic Control. There was excitement at both McMurdo and amongst the Kiwis at Scott Base. They loved seeing the splendid, roaring DC-10s swoop above them. It was, probably, a heart-cheering reminder that there was still normal life in another world, a world of warmth and normality they had temporarily left behind.

Yes, and somewhere up ahead on the ground at Scott Base, ready with his camera and his tripod, waiting patiently for the aircraft's roaring appearance out of the sky, was young Canterbury University political science lecturer Nigel Roberts, who had managed to get himself a three-month secondment to Scott Base as the official photographer for the Antarctic Division of the DSIR. What's more, both Antarctic Division and the university were paying him at the same time. Nigel could not believe his luck. And there was no way he was going to miss this.

Nigel waited with his camera.

So did air traffic control. So did McMurdo. So did Scott Base. In the canteen, for everyone to hear, they broadcast air traffic control and the pilots talking through speakers. Cloud was down to about 2000 feet but, below it, you could see for 40 miles, MacCentre had told Greg Cassin. It was a grey day but not foggy. The DC-10 would cheer the whole place up.

So they waited.

And they waited.

And some 50 kilometres north of them the impossible happened. For much of their waiting, they realised later — and would think about it forever — it had already happened.

Just before the end of lunchtime, at 10 seconds before 1.50 p.m. New Zealand Daylight Saving Time, Jim Collins flew his DC-10 straight into the side of Mount Erebus, killing himself and 256 others.

He smashed into the mountain in clear air in apparently perfect visibility without once seeing the mountain in front of him. Just like that. And none of the four crew on the flight deck with him, not Greg Cassin, not Gordon nor Nick nor Peter Mulgrew, saw it. Not one of them said a thing about a mountain in front of the aircraft. The CVR, the cockpit voice recorder, would later make that absolutely, emphatically and indisputably clear.

The mountain sat there in apparently clear air. It waited for Jim Collins. When he came, at 460 kilometres an hour, the mountain took his aircraft square on. In seconds, the DC-10 was hundreds of thousands of jagged little parts, a narrow black smudge stretching up what had been a pristine slope some 800 metres from the point of impact. All on board were dead. Life was gone. No one survived, not for an instant.

As Captain Gordon Vette would later write in *Impact Erebus*, the passengers were standing up, leaning across to windows, talking to each other, having a wonderful time, beautifully looked after by professional and dedicated people. They died from impact and deceleration. None of the bodies showed signs of frostbite.

All were dead instantly at 10 seconds before 1.50 p.m. on that Wednesday afternoon in November 1979, and then their bodies froze.

Nature is fair. She plays by her rules. She waits for the player to make a mistake and then she kills. And the sudden, monumental impact of the man-made machine against her mountain; this tearing and sundering of metal and plastic and human flesh; this murder of human and engineering wonder; this was a mistake of legendarily catastrophic magnitude. This mess; this mangled mess of sharp metal, torn metal, broken seats, empty trays, open lockers, purses, handbags and wallets; this raw and ruptured mess of blood and heads and arms and legs lying cold and dead and soon to freeze across the virgin ice; this awful scattering of bodies ripped naked by the power of the deathly collision of a complex, convoluted machine slicing effortlessly through the air at 460 kilometres an hour and striking an ancient, merciless mountain named after the god of chaos himself; no one could survive. The tears will stain the soul of a nation forever. The fate of these 257 broken, beloved people, whose remains teams of good men would soon have to see and remember in their minds and hearts forever, was final. There was no putting it back together. It had happened.

And within seconds of the impact, perhaps a few minutes, after the fuel garrumphed, gushed and erupted into the clean air, and the flames had swept across the thousands of little metal parts which were all that remained of ZK-NZP, and the fire had burned out, there was silence again, beautiful, white, timeless, frigid Antarctic silence. The only signs of man were a long black oily, kerosene-stinking smudge. And there, halfway up the wreck site, lying out on its own, lying on its plaintive side, was the once proud high tail of the aircraft with its distinctive koru. And there, towards the top of the slope, that blackened twisted piece of fuselage, crumpled and lost amidst hundreds of bodies and body parts scattered and abandoned across the hard white ice.

In the moderate mountain wind that early afternoon, deathly dry and waterless Antarctic snow wafted a few metres above the ice slope. Upon the wind in the silence fluttered papers from the wallets and handbags of passengers. Documents from the flight deck, perhaps from Jim Collins's flight bag, bank notes, scraps of paper, maps, instructions, and whatever the wind could carry, blew over the ice and into jagged crevasses that gaped deeply all the way up the slope of the lethal mountain and over the filthy, burnt-out, blackened ruination of the wondrous machine.

They were all dead. Jim Collins and his crew and all the passengers were dead. Jim Collins's girls would weep, not just for his loss and for the love taken, but for his inability, any longer, to speak for himself.

For the dead can never speak.

2

The Daughters

They are all smart, the Collins girls — Maria and Kathryn, Elizabeth, Philippa (whom they call Pip) and Adrienne (whom they call Didi). They all have clear, watchful blue eyes. They are all witty, sometimes brilliantly so. They can all make you laugh with a black humour. They can laugh at themselves. I told them at our first meeting that I thought them all funny. Elizabeth suggested I call the book, 'The Funny Girls and their Plane Truth'. One of the seven titles she jotted down on the exercise book I took to the meeting has become the title of this book, *Daughters of Erebus*. Elizabeth wrote the phrase lightheartedly. Later I came to see it as perfect.

They all believe Jim Collins, the commander of Flight 901 to Antarctica on 28 November 1979, was cruelly wronged by the Chief Inspector of Air Accidents. They have all suffered terribly from the injustice of his findings. The Chippindale Report caused them unspeakable pain. Their father had apparently killed himself and 256 people by flying in cloud into a mountain.

They are a proud family. They have seen it all and they notice everything, all of them, and they watch in their individual ways. They have watched people watching them for years and they have learned to watch people carefully back. They observe, they assess, they size you up and make you out. They have acute antennae.

They were all deeply hurt. Their souls have wept for their father with the impotent tears of injustice for more than 30 years.

Jim Collins was killed. He went to work and he never came home. His body and those of 256 others lay frozen on an Antarctic mountain, his aircraft catastrophically destroyed. But life went on for the Collins girls. With all of the burdens of pain we have to carry, it does. Life goes on. So it did for every one of the thousands of people who lost family and loved ones in the Erebus disaster of 1979.

Maria taught the girls this. Maria was born in Vienna into a Jewish background in 1935. She was three years old when her parents escaped the Nazis and made it to New Zealand in late 1939. Maria knows that you have to deal with what life throws at you. Maria was 44 when Jim Collins was thrown from the broken cockpit and onto the frozen mountain slope 32 years ago. She had to deal with that. Maria admires wisdom above all else. It is how she defines intelligence. She measures wisdom and that is enough. After the pain and poor helpless silence of the dead, in the end, there are love and the girls, and there are acceptance and wisdom.

They are all proud of who they are, these Collins women. They are special and they know they are. They are Jim Collins's girls. He was a fine, popular and well-respected man. He had many friends. Eight hundred people came to a memorial service for him when his body returned home. The girls adored him. Jim Collins was the light of their lives, a light extinguished so suddenly and so violently. Maria, Kathryn, Elizabeth, Pip and Adrienne know in their hearts and minds that Jim Collins was not at fault that distant day.

They are exceptionally close. They all treasure their mother for the love, strength and courage she displayed in the darkest of times. They admire her infinitely. They see her often. They are deeply loyal to her.

The daughters form two camps: the older two, Kathryn and Elizabeth, and the younger two, Pip and Adrienne. Fate drove them closer to each other. Tensions between the older two have occasionally perplexed their sisters but no outsider can drive a wedge. The Collins girls have been through too much. They know they have to stand together. They know they must always pick themselves up and carry on. Maria taught them this. Yes, your heart is breaking, but pick yourself up.

These four would be special even if Erebus had never happened. It may be, I've thought many times during the course of this project, that the intelligence and honesty, the dignity and courage of the girls tell us all we need to know about the integrity of Jim Collins himself. The girls insist that you accept the competence of Jim Collins. Their eyes burn with it. They can hide the fire, of course. Life goes on. But when they contemplate Erebus and open themselves to it, they smoulder and burn and they die a little more. Speak of Erebus to the older girls, to Kathryn, to Elizabeth, and you will feel the heat from uncooling embers.

In a group they can be wickedly funny. They got this quality, I am told, from their father. The youngest, Adrienne, is a fine mimic. Much in their lives is run past Maria. She has always been honest with them. Maria's rulings and advice, if not obeyed, are nevertheless listened to.

They are all highly educated and creatively talented. Kathryn is an architect and a painter. Elizabeth is a fine classical musician, a flautist, who has managed some of the world's great orchestral conductors in Europe. Pip has been a New Zealand diplomat in Paris. Adrienne was a journalist.

They are all successful. Pip is ambitious and admits it. Elizabeth is a splendidly efficient organiser. Kathryn is dedicated to her husband, her children, to good works in the community and to achieving justice for her father. Pip speaks French, Elizabeth Danish, and Adrienne and Kathryn some Italian. Kathryn and Pip have some knowledge of German.

Pip has been to Erebus.

They have a mother who knows them perfectly and understands them well. Maria is intelligent, cultured, interested and kind. She is passionate about her music. It sustained her soul and got her through the time of hardest grief. In one long all-afternoon interview for this book, Maria was open and vulnerable. Her matter-of-fact recitation of the way things were in the first days and weeks after Erebus, the simplicity of her descriptions of the betrayals, her acceptance, were moving. I wanted so much for time not to exist and for the Erebus disaster never to have happened. But it did. We cannot undo it. We cannot undo pain and loss. We cannot put that aircraft together again.

Maria is relentlessly active, a lecture here, a concert there, a tramping trip here, a trip to Vietnam or to Europe, or a walk round Uluru with her group of friends. Perhaps tonight, a three-hour version of Handel's *Messiah*, which she has sung so often in the Choral Society. She is driven. Keeping busy got her through the dark days. Keeping busy gets you through, and Maria got through. For Jim's sake and for the girls, in front of the eyes of the world, Maria got through. Maria is 75 now.

The Collins girls value kindness and loyalty, loyalty perhaps above all else. The loyalty of old friends. Loyalty was what mattered.

The two oldest girls went to hell when their father was killed. They have almost made it back. The other two watched and wondered and as the years go by feel the loss of their father more and more. As Adrienne says, 'In a way it gets more significant as time goes by.' Erebus has stamped them all.

The two oldest, Kathryn and Elizabeth, may always exist in a certain kind of confinement that no one can ever deserve.

Still, at heart, they are all normal people, entertaining people from a normal family with all of a normal family's ups and downs, a normal family's light and shade — except that one day the man they loved flew a DC-10 into a mountain in broad daylight and not only did he not come home but he got the blame for killing himself and 256 other people. Even Justice Mahon, when he first read Ron Chippindale's report, thought it quite reasonable. The pilots, sadly, were to blame.

But it was not, of course, the fault of Captain Collins. Not remotely, not even near it.

The girls have all felt deeply, and will feel forever, the injustice inflicted upon their father's good name. They do not remember a time when they did not feel this injustice. Maria waits for the history books and the official world to tell the truth and clear the name of her husband. Nothing less will she accept. Nothing else will satisfy her. Jim Collins, she will tell you, was a good and decent man and a thorough and diligent airman. He was a wonderful father and the girls adored him and one day he could not come home. He was lying face down frozen on a mountain. He could never come home.

The collision of the Air New Zealand DC-10 with the mountain is simple to understand. Yet so many New Zealanders have never been able to grasp it. It was in the interests of many at the time to make it complicated.

It was not complicated at all.

It was just the damnedest and simplest of things.

3

It Got Too Hard

The Erebus story got too hard. That's what happened. You no longer knew which side was right.

It got too hard. The arguments were intensely complicated and, the harder they were fought, the more complicated and arcane everything became.

It got vicious and nasty, too. Greg McGee, who scripted the splendid four-part television series *Erebus: The Aftermath* in 1985 and 1986, laid down four conditions to TVNZ before he undertook the job. He was to be immune from action for defamation. TVNZ would have to wear that. He wanted a researcher. He wanted an independent legal adviser and he wanted — and got — security for himself and his family when the series went to air.[1]

Hours after the Air New Zealand DC-10 under the command of Captain Jim Collins crashed on the northern slope of Mount Erebus, the New Zealand Government instructed the Chief Air Accident Inspector to investigate the cause. His name was Ron Chippindale. He had never investigated a disaster anywhere near this scale. He had never led any investigation into the destruction of a wide-bodied jet airliner.

While the families of the dead crew and the passengers grieved, in New Zealand and round the world, and wondered what on earth could have caused such a monumental catastrophe on a sightseeing flight that the airline had conducted more than a dozen times and that had been enjoyed by more than two thousand passengers, Mr Chippindale began his investigation. We do not know how he went about it because his investigation was conducted, incredibly though it seems now, in secret.

The destruction of the 200-tonne airliner happened in the early afternoon on 28 November 1979. Within a fortnight, a mere fortnight, Ron

Chippindale was already leaning towards pilot error. We know this because when he came to see Maria Collins, Captain Collins's wife, on 14 December, he kept repeating, as they sat at her table, 'Jim was too low, Maria. Jim was too low.' Maria knew then that his finding would reflect that view.

And that is how it turned out. As Chippindale began, so he finished. Until the end of his life, no matter how solid and convincing the alternative evidence, no matter how complete the logic of the brilliant investigation of Justice Mahon, nothing inspired within him even a flicker of doubt that he was right in his determination that the actions of the pilots had caused the accident. Chippindale had 4000 hours of flying time. Jim Collins and Greg Cassin, the two pilots on the flight deck of the DC-10, had 19,000 between them — Jim Collins alone had 11,000 flying hours. Chippindale, who had zero hours on passenger jets, would approach what Collins and Cassin did on their fatal flight as if they were low-timers.

His refusal to move from his position provoked amongst many of his contemporaries admiration for him as a principled man. Now, with the passing of time, it is easier to see his conviction for what it really was, the clever dishonesty of a man of unwavering arrogance. His arrogance never faltered. Right to the end Chippindale knew that Chippindale was right and that Mahon had got it wrong.

The accident was pilot error. The 'probable' cause, he wrote in that strangely uncommitted and strangely constructed sentence was simple: 'The probable cause of this accident was the decision by the captain to continue the flight at low level towards an area of poor surface and horizon definition when the crew were not certain of their position and the subsequent inability to detect the rising terrain which intercepted their flight path.'[2]

What he appears to be saying is that an 11,000-hour man with a DC-10 full of passengers continued to fly towards and into cloud at 1500 feet knowing that in the cloud there was a 13,000-foot mountain. It was a preposterous notion.

Well, he was right, wasn't he? How else could you explain what had happened? How else could Jim Collins have flown into a mountain if he hadn't flown into cloud? Justice Mahon admits in *Verdict on Erebus*, his Erebus memoir, that in the weeks before the start of the Royal Commission hearings, as he read Chippindale's accident report several times, he found himself agreeing with the Chief Inspector and he imagined his inquiry would be over quite quickly.

To the public it sounded more or less fine as well. What Chippindale said happened was probably what happened. The transcript of the cockpit voice recorder had the crew sounding vague about where they were. God, they were all over the show. The whole flight deck seemed vague and unfocused. As for those circles Collins was making in the sky, well, maybe Chippindale was right and the crew didn't know where they were.

The release of Chippindale's report No. 79-139 at midnight on 20 June 1980, a political act of infinite cynicism coming as it did just days before the start of the Royal Commission hearings, had a serious effect on what people thought.

The headlines Mahon quotes in *Verdict on Erebus* were very damaging to the crew.

> CRASH REPORT POINTS TO ERROR BY DC-10 CAPTAIN
>
> CREW UNCERTAIN AS PLANE NEARED SLOPE
>
> FLIGHT THOUSANDS OF FEET TOO LOW
>
> AIRCRAFT RADAR SHOULD HAVE SEEN MOUNTAIN

In fact, as Mahon would soon be shocked to realise, the Chief Inspector was wrong. He was fundamentally, absolutely wrong. There was no pilot error. The crew was not remotely uncertain of where they were. They were not thousands of feet too low and the aircraft radar could not have seen the mountain. In fact, the cockpit voice recorder showed that the pilots believed they knew exactly where they were even though they were wrong. But that was not their fault. They had no reason whatsoever to doubt where they were. They were not uncertain of anything.

What Mahon and everyone in that hearing would soon learn was that Ron Chippindale had doctored the cockpit voice recorder transcript in order to strengthen his argument. Some of what he heard on the cockpit tape no one else ever heard or was able to hear. For it simply wasn't there.

It became clear that Chippindale's determinations as to the cause of the accident were wrong and his process of investigation extremely questionable.

The very night of the accident Chippindale engaged as his technical adviser Air New Zealand's chief pilot, Ian Gemmell. Incredible as it now may seem, Gemmell, a senior officer of the most interested party in the accident, the very architect of Air New Zealand's Antarctic flights, the man with everything to lose, became Chippindale's main assistant and was able to move freely and unsupervised — except for his tether to a mountaineer for safety reasons — anywhere he wanted on the crash site.

Mahon found that all of Chippindale's evidence was hearsay. Chippindale would say forever, of course, that he never used the term 'pilot error' and I do not think he ever did. He was too smart to be so emphatic. Chippindale lived in the grey. His finding of 'probable' cause is classic Chippindale.

He would later say he was merely following the format for aircraft accident reports laid down by the International Civil Aviation Organization in Montreal and that he was required to record as the probable cause 'the last thing which occurred in the sequence of the flight which made the accident inevitable'.[3]

In other words, it was the actions of the pilots. In making the pilots' last actions the probable cause, of course, he could ignore the series of blunders in the days and hours before Jim Collins even got up to go to work that made the crash inevitable.

His report was clear. He knew what he had to do. He would blame the pilots. Dead pilots could not speak for themselves. As the old saying went in crew rooms round the world, 'If the accident doesn't kill the pilot, the inquiry will.' It was quite usual in those days for inexplicable air accidents round the world to be blamed on the pilot. Even the inquiry into the Chicago DC-10 crash just a few months before Erebus initially blamed the pilot, even though he had, through no fault of his own, lost all control of his left wing.

But the great question hung across the nation. Why in God's name would Collins have done what Chippindale claimed he did? Why would a sane man, a man with four daughters and a strong wife who loved him and made his coming home a pleasure, a man known to be one of the most cautious airmen in the fleet, fly an aircraft full of innocent passengers into cloud at 1500 feet with a 13,000-foot mountain in front of him?

For that is what the Chief Inspector of Air Accidents in New Zealand said Jim Collins did and the Chief Inspector knew his stuff because . . . well, that was the title he held. He was the Chief Inspector. The rest of us knew nothing about the intricacies of flying, but he must. Surely. He'd been a squadron leader, a base commander in the air force, so he must know these things. And, indeed, he looked efficient, authoritative and military. That was New Zealand then, of course. You held the title, so you weren't to be doubted. The title meant you knew. That was how it worked then. And never has a man looked more like the person for the job than did Ron Chippindale — tall, tidy, erect and military. He looked so credible.

Ron Chippindale's findings carried authority and weight within the New Zealand community. We had only heard of him before when a Cessna crashed into a hill. Now everything he said was indisputable. Suddenly an obscure backroom man was central to one of the greatest, cruellest and most incomprehensible stories in the history, not only of the nation, but in world aviation as well. The news media and the public hung on his every word and tried to interpret the thinking behind his every gesture. It must have been heady stuff for a man of such Robespierrean righteousness, such unshakeable self-belief and, as we shall come to see, an arrogance that knew no bounds.

And the public release of those findings, just weeks before the opening of the Royal Commission of Inquiry into the crash of the DC-10, had a powerful, fundamental and enduring effect on the views the New Zealand public held about the catastrophe. As Mahon would observe much later, nothing convicts a pilot so effectively in the public mind as an allegation of low flying with passengers on board. It was exactly what Robert Muldoon and his government, Civil Aviation and the management of Air New Zealand wanted and counted on.

Chippindale's essential absolution of the airline and its regulator, Civil Aviation, was a godsend. When it came to the blame game, when it came to the liability and the looming nightmare of hundreds of millions of dollars' compensation facing both the airline and Civil Aviation, Chippindale had delivered manna from heaven. Never mind the permanent stain on the names of Captain Jim Collins and First Officer Greg Cassin. Chippindale for his part was perfectly sanguine about this and never showed a flicker of concern.

Before that public release, Chippindale's interim report went up to the Minister of Transport and copies were sent for comment to those whom the inspector was going to find blameworthy. As everyone expected, copies went to Civil Aviation, Air New Zealand and the counsel for the dead pilots. Word got around. But controversy was beginning to grow. The airline pilots were not happy with what they were hearing. What's more, there was the leak from inside Air New Zealand that a certain bungle by the airline's Navigation Section might have played a part.

Muldoon knew he had to shut it down. He wanted nothing to distract from the Springbok tour the next year, which he knew was going to tear the nation apart and win him the 1981 election. And he wanted a sensible fellow who would understand that the airline could not go under, and that the New Zealand courts could not be allowed to fill up with legal claims for tens of millions in compensation from the families of those who died on Erebus. He wanted a good conservative judge. He appointed a one-man Royal Commission of Inquiry to be conducted by Justice Peter Mahon. Peter Mahon was a great buddy of Lloyd Brown QC, who would lead the case for Air New Zealand.

Muldoon had just made one of his biggest mistakes. Suddenly, into the whole confusing, impossible affair came a man not only honest but brilliant, and a man of legendary probity amongst his peers. In God's name where did he come from, this tireless, gigantically brained Christchurch fellow from whom no falsehood could be hidden? From over the mountains, beyond the rivers in the mists and from the plains beyond the sea, at last he had come. Gandalf the Grey, the intellectual wizard, had arrived.

Suddenly the families got a break. After the silence of the airline and the bankrupt, crooked findings of Chippindale, the families of the crew and the passengers got a break. They got a decent, honest High Court judge, a man dedicated to duty and justice. Peter Mahon QC, a man said to be the best barrister of his day, famous at the bar not only for his skill but his integrity. He was a man who could handle difficult, minute and confusing detail. They got a family man, infinitely courteous, a man who loved his duck shooting, loved his golf and a bet on the horses after a diligent study of the form. They got a man of whom his son Sam would say, wistfully, many years later, that he was never more relaxed or in happier company than when alone in his study with a scotch in one hand and a volume of the poets in the other.

They got a courtly man with an old-fashioned formality but a fine sense of humour, as the published letters to his children show us. They got a man who could solve the most complicated problems. They got a man of common sense, a man who could not be lied to. A man who could deduce.

Chippindale had known about the coordinates being changed without the pilots being told before they took off but gave this no weight.

Mahon, of course, would find that position 'untenable'.[4] He would find that the 'single dominant and effective cause of the disaster was the mistake made by those airline officials who programmed the aircraft to fly directly at Mount Erebus and omitted to tell the aircrew'.[5] The change of the navigational coordinates moved Captain Collins's flight path 40 kilometres east of where he had been briefed to fly. In his eloquent, gripping and powerfully written accident report, Mahon declared that the pilots were convincingly cleared of any blame.

What's more, Mahon stated, in the kind of language one never heard from a judge, that he had been confronted by the airline with a 'predetermined plan of deception' and had to listen to 'an orchestrated litany of lies' from the airline's management.

Prime Minister Robert Muldoon retaliated. Mahon was flat wrong. Morrie Davis, the airline's dictatorial Chief Executive — created so freakishly and uncannily in Muldoon's emotional, attitudinal and even physical likeness — turned vindictively upon the judge who had, obviously, not played by the rules.

But this was Peter Mahon. Mahon stood up to Muldoon. And he stood up to Morrie Davis. In doing so he became a hero.

So the airline, that is to say Davis, and his chief pilot, Captain Ian Gemmell, went off to the Court of Appeal for a judicial review of Mahon's finding that there had been a conspiracy amongst senior Air New Zealand management to perjure — the so-called 'orchestrated litany of lies'. This was the closest they could get to a defamation hearing. The Court of Appeal could not review the Commissioner's findings. It could only decide if the Royal Commissioner had the right to convict management of a crime, namely conspiracy to perjure. Both the Court of Appeal and — later — the Privy Council decided he did not.

The Court of Appeal found that Mahon had gone beyond natural justice by describing any untruths told under oath as orchestrated without warning various parties he was going to say what he did. Two of the five judges who heard the appeal wanted to tear apart Mahon's entire findings as to causation, but they were not allowed to go that far. Effectively, however, they said Mahon was incompetent in deciding what evidence to believe and what not to believe — the very essence of being a judge.

Mahon was furious. He took his case to the Privy Council and they too found against him on natural justice. He should have warned people he was going to accuse them of conspiracy to perjure. And for the incompetent administrative blunders and a cover-up by Air New Zealand, no one was ever held to account.

It was mad. But Robert Muldoon and Morrie Davis used the chinks in the Mahon Report that the courts gave them to propagate and broadcast the scandalous lie that both the Court of Appeal and the Privy Council had overturned Mahon's findings as to causation. Neither court did so. The Privy Council made it clear Mahon was wholly right in his judgement.

The Council went out of its way to compliment Mahon on a brilliant investigation. However, in a famous moment of fatuousness, it said that it was time for everyone in New Zealand to let bygones be bygones — 257 people had needlessly died and bygones should be bygones? But then the Council also forgave some obvious lying by the airline people.

All of which allowed Ron Chippindale to rear up again and cry, 'I told you so!' If only the judge had listened to me! If only the judge had consulted my office and my advisers! If only the judge had known more about 'aviation lore', whatever 'aviation lore' meant. Well, what it meant of course, in Chippindale's old air force mind, was that in any accident the pilot is always to blame.

Chippindale said all of this in a ranting tirade of a press release in February 1982, a few weeks after the Court of Appeal judgement was handed down. In it, he also accused the Collins girls of lying in their evidence to the Royal Commission. He also claimed that he could hear words on the poor quality cockpit voice recorder that no one else could.

The matter of wonder, looking back 30 years later, is that if there had been no Royal Commission, with all its evidence out in the open, evidence subject to cross-examination and the daylight of media coverage, no one would ever have known just how the accident happened and how silly Chippindale's findings were. We probably still don't know how he formed his conclusions or whom he consulted. We do know that he spent considerable time consulting Captain Ian Gemmell, the man who ran Air New Zealand's Antarctic flights.

Grandly, in his strange 1982 press release, Chippindale asserted that he had consulted widely amongst authoritative international experts and that they backed his views completely. But he never stated who they were.

It seems incomprehensible now — and hopefully it could not happen these days — that the senior pilot of the airline that operated the aircraft which had just crashed with the loss of 257 souls, the senior pilot of the main interested party in the whole affair, Air New Zealand, could be there on the mountain advising the man leading the investigation into the cause of the accident. In this way, Air New Zealand, the old Air New Zealand, the Air New Zealand of Morrison Ritchie Davis and Robert Muldoon, controlled Chippindale's inquiry. This was the way in which the company moved blame away from itself and Civil Aviation and moved Chippindale's findings towards their final, fatuous and demonstrably false conclusions.

Worse, the Chief Inspector's investigation, conducted with Captain Gemmell's help, took place entirely in secret with written statements taken from only a few witnesses; for example, American military personnel at McMurdo. What's more, in Ron Chippindale's interviews with other DC-10 pilots who had flown to Antarctica, Ian Gemmell, the powerful chief pilot, sat in to hear what they had to say.

The news media hung on every word Chippindale uttered for signs of the aviation oracle's thinking and Chippindale seemed to love the publicity his all-powerful, uncontested position brought him. He came to believe himself to be the air accident deity. And he seemed never to have to answer to anyone. All his work could be conducted away from any scrutiny.

As Winston Churchill once remarked, a lie gets halfway round the world before the truth has a chance to get its pants on. So it happened now. The public of New Zealand had complete faith in Ron Chippindale, not because they knew anything about him but for no other reason than he was the Chief Inspector of Air Accidents for the New Zealand Government.

That faith was misplaced, as the determined and painstaking inquiries of Justice Peter Mahon's Royal Commission would reveal. But Chippindale's findings suited the government of Robert Muldoon, the diminutive man with the demeanour of a murderous troll who, as mentioned, came to power asserting his genius in economic matters and was evicted from office with an economy in ruins. His regime is remembered for the rudeness of its leader, for the impotent, talentless yes-men with whom he surrounded himself and for the derision he directed towards those who were different or who dared to express a contrary view.

Muldoon and other powerful people who found Chippindale's findings so breathtakingly convenient continued to perpetuate the lie that Chippindale was right, Mahon was wrong and the superior courts had overturned what Mahon had found.

Because there was one thing Muldoon was never going to allow. The state-owned airline would and could not carry the blame. There was too much at stake. Its credibility was at stake. Its licence to fly in the United States might be challenged. Air New Zealand was not to be seen as incompetent. The pilots, who couldn't speak, could not tell their tale, would take the blame.

So the Chippindale Report suited Muldoon perfectly. The report suited the Civil Aviation Division (CAD) as well. They could have been up for millions too, for failing to stop the airline sending to the ice captains who had never been there before. Muldoon was not only Prime Minister, but Finance Minister as well, and the potential numbers were frightening. Sure, both Air New Zealand and CAD received minor scoldings from Chippindale but they were manageable. Both organisations had much to hide.

But most of all, Chippindale's report suited Air New Zealand because, although he knew about it, Chippindale, for some unfathomable reason, gave no weight at all to one salient fact revealed to him. Air New Zealand's Navigation Section had, at 2.16 on the morning of the day Jim Collins took his DC-10 to Antarctica, altered the course he programmed into his flight deck computer and sent him 40 kilometres east of the course on which he and First Officer Greg Cassin had been briefed. This had no effect on the fate of the flight, concluded Chippindale. That was that.

Yes, it got too hard. Who was right? If it was Mahon, then why did the Court of Appeal and the Privy Council do what they did? And what did the courts actually say in those long, complicated judgements? Did they overturn Mahon on causation as Davis and Muldoon appeared to be saying?

So, in people's minds, I believe, the questions arose again — including the greatest one of all. How, with his 11,000 hours of flying, with his reputed skill and his apparently legendary caution, did Jim Collins manage to fly his aeroplane into the side of that Antarctic mountain in broad daylight, with the passenger photographs showing sunshine streaming into the aircraft's cabin? Maybe, just maybe, Chippindale was right. Collins flew into cloud.

It all got too hard. So, we stopped thinking about it. Who to believe? We could not resolve it. So we put Erebus on a shelf in our minds. We put it away, let it rest, unresolved, bitter, sad, lost and hanging, with question marks forever over the reputations of the pilots.

But for the Collins girls, this awful, highly publicised crash of the great airliner, the death of hundreds of people with their father at the controls, the prolonged, bitter investigation with its lies, allegations and obfuscation and its arcane and tortured legal argument and attendant, outrageous covering-up — for these daughters of Erebus, this one great terrible thing has never gone away.

4

McMurdo

Look to your men. Men are the most doubtful quantities in the Antarctic. The most thorough kind of preparation, the shrewdest plan can be destroyed by an incompetent or worthless man.

— Roald Amundsen's advice to Commander Richard Byrd, first man to fly over the South Pole in November 1929

No one knew a thing, of course, about what had just happened on the low northern slope of Ross Island, beneath Mount Erebus. No one knew about the seconds after impact when the broken-off tail engine of the DC-10 continued to roar and thrust itself up the slope through everything like a crazy firecracker until its fuel died, just as everything and everyone else had died just a second or two before.

No one knew anything at McMurdo Base or at Scott Base or at Air New Zealand Headquarters in Auckland. No one knew a thing. Not yet. Not one of the families had any idea of the catastrophe. Not yet. But it was real; it had happened. The aircraft was a black, dirty smudge spread like Vegemite on the snow and ice.

All anyone at Scott Base and McMurdo knew was that today was DC-10 day — something to break the routine, a dramatic sight to treasure. The weather wasn't blue and white and pristine, but it was fine enough, and the overcast would bring the pilot down nice and low and noisy around 1500 feet. In any case, most of the flights came in at around that height.

In the usual scheme of things, they came straight down McMurdo Sound and over Scott Base and McMurdo Base, circled the Scott Memorial Hut a bit further south, turned round, came over the bases again, headed left and north over the great rugged mountains of Victoria Land back up to Cape Hallett before climbing to altitude for the five-and-a-half-hour flight back to Christchurch.

And everyone hoped to hell that nothing would go wrong with the aircraft. There was no way the DC-10 could land on the ice runway. By late November the ice runway was probably too thin for a 200-tonne fully laden DC-10. And even if, in a last gasp of desperate hope, a DC-10 had to put down on the ice there was another problem straight away, a human problem, the matter of caring for some 250 people in an environment that was hostile to human life, even in late November.

Make no mistake, this was Antarctica, this was the monstrous continent of ice and meteorological evil, which could almost instantly grind all human activity to a halt, the monstrous heartbreaking land of the heroic Shackleton and Scott, where brave and gallant men fought death and fear, loneliness and scurvy. For this climate, the passengers were most certainly not dressed.

No one knew a thing. No one would for hours yet. The aircraft had crashed, everyone was dead, and no one knew or suspected a thing.

Maria Collins, at home in Auckland, was planning to collect her youngest, Adrienne, and take her to a friend's birthday party after school. Kathryn, the eldest, was also at home studying for her School Certificate science examination in two days. Elizabeth, the girl with the wonderful musical talent, was at Epsom Girls Grammar, nearing the end of her third form year. She had eaten lunch in a part of the school garden called 'Paradise' just as her father's huge aircraft rolled to the right at Cape Hallett for the 337-mile leg to his destination waypoint at West Dailey Island at the head of McMurdo Sound.

In Wellington, 33-year-old Sergeant Gregory Gilpin had been at a police disaster victim identification team refresher course at Police Headquarters. Greg was an experienced officer. He had already pretty much seen it all. Human death, human decay, rotten bodies, bodies fished out of water, incineration, murder, mutilation, and myriad other human degradations, human sufferings and human fates.

Also on that same police course and travelling in a car back to where he was stationed in Lower Hutt was a young 22-year-old police constable, Stuart Leighton, who hadn't seen much at all. Stuart had joined the disaster victim identification team the year before when his sergeant asked for volunteers. Stuart had figured that the most likely disaster he would ever have to deal with was a massive earthquake in Wellington and since he was there anyway, he might as well find out what to do. He put his hand up.

As Stuart Leighton was travelling back to Lower Hutt, probably an hour before Jim Collins's DC-10 slammed its belly into the slope of Mount Erebus, right near the Petone overbridge, a world-weary senior constable in the car with him said, 'You know, I've been in the police for over 25 years and we've never had to use these procedures and we never will.' This avowal haunts Leighton still.

Later, when he finished his shift, he rode his motorcycle over to the house of the girl he later married. They were going to a movie. Round dinner time, his girlfriend's brother appeared with strange news. The brother worked for Post and Telegraph and he told Stuart that his colleagues had been monitoring radio communications and an Air New Zealand DC-10 was overdue in Antarctica.

Stu Leighton remembers feeling dread.

Morrie Davis, the airline's Chief Executive, was doing what he did so well. He was schmoozing and hobnobbing at the Air New Zealand Golf Open, at the Royal Wellington course in Heretaunga, Upper Hutt, not far from where Stuart Leighton heard the senior constable utter his immortal line. It was only a geographical proximity. Morrie was operating in another world. At the Golf Open, Morrie was the grand seigneur, the effusive host, social climber supreme, laughing and shooting the breeze with some of the most powerful figures in the land and more than a few of the most famous golfers in the world.

Morrie Davis was charming, dictatorial, pugnacious and believed in hierarchy. He thought nothing of throwing the good names of a competent, highly trained and loyal flying crew, who were now deceased, to the wolves. The accident killed them but Morrie would have to kill them more. There was no danger for him there. The dead could not protest.

He was a self-made man who joined the company as an office boy at the age of 16 in 1941. In the early 1970s he became Chief Executive. His rise in terms of power seemed to track that of his good friend Robert Muldoon. Just after Morrie became Air New Zealand's Chief Executive, Muldoon became Prime Minister. Muldoon, as Finance Minister as well as Prime Minister, was the sole shareholder of Air New Zealand. Obviously Davis and Muldoon would have a lot to do with each other. They were drinking buddies, everyone in the airline knew that, but also, Muldoon had a passion for aviation.

Davis ruled Air New Zealand with an iron fist. No one, especially no one he perceived as junior, questioned Morrie Davis. MP Maurice Williamson, who worked for Air New Zealand as a young man, says Davis was Muldoon's exact replica. The myths were similar. Remember, Muldoon was hailed as an economic genius. In fact, he was an economic dunce. He was a brooding, vindictive, ruthless thug. He thought nothing of ruining lives and reputations. He was a man who wrecked the New Zealand economy, failed to take the measures necessary to improve it, and was even prepared, when the country rejected him in July 1984, to bury the economy out of spite. The whole nation would have to suffer because it had let him down. He resigned only when certain members of his cabinet at last stood up to him and threatened to go to the Governor General and have him sacked.

But right now, Sergeant Greg Gilpin and Constable Stuart Leighton were getting back to their police stations. Jim Collins's wife was getting ready to take Didi to a birthday party. Kathryn was pondering cell division in plants. Elizabeth, Pip and Adrienne Collins were at school.

Justice Peter Mahon was in the High Court in Auckland. Mahon was a returned serviceman who was sent to the Italian Campaign in 1944. He saw serious military action amongst the horrors of Cassino and he fought with the New Zealanders all the way to Trieste and the German surrender. Mahon left New Zealand as a private and returned as second lieutenant.

After the war in his native Christchurch he built a name as a fine barrister with an extraordinary eye for minutiae and acted frequently in court in many complicated commercial and financial cases, taxation being his specialty. Mahon loved literature and could quote screeds of it. As Jim Collins headed south from the Balleny Islands in the Southern Ocean, Mahon, who had become a judge less than a decade before, was hearing a compensation case. A young man had been injured. The company admitted liability. It merely remained, he tells us in *Verdict on Erebus*, for the jury to say how much compensation he should receive.

And way over the sea to the south, 4000 kilometres away over the frigid Southern Ocean with its melting, cracking sheets of ice, its majestic whales, its breaching orcas and its wandering lonely birds, waiting with his camera at Scott Base was Nigel Roberts. Nigel was going to get a good photo of the DC-10 today. He was determined. The DC-10 coming over was quite a thrill. It wasn't just the noise or the size of the machine. It was like a visit from home.

A previous flight, a fortnight ago, had come over too high for a decent photograph. The previous week's, that of Captain White, who approached the bases as he believed he had been briefed to, straight up the middle of McMurdo Sound,[1] came over brilliantly low at 2000 feet, later flying past Erebus itself at 4000 feet. But Nigel had missed it. He was not going to miss this one. Yes, it was going to be Good Picture Day today at Scott Base. Air New Zealand, who seemed to delight in dramatic pictures of their aircraft flying nice and low over Antarctica and used them frequently in their publicity material, might even pay something for a good shot.

Nigel Roberts, who would become Professor of Political Science at Victoria University and one of New Zealand's leading television political analysts, remembers the weather at Scott Base as being 'all right'. There was cloud, but it wasn't mad. It was grey. It wasn't Antarctic blue and white. It was, he told me, the colour of a Wellington winter's day.

Way to the north of Nigel Roberts was the DC-10. About an hour behind Captain Collins was an American Air Force Starlifter under the command of Major Bruce Gumble. The major had some high-class Easterners on board, a crowd of Old Virginians, members and friends of the elegant Byrd family. United States Senator Harry Byrd and his party were coming to the ice to commemorate the famous and courageous flight over the South Pole by the senator's uncle, Commander Richard Byrd, in a Fokker Trimotor machine 50 years ago in 1929. Senator Byrd was expecting a big day.

Gumble had been chatting to the DC-10, as you do when you are two lonely crews way out in the middle of the Southern Ocean with no help in sight should anything go wrong and when the last thing you want is a collision of the two aircraft. But Major Gumble hadn't heard from Collins or Cassin for a while. The silence would not particularly have bothered Gumble. He would simply have liked to speak to the DC-10 to check where it was in relation to the Starlifter, which was soon to begin its own descent. But whatever, McMurdo Station would always know where the DC-10 was.

Captain Jim Collins monitored the flight as the DC-10 swept smoothly south and east from the Balleny Islands towards Cape Hallett, the northeastern extension of Victoria Land, a region of towering mountains and vast glaciers that stretches way to the north of McMurdo Sound. Victoria Land was a scenic bonanza in its own right. At Cape Hallett were some abandoned American huts. That was your landmark.

Collins's flight was as simple as that. That was all it had to be. Five and a half hours there, sightseeing for half-an-hour, five and a half hours back over the 3800 kilometres to Christchurch, and that more or less used up your fuel.

Now that the DC-10 approached Antarctica, there would be great excitement on the aircraft. But neither Collins nor Cassin actually had to see Cape Hallett. The aircraft's state of the art navigational computer knew where it was, recognised the waypoint and turned south automatically. Where he could have, Gordon Vette always asserted, Jim Collins would have taken visual fixes on Buckle Island in the Balleny Islands and as he approached Cape Hallett to assure himself he was on track. Such fixes would have reinforced his faith in the accuracy of the AINS.

This was something that was, perhaps, little understood back in 1979. The DC-10 and Boeing 747 aircraft had moved to a new age. These great, sophisticated machines, which already moved thousands of people round the world daily and nightly, high above the land and the seas, were navigated by computer. They negotiated their way round the globe themselves, with pinpoint accuracy second by second.

The DC-10 was guided by the area inertial navigation system (AINS). Wherever the aircraft was in the world, the AINS knew where it was. This was what Mahon realised so clearly. The DC-10 was a flying computer. As Mahon says in his report and in *Verdict on Erebus*, Captain Collins was not leaning out the window negotiating a World War Two bomber back to the nearest base in England. Aviation had moved to the computer age. The AINS, all DC-10 pilots knew, was extraordinarily accurate. Air New Zealand crews flying their DC-10s on AINS at night to Honolulu would see the lights of their fellow DC-10s directly above them as they passed above and beneath each other, dead on track, both of them.

The point of all this is that Jim Collins could be sure that if he was flying on Nav Track, the aircraft would be flying exactly as programmed. But the imminent tragedy of this flight was that the aircraft had been misprogrammed. So, of course, had the pilots.

So above Cape Hallett, with the old American huts possibly in sight below, the DC-10's computer rolled the aircraft gently right on to a track south towards the centre of McMurdo Sound, some 450 kilometres ahead. Jim Collins and Greg Cassin would have expected and would have felt the simple and reassuring pleasure pilots gain from the aircraft they are flying coming onto track. Things were exactly as they should be. Jim Collins had been briefed that he would be flying up the centre of McMurdo Sound before turning left and ambling across to McMurdo Base and Scott Base, another two kilometres further on.

But it was here, at Cape Hallett, that the jaws of a trap began to open. For while Jim Collins's area inertial navigation system turned him quite a way to the right, it did not turn him sufficiently right. The aircraft rolled out of the turn some 2 degrees too soon. The aircraft was now aiming not at the centre of McMurdo Sound but at a giant mountain, Erebus.

It rolled out too soon because, unknown to any of the crew, there was a flight plan change effected at 1.40 that very morning and the crew were not told about it when they reported for duty at Flight Despatch. The change in the navigation coordinates for TE901 — indeed, the entire history of the routes of all the Air New Zealand Antarctic flights — is a perplexing mystery in itself and we shall come to it soon enough.

But all that mattered now, in terms of understanding why Jim Collins would, in less than an hour, crash his DC-10 on Mount Erebus where it rises from the ice-covered sea, was that the unforgiveable had happened. Captain Jim Collins was not told of the change to his new destination waypoint and, therefore, where exactly his new track south was to end.

So an oversight had occurred, an oversight as bad as anything that can happen in aviation, and Collins knew nothing of it. He had no way in the world of knowing it and he had no reason on earth to suspect it. What's more, when Jim Collins looked out the cockpit window at the vast and sprawling landmass below him, so slight is the discrepancy at this early point of the new track, a mere 2 degrees, that he would have been sure that the aircraft's navigation system had just tracked him perfectly towards the Chute, as pilots called the safe military route down the middle of McMurdo Sound before the turn left to Williams Field.

First Officer Greg Cassin would have been of the same mind. So would flight engineers Nick Moloney and Gordon Brooks. Everything was spot on. Nice and easy. Nothing simpler.

As he flew south from Cape Hallett his deviation from the safe track increased, but Captain Collins would never know this. The gap between where he was and where he thought he was became wider. The fates were malevolent this day. The fates were conspiring. The fates wanted to kill this day.

But while he flew this route south he did come closer to the entrance to McMurdo Sound and for a while he cut a long, oblique swathe across it. As he flew closer to McMurdo Station, VHF radio communications between MacCentre and the DC-10 were excellent, readability five, as they say. The DC-10 was discussing descent, agreeing with MacCentre to maintain VMC (to fly visually in visual meteorological conditions), agreeing to advise altitude and hearing from the tower of the availability, should the crew 'desire it', of a radar let-down to 1500 feet up McMurdo Sound. Air traffic control invited Collins down.

'Roger, New Zealand nine zero one, that is acceptable,' replied Cassin.

As Collins headed south above a sprawling cloud layer, he was also heading increasingly east of the presumed track as the miles increased. The little navigation programme error at Cape Hallett was exacting its real price the further south the aircraft flew. Instead of sweeping straight into the centre of McMurdo Sound, the DC-10 made its way obliquely down left of the mouth of the Sound and headed towards Lewis Bay and the rising ground of Ross Island. It was pretty much parallel with where Collins should have been but still heading good and south. Erebus was right in front of him but at this stage well below him.

MacCentre cleared him down to 18,000 feet.

They had told the DC-10 crew that the overcast at McMurdo itself had a base; that it came down to a height of 2000 feet, plenty of room to give the passengers a tour underneath it in the clear air. Visibility was, MacCentre told him, 40 miles in all directions, which to a pilot is infinity. Forty miles visibility is more or less heaven.

So, it being a sightseeing trip, and given Collins knew the passengers' expectations and wanted to give them value for money — and probably with the normal desire of a pilot approaching unfamiliar terrain to see the ground below him — he looked for an early way down, under the cloud. Perfectly normal flying; pilots fly under cloud every day of the week.

He saw his opportunity. He saw wide breaks in the cloud with the sea and the sea ice clear below. He'd go down through the clear air, get under the cloud and head straight up McMurdo Sound and he'd have the safety of both clear visual flying and MacCentre's radar as well. It is important for the reader to understand at this point that from the moment he began to descend, he was flying visually.

The AINS told Collins he was about 10 minutes from the waypoint at which he'd turn left for the last 30 miles to McMurdo Station.

Captain Collins and the crew would have had a good scan of the sky round them. That's what you do. You always want to know what's in the sky with you. You always know where you are in relation to any object. Pilots call it spatial awareness.

At 1.31.20 Collins told his co-pilot, 'Tell him we'd like further descent. We have contact with the ground and we could, if necessary, descend doing an orbit.' In other words, they could see the wide sea below them.

The Americans replied, at 1.32.08, 'Roger Kiwi New Zealand, VMC descent is approved and keep MacCentre advised of your altitude.'

So Collins could descend — he was told to a minimum 1500 feet — and he would have to stay visual. In any case, as Gordon Vette says in *Impact Erebus*, Collins would never have gone lower than 16,000 feet, AINS or no AINS, without being visual.[2] He would not have gone to McMurdo Station without being visual. What would be the point, anyway, if no one could see anything?

Having established that they 'had the ground', and in an example of excellent and professional airmanship, he took the DC-10 down in two great orbits, neither of which — it must be noted — took the aircraft any further south. He is about to descend, as it were, in a couple of vertical spirals. The first orbit is a great right-hand arc, the second a long elliptical orbit which heads him back in the direction from which he'd come, north, descending all the while.

He did this by switching the aircraft from Nav Track to Heading Select. Heading Select meant the aircraft was still flying on autopilot but Jim Collins then turned a knob to direct the aircraft where he wanted it to go. He was all the while flying visually. Between the start of the first orbit and the point of impact, the crew confirmed with themselves no fewer than six times that they were flying visually.

When he had descended to 10,000 feet, flying north, Collins locked the aircraft back on Nav Track and the machine, accepting the command, turned 180 degrees back to the south on track to what he believed was McMurdo Sound. As he flew south in clear air, descending visually at all times, Collins continued down to 2000 feet before 'dropping' down another 500 feet to 1500 feet. At all times they were visual. No one at any stage on the flight deck argued that they were not flying visually.

The two pilots were certain where they were. That is why they so safely locked the aircraft back onto Nav Track. Captain Gordon Vette, in this respect, makes another shrewd observation. There is, on the tape, a rustling of paper and an obvious reference to positions on a chart. Vette observes:

'Airmen are trained from ab initio training that, when tracking normally, they read their expected position on a map and then identify visually the terrain features on the ground.'[3] He believes that this is what this crew was doing.

There is an opposite way of reading a chart, the 'lost procedure'. If you are lost, you look to the ground for significant terrain and try to identify those features on a map. Vette says, 'the CVR suggests the crew were getting confirmatory sightings and were, indeed, seeing what they expected to see.'[4]

The horrific thing, however, was that what they were seeing below them looked uncannily like what they were supposed to be seeing. In other words, the entrance to Lewis Bay looked exactly like the entrance to McMurdo Sound and in front of them was whiteout.

It was the emphatic locking of the aircraft back onto Nav Track that convinced Justice Mahon that Collins was in no way uncertain of his position, as the Chief Inspector of Air Accidents would later so oddly assert. Collins, knowing of the high terrain around in all directions, would hardly lock himself on to Nav Track at 2000 feet unless he thought he was going straight down the middle of McMurdo Sound. Captain Cautious was leaving nothing to chance. He knew exactly where he was when he locked the aircraft back onto its programmed course to what he thought was the head of McMurdo Sound. He was locked onto Nav Track when he struck the mountain, and still flying visually. But what no one on the flight deck knew, Collins's understanding of the meaning of flying visually bore no relation to the realities of Antarctic flying. The normal VMC requirement round the world is that you must be able to see anything eight kilometres away. Air New Zealand had increased that requirement to 20 kilometres in Antarctica but it wasn't enough. In fact the visibility requirement *meant nothing* in whiteout. Whiteout is a unique and fatal trap. Collins didn't know this. MacCentre had told him he would have 40 miles' visibility which, in aviation terms, is infinite.

Air New Zealand had never discussed the kind of whiteout he was now flying into and had not advised the Antarctic pilots never to descend beneath cloud with white snow and ice beneath them and a low sun behind them. The failure to inform the crews about the dangers of whiteout was a grossly negligent omission. It was a gross dereliction. If the airline had arranged for the briefings to include instructions into the variety and perfidiousness of Antarctic whiteout, then even in what he perceived to be visual conditions, Jim Collins would never have flown beneath cloud in Antarctica with mountains all round him, and the crash would not have happened.

The whiteout into which Jim Collins was flying was sector whiteout, the most dangerous of all. Captain Collins and First Officer Cassin could see the black rocks of the capes on the right and left sides of the cockpit. This reinforced their belief that they were flying in visual meteorological conditions (VMC). Normally they would be right. But ahead of them, the low overcast, interacting with the clean, unbroken white of the snow and ice, with the low sun behind them, had made a mountain disappear. And Jim Collins thought he had McMurdo Sound beneath him. That is what he was programmed to believe and that, he was sure, was where his eyes and his navigation computer were taking him.

McMurdo Station assumed Collins would come down the middle of the Sound as all the DC-10s did. It was about 1.45 in the afternoon. Any minute now, they'd see him.

There is another little component in the devilish conspiracy now unfolding. For some reason — which Mahon will explore but never really fathom — the flight plan sent that morning from Air New Zealand to MacCentre named Collins's destination waypoint as 'McMurdo'. No latitude and longitude were given and McMurdo Station, like Nigel Roberts, was expecting to see the DC-10 come roaring straight across McMurdo Sound. Had MacCentre seen the actual coordinates, they made plain later, they would not have accepted the flight plan.

At 1.45, Cassin had become fed up with the inconstant behaviour of his VHF radio. He hadn't realised that the true reason for the difficulties in radio communication with MacCentre was that the DC-10 was now low behind a mountain — VHF is line-of-sight radio. Because of the difficulties, he was transmitting to MacCentre on high frequency (HF) — high frequency radio is not bothered by hills because its signals bounce off the ionosphere.

1.45.00, Cassin: 'Affirmative, we are now at 6000 ah . . . descending to 2000 and ah . . . we are VMC.'

MacCentre: '901, Roger.'

Those are the last words McMurdo Station ever heard from Kiwi 901.

Jim Collins was flying visually but nevertheless had his state of the art navigation computer locked onto the navigation track designed for him back in Auckland by the Navigation Section — which had him, he thought, heading straight for the headwaters of McMurdo Sound, overhead the final waypoint at West Dailey Island. The crew on the flight deck was, they thought, looking ahead over miles of flat white sea ice. Collins knew that when he reached the head of McMurdo Sound, he would bank his aircraft to the left, and fly it an easy 40 kilometres to the American and New Zealand bases where she would be the great star of the ice that day and have them talking for weeks.

A relaxed Jim Collins, no doubt wishing the radio communications were tidier, flew on, waiting for signs of human activity to appear in front of the cockpit, for signs of human activity to come towards them through the frigid air at 460 kilometres an hour.

Now the second deception comes into play. To his right he could see the long black rock face of Cape Bernacchi. Except it wasn't Cape Bernacchi. It was Cape Bird. To his left he could see Cape Bird. Except it wasn't Cape Bird. It was Cape Tennyson. While it is universally agreed that the entrance to Lewis Bay bears an uncanny resemblance to the entrance to McMurdo Sound, Jim Collins, locked onto Nav Track, has no need even to wonder. Why would he wonder if this was McMurdo Sound? In any case, he was visual in VMC conditions. Had he had a previous supervised flight, Jim Collins might have cottoned on.

The most important clue that could have told the crew they were off course, or rather they were headed into Lewis Bay, was the distinct form of Beaufort Island, to the north of Lewis Bay. Passenger photographs make it clear that Beaufort Island was visible. If the crew had recognised Beaufort Island and noted it was on their right instead of being way across to their left, as it should have been, they might have realised something was badly wrong. But no one on the flight deck said a thing about Beaufort Island.

Later, an expert in polar flight whom Mahon consulted in Canada, Mr G. W. Shannon, who had experience flying not only in Northern Canada, but in Antarctica as well, said if Collins saw the island he probably thought it was Dunlop Island, which is off the coast of Victoria Land at the entrance to McMurdo Sound.

Arthur Cooper, a former Air New Zealand DC-10 captain, says we have to remember that the DC-10 flew 5 degrees nose up when straight and level. And the faster your aeroplane flies, the further ahead you have to be looking. This crew wanted to know what was 30 miles in front of them, not what was underneath them.

But Mahon probably put it best. On page 115 of his report, he showed his understanding of mindset. He said the five on the flight deck undoubtedly saw Beaufort Island and thought it Dunlop Island. But more importantly, in the minds of the crew, the island could not have been Beaufort Island because they were nowhere near Beaufort Island.

And now the third and conclusive part of the trap that will destroy the DC-10 and all on board comes into play: the weather. But not any weather. It was bad weather that looked as if it were perfect. And it would provoke the most perplexing question of all. Why did Jim Collins, one of the most cautious and most competent men on an Air New Zealand flight deck, fly in clear air into the side of a mountain?

The true answer is that Captain Collins saw perfect conditions and did not see a mountain — not even in the last second. Neither did First Officer Greg Cassin. Neither did Flight Engineer Gordon Brooks. Neither did Flight Engineer Nick Moloney. Neither did the Antarctic explorer and Antarctic veteran, the man who had acted as guide on four of these flights, Peter Mulgrew.

We know from passenger photos that Captain Collins was flying in clear air, and that sunlight was streaming through the windows of the passenger cabin. You can see the capes each side of the aircraft in the distance. And the flight crew repeated time and again to MacCentre and to each other that they were flying VMC. Passengers were taking photographs at the point of impact.

But ahead of them was perfect sector whiteout.

The Chief Inspector of Air Accidents, who understood whiteout, refused, strangely, to link it to what happened. Air New Zealand didn't like it either. Neither did the Civil Aviation Division. Its director, Captain Kippenberger, would testify later that whiteout did not exist in this case and, if it did exist, it played no part.

It would take a fellow DC-10 pilot, one of the most senior in the DC-10 fleet and the man who, back in the air force days, taught Jim Collins to fly, to show its importance to the loss of the DC-10 that November day. He was Captain Gordon Vette.

In the days after the accident Gordon Vette went to Maria Collins and shook his head. 'This isn't Jim, Maria. This is not Jim's behaviour. Jim doesn't fool round in low cloud. Something's wrong. I'm going to find out.'

Visibility was excellent. The five on the flight deck could see for miles ahead of them — so they thought. Out the window of the cockpit in front of them was a flat white surface which extended as far as their eyes could see. Collins was flying into air that seemed as clear as a bell. And there was a 13,000-foot mountain right in front of him. And no one ever mentioned on the cockpit voice recorder, even in the last seconds, a mountain in front of them.

They were as good as dead. Super cautious Jim Collins, one of the best of the best but unschooled in the tricks of polar light, had flown into full and perfect polar whiteout. The insidious evil of whiteout is that a pilot has no reason whatsoever to think anything is wrong or that anything is other than what the eye is telling him or her. They have no reason whatsoever to think that what they are seeing is not what is there. They have no idea that they are flying into the ultimate optical illusion.

Collins was looking through the cockpit window at a scene that accorded exactly with what he expected to see. He was not flying into cloud. There was no cloud to be seen in front of him. But the base of the cloud had merged with the mountain to create an illusion of a flat surface way into the distance. And if Jim Collins was flying down the centre of McMurdo Sound, that is exactly what he should have been seeing. Innocent Jim Collins, locked diligently onto the programmed Nav Track, First Officer Greg Cassin and 255 others were hurtling towards immoveable rock at 460 kilometres an hour.

In a nanosecond everyone on board was dead. They were scattered all the way up the wreckage site, 700 metres of it.

In seconds the mountain was silent again.

No one yet knew any of this.

But the silence of the aircraft was starting to be deafening at Scott Base and McMurdo Base. Operation Deep Freeze in Christchurch, the headquarters of the US Navy's Antarctic operation, received a telex timed at 4.43 p.m., advising that there had been no contact with the aircraft since just before 2 p.m., New Zealand Daylight Saving Time. Within an hour and a half of the start of the great silence, the US Navy at McMurdo Station threw every resource it could muster into the search for the DC-10.

Just after 12.30 a.m. on 29 November, an American Navy Hercules, X-Ray Delta Zero Three, flew across the northern side of Ross Island. The pilot in command reported in. 'MacCentre, Zero Three. We have located the wreckage. I say again we have located the wreckage of the DC-10. Position 76.26 South, 167.27 East. There appear to be no survivors. I say again, there appear to be no survivors.'[5]

MacCentre said it would despatch a helicopter immediately. Zero Three advised he would 'orbit the scene off the beach 1500 feet and stand by for helo [helicopter]'.

The news was flashed across the Southern Ocean to Operation Deep Freeze in Christchurch.

Nigel Roberts never did get the picture he was after. The DC-10 never arrived. What he remembers most of that afternoon and late into the night was the thwack-thwack of the rotors of helicopters departing to search and returning for refuelling, and the screams of the Hercules engines as every aircraft available searched for a downed DC-10.

But the picture he did get next day would become one of the most iconic photographs in New Zealand — and aviation — history. It was the broken, battered tail section, lying forlorn on the ice, the proud koru in the mist on the Antarctic mountain ice.

5

The Family Waits

Time seems so long to a child who is waiting — for Christmas, for next summer, for becoming a grownup: long also when he surrenders his whole soul to each moment of a happy day.

— Dag Hammarskjold

And back in Auckland, no one knew a thing.

The cruellest part of it all was that they were such a happy family. Jim Collins seems to have had a gift with children. There were endless summers at Matapouri Bay in the Far North of New Zealand. There were silly jokes and fun. He made them laugh. He took them out in the boat. And he was a DC-10 captain. Any kid was going to be proud of that. The children doted on him. And he adored his girls.

And this was just a normal day. Dad would be home about 9 o'clock, no doubt with the blue cod and with stories about the flight, the passengers and the Southern Continent. The Erebus flights were known as all-day cocktail parties. Jim would have stories. Jim Collins loved knowledge and he loved to impart it. He might even have little mementos of the flight.

Kathryn did not hear her father go in the early morning. She awoke a bit later to face another day of study. She would sit her School Certificate science examination the following morning, 29 November.

It was turning into a warm, sunny day. Kathryn studied through the morning and was pleased when lunch-time arrived. She went to the kitchen, made a salad for lunch. 'I remember getting out the vegetables and the lettuce and tomato and deciding to add pineapple for a bit of variation. I made a huge salad in the large blue Swedish bowl Mum used for serving vegetables. I could toss the salad easily in it. I sat outside on the deck by the kitchen and in the sun and launched into it. It was hot, still and sunny on the deck. About one o'clock I remember thinking that Dad would be over Antarctica and the contrast between where he was and what I was doing would have amused him.'

Captain Collins, as his eldest daughter sat there in the sun thinking about him, was probably about halfway between Cape Hallett and the entrance to Lewis Bay. He had less than an hour to live.

Kathryn remembers nothing unusual about the afternoon until the early evening. At about 7 o'clock the Collins world began to change forever. Maria took a phone call from Captain Dave Eden, Director of Flight Operations at Air New Zealand.

'I think Jim was due home at nine and I'd have dinner with him later. I'd feed the children first. Dave Eden from Flight Ops rang me and said, "We're just a bit concerned about Jim's flight. We haven't heard from him for a while. Are you on your own?" And I said, "Well, the kids are here." He said, "Have you got another adult there with you?" And I said no, and he said, "Might be an idea." And that was when cold fear struck me.'

'Might be an idea.' Maria called her parents who lived round the corner and they came round to be with her. Maria's parents adored Jim Collins. He was tall and good looking, smart, loved Maria and loved his girls. They liked that he was liked by his children's friends, they liked that he commanded great airliners, that he was gently funny, that he was sober and faithful and so good with his children.

His girls idolised him. Everyone could see that. When Dad came home, the world was radiant and complete. They were immensely proud of his career. And in those days, at least, the job came with great privileges. Dads who were DC-10 captains could come home from the world with all kinds of treats. Not lavish, silly, spoiling treats. That was not Jim or Maria's style. Elizabeth, at the time her father was killed, was collecting First Class menus, which Jim brought her. On the covers were pictures of native birds. Elizabeth loves her animals.

Later, much later, Elizabeth, the second daughter, would write of her life. She would choose to write much of her short memoir as if she were still an adolescent and it was in this style that she approached the events of 28 November 1979 and the subsequent days and weeks. There is a chapter in which she is anticipating her fourteenth birthday. It is two sleeps to go. All she wants is a simple picnic.

Dad has been away for two weeks on an Auckland/Honolulu/ Los Angeles return trip. Mum has said that Kathryn and I can come with her to the airport tomorrow night to pick him up and a babysitter will look after the two younger girls at home. I am so excited. I love going to the airport because it means that Dad is coming home. I love the anticipation, the adventure, the smell of kerosene, the giant planes, and glamorous hostesses with perfect hair, long nails, lipstick and lots of perfume.

Dad always comes out of the immigration hall last. He waits for his crew to be processed ahead of him and makes sure each one has transport home from the airport. He looks dashing in his sleek black uniform with four gold stripes on each cuff and shiny shoes. He is tall and slim and everyone looks at him as he walks towards our car. I always get a lump of pride in my throat when I see him and Mum has tears in her eyes when he kisses her, gently. 'Hi Jum,' she says. His name is Jim but Mum has her special name for him.

He hasn't brought me a bird menu this time, but I don't mind because he is home for my birthday and that is what counts. I tell him I am now learning the flute instead of the violin and that I passed my ballet exam last week with Honours which was the highest grade in the ballet school and he says I am a very clever Groodle. I love it when he calls me that.

28 November 1979. Early evening. 'Immediate adulthood,' Elizabeth calls it in her memoir. She watches the 9 o'clock news. She remembers hearing newsreader Phillip Sherry saying that the aircraft had by now run out of fuel and there was still no sign of it. The aircraft had, therefore, to be down. 'We couldn't believe what we were hearing. Phillip Sherry must be wrong.'

According to Elizabeth, Maria then rang Jim's very good friend, another DC-10 captain, Ross Gordon, to ask if he had any idea of what might have happened. Ten minutes later Ross and his wife Marg arrived round at the Collins's. In the hours, days and years to come, Jim Collins could wish for no finer, more protective friend for his grieving family than Ross Gordon. Ross Gordon is dead now, but in the frightful days of grief about to erupt upon the home of Jim and Maria Collins, Ross and Marg Gordon performed as if God himself had sent them. Ross handled the phone calls and the news media. This was how six-year-old Adrienne learnt the word 'residence'. Ross answered the phone with, 'Collins residence.' Adrienne says that in those days she also learnt the word 'sympathy'. Before long, she says, she would also learn the word 'error'.

Marg ran the house and made sure Maria remembered to eat and drink. Marg sorted the hundreds of letters and cards that poured in from round the country from complete strangers, and arranged a little thank you note Maria could sign each morning. The house became a mass of flowers. I have wondered, as I've got to know the Collins women, if even then, in those very first days, the country sensed something fine and honourable about this family and about this airman. Perhaps it was simply the regard anyone feels for a mother of four daughters who has just lost her husband and four girls their father.

Elizabeth remembers Ross being straight with Maria that night, telling her Jim must have exhausted his fuel by now. Maria told her parents and Kathryn and Elizabeth that the crew and the passengers would have no chance of survival in the dreadful cold of Antarctica and that if the aircraft had gone down, death would be quick. 'The last thing she would want was for Jim to suffer in any way.'

Kathryn says: 'I remember the black, gold and brown patterned sundress Mum was wearing. And I can remember thinking about icebergs and landing in Antarctica and that if the plane had landed on the icy sea, Dad would be the last one off. I pictured him stepping off the wing onto an iceberg but being very cold as he was only in summer uniform. He would be very worried about his passengers. He would put them first, before him.'

That thought didn't bode well for his survival.

So they all sat there, waiting for news: Maria, Kathryn, Elizabeth, Maria's parents, Josef and Annemarie Tretter, and Ross and Marg, trying to be bright, trying to be optimistic. The hours were slow. They were joined by an old friend of Maria's parents, Karel Beran. Karel was a Czech refugee in his sixties, a dear and trusted friend of the family with a concentration camp tattoo on his forearm. Karel had been a significant figure in the Czech underground during the war. He survived two and a half years in Auschwitz, then Mauthausen, then the Death March at the end of the war from Mauthausen, the concentration camp outside Vienna. Kathryn remembers Karel looking worried and thinking that if he looked worried, after everything he'd been through, and if he had no answers and none of the adults had any answers, then things were bad.

Kathryn went to bed after the 9 o'clock news. Her grandfather, Josef, suggested there was nothing she could do by staying up and that she should try to get some sleep ahead of her science exam the next morning. Josef the survivor, the one who knew things were getting very bad in Vienna though so many others told him they would blow over, who knew you had to carry on, believed Kathryn had to sit her School Certificate exam the next morning. That was what life was about. Carrying on. Enduring and carrying on. Kathryn says it was just assumed she would sit the exam. There was never any doubt, never any discussion. So she went to bed. The lights remained on upstairs and there was the opening and closing of doors. She slept fitfully.

Philippa, or Pip, says of this day, 28 November 1979: 'Dad left early that morning. It was still dark. I crawled into bed with Mum. After school, I went to Brownies. I came home late afternoon. We had dinner. It was still light outside and the weather was calm. Mum took a phone call. I remember standing in the kitchen looking at the *World Book Encyclopaedia* open on the bench where I had been looking something up for my homework, and knowing something was terribly wrong.'

Jim had bought the girls the *World Book Encyclopaedia* with a small inheritance from a deceased English relative. Like his father-in-law, Jim was passionate about education. Jim had failed School Certificate the first time and it weighed on him. He was educated in the air force. Maria was a Bachelor of Science from Otago University.

'I remember my grandparents, Mum's parents, Josef and Annemarie, sitting in our living room,' Pip says. 'It was still light outside. My grandfather sat solemnly in a big brown chair. It was so out of the ordinary. When Josef and Annemarie came over, we never sat in the living room. We talked and moved round and there was a sense of vibrancy. This was very different.'

Somewhere in that earlier part of the night, Maria took Pip and Adrienne to bed. Maria remembers one of the girls asking if there was something wrong with Dad's flight. Maria says she made light of it. 'I said, "Oh, they're a bit worried, but don't worry about it, go to bed." Or maybe I just hid it from them. There's a childish thing in me that if I don't talk about it, it isn't there. You know what I mean? I know it's infantile but there is this sort of, "Don't say anything . . .".'

It was gone 1 a.m. Still no news. No further phone call from Air New

Zealand. No official visit from anyone at Air New Zealand. Nothing. Ross and Marg Gordon went home. Still up and waiting were Maria, Elizabeth, Maria's mother and father, and Karel Beran.

Elizabeth knew she had to stay up and be with her mother. 'That was my calling, to be there for Mum. Mum, Dadum and I sat in silence at the kitchen table hoping for a phone call. We waited and waited. I felt I must be there to support Mum.'

Maria says she felt it was a bad dream. 'It was difficult to believe that we were living through this.'

The call that changed their lives came, Maria thinks, between 1.30 and 2 in the morning, from Captain Dave Eden.

Elizabeth does not recall her mother's words during the phone call but remembers that Maria's responses were short. 'Something told me the outcome was pretty serious. When Mum got off the phone she explained what it was and burst into tears.'

Eden's message to Maria was two pronged. Wreckage of a DC-10 had been sighted on the lower slopes of Mount Erebus and the wreckage was such that there could be no survivors.

It occurs to me as I listen to the stories of this fateful night that there was something seriously wrong with the way Air New Zealand handled the looming trauma about to be endured by the families of senior skilled and loyal staff. Air New Zealand knew, from at least 3 p.m., that TE901 was out of radio contact and had gone silent. By 7 p.m. the aircraft was out of fuel. It was now after one in the morning and any reasonable aviation mind knew the aircraft was lost, that it was down and probably all on board were dead. There could be no search and rescue. There was no point. This was Antarctica. The cold would have finished any survivors off.

At no point did anyone from Air New Zealand come to the Collins house in an official capacity. At no point. By the time Captain Dave Eden made his call to confirm the aircraft was smashed on an Antarctic mountain, the airline had had some 10 or 11 hours to organise someone to go round officially to comfort the captain's wife — a woman with four young daughters, a woman about to enter the hell in which she has lost a loved husband forever and in which she would have to comfort, on her own, four young and breaking hearts.

This has always intrigued me. An airline, like a broadcaster, say, is not about the equipment it uses, although of course aeroplanes and microphones and cameras are an essential part of it. Ultimately airlines, like broadcasters, are about people. Ultimately they are about people liking you enough to go with you. No people, no money; no money, no company.

At the very moment when Maria Collins was sitting waiting silently for news from Antarctica, Air New Zealand employed 8700 people. They were a fiercely loyal team spread round the country and round the world. Air New Zealand was a proud company. Air New Zealand meant something. People would look at you with respect if you said you worked for Air New Zealand. Air New Zealand was a family. Aviation was still glamorous in 1979. Adrienne and Elizabeth idolised the air hostesses whom they regarded as the personifications of international sophistication.

A few years back, I hosted a special and remarkable evening at which Air New Zealand was honouring staff who had been with the company more than 40 years. No one stays with a company for 40 years, it occurred to me, unless they feel that company supports them and is loyal to them. What's more, also honoured that night were staff whose service to the public and dedication to their jobs had gone way beyond the basic call of duty. What's more, these staff had not put themselves forward. Other staff had nominated them discreetly. One woman had given up Christmas with her own family at the last minute to accompany a child who desperately needed to be taken back to the United States.

So I find myself perplexed that Air New Zealand, that sad night 32 years ago, could send no one to comfort Maria Collins. Yet, at the same time, at TVNZ, New Zealand's biggest and most powerful communications company, I was often dismayed at our inability to communicate with the public, to explain a corporate position and to explain why we were doing something in a certain way. We could be terrified of the public with whom we communicated every day. So I am not completely shocked at the dysfunction of Air New Zealand that night. Sometimes people companies simply forget how to be people companies. Sometimes within the company too, things can paralyse and shock. Probably, the thought of a DC-10 down in Antarctica was such an event.

Maria is not particularly angry about any of this. She expresses some mild indignation that no one actually came and knocked on her door and showed her that respect. She wonders if a policeman could not have come to tell her personally. Instead, she had a cursory phone call from Dave Eden, a man she hardly knew, a man who was not a friend.

Her anger, and it remains intense, will build later, much later. It is reserved for those who did not lay their cards on the table, as Justice Mahon said; for those who lied under oath in an attempt to cover up; for those who were prepared to lie under oath in order to destroy the reputation of the father of her children.

She was a normal 44-year-old housewife then, she says, a mother of four children. 'And all these years later, I'm not nearly as naive and I'm not nearly as intimidated and I'm not nearly as stupid as I was then. I didn't know that prime ministers could do this sort of thing; that they connive with others; that people tell lies at inquiries. I was intimidated. I was a child of that time when authority meant something. So I was an idiot, a naive one, the one that's thinking, well, everyone will do as I do, tell the judge the truth.' Maria Collins is not a romantic. 'Feet on the ground,' she says.

I mention this to Elizabeth. 'You should have seen her with Dad,' she says. Maria is a scientist, a haematologist. She loves her music, her concerts, her National Radio, the talks she attends, theatre, the life of the mind. But in getting to know her, one is not exposed to any sense that she is tormented by the vulnerabilities of the excessively romantic.

I was talking one day to Maria's best friend, Kathryn Schollum, who is just a couple of years younger than Maria. They met in 1956 in the laboratory of Auckland Hospital where they both worked. They have been friends ever since. Schollum is a Catholic, very active in her church. Her people came from Bohemia. Schollum says that she and Maria have great arguments about religion. In the years after the disaster, Kathryn Schollum would be a loyal and fundamental buttress of support for Maria and her emotionally burdened girls. Kathryn Schollum would come round on Friday nights. She would bring sweets and treats and have a sherry. She likes a cigarette. Kathryn Schollum threw life and fun and laughter at the girls when she came to visit.

Kathryn Carter told Kathryn Schollum years later that without her she doesn't know how they would all have survived.

Maria Collins is a remarkable thinker. And she knew her husband profoundly. She says she hoped, at the point of Dave Eden's phone call, that Jim had not survived. She wrote for me in the exercise book I gave her: 'Jim's heart and mind could not have withstood the catastrophe which I knew he'd be convinced he was responsible for. Were he to survive, he'd be a haunted human being forever. He told me on several occasions the company would be merciless on any crew member involved. That wonderful person to whom I was married would be changed for the worse forever.'

Later she tells me: 'I began to hope that if they had crashed he died quickly because he would . . . the torment in his mind would be unbelievable. It would have destroyed him. It would have destroyed him mentally if he'd survived.'

Maria put the phone down from Captain Eden and cried out. 'I howled loudly. I didn't want to bring up the girls alone and be lonely, lonely, lonely! I remember shrieking, "Now I'm going to be alone and these poor children won't have a dad".' She thinks that was the only time she was 'poor me'.

Kathryn, in her bedroom, can't quite remember what caused her to get up. Her grandfather may have come downstairs to wake her or she may have heard her mother's broken-hearted cries. She doesn't remember exactly. Kathryn, 15 years old, got out of bed and went upstairs to the kitchen. There, Karel told her gently that aircraft wreckage had been found and that everyone was dead.

'I couldn't really quite believe what that meant. Other than that my life had changed forever and that now I'd have to try and work out what Dad would have wanted me to do. The thought was daunting. I was looking at the faces of my family and the devastation I saw there. I felt so sorry for my mother. I was heartbroken. The memory still brings tears to my eyes thirty years later.'

Pip remembers being woken by Elizabeth: 'I lay in bed as she opened the door and the hall light shone in. She told me the wreckage had been found, on a mountain. I had an instant mental picture of a green forested mountain, like in the Rockies. I think I'd assumed Antarctica was flat. I got up and went into the kitchen. Mum was at the kitchen table, by the phone. I had never seen her look the way she did. I'm not sure what it was — her pallor, her demeanour, sense of devastation — or just the fact that she was crying. I had certainly never seen her cry.'

About three in the morning, everyone went to bed. Maria lay awake. There were things she had to do. All of the schools had to be called in a few hours.

Elizabeth had watched her mother carefully all evening and into the frightful, empty morning hours of hopeless desolation. She watched her with those same large blue eyes that followed Jim everywhere, watched the way he drove the car, watched the way he changed the oil, watched the way he used his carpentry tools and watched the way he walked in his black uniform. Now her beautiful father was dead. He would never come home. How was this possible?

She slipped into bed with Maria. She lay in the dark next to her mother asking many questions. How did she think Dad might have died? Should we wash the shirt he had left on his spare chair? What should we do with his clothes? Would Mum get married again? Mum gently suggested Elizabeth try to get some sleep and they could talk about all of those things in the morning. Elizabeth could smell her father in the bed, could smell his hair on the pillow.

'I knew he was dead,' she says. 'But I couldn't comprehend it. I mean, I absolutely understood what it meant but I couldn't, you know . . . there was a chair in his room that had his home work clothes on it. His jeans were folded, his shirt was folded, his suede shoes with the socks coming out of them ready for him to pop on when he came home. There were the clothes in the corner of the room but there wasn't going to be anybody coming home to wear them.'

Should they wake the little girls and tell them what had happened? No, said Maria. Let them sleep. Let them be normal for a few more hours. Switch your brain off and go to sleep.

Adrienne, at six years old, had few memories of the early evening of 28 November 1979. 'I remember it was light, dinner time-ish and Kathryn and Elizabeth had been fighting and the next minute they were crying. That's all I remember of the night.'

She recalls more of the next morning: 'I wake up. It's early. I get up and walk out of my room, see that my parents' room and my sisters' rooms are empty. Everyone is up already. That doesn't surprise me — something serious was happening last night. I walk up to the living room. Mum, my three sisters and an older family friend — probably Karel Beran — are seated round the coffee table. There is sadness and crying. I kneel down beside my sister, Pip, and say, "He's dead, isn't he?" Pip nods. Her face is sad. I don't feel like crying.'

Of the four daughters of Jim and Maria Collins, Adrienne is perhaps the hardest to reach. A hidden jewel, her mother calls her. Adrienne uses the word 'fraud' once in our conversations, as if she knows she was part of it all, the great loss, the great national tragedy, but doesn't really know in what way she was part of it. She is charming, funny and sharp. She is very direct.

Adrienne is a watcher. When I suggested the idea of this book to Kathryn at the time of the thirtieth anniversary of the Erebus disaster, we arranged that I should meet her sisters at Maria's so they could make an assessment of this man Holmes, whom Kathryn had known vaguely over the years. Maria made a light lunch. Two hours of intense conversation were broken by sharp humour and warm laughter. That is the day on which I first noticed that Kathryn's eyes can sing with life one minute and be lost and sad the next. I saw how quickly Pip can laugh, how quick and light she is and how intense. Already, Elizabeth had taken possession of the red Collins exercise book I brought with me and was writing down phone numbers, family history and possible book titles. She is the organiser, the note taker, the record keeper and the black humorist. And next to me, on my right, was the quiet one, the watcher, the youngest, the assessor, who every now and then interjected a very clever comment.

The Collins girls, as I call them — though of course they are women now, and Kathryn the mother of four children herself — all have extraordinary blue eyes. And Adrienne's eyes watched me. I could feel them.

I mentioned these watching eyes later to Kathryn Schollum. I told her Adrienne has the ability to sit there and be there and make you not notice her, but you remember the eyes, and how they watch.

'Jim's eyes,' she said immediately. 'Jim's eyes. Jim had the most amazing eyes. Jim's eyes were fantastic. Deep, deep blue eyes. I forgot to mention that. Incredible eyes, brilliant, brilliant eyes. Adrienne's got them. I think Kathryn's got them. They've all got them.'

Kathryn Schollum never married. ('Not for want of offers, Paul.') In those days, the fifties and the sixties, you had to choose. Kathryn enjoyed her work. She loved her sport. And bugger it, she loved her independence. But she adored Jim Collins.

'Jim had the most wonderful, almost lopsided grin,' she says. 'His teeth were slightly irregular but he had these enormous bushy black eyebrows and, you know, he was a real clean-cut guy. And he was lovely, he was a gentleman, he was fun, he was serious, he was a great conversationalist, he had wide interests. And the parley round the dinner table was fantastic, just excellent conversation. Everyone contributing, not everyone agreeing of course, but it was really good stuff. And Jim would always, I can just see him sitting there, he'd listen, listen, listen and then he'd make some profound statement. He was a neat man.'

Then one day, Adrienne, who does not speak as easily of her heart as her sisters, told me a story. 'I know Pip's had a similar dream. On the rare occasions that I've dreamt he's alive it's like, it's like the answer to life, the universe, everything. You know, when he's alive it's like there's nothing else I need. You know. And then you wake up and you realise it's like I've been living with half my limbs or something. You feel this massive sense of what you've lost. It's hard to describe. But it's only in that dream I get the feeling "Wow, this is actually what it would be like if he were alive and it's the answer to everything." And when you can experience that feeling and then you go back to what you have, it's like, oh fuck.'

The conversation continued.

'So when Dad's in the dream it's all you need?'

'Exactly,' she replied. 'And I mean, I feel that way now. If he could be alive, that's all I'd ever want, in a way. I mean, I'm sure there are other things I'd want. It would just be, it would just be . . .'

'So growing up without Dad, something big was missing?' I said.

'Yeah, but this is with hindsight, you know. Growing up I never felt this way.'

'So it's more important now?'

'Yeah. Yeah, definitely. Because, as I grew up, I always thought it was actually an advantage, in a way, that it had happened when I was young because I didn't know what I was missing. And to a certain extent maybe you can still argue that point, but I think as you get older, and I think Pip's the same, we've come to realise more what the loss is. But I don't know what it was like to have known him or lived with him so I can't — I don't know him.'

It was one of the first things Adrienne ever told me. Jim's death get's bigger as she gets older.

The morning of 29 November 1979 is the first day of the rest of their lives. The entire country is in shock. A nation is grieving. Hundreds of families have lost loved ones. Soon, the subtle process of pointing the finger will begin. Soon, Air New Zealand and the Muldoon government will have made the decision. The names of the pilots must be sacrificed in order to save the airline. It won't be long before Adrienne learns that new word, 'error'.

By 9 o'clock, Kathryn remembers being lined up alphabetically to sit her School Certificate science examination. Later her friend, Rebecca, will tell her that they took her out of the 'C's and put her with the 'H's so as to give her a front row where the supervisors could keep an eye on her and help her if she became distressed. Rebecca told Kathryn later that she sniffed and sobbed all the way through the exam. Kathryn has no memory of this. She passed with a mark of 65 per cent. Not her best work, she says, but then she didn't need an aegrotat pass either. She turned up. She sat the exam. She passed. She carried on.

And now, so did Maria. The way Maria carried on has earned her the eternal respect of all who know her, and her daughters will love her forever for it. What had to be done was done. For weeks, the house was full of people. Maria, says Elizabeth, became fixed to the couch as visitors and well-wishers paraded through.

Elizabeth describes this as the time she became an event organiser. Elizabeth needs to see things running smoothly. She likes a plan and she likes to see the plan kept to. So she helped Ross Gordon keep order, keep the machine working. It was at this time, she says, they all learned to deal with a range of people from a variety of backgrounds and seniority. It's been something she's been able to do all through her working life. 'I've never really had an issue dealing with people wherever they sit in an organisation.' And she 'learned to have the confidence to deal with media people when they rocked up at the front door, courteously and informatively but without being rude'.

And all the time their hearts were breaking, hanging open, broken, exposed, inconsolable and wounded. And, one would have thought, beyond repair. The emotional stress on Maria and her girls would become immense. Things would be hard and sad and bleak for a long time.

Just round the corner lay the triple whammy. Not only was Jim Collins dead, next he would get the blame for the deaths of 257 people, then he would be exonerated by a Royal Commission of Inquiry only to have that rubbished by a brutal, cynical prime minister determined to muddy the truth. The winds of fortune would be vile. The pain of the loss of Jim and the blackening of his name would never end.

Elizabeth was having a difficult adolescence. She admits to being hard on her mother at this time. It would not be long before Maria would stand at the top of the stairs one day when Elizabeth was being particularly tough on her and scream, 'I miss him as much as you do, you know!'

And Maria was getting a bad feeling. She sensed it. Things were going to get very hard for the children. One of Jim's best friends was an executive captain, Barney Wyatt. There was a distinction between the executive captains and the line captains. The executives had management responsibilities; Jim simply flew the DC-10s. But Jim and Barney were buddies. Jim was groomsman at Barney's wedding.

Barney came several times in those first few days. He told Maria that the company would 'hang' for the accident because of 'a massive computer error'. Then he stood in the doorway and turned to her. He said, 'Maria, I won't be able to see you any more. I've got to be with the company and the executive pilots.'

Maria was on her own. She knew it. And she understood it perfectly. If there was indeed a computer error by the company, the company could not be allowed to wear the blame. Jim would be made to pay the price. That's what he had always said. That's what he had always meant. If he ever bent an aeroplane, he would pay a terrible price. In aviation, in those days, the dead were always guilty.

Barney Wyatt was as good as his word. Maria never saw him again.

A month after the accident, on 31 December 1979, Air New Zealand stopped Jim Collins's pay.

6

Alan Dorday Works it Out

All truths are easy to understand once they are discovered; the point is to discover them.

— Galileo Galilei

Where was the damned aircraft? That was the question tormenting half the world on the afternoon of 28 November 1979.

Where in God's name was it? There were 257 lives on that aeroplane. Please let it still be flying. Please let it be a communications failure. Please let it be that Jim — safe, dependable Jim — is making his way back to Christchurch on two engines or even one engine. Let him be limping home at low level on even one engine and the smell of an oily rag and about to pop up on radio to request a straight-in emergency approach. Let this not be another DC-10 fiasco.

By 8 o'clock Jim Collins had to be out of fuel and down. Everyone knew that by now. But where? On the ice? In the Southern Ocean? Everyone knew the chances of survival for passengers and crew of a ditching in the Southern Ocean to be non-existent. Heaven knows, the Americans at McMurdo Station didn't even maintain a marine search and rescue facility. There was no point, in those waters. No one survived. It was shock, hypothermia, go to sleep, die, and all of it in minutes.

The world waited on tenterhooks, concern and disbelief building in every city, town and village and in every building and on every farm across New Zealand. Everyone, the country has always told itself, knew someone — or knew of someone — on that flight. The country waited. Air New Zealand waited. The Americans at McMurdo Station waited and threw everything they had at trying to find the airliner. The evening drew late.

But what no one outside Air New Zealand knew was that two Air New Zealand flight despatchers, navigators themselves, were working out what had happened. In fact, by 10.30 that night they had cracked it. They worked out what was different about this flight compared to previous Antarctic flights, with the result that Air New Zealand, once it heard that the DC-10 had struck the side of Mount Erebus, knew the reason it had. It was all so diabolically simple.

Flight Despatch, obviously, was at Auckland International Airport. It was the last port of call for departing aircrews. The crews read briefs of weather, received their flight plans and heard any last minute necessary information before heading out to the flight decks of their aircraft.

Alan Dorday came on duty at Flight Despatch at 3 o'clock on the afternoon of the fatal flight. The DC-10 was already causing some concern. His immediate superior was an English, marine-trained navigator, David Greenwood. Greenwood informed Dorday that there was some concern that the Erebus flight had been out of contact for more than an hour. Collins should have been in contact with McMurdo Control. What's more, McMurdo hadn't even seen the aircraft, let alone heard from it. The aircraft had gone completely silent.

According to Arthur Cooper, Jim Collins should have been reporting to Auckland Oceanic Control as he crossed each waypoint above 60 degrees latitude south on the way home. Before that, he should have been reporting to McMurdo Station. Instead, there was silence. Greenwood told Dorday that at this stage air traffic control regarded the issue as one of faulty communications only. Surely it had to be.

We know much of the detail of Dorday's subsequent hours because, two days after the accident, he wrote a detailed record of his and Greenwood's process of discovery that evening, which, while Air New Zealand would never show it to Justice Mahon, would eventually find its way to the Court of Appeal as evidence.

As concern mounted through the late afternoon and evening of 28 November, Alan Dorday and David Greenwood occupied themselves making various calculations about engine failure and fuel consumption and where Jim Collins might be in relation to Christchurch. It might be useful. It was something to do. It became apparent that Captain Collins's aircraft had passed its fuel endurance. The aircraft had to be down.

Shortly after 8 o'clock, says Dorday in his statement, Milton Wylie, one of Ron Chippindale's air accident inspectors, and First Officer Peter Rhodes, an Air New Zealand DC-10 pilot with strong accident investigation qualifications, who represented the airline pilots, arrived at Flight Despatch. David Greenwood became busy providing them with information and documentation. For the next couple of hours, Dorday says, he took phone calls and brought visitors to the office up to date on what he knew of the deepening situation.

Suddenly, Keith Amies, a navigation systems specialist, an authority, actually, on the DC-10's brilliant navigation computer, the AINS, was on the phone. He had seen the television news. Amies told Dorday that there had recently been an amendment or two to the Antarctic flight plan and could Dorday check that all the longitudes on the digitised flight plan were easterly.

In navigation, just as all latitudes are north or south, so all longitudes are easterly or westerly. Amies was asking for an assurance that Captain Collins had not programmed his aircraft to depart McMurdo and track to Madagascar. Dorday put the phone down and checked. Yes, he told Amies, all the longitudes on Jim Collins's flight plan were easterly. A relieved Amies hung up.

But Alan Dorday was about to discover something very odd. In fact, he was about to discover the core reason for the fate that had befallen Flight 901. Keith Amies' informing him of certain amendments to the Antarctic flight plan had sparked an idea.

He did a very simple thing. It was 28 November. The previous Antarctic flight had been exactly a week before on 21 November, commanded by Captain White.

He compared the flight plans:

> I did this by working my way from top to bottom of both plans, checking every item printed. When I came to the McMurdo waypoint, I discovered what I considered to be a significant difference in the coordinates of TE901/28 [November 1979] and TE901/21 [November 1979]. The difference amounted to some 2 degrees of longitude and some small difference in latitude, the significant part being the 2 degrees in longitude.[1]

Intrigued and slightly alarmed, knowing what a difference 2 degrees of navigation variance can amount to on a flying leg of 337 miles, the Great

Circle distance from Cape Hallett to McMurdo, Dorday went back to the computer and pulled up the flight plans for all of the current season's flights to Antarctica. He found that all of the previous flight plans of November 1979 had the same latitude/longitude McMurdo waypoint.

Jim Collins's flight did not.

Dorday got David Greenwood's attention. He did so without fuss. At no point did it seem to occur to Alan Dorday to take into his confidence the accident inspector, Milton Wylie, or ALPA's Peter Rhodes, both of whom were right there in the office with them. If it did occur to him, he does not mention it. In fact, this is the most peculiar part of the entire Dorday statement. Neither he nor David Greenwood ever thought to inform either accident inspector, right there in their office during the entire period of their process of discovery.

Together, Dorday and Greenwood took out the relevant chart and plotted the course difference between the previous week's leg from Cape Hallett to McMurdo and the leg programmed for Jim Collins. With great concern they saw that the new plot, the 2 degrees difference in the course from Cape Hallett, put the DC-10 directly in line with Mount Erebus, the 'old' coordinates, as he calls them 'being approximately 20 miles to the west', meaning right over the middle of McMurdo Sound, where all the other 1979 flights had flown.

'As a result of these findings, and considering the overdue situation of TE901, we both had fears, at this stage, and I emphasise at this stage, that the aircraft may have collided with Mount Erebus,' Dorday would later state.[2]

Bingo. It was that simple. A flight despatcher had worked it out even before the wreck had been found.

Greenwood got back on the phone to Amies at his home and told him what he and Dorday had discovered. Greenwood told Dorday that Amies 'was shocked at the discrepancy in the coordinates'. Amies too realised what the 2 degrees could mean on a sightseeing flight when the entire company — though its senior flight operations men would deny it forever — knew from published articles that flights regularly went down to 2000 feet, or even lower, in McMurdo Sound. Amies told Greenwood to advise Brian Hewitt, the Chief Navigator, immediately.

It was Brian Hewitt whose finger trouble in mid-1978, when the flight plans were being computerised, changed the crucial digit in 166 degrees of longitude to 164 degrees of longitude east: 166 degrees took you straight to Erebus, 164 degrees took you nice and safely up the middle of McMurdo Sound. And now it was Brian Hewitt's late amendment that had caused the last minute change back to 166 degrees of longitude, in the early morning, just hours before Jim Collins took off.

Having plotted the 2-degree change that aimed Jim Collins at Erebus, an active volcano, Greenwood headed back over to assist Wylie and Rhodes. Again he told them nothing. They knew nothing of what was going on. Of course, there was at this stage no accident, although the aircraft had to be down somewhere. At 11.45 that night, Dorday recorded, he phoned the Chief Navigator, Brian Hewitt. The telephone rang for a long time.

Dorday remarks in his statement that the office was by then 'fairly well crowded'[3] and the only available telephone was on a counter in a place busy with people anxious to find out what they could about the looming disaster. Eventually, Hewitt answered. He was ill-tempered.

Dorday identified himself and told Hewitt that Keith Amies had asked that he call him to advise him that he and Greenwood had made a discovery about the difference between today's flight compared to previous Antarctic flights. Instead of reacting as Dorday expected he would, by asking what the difference was, Hewitt snapped Dorday's head off.

> Mr Hewitt interrupted me before I could go further and stated (quite abruptly, I recall thinking at the time), that there had been a change in the coordinates of McMurdo, some two nautical miles, due to the repositioning of the NDB [non-directional beacon] from one side of the [Williams] Field to the other and it was of no concern to us.[4]

Meaning, Dorday assumes, of no concern to Flight Despatch and of no concern to the flight plan.

Now, that had Dorday stumped. He couldn't figure Hewitt out. But Dorday had a roomful of ears desperate for information. He wondered if Hewitt even knew that there was a DC-10 overdue, probably lost. He asked Hewitt if he knew what he, Dorday, was talking about. To Dorday's consternation, Hewitt said that of course he did and that the longitude and latitude discrepancies were of no concern.

Dorday didn't want to push it or explain things more graphically to the

Chief Navigator. There were too many people within earshot and what he'd discovered was dynamite. Note the immediate instinct to hush things up, to keep the story close. So he decided to leave it there. He simply told Hewitt that Amies had asked him to call. He related the nature of the conversation to Dave Greenwood. Both agreed Hewitt's reaction 'was somewhat extraordinary'.[5]

It is likely — this will become clear later — that Hewitt genuinely thought the change to the flight plan was two miles. He had not yet realised the series of mistakes he had made nor the entire fatal and fateful chapter of errors and omissions by him and others which will become evident later in our narrative. The reader should not at this stage become bog-eyed and baffled about the 2-mile movement of a radio beacon versus a 2-degree difference in the flight plan. We will sort this out later and we shall keep it simple. It really is simple.

So Alan Dorday kept his counsel.

But then something else started to nag at him. He began to wonder if Jim Collins had been briefed on the new course. He had serious doubts. He could see no 'ops flash' on the Jim Collins flight plan. So, obviously, he concluded, the course had been changed at some stage between the previous Wednesday 21 November and this day, Wednesday 28 November. He knew that Air New Zealand's computer updates and amendments were generally effected early on Wednesday mornings.

This week, therefore, that change would probably have been made just a few hours before Jim Collins departed for the ice with an aircraft full of passengers, without any ops flash attached to the computer flight plan. Jim Collins really might not have been briefed on the change.

Dorday took the next terrible step. He went back to the records. He found no record of any RCU (Route Clearance Unit) pilots' briefing for any flight to Antarctica within the previous fortnight.

Collins and Cassin had, in fact, been briefed on 9 November, nearly three weeks before, along with Captains Gabriel and Simpson and First Officer Irvine. Captain Simpson will assume considerable importance later in our story. Suffice it to say now that at the Royal Commission, Captains Simpson and Gabriel and First Officer Irvine will all swear under oath that neither of the briefing officers, Captains Wilson and Johnson, said anything about flying over Erebus. But that is all well ahead.

Dorday said in his report: 'It seemed apparent to me, therefore, that Captain Collins could have been briefed on different coordinates for

McMurdo than those on his flight plan for TE901/28. The implications behind this further heightened my apprehension.'[6]

At half past midnight, Dorday said, there being nothing more he could do, he headed off home. His report shows that he neither told nor even contemplated telling the two obvious people he should have been relating his concerns to, the two men who left Flight Despatch with documents just before midnight, Wylie and Rhodes. He didn't even wonder if he should have. There is, in his report, not even any real link made between his discovery and the use it might be to the two visitors to his office. They seem to exist for him in a different universe.

When he got home he took down from the shelf his volumes of *Scott's Last Expedition.* These, he says, have been in his family for some years. The books contain maps and charts and photographs, including photographs of Mount Erebus. Dorday didn't like what he saw. Then he heard the news. The aircraft had been found, a broken wreck on the slopes of Erebus.

All of this was going on deep into the night, while Maria Collins, Anne Cassin and their children sat, their hearts breaking, waiting for news of the fate of the overdue flight. So were the families and loved ones of 255 other passengers and crew. The waiting and then the confirmation of the destruction of the aircraft sucked the breath out of the nation. It was a huge disaster, a once in a lifetime disaster.

Mystery would surround the truth of how the aircraft ended up a black smudge on the side of a mountain for another year and a half, until the release of the Mahon Report. But that very night, out at Flight Despatch, Alan Dorday and David Greenwood knew what they were dealing with. They knew what had happened.

So whom did they tell? If we believe Air New Zealand's Chief Executive, Morrie Davis, Flight Operations Manager Dave Eden, and Chief Pilot Ian Gemmell, they told no one in a hurry. Davis would say he did not find out about the coordinate change until Monday or Tuesday, 3 or 4 December. Morrie Davis doesn't play with a straight bat here. He always claimed that while he was initially told of the course change on 3 or 4 December, he wasn't told until 8 December that the pilots might not have been briefed. It was not a credible story. It was cunning old Morrie's attempt to downplay the importance of the coordinate change.

Preposterously, in 1987, in *Metro* magazine, Davis finally conceded that he believed that the pilot was not told of the course change. This is Davis still in a state of extraordinary denial. It was clearly, emphatically established by both Chippindale and the Royal Commission that the pilots were never told.

Mahon did not believe any of the airline management witnesses' evidence about when they knew.[7] He believed that the discovery of the coordinate change without the pilot being notified was so crucial and so explosive that the senior people in Flight Operations, right up to the Chief Executive himself, most certainly must have been informed the very night of the accident or very early next morning. It had 'administration error' all over it and the loss of life was catastrophic. Mahon never got to see Alan Dorday's report. Air New Zealand kept it to themselves.

This was the world's fourth worst air disaster. Senior management would have known immediately that they could all be in very serious trouble. This is why the cover-up started when it did. It started the moment Dorday plotted Collins's changed course on the big chart with David Greenwood, and when they chose to say nothing to Wylie and Rhodes.

Chippindale testified at the Royal Commission that he was told of the changed coordinates on or about 11 December 1979. But the fact that the aircraft's commander was not told of a new destination waypoint would never matter to Chippindale because he believed what was in fact a crucial airline untruth, that there was a strict 16,000-feet minimum safe altitude for an aircraft to pass well over past Erebus and arrive overhead McMurdo a short time later.

But, as Mahon would establish much later, no one had been over-flying Erebus for 14 months of Antarctic flights. They had all flown safely up the middle of McMurdo Sound at sensible, low, sightseeing altitudes which McMurdo Control invited them to fly.

So given this, if the coordinates upon which he had been briefed had been changed and Collins had not been told that his new route took him directly to Erebus, then the airline was seriously exposed to negligence allegations. And not just the airline. Senior individual officers of the company might have to face the possibility of manslaughter charges.

And, since Air New Zealand had ceased to comply with the Civil Aviation demand since the third Antarctic flight, in 1977, that every command pilot of an Antarctic flight had to have undertaken at least one flight under supervision before commanding his own aircraft to the ice, then it had become crucial that the pre-flight briefing made it absolutely clear to the pilots where the pilots were going to fly. It was obvious, therefore, that a good number of people from the airline, and from Civil Aviation as well, who had rubber stamped a dispensation weeks after the fatal accident, might be in serious legal danger.

I believe that in such a business as an airline, responsible for the lives of thousands of people, and an airline that was a state-owned company where the ultimate boss was the fearsome Prime Minister Rob Muldoon himself, senior management would have had in place a firm and general policy that they should be told dangerous, unpleasant and important information immediately it was discovered. And this was all very dangerous, very unpleasant and very important indeed.

But Gemmell was always adamant, under oath, that he was not informed of the coordinate change before he joined Chippindale on the flight to the ice on 29 November, the day after the accident.

Alan Dorday has been dead for some years. But there is a late sequel to his report of that dramatic evening back in 1979. Thirty years to the month after Dorday's revelation, in November 2009, Paul Davison QC, representing Maria Collins, recorded a conversation with the flight despatcher, David Greenwood, by then long retired. The transcript of the conversation, which he sent to Maria Collins, explored what Greenwood remembered of those shocking first days. Davison showed Dorday's account to Greenwood, written two days after the accident in 1979. Greenwood agreed that Dorday described the evening and their discovery correctly.

Remember, according to Alan Dorday, the air accident inspector, Milton Wylie, arrived at Flight Despatch with the purpose of impounding documents and whatever other information might be useful, at 10.40 p.m. He and Rhodes spent a lot of their time with Dave Greenwood. They did not leave until 11.50, just before midnight. In over an hour, apparently, neither Dorday nor Greenwood informed Wylie of their joint discovery of the dangerously altered Jim Collins's flight plan and the lack of an ops flash to alert him.

Yet, in November 2009, Davison put it to Greenwood that the information they had uncovered, the 2 degrees of course variation on the last leg of the flight to McMurdo, 'was it significant enough for you to think, well, gee, that might be a key answer to the question of how this accident occurred?'

Greenwood replied, 'I'm sure it was, yes.'

So Wylie was there, and Dorday and Greenwood had made their discovery. Greenwood accepts he did not inform either Wylie or Rhodes.

But, he said: 'I was in the Nav Section the following morning and I certainly told Ian Gemmell.'

Greenwood said he stayed on for a while into the night at Flight Despatch. He told Davison that he got home about 1.30 a.m. and went to bed. But he could not sleep. His wife was terribly upset. He got up early. The 2 degrees of longitude were obviously haunting him. Between 6 a.m. and 6.30 a.m. he went into Air New Zealand House, he said, to the Navigation Section: 'Seventeenth floor, I think it was.'

Davison: 'You just went in because . . .'

'Because I was pretty concerned about what had happened and I think I was probably pretty sure that Keith Amies and the navs would be there and I just wanted to be there to see if I could contribute anything.'

Davison: 'So you went up to the seventeenth floor and . . . just explain to me what you can remember happening up there.'

'Well . . . I'm certain Keith Amies was there. I think Brian Hewitt [and] . . . probably all the navs were there . . . Which pilots were in there I don't know, certainly Ian Gemmell and [First Officer] Peter Rhodes were there.'

It is, at this point, interesting to speculate why 'all the navs' were in so early. In those days, if a DC-10 crashed, the immediate assumption was that it was an engineering failure. Had word got round Flight Operations already that the secret of this disaster might lie with the Navigation Section and the last minute change to the destination waypoint coordinates on Jim Collins's flight plan? Why would 'all the navs' be there at Air New Zealand House at 6.30 in the morning?

Greenwood described a big office with a broad chart table in the middle of it with great drawers that slid in and out of the table on which the charts lay. People were coming and going, he said. Greenwood had brought no paperwork with him. He had not brought, for example, the two different flight plans. Well, said Greenwood, curiously, the relevant stuff had already been impounded.

Davison: 'Were you focusing your attention, David, on that whole business of the 2-degree change that you'd found?'

Greenwood: 'Yes, I imagine . . . I would think so, yes.'

(Throughout the Royal Commission, all through the transcripts, you can see, in his interrogations and his cross-examinations, how patiently and lethally Davison stalks his prey.)

Davison: 'And at some point you had a conversation with Ian [Gemmell]. How did that come about or what can you recall?'

Greenwood: 'I think I just wanted to make sure that he knew before he went down [to the ice] that there'd been a discrepancy in the position of McMurdo.'

Davison: 'And so what did you do?'

Greenwood: 'I can't remember what I told him, whether it was 2 degrees or 2 miles or what.'

Now that is an extraordinary statement. That is the same old loss of memory that so conveniently affected so many of the senior Air New Zealand Flight Operations people at the Royal Commission, right up to Chief Executive Morrie Davis who could not recall seeing a brochure the airline made of an article about flying at 2000 feet with Air New Zealand in Antarctica, distributed to nearly a million New Zealand homes.

The important, dramatic and unforgettable discovery Dorday and Greenwood had made was 2 degrees, not 2 miles. Two miles was nothing. Two degrees was everything.

Davison: 'Well, what you'd found out was a 2-degree change, hadn't you?'

Greenwood: 'I did want him to be sure or to be aware of the fact that there was a discrepancy in the flight plan from the previous week.'

Davison: 'Just let me step you through this. What you had found was the result of a comparison of the two types of flight plan, which demonstrated that there was a 2-degree variation, right?'

Greenwood: 'Correct.'

Davison: 'And so any conversation you had with him would have involved you communicating to him that the variation you were talking about was what it was. You wouldn't be talking about a 2-mile variation when the day before you'd found a 2-degree variation, would you?'

Greenwood: 'I can't be absolutely sure whether I said 2 degrees. I just don't know at this late stage, but I'm aware that I wanted to make him aware of the fact that there had been a change to the coordinates.'

Davison: 'Let me step you through this in a slightly different way. What you had found the evening before, the night before, was that there was a 166/48 and a 164/48, I think it is.'

Greenwood: 'That is correct.'

Davison: 'So, fresh and prominent in your mind would have been a 2-degree shift.'

Greenwood: 'Yes.'

Davison: 'So if you were communicating any information to Ian Gemmell, you would be wanting to communicate to him what you knew.'

Greenwood: 'It's logical to suppose that.'

Davison swung away and they spoke of how Greenwood was later put in charge of the Navigation Section by Captain Eden and had the discomfort of considerably more experienced men reporting to him. And how, when Eden gave him the senior navigation job, in Eden's office at the time was Captain ET Kippenberger, the Director of Civil Aviation. What on earth would he be doing there?

Davison had had enough. He swung back to the essence of what Ian Gemmell knew when he went to the ice.

Davison: 'This is what I had noted in our conversation the other day. You can just tell me whether this is correct or not. DG (which is you) said that on the morning of 29 November, he went into Air New Zealand House to the Nav Section at 6.30 a.m. He said he didn't know quite why he went, but he went in there anyway. And whilst there, [he] encountered Ian Gemmell and Peter Rhodes who were preparing to head off [later that day] to Antarctica. DG says that he recalls telling Ian Gemmell that there had been a McMurdo waypoint change of 2 degrees. He told him this whilst the two men were in the Nav Section. He said it wasn't a formal meeting, but he "categorically" remembers telling Ian Gemmell about the 2-degree change in the McMurdo waypoints between the flight plans that had been checked for 21 November and earlier. DG says that navigator Keith Amies was also present in the Navigation Section early in the morning of 29 November. DG says he did not have a copy of the flight plan with him as the one that was at Flight Despatch had been given to Milton Wylie . . . What I've recorded is pretty much what you've told me this afternoon.'

Greenwood: 'Fine, yes.'

Davison: 'Did you ever become aware of the fact that Ian Gemmell was claiming not to have known about the 2-degree shift [before he went to the ice]?'

Greenwood: 'No, I didn't know that.'

Of course, accident inspector Milton Wylie being given a copy of the flight plan doesn't actually mean much. Mr Wylie needed to have been given a previous flight plan as well.

Paul Davison finished the conversation with David Greenwood, stating that he did not think 'there would be any prospect of a pilot such as Captain Gemmell forgetting that there was a 2-degree variation between the waypoints. That's all that needs to be said about that.'

Captain Ian Gemmell always claimed under oath that he did not know the crucial information before he went to the ice.

Ross Land

Maria Collins and, from left, Elizabeth, Pip and Kathryn. Photographed at Maria's home, April 2011. Missing is Adrienne.

Collins family

Flying Officer Jim Collins, RNZAF (centre), having just received his wings, mid-1950s.

Collins family

Jim and Maria Collins on their wedding day, February 1962.

Collins family

Pip, aged 4, with Jim in the Collins's garden, February 1974.

Collins family

Elizabeth and Jim in Maria's parents' garden, St Heliers, December 1978, just under a year before the accident.

The Collins family on holiday, Matapouri Bay, January 1978. Possibly the last complete family photograph before the accident. From left: Kathryn, Jim, Elizabeth, Maria, Pip and Adrienne.

Kathryn Carter

ABOVE: Painting of Kathryn by Mark Bassett, January 1981, 14 months after the Erebus accident. Kathryn is 17. She is wearing Jim Collins's summer issue Air New Zealand shirt. Painted at Kaiteriteri, Nelson.

Collins family

RIGHT: A perplexed Adrienne, mid-December 1979, aged 6, just a couple of weeks after the Erebus accident. Photo taken by John Collins, Jim Collins's older brother.

Collins family

Elizabeth Collins

ABOVE: Pip Collins, left, and Adrienne Collins, Matapouri Bay, January 2009. Later in the year, Pip would journey to the ice.

LEFT: Elizabeth Collins has a special bond with animals, May 2009.

Collins family

Jim Collins, husband and father of four.

7

The Body Recovery

The conduct of the Police DVI [disaster victim identification team] was beyond praise.

— Hon Peter Mahon QC

Hugh Logan, a slight young man of 26, was one of three mountaineers at Scott Base, stationed there in a search and rescue capacity. The morning of the fatal flight he and his two colleagues, Daryll Thompson and Keith Woodford, had gone to Vanda Station in the Dry Valleys on an exercise. By 2 o'clock in the afternoon it was clear from the radio that McMurdo Air Traffic Control was looking for a DC-10 that had gone unaccountably quiet. Vanda put its radio on loudspeaker. The entire American and New Zealand Antarctic communities were being dragged into a gripping and potentially fateful drama.

Hugh Logan and his colleagues were placed on standby. All afternoon they listened as greater numbers of aircraft became involved in the search for the Air New Zealand airliner. At one point they heard transmissions from the RNZAF P3 Orion which had taken off from New Zealand to head south over the yawning ocean to look for any sign of a broken DC-10 in the infinite blue-grey waste. Perhaps the DC-10 had suffered a serious engineering malfunction, such as the loss of an engine, perhaps two engines, and the pilot was nursing the crippled aeroplane back to Christchurch with all of the flying skill and coolness for which he would later be praised by the flying fraternity.

The day grew long, the middle of the night approached, hope beyond hope was fading. McMurdo heard nothing. Christchurch heard nothing. Auckland heard nothing. Then, around midnight, Logan and his colleagues over at Vanda heard the appalling call from the flight deck of a US Navy C130 Hercules. The flight crew could see wreckage of a DC-10 on the northern slopes of Mount Erebus. There did not appear to be any survivors.

No doubt everybody listening to that would have wondered how the Hercules skipper could make that assumption. Later, those who saw the wreck would understand. Apart from a few larger aircraft components, an engine or two lying loose, a broken set of wheels and some twisted, blackened fuselage, the DC-10 was now a flat black smudge on a wide white mountain. The Hercules captain circled the crashed aircraft for many hours, looking for survivors, guiding other aircraft in and, perhaps, standing guard, as military people do, unwilling to leave the dead. There was a very close relationship between the folk at Scott Base and those at McMurdo Station.

Logan and the other mountaineers were brought back from Vanda to McMurdo Station. No aircraft could land yet at the crash site because of the weather. The boys had an hour's sleep, were woken and got their full mountain gear on. They assumed the aircraft was on steep terrain. They kitted up to abseil out of the helicopter, something none of them had done before. Logan had seen the odd dead body in his rescue work over several summers at Mount Cook but only God knew what they were going to find when they got round to that northern side of Erebus.

The chopper pilots were Vietnam veterans. They were hard men and dry-witted. Nothing was to be taken seriously. As they flew over the saddle between Mount Bird and Mount Erebus, they could see the long sprawling mess ahead of and below them. Logan and the boys noticed that the slope was quite flat, an easily manageable 14 degrees. The wreckage was smeared 600 metres from bottom to top and it was 120 metres wide. At the top was the huge, deformed piece of green and white fuselage, burnt out by what had obviously been a savage, raging fire.

The pilots brought the helicopter down closer. They seemed to become mindful that their passengers were Kiwis and that below them was a New Zealand catastrophe and a mountainside of dead New Zealanders. One of the pilots said, 'God, look at all those fucking bodies.' The Kiwi boys said nothing. The skipper said, 'For God's sake, shut up!' Logan was appalled at the sight below them. He couldn't believe that black smudge was once a DC-10. 'Hell, look at that.'

The chopper pilot could not land on the slope of the mountain but he went as low as he could and hovered. Logan, Woodford and Thompson jumped out onto the snow, the first men on the mountain, the only men on the mountain.

Logan remained in awe of the sight that greeted them. 'It was a hell of a mess. And the thing is,' he says, 'when you looked at it, particularly when you walked into the middle of it, all you could see were broken bits of everything, including broken bits of bodies everywhere. And it was just, how can I describe it? The area was very blackened where the fireball had been the most intense. But you could recognise bits of bodies and bodies sort of everywhere. And after a while you sort of think, "Whoa, shit, shut down here a bit!".'

This was Logan's way of telling himself to distance himself a little, to shut his senses down a little. This scene was overwhelming. This was stuff that could make you scream and keep you up at nights for a very long time.

The mountaineers made their appraisal, flew back to McMurdo and briefed the senior people. How in God's name was this unbelievable event to be handled? No one yet knew. Perhaps nowhere in the world had there ever been so many bodies to recover from so remote a part of the world. Never. God, there were probably hundreds of bodies up there.

As Logan tells it, the enormity of what he saw on the mountain never really hit him until he went back to Scott Base after that first reconnoitre of the crash site in the middle of the polar night. 'We were knackered because we'd been going nearly 48 hours on the run. We had a bit of a feed, bit of a sleep and a wash because we knew that in about six hours we'd have to fly back in there and get ready for the camps.

'I remember walking into the mess or one of the other rooms down there and they were playing Radio New Zealand. And all I could hear was these names being called out. Name after name. And I remember thinking, "What are all these names?" And I remember this incredible emotion, thinking, "Holy hell, this is all the people on the plane." Because to me they weren't necessarily . . . they were just, we'd seen this stuff, we didn't know who they were. And it just went on and on. It was connecting what I'd seen with real people.'

It was giving names, of course, to those sometimes naked, torn and wretched pieces of flesh that lay upon the side of the frigid mountain.

Logan, Thompson and Woodford went back up to the wreckage site and began to build a camp for some 20 people. Over the next few days there was much industry on the mountain. A mountaineering team arrived from New Zealand and began marking the site out in red and green flags on tall stakes.

A red flag meant there was a dangerous crevasse. A green flag indicated a body or a body part. A surveying party began construction of a grid covering the entire site. The grid was marked out in 30-metre squares, each defined by black flags on tall stakes. When copied onto paper this grid enabled an accurate and permanent record of the location on the site from which each body was recovered.

During this time too, the Chief Inspector of Air Accidents had made his way up the mountain looking for clues. He found very little to assist him to decipher the unfathomable and he hung round Scott Base and McMurdo Station for almost a fortnight. Later, Justice Peter Mahon would opine that Chippindale would have been more usefully employed at Air New Zealand's Head Office in Auckland securing documents before they went to the shredder.

Chippindale knew very little about wide-bodied jet aircraft. The largest aircraft whose demise he had investigated until then was a Fokker Friendship that landed in the Manukau Harbour just short of the runway at Auckland Airport earlier in 1979.

Up there on the mountain, wandering round the crash site with Chippindale was his new adviser on the technicalities of wide-bodied jet airliners, one of Air New Zealand's most senior figures, the chief pilot, Captain Ian Gemmell, about to be promoted to Flight Manager, Technical.

Justice Mahon would later paint a portrait of a cold and calculating Ian Gemmell on the mountain over this period of time. There was always the allegation, never proven, that Gemmell had somehow retrieved for Chippindale only documents detrimental to the reputation of the crew, or may have secured other documents and safe-handed them back to Head Office in Auckland for the shredding committee. This was a matter of intense cross-examination of Captain Gemmell by Paul Davison.

But curiously, one of the mountaineers who remembers Ian Gemmell on the mountain at that time felt that he appeared deeply disturbed, deeply stressed, and in the view of this mountaineer was in no state to be on a mountain in Antarctica. This might speak of Gemmell's compassion. It might also be because of what he already knew before he left Auckland for the ice, that there had been a last minute navigational coordinate change for this flight that had sent it into the mountain and that some people, and the airline, were going to be in serious trouble.

Within a day or two, both the cockpit voice recorder and the digital flight data recorder were found and sent back to New Zealand and, before long, the cockpit voice recorder would become a legend all of itself.

So far, on that silent hill of death, no one had touched the bodies. Removing the bodies from the mountain was going to require a mountain of an effort. Of course, the removal was the straightforward part. Identifying the bodies and reassembling them would be the challenge. It would be a psychological ordeal that would haunt the policemen who undertook it for the rest of their lives and the lives, too, of those in Auckland identifying the bodies and body parts as they arrived.

Of the 10 officers who worked on the mountain through those eight days and nights of misery, only two remain in the police. They were, as it happened, the first two officers on the mountain, the police advance party. They are both police inspectors now but, then, one was 33-year-old Sergeant Greg Gilpin and the other was 22-year-old Constable Stuart Leighton, both members of the newly formed police disaster victim identification team.

Stu Leighton retains a boyish enthusiasm but one can have no doubt that no experience affected him as deeply, before or since, as the time he spent on the side of Mount Erebus with the frozen dead. Greg Gilpin is now the longest serving New Zealand police officer and he also carries burdens from the mountain. He tells me softly at the end of the second of our long conversations that not a day goes by, not a day, without his mind turning to the mountain, to what he saw there and what they did there. He says the body recovery on Mount Erebus similarly affected all of the police who were there.

The DC-10 slammed into the slope with 257 souls on board at 460 kilometres an hour. During their eight days and nights on that sometimes unforgettably beautiful, sometimes hateful and frequently terrifying mountain, performing their shitty and horrible job, the police DVI team regarded each body part they found as a separate body. They would pick up and send back to McMurdo 340 bodies. Some bodies had simply disintegrated. Some had assumed grotesque shapes. Some bore no likeness any longer to anything human. Some were monstrously distorted and disfigured. Some of the photographs I was shown in good faith during the course of researching this book I wish I had never seen. These were mere photographs. Greg Gilpin, Stu Leighton and their police colleagues confronted these horrifying mannequins of frozen flesh for 12 hours a day for over a week.

Some bodies were never found. Some may rest under the large, twisted, immoveable section of fuselage near the top of the crash site. Some may have vaporised in the fireball. The effects on the bodies of the instant deceleration from 460 kilometres an hour to zero were frightful. The site was its own kind of hell.

Erebus, son of Chaos, guardian of hell, had opened his gates. For over a week, the police DVI team would live in the bowels of mythology. It would change their lives forever. None will ever forget it.

Neither Greg Gilpin nor Stu Leighton had been on a mountain or in snow before they were sent to Antarctica. Back in Wellington, advised he was going to the ice, Stu was told to grab some warm clothes. He was possessed of a mixture of excitement and dread. What was this mountain going to be like? How do you work on a mountain?

Greg Gilpin, on the flight south, was seriously concerned about the difficulties of the task ahead. This dedicated family man had genuine fears that he would not see his wife and children again, but he knew he had a job to do that had to be done and he retained some faith that the police would not send him anywhere too impossible. Still, as the Hercules ground its way south through the night, he could not completely expel from his mind the idea that he might soon be clinging to the side of a very steep hill.

The four Auckland officers in the party of 11 police who flew to the ice the day after the accident had search and rescue training. Gilpin and Leighton did not. Now, all DVI personnel are search and rescue trained but when Gilpin and Leighton set off to do the job they were asked to perform, the unit was newly formed. There was much learning to be done and it was about to start.

At Scott Base, Gilpin and Leighton cooled their heels as they waited for the weather to allow their transportation to the wreckage. They were given some basic snow and ice training, told some basic do's and don'ts. During this period Gilpin was appointed Officer in Charge at the crash site.

On the morning of 4 December, a week after the aircraft had bought the mountain, Greg Gilpin and Stu Leighton were flown to the sad and blackened remains of the DC-10. Their DVI gear, the tools of their trade, were carried in heavy cardboard suitcases; normal civilian suitcases, the kind you'd take with you on the railcar. They threw them off the chopper and watched them slide down the hill. They jumped out themselves and slid down the hill to retrieve the suitcases.

As I spent time with Greg Gilpin and Stu Leighton, I began to wonder if New Zealanders have ever really understood the hostility, the sheer formidable violence of the environment into which these men and their colleagues had been dropped and in which they were expected to perform this grotesque work of body recovery. There has been a perception, I think, that whilst the police were operating in difficult conditions, they were conditions that were still within the bounds of routine.

But this was not in any way routine. This was an Antarctic mountain. This was the land of Scott and Wilson and Oates and Shackleton. This was Antarctica. This was the end of the earth. This was a place that liked to kill people and a person could die here and be disfigured forever here very quickly. In this place you were a mere bloody, soft-tissued speck with skin on, completely at the mercy of untamed, unknown and unimaginable weather and whatever the continent chose to throw at you.

With all the modern equipment and communications in the world, Antarctica was still the boss. If the weather wasn't right, the team on the mountain could not be supplied. You were up there and cut off. That was that. And this was where Gilpin and Leighton and their colleagues were expected to locate, tag, photograph and bag in excess of 250 human bodies.

Stu Leighton vividly remembers arriving at the site that December morning long ago. He remembers looking up and down the site unable to believe that this black mark, this flat expanse of tiny bits of smashed metal and plastic littering the slope so thickly, had been a DC-10. Apart from one or two bigger objects like a jet engine or two, or an aeroplane tail or a set of broken-off wheels, there was nothing to suggest this mess had ever been a DC-10. He remembers the awesome enormity of the destruction. He recalls the entire scene as one of complete, utter human and engineering destruction, 600 metres long, 120 metres wide.

The mountain's baptism of the two men came quickly. Both learnt that day the astonishing speed with which Antarctic mountain weather can turn. Gilpin was taking it all in, noting with some relief that the slope was quite gentle. He would not be clinging to the side of a mountain, but across the site there were dangers in the form of crevasses. They had been marked with flags but they still had to be very careful. There were holes everywhere. There was the jagged metal from the aircraft. This is something anyone who was there will tell you about.

The treacherous, jagged little pieces of metal. Hugh Logan remembers the senior man from General Electric showing him a flat piece of steel which had been torn apart by the wrenching of the impact. In high winds, these scraps of metal could be picked up and they could see them, along with other debris from the crash, flying round in the air. When they saw that, they left the site.

But suddenly, that first day, the weather changed without warning and a major storm swept across the slope. The two men had just arrived there and they knew nobody else on the site. Neither had been on a mountain before and a ferocious blizzard was screaming down upon them. They leapt into their little tents. Suddenly, the wind chill temperature dropped to minus 40. The wind howled and screamed from hell. Erebus was thrashing them. Erebus was out to kill them. Greg Gilpin was wondering if they were going to survive it, such was the extremity of that wind. This was a storm the like of which neither man had experienced before or has since. There they were, at the bottom of the world, totally isolated and new on the hill, straight out of Wellington, each man fearing for his life.

Stu Leighton says he told himself that this was reality and they were in survival mode now. This was touch and go. This was the wildest place on earth. There are no indigenous people there. No one lives there or survives there. It is horrendous. This is Antarctica.

There was the isolation. They were dependent on the weather for everything. If a whole set of circumstances did not align, then they could not be resupplied. And just when they had finished the body recovery job, when every body or piece of body had been accounted for, and the men wanted to get off the mountain and get back to Scott Base and strip off their filthy, stinking clothes, have a hot bath and get ready to go home and hold the people they loved, the weather closed in. They were cut off. It was still, grey, misty, dreadful and cold. Gilpin realised how dependent and totally reliant they were on the Americans for transport and equipment. He says they were fantastic and that he cannot speak highly enough of them over the more than a week the body recovery took.

The Americans lent the New Zealanders four photographers, one for each of the four recovery teams. They were young men who had probably never seen a body before, says Gilpin, let alone what Erebus was showing them. 'They were fantastic. Not only did they photograph the bodies in position but when they'd taken their photograph they'd then pitch in and help get the body out of the ice.'

Gilpin hardly slept the entire time. The job played on his mind. They were finding, excavating and carrying bodies all day. Some were grotesquely insulted by the impact. They floated in their minds at night as the men tried to sleep. They were living on the job, living with the dead and ruined just inside the gates of hell.

And there were the skua gulls, Antarctica's carrion, large brown birds, twice the size of a seagull with a vicious beak. Their main prey was penguin chicks. The skuas went to work on the DC-10 dead very soon after impact. They preferred the softer pieces of the human body. They never left the site. They seemed never to sleep. They squawked day and night. They swooped in and ripped at human flesh. Gilpin, Leighton and the other police waged a constant battle against them in an attempt to protect the dignity of the bodies. Eventually when they recovered a body and slipped it into the body bag, they covered it with ice and snow. This appeared to do the trick.

Stu Leighton will not even discuss the skua gulls with me. 'I'd prefer not to. Suffice to say there were scavenger birds on the site, Paul and that's all I'll say about it. There were scavenger birds on the site.'

Holmes: 'Okay.'

Leighton: 'And we had to protect the bodies from them.'

H: 'Did they torment you, the living, as well?'

Leighton: 'No. We were rescue people, we were body recovery people. We owned the people there. We were responsible for their dignity. We were responsible for looking after them, and so therefore we wanted to do the best by them to protect them and that's what we did.'

H: 'What was the drill? When you found a body, what did the DVI team do?'

Leighton: 'DVI on the site, which is part of a bigger picture of disaster victim identification, was just to locate the bodies, tag them, photograph them with that tag on them which was a temporary identification number and then simply put them into a body bag and return them to New Zealand. So that the experts in the mortuaries could then go and do their post mortems and record the specific details of the recovered people.'

H: 'Yes, what did you call it?'

Leighton: 'Locate, Tag, Photograph, Bag.'

The bagging was often a challenge. Many of the bodies were merely body parts, many had disintegrated and many had frozen with arms or legs extended at all sorts of odd angles. Leighton says they simply coped. They improvised. They might have simply cut a bag in half and wrapped the body in the plastic. He says they sent an SOS back to New Zealand and they manufactured some wide bags quickly.

H: 'Did you consider bending arms back closer to the torso, or . . .?'

Leighton: 'No. No, you never considered that because it was not an option.'

H: 'From the point of view of humanity . . .?'

Leighton: 'No, from a practical point of view. I mean, if a body is frozen solid . . . yeah, it's just not an option.'

H: 'Frozen flesh?'

Leighton: 'No, they were humans.'

The frozen nature of the bodies made them easier to handle in one sense and made the job obviously less onerous — the bodies had been there over a week now — but it also meant they were frozen in ice. Bodies had to be chipped out of the positions in which they had ended up. It was excavation work. They sometimes had to hack away at the ice with the diligence and patience of archaeologists.

Across the entire site, day and night, inescapably, was the smell of kerosene. Every piece of wreckage — and Gilpin still shakes his head at how much wreckage there was — every piece of clothing and every body or piece of body reeked of jet fuel. Jim Collins's tanks would still have been more than half full when he impacted the mountain. But the anti-freeze, or icing inhibitor in the airliner's jet fuel, reacted upon the bodies in the sun in a strange and unpleasant way. It created a smell of death that Greg Gilpin had never experienced before. Gilpin had dealt with plenty of death. On the mountain, the police officers found that some of the bodies were not as frozen as they expected when they touched them. Even today, the smell of kerosene at a service station or at an airport or from an indoor heater transports Gilpin straight back to the mountain.

In the first few days in that 24-hour light, Gilpin and Leighton and their team worked ferocious hours: 16-hour shifts at first, then, when the other teams arrived, a routine of 12-hour days. It was hard work and by its very nature it became harder and more oppressive. They needed regular breaks and going for a cup of tea meant trudging up the hill in soft snow. They sometimes needed to talk to someone, just to get away from it. And after a sleep, they knew they had to go and face it again. It didn't matter how much experience they had, how much training they had, or how much involvement in dealing with bodies, none of them had ever been in anything like this before. The sheer number of dead and the nature of the human destruction made this different from anything else.

And it was bitterly cold, says Gilpin. 'There were terrible days of no sun at all, when . . . and it was just misty and dull and oh, it was very cold then. Towards the end of the recovery operation, I always remember they were the most miserable days of my life because all we could do was shelter in our tents because it was so cold and miserable. And the job was over and all our minds were on getting back to McMurdo and getting home. We'd done the job but we couldn't get out of there, we were stuck by the weather.'

They had been in the same clothing for over a week. They were filthy and they stank. They had each been issued with gloves, which they wore when they worked, when they lifted and carried bodies, when they drank, when they slept and went to the lavatory, the hole in the ice. Gilpin insists he took his gloves off when he ate. Both men remember the gloves being too short at the wrist. Human remains worked their way inside and over their hands. Gilpin says, 'We stayed in the same clothing while we were on the mountain and all our equipment became extremely soiled by the human remains.'

The men were promised that the supply of gloves would be replenished. It never happened. So while they were in the same long johns, the same underclothing the whole time, Leighton remembers the woollen gloves being the worst because they got covered in moisture, covered in body fats and fluids. 'And you couldn't take them off to eat with because it was too cold and so you were picking up food and eating with the same pair of gloves and it wasn't particularly good. They were gooey and they went hard. But you do what you do. And we did.'

They did. They gathered the broken dead and brought them off the mountain. Stuart Leighton remembers: 'You had to motivate yourself, you had to call on your inner strength towards the end when we were physically and mentally exhausted. You had a goal that you had to achieve and you just got on and did it. But it became harder and harder the longer you were there to do it . . . at the very end, I could not have done any more. If someone had said to me, "There's another body to be picked up," I wouldn't have done it, I couldn't have done it. I had pushed myself to the total limit of my endurance and I suspect I am no different from any of the others who were there. So, when we left for the final time, that was it. There's no going back . . . we kept it together whilst we did the recovery, but once we'd mentally hung up our hat, that was it, you couldn't pick it up again.'

On about Thursday, eight days after the accident, Greg Gilpin and his team were working on the recovery of the body of a man wearing a short-sleeved shirt with four gold stripes on each shoulder about 50 metres downhill from the wreck of the flight deck. They have identified him as Captain Jim Collins, the commander of the airliner. He was lying towards the top of the crash site below the mangled metal and wiring and instrument panels of what was obviously the cockpit. He was to the left of the main trunk of the destruction. Near him was First Officer Greg Cassin.

Captain Collins was relatively intact compared to many other bodies. The post mortem would reveal his death to have been the result of multiple internal injuries. It was the same for many of the dead. They found him lying on his front, his head on a piece of plastic, his middle section propped up on his elbows.

Greg Gilpin did not know until 2007, almost 30 years after the disaster, that the Collins family were never told where Captain Collins was found on the mountain, or that they were not told of the condition in which he was found.

While Jim Collins's body was being processed, Constable Stuart Leighton was about 50 metres away. In the area of the flight deck he made a fascinating discovery. He found a small black plastic ring binder. It had Jim Collins's name on the cover and his address. Leighton looked through it, thinking that he might have found something evidentially important for the accident inquiry. He saw there were about 30-odd pages. Perhaps seven or eight pages had writing on them: notes, numbers. The ring binder itself and the pages, he noted, were undamaged.

Leighton wandered over to his supervisor, Sergeant Gilpin, who agreed that it was a very important find indeed and that they must secure it and send it back to McMurdo Station for the Chief Inspector of Air Accidents. That was the kind of document they had been asked to look for. They sealed it in one of the small plastic bags they carried with them for small body parts, a bag with a squeeze-seal top.

Together they took the ring binder up to the campsite and placed it in a bigger plastic bag set aside for such special pieces of evidence. That bag would also be sealed before being placed inside a helicopter to be carried back to a shed at McMurdo Station.

That is the last Greg Gilpin and Stuart Leighton saw of the ring binder and for a long time neither man gave it another thought.

They didn't know it then, but what they handled that day would become one of the most important pieces of evidence in the entire Erebus affair, suggesting there was a cover-up at powerful levels.

After the Royal Commission of Inquiry was over and after Mahon had been publicly insulted by Muldoon, and after the Court of Appeal had pronounced, and after Mahon had resigned as a judge in protest, Greg Gilpin sat down at home and watched a documentary about the Erebus Royal Commission.

There on screen was Peter Mahon at his Commission hearing. He was holding a small black ring binder. There were no pages in it. They had all been removed and Mahon was questioning an Air New Zealand person fiercely about where and why the pages had gone and who was responsible.

Gilpin was shocked. When Stu Leighton found that ring binder it was full of pages. There was writing in it which Greg realised immediately was technical writing: numbers, of obvious evidential interest to an inquiry into the air disaster. The ring binder was in 'very good condition', says Gilpin, when he and Stu Leighton sealed it and took it to the campsite. 'The contents were perfectly legible. It was not damaged in any way that would have justified anyone disposing of them.'

By the time the ring binder got to the hands of Peter Mahon, the Royal Commissioner, the pages had disappeared.

Gilpin had no doubt what had happened. And it was anathema to him. The only reason someone would have removed those pages would have been to conceal the contents, he believes. Someone had perverted the course of justice.

What did Jim Collins write on those notebook pages that someone somewhere along the long journey of that ring binder saw the need to destroy? For the next 30 years the ring binder and the missing pages would gnaw at Gilpin. He tells me he thinks about this every day.

For Greg Gilpin, this is about justice. And the deaths of 257 people.

Every day. Not a day goes by.

8

The Ring Binder

Where the instrument of thinking mind, Is joined to strength and malice, Man's defence cannot avail, To meet those powers combined.
— Dante, *The Inferno*, quoted by Peter Mahon
to author Greg McGee

One of the problems with evidence from the crash was the legal status of the site. That is all it ever was, a crash site. It was never a secured scene. It was never quarantined. Had that status been applied to the wreckage it would have been secured, and evidence would have been carefully protected.

As it was, the police were there for the recovery of bodies. That was clearly spelt out to them. They had no other function. They were to endure the cold and the mountainous misery, the hard slog up the slopes in soft snow, the terrifying wind and the awful sight of whatever bodies could be retrieved and whatever bodies still existed, and that was it. They had no business watching what everyone else wandering round the site was up to.

If they found some paperwork that appeared as if it may be of interest or value to an accident inspector, they were asked to take it up to the tent site and put it in a big plastic bag designated for such evidence and thence flown round the mountain to one of the sheds at McMurdo.

But the Erebus affair is very much one in which documents are never found or are found and disappear or are never produced or are shredded.

A large part of the debris which lay or flew round across the length and breadth of the crash site was paper. Greg Gilpin says there was a fortune in folding money in a multitude of currencies blowing round him across the crash site. Or it lay in bundles, thrown out of wallets or purses and passengers' pockets.

It was not a poor man's flight. It was not necessarily a rich one's, either. Very early on, the Antarctic flights were treats people bought for friends or loved ones or by bosses rewarding diligent staff, or won in raffles at the sports club. A couple of the passengers were in their teens and the remembrance websites for the passengers are profoundly moving to read.

There were high and frightening winds and so many crevasses in which paper could disappear that it is a surprise any remained on the site at all. But remain they did. There was a lot of paper. It was therefore a matter of consternation later to the Air Line Pilots' Association (ALPA) that of only three flight deck documents alleged to have been found at the crash site, all were detrimental to the case for the deceased pilots.

One of those documents was a 1977 flight plan. What a 1977 flight plan was doing on a flight in late November 1979 is anyone's guess. The flight plan went over Mount Erebus.

The only member of the flight crew to have flown to Antarctica before was Flight Engineer Gordon Brooks and, indeed, he flew on 22 February 1977.[1] The destination waypoint of Gordon Brooks's first flight had been at Williams Field, at the dissection of the two runways. On 10 October 1977, the destination waypoint was changed slightly to the airfield beacon, the McMurdo NDB.[2] The destination waypoint on the flight plan 'found' at the crash site was the McMurdo NDB. It could not have been Gordon Brooks's flight plan. So how did it get there and why?

There was another key document that Chippindale swore had been recovered from the crash site. He called it 'Annex J' in his report. This was a track and distance diagram, which, if plotted on a map, put the last leg of the flight route south directly over Mount Erebus.[3] Chippindale swore under oath that Annex J had been recovered from the ice. But Annex J had ceased to be issued in the flight envelopes after the flight path was changed to McMurdo Sound in 1978, after which a document that came to be known as Exhibit 164 was included. We shall meet Exhibit 164 later. Exhibit 164 is a fascinating document.

Mahon decided that 'in my opinion Annex J never formed part of the 1979 flight documents'.[4] As Alister MacAlister reminded the judge in his final submission for ALPA, 'One witness said he would not be prepared to navigate his row boat with such a document.'

The reason Chippindale was so keen to promote Annex J was the implication that Collins had failed to note his flight track lay straight across Erebus.

It later emerged, however, that Annex J wasn't found on the ice at all. Chippindale went to Air New Zealand and asked if they could provide him with the documents pilots are given before departing for the ice. Air New Zealand gave him Annex J 'and told him it had formed part of the flight documents carried by the crew of the fatal flight'.[5]

Then having been shown to have been wrong at the Commission, Chippindale defended himself in his press release of February 1982 by saying, 'Annex J is listed in the contents of the Antarctic envelope, was included in the Antarctic envelope and Mr I.A. Johnson [the despatch officer on the day of Collins's flight] stated on oath that it was there before handing the envelope to the crew.'

In fact Johnson did no such thing. He could not in fact say which track and distance chart was in the envelope.[6]

One simple map, which the company consistently failed to provide to its Antarctic crews, was a topographical map of the Ross Sea and McMurdo Sound areas with the flight plan printed across it. Mahon regarded this very seriously. Such a chart with the route printed on it would have been the simplest and clearest of aids. Had the crew of the fatal flight had such a map, the accident could conceivably have not happened.

Jim Collins had his own topographical map, of course. That was the chart he was following, and on it he was following the route he had been briefed on three weeks earlier. We know that because this was the map he was working on the night before that flight, so big he had to open it on the floor to show his course to his girls.

Chippindale would deny Collins could have had such a map. In fact we know he did and we even know where he acquired it. Chippindale knew too, but said nothing. We shall discuss this in a later chapter. Chippindale was not above a lie.

Everyone said — even those who tried to blame him for the crash — that Jim Collins was always methodical and cautious and he never broke the rules. And on his own topographical map, Jim Collins had plotted the route south upon which he had been briefed, the route of the 7 November 1979 Antarctic flight, a copy of which he had taken home with him from the briefing on 9 November, with the destination waypoint highlighted in some way.[7] In the days after the accident, Captain Dave Eden asked Captain Ross Gordon to have a look through Jim Collins's papers to see if he could find a copy of the flight plan issued at Collins's briefing. It would never have occurred to Jim Collins that the flight plan he'd been briefed on would be changed without his being told.

The maps Collins plotted his flight plan on were never found on the mountain. Neither was his copy of the flight plan. Given Greg Gilpin's description of the winds up the mountain, even the winds of his first night alone, it is conceivable that maps from the mangled wreckage of the cockpit simply blew off to infinity.

There was also found on the mountain the famous memorandum from Captain Johnson of 8 November 1979 advising the procedure for 'Descent to 6000 feet for cloud penetration at McMurdo'. The pilots believed that was all the memo ever was, a procedure for cloud penetration in order to be well clear of cloud by 6000 feet, after which McMurdo Air Traffic Control could clear you lower. The airline and Civil Aviation were adamant that the memo made it clear to pilots that 6000 feet was the minimum safe altitude. In fact it would emerge later that the pilots flew at whatever altitude McMurdo Air Traffic Control invited them to.

But Captain Collins also carried his New Zealand atlas because, as Justice Mahon would observe, Captain Collins had found very good maps of the area into which he was going to fly on pages 184 and 185. Page 184 was the whole Ross Dependency, but page 185 focused on the McMurdo area. No one disputed that Collins took his atlas to the briefing on 9 November 1979 'and that he was seen to be closely examining the pages when he was in possession of a flight plan showing the incorrect coordinates. It is also common ground that he took this atlas with him on the fatal flight'.[8]

Chippindale came to Maria Collins's house looking for the atlas a fortnight after the accident. Pilots had no doubt mentioned to him that Jim Collins had found a very good Antarctic map in his atlas. Maria couldn't find it. Jim must have taken it with him, she told Chippindale. Chippindale must have been wondering if Collins had marked the waypoints of his flight path on the page in the atlas. If he had, it would make it impossible for Chippindale to claim that Captain Collins had not been misled.

But the atlas was never found.

Well, not officially. Yet an atlas was too heavy and flat, one would think, to have blown away in the Antarctic wind. But there are a couple of strange, inconclusive stories that carry some weight. The evidence is strong that the atlas was found and handed in.

One of the mountaineers at the crash site, John Stanton, came to stay at the time of the Erebus affair with his friend John Maine, also a mountaineer, who later swore an affidavit about that visit before J. M. Savage, Barrister and Solicitor of the High Court of New Zealand. Greg Gilpin remembers John Stanton as a good man who pitched in and helped with body recovery.

Maine's 25 November 2009 statement says:

> In the course of our conversation that evening John told me how he had found the captain's atlas, that he had found it inside the captain's flight bag and that there were some other items in the flight bag. He mentioned either a map or a chart. He said he had handed these items in, although he was not specific as to who he handed them to. He was very concerned that the items had not been presented in evidence to the Royal Commission and had apparently not been made available to the investigators. He commented to me that he could understand that people might think there was a cover-up. John seemed genuinely concerned about that topic and I had no reason to doubt that he was telling me the truth about what he was describing.

The pilots' flight bags made it to the shed at McMurdo. Greg Gilpin found Jim Collins's bag and took it up to the campsite. The atlas probably made it to the McMurdo shed. They were never seen again. No one, to this day, has ever said what became of the atlas and the flight bags. Someone, of course, knows. But neither Maria Collins nor Anne Cassin ever saw their husbands' flight bags again and Maria Collins has never seen the atlas.

And then we have the ring binder.

The little black ring binder with Jim Collins's name on the cover would become one of the most famous pieces of evidence at the Erebus inquiry. Inside the ring binder and in almost perfect order, say Gilpin and Leighton, were about 30 loose pages on some of which were written numbers which, to Greg Gilpin, who knew nothing about flying, 'seemed to have something to do with the flying of an aircraft'.

Inspector Stu Leighton says the crash site was like a rubbish dump. There was paper everywhere. There were diaries everywhere. Leighton picked a few up. One had a page headed up 'Antarctica 1979'. The page was blank. Another that he read described radiantly the wonderful view of the

Antarctic sea ice. The last words written in the diary were, 'Gee, it's great to be alive.'

But up near the wreckage of the flight deck, which was slightly off to the left-hand side of the main axis of the crash itself and which had not been engulfed by fire in the seconds after the impact, on Thursday 6 December, Constable Leighton found a black ring binder with the aircraft commander's name on it. Gilpin says it may have been slightly stained but you could still read its contents.

'It had a thick wad of paper in it and at least the first three, four, five or six or so pages had writing on it,' says Stu Leighton. 'It was undamaged, it was easily readable and it contained, I did not recognise what I was seeing, I didn't know the significance of it, but I did know that it contained things like radio frequencies and it had other sets of numbers. Some of them looked to me to be coordinates.'

Holmes: 'You mean degrees and minutes? Latitudes?'

Leighton: 'Lats/longs. That's just the way it looked to me.'

H: 'Would you have recognised such things?'

Leighton: 'Yes, I would have because I'd done some bush work in the past. This was a work in progress. Something in which you'd scribble information down as it was given to you during a flight.'

Both Leighton and Gilpin recognised that this was an important document. They saw what appeared to be latitude and longitude coordinates. They sealed the ring binder in one of the bags used for valuables and body parts and took it straight up the hill to the campsite for shipment to McMurdo Base with other documents. They never saw the ring binder again until well after the Royal Commission. But, again, once it was out of their hands it was gone. The police were there to get the bodies. The Inspector of Air Accidents was there to take charge of documents and to think how the whole frightful mess came about in the first place.

When the police officers handed the ring binder over, 'there was no documentation of our doing it,' says Gilpin. 'We didn't do an exhibit form or anything like that because that wasn't our role. Everything was just collected and dumped in a big pile of all these important documents.' There would be no chain of custody over the ring binder from the time it left Leighton's and Gilpin's sight.

Shortly after the ring binder was flown back to the shed, its journey became unclear, and it made only fleeting appearances before it was returned to Maria Collins without its pages, and then showed up at the Royal

Commission. We do have a fairly good idea that things were very loose for the first few days and that people wandered in and round examining diaries and so forth. Some of these might have been Air New Zealand people. This situation was brought under control with the arrival from Christchurch of Senior Sergeant Muddiman, who took charge of property. But people, nevertheless, had generous access to retrieved property.

Captain Ian Gemmell held the ring binder once it arrived at McMurdo Base. There was a moment of revelation at the Royal Commission in which he admitted this and then immediately pulled back. It happened just after 10 a.m. on Monday 8 December 1980 at the start of the day's proceedings. David Baragwanath, counsel assisting the Commission, read a long letter from one of the mountaineers, Keith Woodford. Suddenly, without any warning, Baragwanath asked Gemmell, 'Referring just briefly to the first part of this letter, at what stage did you first see the black ring binder, the one that has all its pages missing?'[9]

Gemmell replied: 'As far as I can remember it was Thursday when it was given to me. I could qualify that and say that I may possibly have seen it but not recognised it.'

Thursday was 6 December, the day the ring binder arrived back at the McMurdo shed. So at what point did Gemmell have hold of it and what did he find in it? By next morning, the Friday, he was back at Air New Zealand House at a meeting with Mr Oldfield's committee. George Oldfield was Air New Zealand's safety officer. He was secretary of the Investigating Committee appointed by Chief Executive Morrie Davis, whose main role appears to have been to sort out what documents should be shredded.

But, in the inquiry transcript four days earlier, during cross-examination by Paul Davison, we have this exchange in which Gemmell denied ever seeing the little ring binder.[10]

Davison: 'My information is that you were in possession of a blue plastic folder, which you were seen leaving McMurdo with when you departed.'

Gemmell: 'That's news to me. I've no recollection of any blue plastic envelope.'

Davison: 'You've seen the little ring binder that Captain Collins's family had returned to them?'

Gemmell: 'No, I haven't.'

Davison: 'Perhaps there could be shown to the witness . . . Do you remember seeing that before or recognise . . .

Gemmell: 'No, I don't recall seeing that.'

So Gemmell was inconsistent. The story of the black ring binder is strange indeed.

First Officer Peter Rhodes, who was on the ice as an accident inspector for ALPA, has always said he was shown the ring binder at McMurdo by a policeman, although he no longer remembers his name. In an email to Kathryn Carter in November 2009, he wrote: 'I had a good look at Jim's notebook at McMurdo which contained the usual stuff we used to write in our work diary (flight/duty hours, crew names, etc) but also included a lot of lat/long numbers which I did not copy but were definitely Antarctic lat/long numbers which, at the time, meant nothing to me other than to look at later.'

Rhodes realised they were Antarctic coordinates because the latitude numbers were very high, numbers of latitude increasing the further one extends from the Equator.

But where were the pages which were presumably in Captain Collins' ring binder? Where had they gone? After the inquiry was over, Justice Mahon asked Gary Harrison, counsel assisting the Commission, to follow up the issue of the ring binder with the commanding police officer on the ice, Inspector Bob Mitchell. Mitchell told Harrison in late 1980, when you would think the memory would be fresh, that he had been given the ring binder in the course of the recovery operation in Antarctica, that he had examined it and found it to have no pages. He may, of course, have been telling the truth.

Jim Collins's flight bag was never registered on the police property sheet at McMurdo. The bag was never seen again and, as I have mentioned, was never returned to Maria Collins.

The ring binder, along with a red pocket diary belonging to Jim Collins, was, on the day it was found, entered onto the property sheet at the McMurdo shed. This was revealed by Inspector Malcolm Burgess, who conducted a police inquiry into the fate of the ring binder in 2007, after Maria Collins lodged a formal complaint. Incredibly, the ring binder was entered as 'Diary and Briefing Notes — Capt COLLINS'.[11]

So Greg Gilpin watched TVNZ's documentary about the Erebus inquiry in late 1981. Mahon's report, released in April 1981, had caused, as he predicted, all hell to break loose. And there to Gilpin's consternation, he saw Justice Mahon holding a ring binder and demanding of a certain Captain Crosbie, who delivered the empty ring binder to Maria Collins, where the pages had gone. Gilpin was astounded. He checked with Stu Leighton. Both men were certain that what they had seen was the ring binder they found in the wreckage. But where had the pages gone?

There was Mahon on the screen, an angry Mahon, rubbing that ring binder on his chin, demanding an answer.

Mahon to Bruce Crosbie: 'Mr Davison means paper secured inside the ring binder. How could the ring binder cover itself be intact yet the pad of writing paper disappear?'

Crosbie: 'I suggest the cover survived the water and kerosene but the paper didn't.'

Mahon: 'There were some folded pages in it? [inside the front cover]'

Crosbie: 'I noticed in Mrs Collins's evidence that this was so. When we received Captain Collins's wallet it was in a very damaged state and it would have caused some distress to have returned it in that state so the contents were removed from [the] wallet, placed, I presume in an envelope, but separated, but the wallet itself disposed of.'

What on earth was Crosbie talking about? Who was talking about a wallet? It was waffle. Gibberish. And if the ring binder pages were wrecked by water and kerosene then why were the folded pages slipped into the pocket inside the front cover of the ring binder in perfect order? They remain so to this day, inside the empty ring binder at Archives New Zealand.

Mahon: 'Pass that to the witness, Exhibit 251. The ring binder with the plastic cover is not damaged at all?'

Crosbie: 'Correct.'

Mahon: 'How do you suppose the pad of paper secured by the ring binder could have disappeared?'

Crosbie: 'I have no idea. As I say, unless they were removed because they were damaged. That would be the only reason.'

Then Captain Crosbie was examined by Gary Harrison, counsel assisting the Commission.

Harrison: 'If papers were removed from the ring binder, who would have done that?'

Crosbie: 'I would have myself, I presume.'

Harrison: 'Do you recall doing that?'

Crosbie: 'No, not specifically. I was involved in destroying papers that were damaged and would have caused distress, some of that and because it was the obvious thing to do.'

Greg Gilpin was watching this astounded. He thought, 'This isn't right. Where are the pages?' He listened to Crosbie. He became suspicious. He knew the pages were not so soiled as to be unreadable. Gilpin was shocked and suddenly very disturbed at the fate of the ring binder he and Stu Leighton had found and handed in so diligently in those early days when he assumed everyone was on the same page, working together with honesty to discover the cause of the accident.

'I read into this that someone had removed the pages. And this could only have been done to conceal something because why would you remove the pages from a document that was going to be produced at a Commission of Inquiry?' he says. 'Why would you produce it in an altered state to how it was found? There's no reason to do that, despite whether they were stained or not.'

Inspector Bob Mitchell, meanwhile, the man in charge of the overall police operation on the ice in those first days after the crash, unbeknown to Gilpin and Leighton had told David Baragwanath that it would not be possible to find out which police officer or officers found the ring binder. To this day, Gilpin finds this assertion frustrating and finds Mitchell's behaviour extremely unusual. 'All he had to do was ring me,' says Gilpin.

As Mahon observes, in paragraph 360 of his accident report:

> It therefore appears that there were sundry articles and perhaps documents which had been in the possession of the aircrew which came back to New Zealand otherwise than in the custody of the Police or the chief inspector. Captain Gemmell asserted that when he went to Antarctica he was unaware of the changed coordinates, and the inference was that he would have no motive for searching for any documents relating to that matter. I do not accept that Captain Gemmell did not know about the changed coordinates before he went to Antarctica.

In other words, latitudes and longitudes in a captain's ring binder were going to be crucially important to Captain Gemmell.

After watching the documentary, and knowing there was a police investigation into any possible wrongdoing regarding the flight, the crash and the aftermath, Gilpin attempted to contact police in Auckland with his and Stu Leighton's story of the ring binder. He heard nothing. He got no response from the Auckland investigating team at all. Nothing. He got his own boss, Inspector John Thurston, to contact a senior colleague in Auckland. Gilpin received an acknowledgement and an assurance that his information would be passed on to the inquiry head, Superintendent Brian Wilkinson. Nothing happened. Gilpin never heard anything more. Once, he did manage to get through to a police officer in Auckland who said, 'Well, this thing's winding down now so it's not worth pursuing.'

Greg Gilpin formed the conclusion that he was being deliberately ignored. 'But I said to myself and my family that I can't let this go, it is worth pursuing as far as I'm concerned, because here's a document that we saw, we know how we found it and what was in it and it's being produced without the pages in it. Two hundred and fifty-seven people died and I can't let this go. And in those days I knew I was sticking my neck out but I was determined to do it for justice. I knew it wasn't right, what had occurred.'

In the meantime, with the police investigation under way, through his lawyer, Gary Gottlieb, Bruce Crosbie sent Superintendent Wilkinson a statement in which it appeared he could now, indeed, remember taking the pages out of the ring binder. His wife, Lorraine, had been able to remind him on the evening of the day he presented his evidence that 'she cleaned the book, read some of the pages, and discussed this with her husband at the time. Captain Crosbie then destroyed the damaged pages.'

He also sent an undated statement to the airline Chief Executive, Morrie Davis. (A copy is in possession of the author.) It says:

> When the ring binder notebook belonging to Captain Collins came into my possession . . . it still contained the pages. On inspection, these were found to be severely damaged by kerosene and water to the extent that they were wet and messy. I inspected what information I could that was contained in these pages, to see if there was any item that may have been of interest to Mrs Collins. There were only references of a general nature such as shopping lists, names and addresses, phone numbers and the like that could be made out or understood Rather than present this to Mrs Collins, I removed the contents and disposed of them.

Again, it was not Bruce Crosbie's right to tamper with private property in any case. And with an inquiry looming, the last objects to destroy would surely be the pages in the captain's ring binder, and Crosbie must certainly have known this. What's more, wrote Paul Davison QC to Maria Collins in March 2008: 'It is inconceivable that he would take it upon himself to destroy such material.'

But why could Crosbie not have remembered these actions as vividly before the Royal Commission as he did for Gary Gottlieb and Morrie Davis? For the single reason, of course, that he knew the significance of what Jim Collins had written in the ring binder and that removing anything in the circumstances was evidence tampering.

It was also Bruce Crosbie who, the day after the accident, visited Anne Cassin's home and took the flying documents of First Officer Cassin. They were never seen again. They were a gold mine too, because Cassin had forgotten to take his Erebus documents with him to the fatal flight on the morning of departure. They would most probably have revealed that Cassin and Collins had been briefed on a McMurdo Sound flight path, which is why they were never returned.

Greg Gilpin then determined to bring the matter to the attention of Justice Mahon. In mid-1983, he contacted Gordon Vette, another of the heroes of the hour. 'Vette said, "Well, this is important. I want to come and talk to you",' Gilpin recalls. 'So he came to Wellington and met me at the James Cook Hotel and I told him my account of what we'd seen and he says, "Oh, this is just what we've been looking for and I'll let Justice Mahon know".'

On 16 September 1983, Mahon wrote to Greg Gilpin from Christchurch. Mahon told him: 'There is no doubt at all that the ring binder notebook which you saw on the television documentary was indeed the notebook found by Constable Leighton.' Mahon told Greg that Collins used the ring binder 'for recording details of flight operations'.

He was frank: 'There is little doubt that someone from Air New Zealand got possession of this ring binder notebook, either at McMurdo or at Auckland, and removed the pages before handing over the empty hard-back cover to Mrs Collins and the reason for this would have been that the flight information which you saw represented the incorrect navigation data which Captain Collins was given at the briefing for the fatal flight.'

Mahon came to Wellington and interviewed Gilpin and Leighton at Gilpin's house. As a matter of courtesy, Gilpin invited Inspector Bob

Mitchell, the man who had overseen the police operation at McMurdo. What puzzles Greg Gilpin is that throughout the entire meeting, Mitchell said nothing, Mitchell who had earlier told the inquiry that when he saw the ring binder at McMurdo all of the pages were missing. Mahon even told them at that meeting that he knew who had removed the pages. Still Mitchell said nothing.

Mitchell is a curious one. So far he's told counsel assisting the Commission that when he first saw the ring binder it had no pages,[12] and that it would not be possible to find out who found the ring binder. When he found out later that Mitchell had claimed this, Gilpin considered it absurd. Then, in the Greenstone Pictures television documentary *Secret New Zealand*, Mitchell said that when he got the ring binder at McMurdo, he showed it to one of the accident inspectors there, First Officer Rhodes or David Graham. Mitchell tells the programme, 'He had a look at the numbers and things that were written in the book and there was nothing there that he felt could assist and so he handed it back and it just went in the plastic bag and that was the last that I saw of it.' In a police inquiry into the ring binder in 2008, however, Mitchell conceded to Inspector Burgess who conducted the inquiry 'that he could have been wrong about the paper in the ring binder' when he first saw it in the shed at McMurdo.[13]

As to what he claims the accident inspector told him, it seems untenable that an accident investigator would say such a thing and be so dismissive of numbers written in a book that was obviously the captain's property with a massive inquiry bound to be launched into a crash that is already baffling everyone, except, of course, those who already know about the coordinate change.

Inspectors Greg Gilpin and Stu Leighton have only ever told one story. They found a ring binder. It had latitudes and longitudes on the pages. There were other numbers. The pages were undamaged. They saw that it belonged to the captain. They handed it in as they were asked to.

Gilpin believes what happened to the ring binder was a perversion of the course of justice, as Mahon obviously did. 'Definitely. Well, I know from my experience as a police officer that you do not, if you recover a document at a scene, you do not interfere with it, you do not remove pages. Why would you do that? You would only do that for one purpose. That's to conceal something.'

It is the issue of the ring binder that has been the emotional and intellectual focus for Greg Gilpin since he experienced that horror exposure to extreme, violent and needless loss of life on that Antarctic mountain over 30 years ago. 'It's caused me more heartache and stress than the body recovery operation because it's just, it's something that I know is wrong. It occurred and it was wrong. And yeah, I know what we saw. And that someone tried to conceal it. Why would you try to conceal it? There's only one reason.'

Holmes asks: 'Do you think Jim Collins and Greg Cassin should be exonerated? What do you think?' and Gilpin replies: 'Yes, I do, definitely. I mean, I've done this all these years because I wanted to see justice for the crew and for those people who died. This is just one little aspect of this thing. Two police officers with over 80 years of experience between them know what they saw and that was not dealt with correctly and someone interfered.'

What Greg Gilpin could never contemplate was that there was never going to be justice. Justice was not in the frame. It had all been decided. Halfway through the Royal Commission, on 11 September 1980, Captain Arthur Cooper and First Officer Peter Rhodes went to see Morrie Davis to warn him how badly the inquiry was going for Air New Zealand. Davis wouldn't listen. The pilots were 'wholly culpable'. Mahon was an 'amateur'. He was 'incompetent'. He told the pilots that there was 'far more involved in the inquiry than they realised'. On other occasions he would tell staff that he had 'the government right behind me on this'.[14]

So whilst a full police inquiry was under way by the end of April 1981 to investigate whether some senior Air New Zealand executives should be considered for charges of 'culpability for manslaughter, perjury, conspiring to pervert the course of justice and perverting justice'[15] for their part in the deaths of 257 people on Mount Erebus on 28 November 1979, no charges were ever going to be laid. The investigation was real enough. It looked real enough anyway. Senior management were stood down. Morrie Davis retired from his position as Chief Executive and went home to wait for the knock on the door.

But there were Greg Gilpin, with a major piece of evidence that got a retired Mahon excited enough to fly to Wellington to meet him, and Stu Leighton, who could not get any interest whatsoever from the police investigating team in Auckland.

The reason was simple. The head of the Auckland investigation was Detective Superintendent Brian Wilkinson. The detective superintendent was a very old friend of Justice Peter Mahon. He told Mahon that he had been told to make it disappear. Mahon repeated that statement to Auckland Erebus researcher Stuart Macfarlane. The investigation was to make everything disappear. Not overnight. Just make it go away. Evaporate it. Fade it away. And that is exactly what happened to the investigation following Justice Mahon's extraordinary allegations in the Royal Commission report.

Superintendent Wilkinson is now deceased.

The years pass.

The mountain never leaves our police officers alone for long. Another disappointment Greg Gilpin and his entire police team have felt over the years, after returning from those unforgettable, dangerous days on the ice, was the lack of recognition of what the police team achieved in that extraordinary exercise in body recovery. One day he cornered Annette King, then Police Minister, at a function and requested a word. He asked what was being done about the long-standing police request for recognition of the work done by the service personnel on Erebus. He stresses to me that he wasn't after glory. He simply felt that the magnitude and the bravery of the body recovery operation on Erebus had never been acknowledged. 'It shall be done,' said the minister.

And it was. Greg, Stu, and all of their colleagues and mountaineers who had endured those days were to be honoured with the New Zealand Special Service Medal (Erebus) in the Grand Room at Parliament in 2007. And that is where, as we shall see later, Greg Gilpin and Stu Leighton met Pip Collins.

Greg came to Auckland and met Maria and Pip's three sisters. And it was shortly afterwards that Maria, through Paul Davison QC, issued a formal complaint to the Police Commissioner, Howard Broad, about the fate of the ring binder. Broad sent it out to Detective Superintendent Malcolm Burgess, who went through the motions and reported back that it was 30 years on and nothing could be sufficiently or convincingly determined.

The Burgess Report concluded: 'It does seem likely that the pages were removed or dislodged from the notebook at some point before it reached McMurdo.'[16] The suggestion is absurd. The ring binder was placed in a plastic bag and sent inside another bag to the McMurdo shed. We know the pages were seen at McMurdo. The ring binder and Captain Collins's little pocket diary were entered onto the police property sheet as 'Diary and Briefing Notes — Capt. COLLINS.' They remained in the ring binder until they were dealt to by Captain Crosbie back in Auckland.

Burgess also said: 'Accidental dislodgement, while unlikely, cannot be entirely eliminated as a possibility for pages apparently not being in the notebook on arrival at the shed at McMurdo Station.' Sure. And, says Burgess, 'there is no evidence that Greg Gilpin was deliberately ignored [by the Auckland inquiry].'[17] That is because, he said, there is no record on the Auckland file of Gilpin's attempts to bring the ring binder to the inquiry's attention. Fortunately, Greg Gilpin kept his own record of trying to do so and a copy of the written acknowledgement.

As for Mitchell's claim that it would not be possible to find out who found the ring binder, Inspector Burgess said that Mitchell was 'incorrect' and that he had made no attempt to find out, and doing so would have been simple.

And there it lies. The truth of the fate of the pages of the ring binder has disappeared into the mists of time.

Gilpin looks back philosophically on those historic, heroic days on the ice and the way the crash site was managed: 'What would be different now? The scene would definitely be treated as a crime scene.'

Holmes: 'Yes. To me, one of the odd things is that, about the way the accident was handled then. And the governance structures that existed then, with the Chief Inspector of Air Accidents enlisting the chief pilot of the most interested party.'

Gilpin: 'Yes. I know. Exactly.'

H: 'Air New Zealand. To become the technical adviser, to go round the site looking for documents. Would it happen now, do you think?'

Gilpin: 'No, definitely not. It would not happen.'

H: 'No one is impugning Captain Gemmell necessarily, but his wandering round on that site invites comment. Suspicion.'

Gilpin: 'Of course it does. I mean, even at the time, I remember thinking, you know, why are Air New Zealand people on the site? I knew that the Inspector of Air Accidents would be there and his assistants, but I certainly queried, you know, started thinking, "Well, that's a bit strange".'

H: 'Did you?'

Gilpin: 'I did. But, having said that, remember that Inspector Mitchell had told us very clearly we were there for body recovery only.'

H: 'You live with this every day?'

Gilpin: 'Yeah.'

H: 'Some people think you're obsessed, I suppose.'

Gilpin: 'Well, they may do, but I'm not.'

H: 'I wonder if you're obsessed.'

Gilpin: 'No. I'm not obsessed. I know what we saw in that ring binder. It bugs me that we never got the chance to give evidence to the Commission of Inquiry, which would have confirmed what Justice Mahon was thinking.'

H: 'Some funny things failed to happen in the police, though.'

Gilpin: 'Yeah, definitely.'

H: 'In relation to the ring binder.'

Gilpin: 'That's what I'm referring to. Yeah. But getting back to being obsessed. I'm not obsessed with it. I just wanted to see the issue of the missing pages investigated and some sort of conclusion drawn. Two hundred and fifty-seven people died and it was an important document belonging to the captain. I thought this is an injustice. I want to see justice done in some way.'

H: 'It won't be.'

Gilpin: 'And it won't be. Yes, I know that. And I have to accept that now. But I wanted to see a fair go. And there are some people alive today still who know.'

And I thanked God, as he talked to me, for determined, honest police officers like Inspector Greg Gilpin.

9

The Trials of John Blumsky

You can cage the singer but not the song.

— Harry Belafonte, *International Herald Tribune,* 3 October 1988

Another man was struggling to do his job in that place at that time. He still doesn't really know why they chose him to go to the ice. The treatment he got there and the frustrations of trying to gain access to any meaningful information to report to the New Zealand public and the world affect him still.

Christchurch broadcaster John Blumsky was one of New Zealand's most experienced. He was mainly a radio man but was accomplished in television. He was held in great respect in the Canterbury region. He was about 50 years old in 1979. He was the deputy chief announcer at the BCNZ stations in Christchurch and he was one of New Zealand's pioneers of talkback. He had a rich, suave and gravelly voice and he had that special ability to talk to and reach out to people that talkback broadcasters need.

The Blumsky voice. It was probably one of the loveliest, most prepossessing ever to be carried across New Zealand's hills and plains. When I was a boy, and before he went to Christchurch, John Blumsky was based in Napier on my local NZBC station. I have never forgotten a little moment in time when one day I heard him announcing a song. This is what he said: 'Away out here, they got a name for wind and rain and fire. The rain is Tess, the fire Joe, and they call the wind Maria.' Just like that. I can hear it still. And I can often hear the sound of that gorgeous drawl and have often heard the sound of that rich voice moving with such atmosphere through the world.

Maria, as in pariah. As I say, nothing important. Just something, I suppose, that a boy who didn't know it but was about to spend his life in radio would notice.

One day, at 16, I wrote to the radio station to ask if I could audition to be a part-time radio announcer. Blumsky wrote back and invited me in. He sat me down in front of a microphone above a green felt-covered table and placed in front of me the standard NZBC audition material. As I recall, you had to announce some songs, some classical music with German, French and Italian names amongst it, read a commercial and a short news bulletin. I did it quite well. I know I did. Blumsky came out of the control room, walked over to me, examined me and said simply, in that unmistakeable voice out of that already lived-in face, 'Very interesting.' Days later a letter arrived in which he told me the audition was good. Nevertheless, I was probably too young and I should apply in a few more years. Six years later, I became a radio announcer and was sent to Christchurch where John Blumsky was the star. I don't recall if we ever discussed the little audition in Napier.

Now it was 1979. I was long gone from Christchurch. I left, I think, in late 1973. I was working for the Dutch World Service radio in Hilversum and living in Amsterdam where in late November 1979, one afternoon in my small apartment, I turned on the BBC Radio News — on long wave — to hear that there was concern for the safety of an Air New Zealand DC-10 in Antarctica.

Blumsky, on the other hand, was at home in Christchurch when he heard the news of the aircraft's disappearance on television. He called Head Office. They asked him to get out to the airport, to the headquarters of Operation Deep Freeze, the American Navy base at Christchurch. 'So I went out there, I picked up some stuff for *Morning Report*. And the airport was closed for business but everything was alive, lights, cars, everything. That would have been about 11 o'clock at night. Walked over there, sniffed around, was not welcome, spoke to one or two people, got an idea of what was going on, that there was a plane leaving the next day.'

At this stage, of course, Jim Collins's fuel was exhausted. There was still no sign of the wreckage. Blumsky went back into work, edited his report for the morning news programme, sent it down the line and went home to sleep.

Next morning Buzz Hart, head of BCNZ News, wanted to see him. 'You're leaving for the ice at 2 o'clock. Go home, get your toothbrush and your undies.'

So why did they send John? John was no hardbitten newshound. That was not John's style. John was no 'chase the lawyer down the street' type of man, as he says himself. Buzz Hart, dead now, but greatly respected by old New Zealand broadcasting news hands, knew what he was doing. This story was huge, the scale of the disaster horrendous. Blumsky was mature and thoughtful — he had stood for Parliament — and could handle people. There were going to be a lot of difficult people to handle on the ice. Blumsky had the maturity and the charm to smooth his own way given the general attitude to the news media amongst officialdom in the days of Muldoon.

These days, since the advent of CNN, Fox News and live reporting from wherever a story is breaking, those involved in the big stories know they have to accommodate the needs of the news media, which are simply the needs of the world to know. Officials know there is no point maintaining dumb silence or excluding the cameras.

As late as 1989, TVNZ was denounced as ghoulish and preying on people's distress for daring to locate its 6 p.m. news bulletin on a hill above the coastal settlement of Aramoana after the infamous massacre there. Now the world expects to see live coverage of the rescue of the Chilean miners. Now governments actually position all the cameras for such an event. When 29 miners died at Pike River, even local people expected the media to broadcast the story nationally from the scene. By now it is an expectation.

This was not the way it was going to be on the Antarctic ice in the days following the DC-10 disaster. Buzz Hart probably thought he had the right man for such a vast human tragedy, which was going to require extreme sensitivity. In any case, Blumsky was already there in Christchurch. What's more, Blumsky had had dealings with Bob Thomson, the director of the Antarctic Division of the Department of Scientific and Industrial Research. Bob Thomson flew several times as tour commentator on the Antarctic DC-10s and he will make a brief appearance later when the question of altitudes becomes a sore point at the Royal Commission.

I asked Blumsky what Thomson was like.

'Good man. Very fine civil servant, bureaucrat. If ever there was a bureaucrat it was Bob Thomson. He had for years negotiated and was one of the leading negotiators with the treaty arrangements for Antarctica. He'd flown to the ice so many times he'd almost become a mile millionaire. We at 3ZB knew him as very helpful.'

But Blumsky was terrified. 'It had to do with the ability to cope, capacity to perform, capacity to supply information, worries about the equipment, whether it would work and how I'd get on with our American cameraman, Frank "Kaz" Kazukaitis, whom I didn't really know,' he says. 'I had grave fears about being inadequate. And also [I was] beginning to question whether they should have sent a seasoned hard news man down. Because I was the last one to hunt the subject with the microphone, chase him down the street. I'm not that aggressive.'

They flew to the ice. On board, Blumsky says, were about 80 or 90 people. 'We get down there and land, everyone went to their positions at Scott Base. Kaz and I appear at the office of Bob Thomson. He welcomes us. But he made it very plain. "You'll understand, won't you fellas, that you'll have to keep out of the way. We're extremely busy, we don't know what's going on, we don't know what happened, we've got bodies to remove from the hill," and so on and so on and so on.'

Now, one has to judge a man in terms of the time in which he lives. But Thomson's attitude would be seen as outrageous, disgraceful, unacceptable and patronising now, and these days, should a senior broadcasting journalist encounter that attitude from a bureaucratic official when trying to cover such a national and international tragedy — in this case the fourth worst air disaster in history — calls would be made back to Radio New Zealand and TVNZ and a ministerial press secretary, if not the Prime Minister's chief press secretary, would be hearing the riot act.

Blumsky is a conservative, courteous man and also a man of that time. But he knew the job he had to do. 'At the same time, I had this funny, funny, funny thought that I don't necessarily agree that the public have a right to know. I began to doubt even if they had a need to know.'

This doubt was probably not going to be useful to him on the ice. But he had a job to do and was under intense pressure from New Zealand to get it done and that doubt was not going to stop him trying.

Holmes: 'May I say something, John?'

Blumsky: 'You may.'

H: 'Air New Zealand was entirely owned by the taxpayer.'

Blumsky: 'Yeah.'

H: 'Two hundred and fifty-seven people were dead. They had family and loved ones who wanted news. You're a taxpayer — you yourself, you had the right to know what was going on. News dissemination was what those people needed to be mindful of.'

Blumsky: 'Yes. But I wasn't going to get into speculation on the radio about what I was hearing from round Scott Base, from the cook or the chef. I was very conscious that whatever I said from down there would affect the whole country. It's like there's a riot at Paremoremo, right? And you're sent there, you and a cameraman are sent there to find out what's going on and why it occurred, who was going to do what to whom, how it happened. They open the big doors, in you go with your equipment, they shut the doors again and say, "It's too dangerous, we're not letting you out, we'll give you information when we get it. You're on your own." Now, you can't get information from someone who doesn't want to talk and you can't go getting information from someone who's just come down off the hill and has been picking up bits and pieces of air hostesses. I felt conscious of that all the time. And in many ways I was almost the worst one to send down there because of this feeling I had.'

H: 'Yeah.'

Blumsky: 'But in my defence I would say, if John Knowles [who succeeded Blumsky on the ice after some 10 days] went down at the beginning he would have lasted 24 hours and been sent home because he was aggressive and I think he hunted too hard. So in many ways I think Buzz Hart was doing the right thing. Jesus, it's haunted me, Paul, for years, whether I was the right one, whether I did a good enough job. After all, what information did I have? How could I have done it differently? We did two tapes straight away down there, Kaz and I, standing in the snow talking about things. We could only give them to the pilots of the United States Hercules, we gave two tapes to them and they never turned up in Christchurch. They're lost.'

H: 'What do you mean?'

Blumsky: 'They disappeared. They were never delivered to TVNZ.'

H: 'Stop there, John. I think you were the right man to send.'

And I do. My former colleague is decent, intelligent and dedicated. A man who does not have to overcome feeling reluctant to impose himself on someone who has spent the day picking up bits and pieces of air hostesses is not a man I would want on my team. Blumsky's team was him and the cameraman. He had no weight with which to lean on anyone subtly.

What is clear from everything he tells me is that there was a clear attitude of exclusion in that place during those days. He had a real feeling that everyone there wanted to shut it all down. And Blumsky never got up to the crash site to report or to film.

'We were blocked. We couldn't. I use the prison analogy because we were dependent on Scott Base for everything, transport, food, lodgings, the whole bloody works. And if we wanted to move out of Scott Base to go over to the Americans? That was denied us several times. Kaz was an American, used to be a Petty Officer in the US Navy, attached to Deep Freeze. That's why he was sent down as the cameraman.

'Kaz said, "Let's just see if we can go over there and have a chat to some of those fellas of mine." We couldn't get transport across. We couldn't get a helicopter because they were all too busy. And who am I to say, "I demand a seat on transport!" When they're ferrying people up the hill. All sorts of equipment is going up there, who am I to say, what right do I have to a seat? If they tell me they haven't got room for me, I have to accept that. But the sight of that television camera and a tape recorder for the nine, 10 days I was down there, was enough to drive them up the wall. Didn't want to know, too dangerous.'

Blumsky knew the real reason there was no ride up the hill, of course. 'They didn't respect our pledges on the pictures we would have taken. I said, "All right, Kaz will go up, he won't take the big lens, he'll just film long distance, promise you." "No. We don't trust you taking the right sensitive pictures." And I said, "That will all be done back at head office. It's for me to gather the stuff. It's for them to edit it." "No." So we were never allowed to get anywhere. I never went in a helicopter, never went near a helicopter.'

According to Ken Hickson, the buck stopped with Bob Thomson, boss of the DSIR's Antarctic Division.[1] All Thomson ever said, in response to Blumsky's requests to get up to the crash site and report the disaster to New Zealanders and those affected round the world, was, 'We'll see what we can do.' But, as Hickson says, Antarctica was suddenly a top heavy, paranoid, controlling body of people. You had Air New Zealand, Civil Aviation, the Air Line Pilots' Association, McDonnell Douglas, General Electric, the FAA, the National Transportation Safety Board (NTSB, the US air accident investigator) and the US Navy itself, any one of which might find itself blamed for the disaster.

I feel for Blumsky, a dedicated and diligent broadcaster trying to cover a story of crucial, hour by hour importance to New Zealanders, his countrymen. One can be sensitive to the concerns about bodies and body parts, but Blumsky is a New Zealander too, and not a hungry, cunning, tricky young man wanting to make death pornography. He was there representing

New Zealand's state radio and television. He was a safe, middle-aged man. That was why he was sent. The attitude of the New Zealanders there to him can only, even now, be seen as a disgrace. I tell him that their attitude showed a lack of respect towards him as a working human being and a loyal Kiwi. That is what I think. I despise their attitude.

One day Blumsky got sick of interviewing the great Ron Chippindale: '... backwards, sideways, frontwards, we've interviewed the weatherman, we've interviewed the black box people. These are general interviews, nothing special about the crash. They're saying nothing. So about the fourth day there, Kaz and I decide to go down to the ice field. Scott Base, on a hill, overlooks the ice field on the massive Ross Sea. This is where they've set up huts to store the bodies. The helicopters are flying in from Erebus and dropping down to the recovery sheds. So I said to Kaz, let's go and take some long shots of the helicopters coming in, depositing their recovery. Right. So we go down there. Set it up. Believe me, within three or four minutes, a Land Rover comes screaming down the hill. "No. Stop, stop, stop, stop, stop, stop. I'll have you arrested. Now get in here [the Land Rover]. Put that equipment away, you're not going to do it." It was the Scott Base boss and Nelson schoolteacher Mike Prebble. We packed up the gear and we didn't do it. I mean, after that we were kicked in the tweeds.'

It wasn't just the attitude of the Scott Base people that frustrated Blumsky. Live sound feeds back to Wellington would fail. Equipment failed. It seems, by his description, to have been 10 days of misery, humiliation and intense frustration.

Kaz Kazukaitis was furious at the treatment given him and Blumsky. 'It amounted to bloody harassment. We were totally blacked out. I don't believe they had the right to prevent us from doing our job.'

So the company pulled Blumsky out. 'I get on the plane, I get back to Christchurch and bugger my days if I don't meet one of ours going the opposite direction. John Knowles is flying to the ice. So they're getting rid of me and sending Knowles down there. But he doesn't get any more than I got, I don't think.'

Prime Minister Muldoon and the chairman of the BCNZ had intervened. The DSIR was to allow filming of wreckage from the ground. Two weeks after the crash, New Zealanders finally saw close-up film of the twisted, broken wreckage. Knowles got into bad trouble a few days later. He claimed in a report that someone on the flight deck had cried out seconds before the crash, 'Where the hell are we?' Knowles declared his source to be reliable. It was thought to have come from the Americans. It was nonsense, of course. John Blumsky later won a radio current affairs prize for his work on the ice.

I listened to Blumsky and contemplated his undisputed dedication to radio. It was no accident, I found myself thinking, that he married a woman called Mike. Mike made me tea and her own fresh date loaf with lashings of butter spread across it.

The taxi came to take me back to my hotel. Blumsky walked me outside.

He remains deeply angry about Erebus. Not necessarily about the treatment he got. He spoke kindly of Bob Thomson, who failed singularly to help him convey information to the people of New Zealand, essentially the owners of the story. He understands that body recovery from an impossible place was the priority at that time. He is angry about what emerged later, what people in government and people at the airline did subsequently. There was Chippindale at Scott Base, nice as pie, loving being interviewed — he loved the attention — and his report would turn out to be a fraud.

I shook his hand. I hadn't seen him for over 30 years.

'By the way, John,' I said. 'Did I pass the audition?'

He was grinning from ear to ear as I drove away.

Some weeks later I described to Richard Griffin the stories John Blumsky had told me of the obstruction he endured at Scott Base. Richard Griffin is a veteran of the New Zealand Parliamentary Press Gallery and a veteran of New Zealand broadcast journalism. Griffin served five years as chief press secretary to Jim Bolger, Prime Minister of New Zealand. I told Griffin especially of the final hysterical treatment Blumsky received at the hands of Mike Prebble.

Griffin shook his head in disbelief. 'That's extraordinary, isn't it? I wasn't aware of all that. How did they get away with that rubbish? We forget so quickly, don't we? That was the way things were done. But I'm not surprised.'

Holmes: 'That was the way things were done in the Muldoon era.'

Griffin: 'And before, of course. But in the old days there weren't cameras, and journalists were sycophants. I'm horrified to hear that story. So once again, I reiterate, times have changed, thank God, so dramatically that no one in New Zealand can be treated like that and no one in any sort of authority, particularly in that sort of scene, would even try to do it.'

As for Blumsky's inability to get up the mountain to film and report from the crash site, Griffin was indignant: 'Why do those people think they're the high priests of sensibility? We can decide, but you can't. It's extraordinary, isn't it?'

Without meaning offence to either Blumsky or John Knowles — 'Knowles wasn't that hard either' — Griffin says he is ashamed of the news media, looking back. 'We didn't have the gumption to demand proper access to the mountain. In retrospect I'm ashamed at how badly, politically anyway, we handled it. I think we were very lax about the way we handled not just the accident itself but the subsequent hearings and inquiries.'

Richard Griffin was, on the night of the DC-10 crash, in the upstairs bar of the De Bretts Hotel on Lambton Quay, 'the famous bar in town, directly opposite the Supreme Court at the time, and where lawyers, journalists and trade unionists spent untold hours talking rubbish to each other . . . I was with Peter Elworthy. He was at that stage working for Gerry Symmans, who was then chief press secretary to Robert Muldoon. 'It must have been about half past seven and he must have taken a phone call in the bar because they knew where he was and the Ninth Floor had phoned him.'

By 7.30 that night worries were rapidly intensifying. By 7.30 Jim Collins was coming to the end of his fuel. Griffin continues: 'He came across to me and said, "Look, I've got to go back to the office. You won't believe this but one of those flights to Antarctica hasn't reported in." And I said, "Oh, come on." He said, "No, they're panicking up there. I've been told to get straight back." And I'm not quoting verbatim but he was quite exercised. Peter could get quite exercised anyway about almost anything, but you could tell he was jumpy.'

Griffin, who was political editor for Radio New Zealand at this stage, phoned his newsroom and suggested they start calling some people in. He walked back to Parliament.

He called Elworthy about 9.30 because radio was reporting an increasingly serious situation. 'And he said, "Can't talk. Can't talk. Sorry mate." And that was it. Never heard from Peter again. He was locked up on the Ninth Floor. I went back to the office about 10. All the lights were on on the Ninth Floor. It was clear by this time things were extraordinarily serious. Bars were emptying out all over town and people were going back to their workplaces if they were in the media and you could tell there was big tension at the Beehive.'

Just as there was already at a house in St Heliers in Auckland where a mother and her two elder daughters waited anxiously for news.

Griffin went home to bed about two in the morning after he heard that wreckage had been sighted. The aircraft was smashed. There were no survivors. 'I remember going into work the following morning about 9 o'clock and there was tension throughout the whole building but there was a closed shop on the Ninth Floor. And Robert Muldoon, who would hold a press conference at the drop of a hat, was not engaging. Morrie Davis was being even more singularly arrogant. In fact he wasn't dealing. What he was doing was dismissing questions as "None of your business". I don't know when he first started to engage at a relevant level but it certainly wasn't in the first few hours the following morning.'

I asked Griffin: 'What did you see, Richard, of the involvement of the Muldoon government in subsequent months in what the public understood had happened to the aircraft, in the inquiries up to the establishment of the Royal Commission? What were you gleaning of how they were handling things?'

He replied: 'From a personal point of view I was really disappointed from day one that the government didn't seem to be taking into account the dreadful tragedy that had been visited on the families. There didn't seem to be any sort of engagement on a personal level at all.

'At a political level, at an information level, there was no engagement at all. Robert Muldoon became more and more abrupt and more and more dismissive and even grumpier than he always was when it came to dealing with the media. The suggestion that he might have been in touch with Morrie Davis from time to time was dismissed out of hand. Davis and he became, appeared to become, clones, their attitudes were very similar, generally speaking. "Well, what's it got to do with you?" and "We'll know in the fullness of time, process will go ahead."

'And Muldoon on the following Monday [after the crash] at his post-cabinet press conference was so dismissive of questions, it was — and this was a man who could be quite a sensitive human being — as if he had no sensitivity at all, and certainly didn't express it in a news conference. I do remember thinking, "This is just an outrageous way to deal with such a tragedy. This is worse than Tangiwai" — and I was alive for Tangiwai.'

Could it be, and it is only speculation, that Muldoon was particularly grumpy because by then he knew of the coordinates bungle? Air New Zealand was entirely state owned. He, as Finance Minister, was the airline's only shareholder. He was certainly a prime minister who did not appreciate public surprises. Like Morrie Davis, he would have expected to be told. And again, there was no doubt of the effect the coordinate change had on the flight because of the way Air New Zealand kept it all so secretive for so long, telling only the Chief Inspector, who would display kind consideration to the Establishment by keeping quiet and then determining that there was no evidence to suggest the change in the coordinates affected the fate of the flight.

What amazes Griffin about the Erebus story was that so much of it appeared to be so out of character for New Zealand, and the New Zealand way of doing things — for example, the order given by Chief Executive Morrie Davis to shred documents at Air New Zealand House in Auckland in the days after the accident. When it came to the Royal Commission, time and again, Mahon would bemoan an almost complete lack of documentation for any particular action the airline might have taken, such as documentation on how the pilots were briefed for the Antarctic flights.

Griffin said: 'We knew nothing about it. It was so foreign to the New Zealand concept of doing business. This was literally a government-owned company, you know, you just didn't behave like that. And that's why Morrie Davis was so different from everybody else within the state organisations. He was cavalier. When those reports came out, it shocked everyone, that that was going on. And I don't think we really accepted it was going on.'

And that is a very important part of the story. Some of what Mahon discovered seemed to be beyond the realm of possibility in fair old honest New Zealand. It started to look, said Griffin, like some kind of bad novel and we didn't believe it. He included the break-ins at the homes of Maria Collins and Anne Cassin as well.

Strange burglaries indeed. On 29 March 1980, her birthday, Maria Collins took the children to Kathryn Schollum's for dinner. This was the first night since the Erebus accident on which the house had been completely empty. When she got home, the light didn't work. She saw very quickly that the house was in disarray. Photos of Jim Collins and newspaper articles she was saving for a scrapbook had been thrown around the living room. In a draw in her bedroom was a ruby ring and next to it a document or two relating to Jim. The ruby ring was there, the documents were gone. In an envelope had been a small photograph of her husband. It had been ripped in half and replaced.

It might have been a random burglary. Except the home of Anne Cassin, wife of First Officer Greg Cassin, was also broken into round the same time. Some of Cassin's flight documents disappeared. Whilst one burglary might be random, two would seem to be something else. No one was caught; nothing was ever proven.

Of the news media of the time, Griffin said: 'And I think most of us . . . and this is what I'm ashamed of . . . most of us at the time . . . it was deeply embedded into the Wellington tradition . . . thought, "No, that break-in stuff just sounds nonsense. I don't believe it." That was the attitude of most of us, I think. We didn't show the gumption that was called for and we didn't go to the effort to see whether any of these claims were real or otherwise. We lived in our silos. Our political silos.'

Griffin, for his part, has no doubt Muldoon was complicit in a cover-up. He doesn't know, of course. Muldoon never told him he was. You would never prove it. But there were signs, said Griffin. It was the way Muldoon avoided questions on the Erebus disaster. It was the way he avoided mentioning Morrie Davis's name.

Griffin said that Muldoon and some of his people looked cagey, looked guilty. 'They looked like people digging holes and burying things. You knew there were secret meetings.'

He has no doubt that the first impulse of the government, and particularly the Prime Minister, was to shy away from any involvement at a public level with Air New Zealand and the terrible business around it. Then there was a determined effort by a number of them to write Mahon off as a screwball.

Griffin described the Muldoon attacks on Mahon as 'vitriolic'. It was an attack on a man who clearly disagreed with what had become government policy. 'The amount of [the vitriol] I've not seen or heard about before. This man was dangerous, he's demented and we should rid ourselves of him.'

We spoke about the effect of the release, just before the Royal Commission hearings began, of the Chippindale Report, which was so damning of the pilots. And how Mahon admitted that when he read the Chippindale Report he found it eminently sensible, and that he expected the Royal Commission would probably rubber stamp it. Here was Mahon himself, a ferociously intelligent man, who found the Chippindale Report so beguilingly believable and reasonable.

Griffin said: 'I do remember thinking Chippindale was a very inappropriate man to conduct the investigation because this was a jet airliner, it was a passenger airliner, it was in a region that Chippindale, I imagine, had never been near, and for years we'd been used to Chippindale's response to the old Cessna flying into a hill, or flipping in air, or clipping a power pole.

That was about it. So he seemed inappropriate to me.'

Richard Griffin is, as I said, the former chief press secretary to a prime minister.

Holmes: 'Is it likely the Chippindale Report was deliberately released at the time it was in order to affect the public attitude to the crash?'

Griffin: 'Of course. Well, if I'd been in the business, absolutely, that would be the first thing you'd decide to do.'

H: 'If you were the chief press secretary to the Prime Minister.'

Griffin: 'If you were giving advice to the Prime Minister and those associated, you'd say, "This is the best possible way to muddy the water," and possibly, if you want to . . . I presume a decision was made somewhere by someone to take this thing out of the hands of the Mahon inquiry and ensure that, no matter what, New Zealand and Air New Zealand were not going to carry responsibility for it.'

H: 'Yes. If you were the chief press secretary to the Prime Minister and the Prime Minister was facing the possibility that if Air New Zealand is found grossly negligent there could be legal suits for up to a hundred, two hundred million dollars . . .'

Griffin: 'Big money in those days.'

H: 'Yes. As Prime Minister . . .'

Griffin: 'And probably kill the airline.'

H: 'And the government would have to find a hundred, couple hundred million dollars, well, you'd have to protect the airline, wouldn't you?'

Griffin: 'You'd have to protect the airline. And Gerry Symmans was the chief press secretary at the time and if I was in his position you'd either make a decision to go with it, to go with the decision by the government to bury as much responsibility as possible, or resign. If you don't resign then it's your responsibility to come up with the best possible scenario within the framework of the political determination to ensure there wasn't going to be responsibility on the taxpayer.'

H: 'Yes.'

Griffin: 'And that would be the best advice you'd give them.'

H: 'Well . . .'

Griffin: 'This is how you do it.'

H: 'Not right though, is it?'

Griffin: 'It's appalling. It's disgraceful. And it's not the way we used to do things.'

H: 'So this was a new approach, is what you're saying?'

Griffin: 'God yes! Our history has been polluted with errors of judgement but I don't think at any other time in New Zealand history has there been such a determined conspiracy. Possibly during World War Two to keep us from finding out the realities. That's the only time in all my time I've been following politics that I can recall a total distortion of reality, of what happened.'

Griffin spoke of Muldoon's passion for aviation. His office was filled with models of aeroplanes. Air New Zealand was his baby. He said that Muldoon was 'a very sentimental man and the airline was a very important issue to him. Morrie seemed to be very special to him and aviation was almost an obsession. So I can understand Rob Muldoon saying, "Well, this dreadful thing's happened, we've got to get over it, out of it as best we can and the last thing we need now is further fallout".'

H: 'Even if it is means we've got to ditch the pilots.'

Griffin: 'Even if it means we've got to ditch the pilots. He's quite ruthless enough. And that's another thing, he's quite ruthless enough to be able to do that, and not flinch. I think Muldoon would have worked on the assumption that this was what he had to do. Look after the country, look after the taxpayer. It's a terrible business, but let's not make it any worse.'

I put this to Paul Davison QC later on. Davison represented the Air Line Pilots' Association at the inquiry and he was counsel for Maria Collins at the Royal Commission.

'Yes,' he sighs. 'But what price justice?'

10

The Centrality of Chippindale

'So,' I went on, 'if this question comes up in the House, or if the papers start asking questions, I shall announce an inquiry.'
'Excellent idea,' he agreed. 'I shall be more than happy to conduct it.'
I took a deep breath. 'No, Humphrey. Not an internal inquiry. A real inquiry.'
His eyes widened in horror. 'Minister! You can't be serious.'
'A real inquiry!' I repeated emphatically.
'No, no, I beg you!'

— The Right Hon James Hacker, *The Complete Yes Minister*

It was pretty dumb, wasn't it? It was pretty dumb. I mean, how difficult can it be to put those pieces of the jigsaw together and [still] come up with the wrong answer as he managed to do?

— Paul Davison QC

Because it was exactly what he set out to do, is the answer. It was what he was expected to do.

Ron Chippindale emerges upon study as one of the most fascinating creatures of the entire Erebus aftermath. He was a very bright man. Yet his report was very dumb. Impossibly so. Indeed, I now believe him to have been central to the entire cover-up. He did exactly what Air New Zealand, Civil Aviation and the government wanted. Despite the wealth of evidence against such a finding, Chippindale managed to blame the pilots. It was dishonest, cowardly and corrupt.

The first thing we have to realise about Chippindale was that his report was the result of an interdepartmental inquiry. In other words, Chippindale was going to see that everyone alive was looked after. The dead could take the blame. Ron was going to be a safe pair of hands.

Captain Arthur Cooper, the ALPA representative at the Commission, believed for years that Chippindale was simply struggling, that he was out of his depth. He now believes that was quite wrong. He now believes that shortly after the accident Muldoon and Davis had a discussion about how, given the vast financial implications, the fallout of the disaster had to be handled for the sake of the company and New Zealand itself. It would have been made clear to him that the company could not be found to have been negligent. Pilot error would fit the bill. In the world of realpolitik such a discussion would be expected to have taken place.

Mahon realised the potential for this scenario straight away. He notes early on in *Verdict on Erebus* that the Office of Air Accidents was part of the Ministry of Transport, although Chippindale was statutorily independent. Civil Aviation was also a division of the Ministry of Transport. Even the Meteorological Service was part of the Ministry of Transport.

At the Commission of Inquiry, Mahon observed that the Met Service witness wanted but could not quite bring himself to say that there was low cloud in front of the DC-10, despite being seriously pushed to say so by Civil Aviation counsel.[1]

Civil Aviation and Air New Zealand worked, naturally, close together; both were in the gun for the accident, and both knew they could be facing civil claims of tens of millions of dollars from the families of the deceased. Senior Air New Zealand personnel knew by early the morning after the accident that the coordinates had been changed to fly Jim Collins into a mountain and that Collins had not been told. Civil Aviation knew that it had neglected to make sure Air New Zealand had sent to the ice a captain who had flown at least one previous flight to Antarctica under supervision.

What is so deeply disturbing about Ron Chippindale when one examines his report, which so cruelly and unjustly blamed the pilots, is how he got away with it and how officialdom not only took him seriously but tolerated him in the job for another 20 years. The answer is simple. He did what he was expected to do. And he did it very well. There are still people who take him seriously.

Chippindale knew the McMurdo destination waypoint coordinates had been changed, and the captain not told, because Air New Zealand told him.

The company most certainly didn't tell the public, and for one reason. They knew the importance of the coordinate change and the pilot's ignorance of it. They knew on the night of the accident. Senior management would most certainly have been told about the change that very night or early next day. It would have cut through senior levels of Flight Operations with the speed and horror of a straw fire.

Chippindale knew about sector whiteout. His report is very authoritative on whiteout.[2] He knew exactly how treacherous it could be. The Americans at McMurdo had told him all about it. He was told about a loss of depth perception over uniform, snow-covered ground and a low, solid, pale, overcast overhead. In whiteout, you fail to see any rise in the ground ahead, and 'to be aware of terrain changes and the separation of sky and earth'.[3] What's more, they told him — and Chippindale records this — whiteout can exist in normal VMC (visual meteorological conditions) under which pilots think they are flying within safe visual flying parameters. 'The condition may occur in a crystal clear atmosphere or under a cloud ceiling with ample comfortable light . . .'[4] What's more, Chippindale tells us, 'in polar regions these conditions occur frequently'.[5]

For Mahon, whiteout was crucial. 'The obvious ultimate cause of the disaster was quite plainly — if one read the Chief Inspector's report in full — the whiteout conditions operating on the approach to Lewis Bay.'[6]

Yet, incredibly, despite devoting 13 paragraphs to whiteout, Chippindale gives no weight to it as a cause of the accident. He merely speaks of the pilot flying onto an area of 'poor surface and horizon definition'. Which meant nothing to the public except flying in cloud. Justice Mahon would say later: 'The Chief Inspector blamed the aircrew on the basis that they plainly saw in front of them "poor surface and horizon definition", yet elected to fly on and did not detect the rising terrain ahead. This was certainly an ingenious method of attributing the "probable cause" of the accident to the aircrew.'[7]

You learn, as you study Peter Mahon, that when he uses the word 'ingenious', it is code for 'a lie'.

Neither did Chippindale give any weight to the airline's Chief Navigator, Brian Hewitt, failing to fulfil the obvious requirement to notify the aircrew of the waypoint change that sent them to the mountain. He refused to accept the work of the Washington CVR transcription team and went off and manufactured his own transcription to support his bogus arguments and make 55 changes to the detriment of the aircrew.

So, just like that he did it. That is how Chippindale — ignoring the change to the coordinates, the pilot not being told, what he had been told about sector whiteout and the fact that no one on the flight deck, five highly trained professionals, ever saw the mountain — blamed the aircrew for flying on towards filthy weather with a mountain up ahead.

The great compelling question of why a highly trained, highly respected, sane man flew low into cloud with a mountain up ahead, Chippindale never asked. He could not afford to, of course.

Later, after the Royal Commission, after Mahon's report was published, and after the Court of Appeal had overturned Mahon not on causation but on his finding that there had been an organised conspiracy to perjure, Mahon believed that his credibility as a judge was ruined. In January 1982, therefore, he resigned from the bench.

Immediately, a spluttering, vengeful Chippindale was allowed by his minister, George Gair, to release a lengthy and hysterical denunciation of Mahon, despite the thorough analysis and logic of Mahon's exhaustive report. The Mahon Report was riddled with errors, Chippindale claimed. In a letter to the Minster dated 18 January 1982, released with the rambling press release, Chippindale declared:

> If the judge's determination on the cause of this accident had been exposed to any process of review by persons knowledgeable in aviation lore it would surely have been exposed as an illogical conclusion . . . The fact of the matter is that the judge has only expressed an opinion and it is the opinion of one man who does not appear to have accepted sound advice on aviation lore.

Whatever in God's name aviation 'lore' meant. Mahon dealt, of course, in law, not 'lore'. He also always took pains to point out that there was nothing technical about this accident. It was straight-up human error and omission, and it all took place back at Head Office in a dysfunctional Flight Operations Section.

The release of Chippindale's barely literate tirade in February 1982 made it appear that the great Chippindale answered to no one. Or was this infamous press release simply another instance in which the vanity and arrogance of the great inspector of broken Cessnas, mangled helicopters and smashed up top-dressers suited the aspirations of a government determined to discredit a former High Court judge in order for Chippindale's incomprehensible story of causation to prevail — namely that Jim Collins had been flying, against regulations, too low towards cloud in which there was a mountain that Captain Collins knew was there? This was also, of course, the official airline view. And it was also the official Civil Aviation view. And it was exactly what the Übermeister, Robert Muldoon, wanted to hear.

So then. Leaving aside the Chief Inspector's manner of expression, here is what he decided caused the accident.

> The probable cause of this accident was the decision of the captain to continue the flight at low level towards an area of poor surface and horizon definition when the crew was not certain of their position and the subsequent inability to detect the rising terrain which intercepted the aircraft's flight path.[8]

If ever there was an unsatisfactory explanation of the cause of an air accident it is contained in the lines above.

Chippindale knew about the coordinate change which took Captain Collins just under 30 miles east of where he thought he would end up. He knew the change had been made in the early morning hours before Jim Collins took off. He knew the pilot had not been told. He must have known Collins had been briefed to fly down McMurdo Sound. He knew much about whiteout. He knew that no one on the flight deck ever saw the mountain or expressed concern until the last minute of flight. He knew that the flight crew were looking ahead at exactly what they expected to see, the flat sea ice of McMurdo Sound.

And in the 'probable cause' was one of the biggest lies. It is amazing Chippindale got away with this one. He knew that when Jim Collins realised something was not right, instead of deciding to fly on towards this spooky area ahead he in fact elected to fly away from where he was. Away. In the remaining minute in the life of Flight 901, the discussion on the flight deck is between Collins and Cassin about the safest way to climb out. He would also have thought that when the ground proximity warning sounded it was malfunctioning, even though he obeyed it instantly as he was so immaculately trained to do.

None of the above meant anything to Chippindale. It could not be allowed to. It was too awful to contemplate. It meant the problem wasn't on the flight deck. It meant the airline and Civil Aviation would have to face charges of gross negligence.

But in those five lines he blamed the pilots. He wrote them off. The impression was given that Collins flew towards the mountain and, even though there was cloud in front of him, kept going. Management of both Civil Aviation and Air New Zealand were absolved from any blame for or contribution to the disaster.

And Chippindale could do no wrong. What was there to doubt about Chippindale? And, surely, everyone would pull together to find out the truth about what had happened on the mountain that November day. After all, Ron Chippindale was the Chief Inspector of Air Accidents. He knew what he was talking about. And our public service was honest, wasn't it?

It so happened that an aviation journalist of the time, a man with a healthy regard for himself, Ken Hickson, published a book during the Royal Commission, *Flight 901 to Erebus*, an effort which can only be described as both unfortunately premature and more than a little in the thrall of Chippindale. The book is nevertheless instructive of the image being constructed in the public mind at the time, an image of a great and internationally respected giant of accident investigation.

And here are some gems. 'Six months of searching,' writes Hickson, 'and Chippindale knew what had happened.'

'But I still don't know why it happened,' he quotes Chippindale.[9] This was, incredibly, a month before Chippindale released his report, during which time, Chippindale — as we shall see in the next chapter — was doctoring the cockpit voice recorder to shore up his bogus finding of pilot error by making it look as if Captain Collins had dragged the crew down kicking and screaming.

Hickson went on *Eyewitness News* when the Royal Commission was announced on 30 March 1980.

> I didn't think an inquiry into the accident was necessary. I had complete faith in the process of investigation of air accidents in this country, and in the methods and expertise of Ron Chippindale and his team from here and abroad. At that stage — even with the interim report circulated to certain parties — the process of investigation was still continuing. I considered the inquiry call was instigated on emotional and

> political grounds, without an appreciation of the process of investigation and the thoroughness and independence of the investigators.[10]

And if the DC-10 had been, instead, a top-dresser lying mangled at the bottom of a gully with an overloaded hopper, Hickson was probably right. Unfortunately this was one of the largest and most incomprehensible air accidents that ever happened.

Poor Hickson. He might have known a bit about aviation but he didn't know much about the politics of internal departmental inquiries, and the ways governments and departments of state looked after themselves.

For the record, Chippindale had no team from 'abroad'. He loved his international connections, however. Certainly he loved to visit his international contacts, most often in Europe or the United States, generally during the northern hemisphere summer months.

Chippindale was a man of great bureaucratic skill. While damning the pilots, he also showed great humility. In fact, he was covering his backside. He is quoted in a newspaper report shortly after the release of his report, quoted in turn by Antarctic researcher Stuart Macfarlane in his *The Erebus Papers.*

> Mr R. Chippindale said yesterday he had not been able to find out definitely what caused the plane to crash on Mount Erebus last November with the loss of 257 lives. It had been hard to establish a definite cause. Mr Chippindale said he had difficulty in finding 'the ultimate cause' for the crash. 'I have said in the Report what I think is the probable cause — the last thing that made the accident inevitable, though there were other factors or causes leading up to the accident.'

But what that meant was that nothing that occurred before Captain Collins pointed the aircraft at the mountain and continued on had any effect on the fate of the flight. Air New Zealand and Civil Aviation were completely off the hook.

And of course 'the other factors or causes' he never mentioned. He never allowed them. Only Chippindale was right. If a plane crashed, the pilot was to blame. In those days, that is how it was. Management never wore the blame. They weren't going to this time either. They had the right man in charge. Chippindale was old school. As mentioned, a saying in crew rooms round the world was: 'If the accident doesn't kill the pilot, the inquiry will.'

Mahon, in what was a pioneering accident report, would render that kind of thinking obsolete and unacceptable. And he would be put through hell for it. Mahon saw the Chippindale findings for what they were, a gigantic interdepartmental cover-up. Chippindale did the job for the boys and girls and he did it very well.

Why that aircraft collided with that mountain, the really big question, Chippindale would never answer. It was not politic for him to do so.

How could Chippindale have dared to say that the crew was not misled by the coordinate change about which they had not been told? The rest of us could see it. How could he not? For if they had been told, the diligent Jim Collins and Greg Cassin would have worked out immediately that the new track would shoot them straight at Erebus.

The answer is that he did it with cunning. He said, in his report at paragraph 2.5, 'The error in longitude had persisted for 14 months and was not corrected on the sample flight plan showed to this crew at their preliminary briefing.' In other words, the crew had been briefed to fly a course down the centre of McMurdo Sound. Incredibly, again in paragraph 2.5, Chippindale then writes, 'In the case of this crew, no evidence was found to suggest that they had been mislead [sic] by this error in the flight plan shown to them at the briefing.' This was the flight plan that Jim Collins, and all of the other pilots who attended, understood was to take the DC-10 straight down across the safety of the flat sea ice of McMurdo Sound. The destination waypoint was actually underlined or highlighted in some way, Captain Gabriel — who attended Collin's briefing — would later testify.

Surely the most obvious evidence that Collins and his crew had been deceived by the change in coordinates was the accident itself. The aircraft had flown straight at a mountain at low altitude and crashed into it and none on the flight deck mentions at any time either cloud or a mountain.

But it turned out Chippindale did not see this as evidence at all. Evidence was paper. Where were the maps or documents to prove Collins had reason to believe he was over McMurdo Sound? If there were no documents there was no evidence, apparently.

If you believed Chippindale, for it to be established that the pilots had been deceived, someone would have to have seen Collins making notes, or at the crash site a plotted topographical map would have to have been found.

Under cross-examination by Paul Davison at the Royal Commission on 16 July 1980, Chippindale admitted that this was what he meant by evidence. 'We had found no one who attended the briefing was misled by those coordinates or had seen the members of the crew of the subject flight write down the coordinates, nor had we come across any documents such as you suggest indicating a track to the incorrect destination. Or a note of the incorrect coordinates.'[11]

This was all a lie as we shall see in this chapter and subsequent chapters. Chippindale alleged that neither Maria nor the girls ever told him Jim Collins had been working on maps, and when they gave evidence that he had, accused them of lying. He refused to believe that Collins had got hold of a chart such as Elizabeth described. And he kept entirely to himself that he knew Collins had his own topographical maps on the flight with him.[12] The truth didn't suit. We shall see the incredible dishonesty of the Chief Inspector regarding charts later in our narrative.

And here was a most peculiar thing. Chippindale's approach to questions put to him at the inquiry is very strange and highly suspicious. He was just as cagey as the rest of the airline and Civil Aviation management witnesses. Just as getting anything out of those men was likened to the painful process of pulling teeth, so it was with Chippindale. Why was Chippindale's approach not to just speak freely about the facts as he knew or understood them? You have a real sense when reading the transcripts of Chippindale under cross-examination that he too is hedging, that he too is reluctant, that he is adopting the super caution of the liar anxious not to be tripped. What he was doing, of course, was protecting the airline and Civil Aviation.

Never mind the right to the truth for the deceased 257.

What's more, he could spout gobbledegook as well as the rest of them in order to throw interrogators off the trail. Take this exchange between Chippindale and counsel for Anne Cassin, Roger Maclaren.[13]

Maclaren: 'The new flight plan was over it [Erebus]?'

Chippindale: 'Very close to it, yes.'

Maclaren: 'Am I right in suggesting that although you have indicated a probable cause of this accident, that that is not necessarily the only probable cause for the air crash of TE901?'

Chippindale: 'This is correct.'

Ron sees where this is going.

Maclaren: 'May I suggest to you in conclusion, that an equally, if not more probable cause of this accident was the change of the flight plan from the old one to the new one across to and close to an active volcano without notifying the crew of the change and therefore on descent leading them into a collision path. Do you agree with that?'

Chippindale: 'No, I would not.'

Maclaren: 'What part would you disagree with?'

Chippindale: 'Almost the entire statement as I recall it. But primarily that the change of flight plan coordinates resulted in the accident.'

Maclaren: 'Would you agree that a probable cause was the failure to notify the crew of the change of the flight coordinates.'

Chippindale: 'No, again I would not agree.'

Maclaren pushes on. He asks Chippindale whether a failure by the airline to brief the crew in detail about the rich dangers of whiteout was an equally probable cause as the one he had suggested.

Chippindale: 'These I believe may be causal factors and to explain what I consider the difference the statement that I recorded as the probable cause is the last thing which occurred in the sequence of the flight which made the accident inevitable.'

And that was that. It was nonsense and it suited Chippindale's military and bureaucratic rigidity. It also kept blame well and truly away from Civil Aviation, from government and from the airline.

The judge intervened on the subject of the flight plan change.

Mahon: 'Mr Maclaren suggested to you that a cause was the change of the flight route and the suggested non-disclosure to the pilots of the change of route. Now if that combination of events did occur, and I'm not saying it did, would that not be a cause?'

Chippindale: 'I find this a little difficult to unravel clearly, in that it is a matter of chance that had the error remained in the flight plan, then because the aircraft would have been following an unintended track would have averted the accident.'

Gobbledegook. (The reader has not yet been introduced to the maddening business of whether the change in the coordinates was a return to the 'correct' or 'incorrect' coordinates. At the core of the inquiry was the airline's insistence that Collins should have known he was heading towards Erebus. It was an absurd proposition. But 'correct' versus 'incorrect' was to become one of the most baffling debates of the entire inquiry. The reader should not panic. Ultimately, it didn't matter.)

That was that then. Jim Collins had not been misled by the change in the coordinates and his failure to be notified. He was presumably to have noted the change by mental telepathy.

Mahon was incredulous at this finding by the Chief Inspector. Early on in his accident report he erupted:

> With respect, the conclusion just stated is untenable. The evidence adduced before the Commission made it clear . . . that Captain Collins had plotted, on the night before the fatal flight, certainly on his atlas and almost certainly on the other maps in his possession, the flight path upon which the erroneous NAV track would take the aircraft. Apart from anything else, the decision of Captain Collins to arm the NAV mode of the aircraft within a few minutes of impact completely destroys any suggestion that he had not previously plotted the destination coordinates which had been produced to him and First Officer Cassin at their briefing.[14]

How could Chippindale possibly find that Collins was not misled by the flight plan shown at the briefing? Everyone else was. Greg Cassin was. That is why First Officer Cassin voices no objection to Captain Collins flying at 1500 feet. Like his captain, he believed they were flying where they had been briefed to fly, over the flat sea ice of McMurdo Sound.

As for Chippindale's assertion, given in evidence under oath, that 'we had found no one who attended the briefing who was misled by those coordinates',[15] that was nonsense too. Five pilots had attended the 9 November briefing. Three were still alive.

The three gave evidence. At the Royal Commission, Captain Gabriel said he could tell from the destination waypoint shown to them that the flight path was west of Ross Island.[16] Captain Simpson looked at the coordinates at the briefing and realised that the computer flight path ran down McMurdo Sound. They can do that, these highly qualified pilots.

First Officer Barry Irvine said in evidence: 'When I left the briefing I had a clear understanding that we were flying into the McMurdo area up the McMurdo Sound with Ross Island and Mount Erebus well out to our left.'[17]

Captain Simpson had more to tell the Royal Commission. When Lloyd Brown QC took him on, Simpson remained adamant that he (and Collins) had been briefed to fly down McMurdo. What's more, he declared that what he had heard in court from the two briefing officers, Captains Wilson and Johnson, about what they had told the Antarctic pilots about their imminent flight plans, made him think that he had attended another briefing entirely.

Chippindale lied about all three pilots.

There was yet another way in which Jim Collins was deceived. At Flight Despatch on the morning of the flight, the Antarctic envelope the crew were given had a list of contents: 'Spare flight plans; NZAA [Auckland Airport]; Cape Hallett; McMurdo Sound 2; spare computer plans; NZAA; Cape Hallett; McMurdo Sound 2.'[18] This envelope, incredibly, was introduced at the inquiry by the Chief Inspector himself as Exhibit 38. Incredibly, it told him nothing.

The first shock Mahon received at the Royal Commission is that the passenger photos — and people were taking photographs right up to the point of impact — showed that the aircraft was flying in clear air and that there are black cliffs to be seen left and right in the distance. The Chief Inspector's report, and he knew it, had given the impression Jim Collins was flying in cloud. He never disabused anyone. He published no pictures with his report. This has to have been a clear attempt at deception.

The overall effect of the Chippindale Report was to whitewash both the airline and Civil Aviation. Sure, he found both organisations at fault for minor infringements of regulation. Civil Aviation denied any fault. Air New Zealand said the infringements didn't apply any more because all Antarctic flights were finished. In his passionate final submission Paul Davison QC described the Chippindale findings as to cause 'incredible', that his conclusions flew in the face of all the information he had.[19]

One of the main factors that haunted Mahon right through his inquiry — apart from Chippindale's findings not matching the fine reputations of the aircrew — was that after his descending orbital manoeuvre in Lewis Bay, which he presumed was McMurdo, Collins locked his aircraft back onto Nav Track immediately, in other words back on to his programmed course.

Before they left Auckland that morning, the crew had programmed into their AINS what they presumed was the McMurdo Sound route and the AINS, pilots knew, would give excellent guidance. The AINS was never wrong. Nevertheless, Jim Collins was flying visually as he descended. For lower level flight round Antarctica, he would use his eyes. He was required to. Locking his aircraft onto Nav Track was simply further assurance.

This was something Mahon understood. This was modern flying. Mahon was particular to point out the revolution the AINS represented in world aerial navigation and how crews with thousands of hours between them, like Captain Jim Collins and First Officer Greg Cassin, had come to rely implicitly upon it, and how justified they were in doing so. Aircraft were now giant computers. Aircrew flew their great airliners across seas and continents with all kinds of weather below them in complete faith that they were on track. This is why he devotes six pages to the brilliance of it in his accident report and an entire chapter to it in *Verdict on Erebus*. The AINS represented a transformation in aerial navigation.

So, in the last stages of the fatal flight, although Jim Collins was flying visually, he knew he had perfect navigational backstop he could rely on. As Stuart Macfarlane puts it, he not only wore a belt, but braces too.

The moment he began his orbiting descent, he was flying visually. And the airline's rule for visual flight in Antarctica was a minimum of 20 miles' visibility. Passenger photos show that he had such clarity all round him. Captain Gordon Vette wrote back in 1983[20] that there was no way Jim Collins would have departed 16,000 feet unless visual conditions were satisfactory. Once he left 16,000 feet he would be 'eyeballing' it.

Indeed, at 1.31.30 on the cockpit voice recorder Collins tells Cassin, 'If you can get HF contact with him [the tower], tell him we'd like a further descent — we have contact with the ground — and we could, if necessary descend doing an orbit.'

At 1.32.07, Cassin: 'We'd like further descent or we could orbit in our present position which is approximately 43 miles north — descending VMC.'

1.32.08, McMurdo Tower: 'Roger Kiwi nine zero one VMC descent is approved and keep MacCentre advised of your altitude.'

All in all, from when Collins asks Cassin to tell the tower 'we have the ground', there are between then and impact some 11 references to being visual or flying VMC. Just as he begins his first right-hand orbit, at 1.34.21, Collins addresses the passengers, 'Captain again, ladies and gentlemen. We're carrying out an orbit and circling our present position and will be descending to an altitude below cloud so that we can proceed to McMurdo Sound. Thank you.' Note the very important point that Collins says 'to McMurdo Sound'. That was where he thought he was going.

Chippindale, however, along with Civil Aviation and Air New Zealand, believed that Jim Collins should have gained a 'positive visual fix' before descending into what he must have believed was McMurdo Sound and should not have relied so completely on the accuracy of his AINS.

But he was not relying unduly on the AINS. He did have a positive fix. He had 'contact with the ground'. And, of course, he had thousands of flying hours worth of reasons to rely on the accuracy of the AINS.

The Director of Civil Aviation, Edgar Kippenberger, the man who later said he thought Collins must suddenly have become mentally ill in order to fly into the clouded mountain, believed over the distance of the final leg of that flight that Collins could have been up to 15 miles wide of his mark, left or right. That was nonsense, but it was in the Director's interests to degrade the accuracy of the AINS and to dismiss as bad airmanship Collins's reliance upon it. The Director was talking through his hat.

In his pedantic, vindictive press statement of February 1982, 19 pages of single-spaced A4 ranting, Chippindale makes the bizarre statement: 'As Capt. Collins was a trained navigator and experienced DC-10 pilot familiar with the AINS I submit he cannot possibly have been certain of his position.'[21] This was quite wrong. It was because of the AINS, and because of what he was looking at, that Collins was absolutely certain of his position.

Chippindale continued: 'Despite the inroads computers have made into navigation procedures, and the accuracy of the AINS, the crew must know where each waypoint is from an approved checking reference such as an RNC chart or topographical map. Captain Collins may have been misled into thinking he was somewhere else but certain enough of his position to make a safe descent — never.'

It was nonsense. Captain Collins was certain. He had his eyes and his charts and the AINS and the briefing three weeks before.

In any case, as the various island waypoints came into view and disappeared underneath the aircraft, Collins could see that his AINS was working perfectly, as it always did. He was following the projected and predicted course. It cannot be stated strongly enough. Jim Collins had been briefed down McMurdo Sound. He had no reason whatsoever to believe he was flying any other course. You never changed a flight route without telling the pilot.

Chippindale's dismissal of Captain Collins's reliance on the AINS is Chippindale at his most patronising and devious. The implication was that Collins wasn't looking out the window carefully enough. But as Mahon would point out later, everyone in aviation knew of the 'extreme accuracy' of the AINS.

> Captain Collins and First Officer Cassin had flown between them some thousands of hours, and had seen the system [AINS] proved to be of extreme accuracy over all that time. The crew in my opinion was perfectly entitled to rely upon the AINS to take them, on the approach to McMurdo Sound, within a mile or two either side of a line representing the nav track.[22]

The opening to McMurdo Sound is 40 miles wide.

Mahon also stated: 'This [the AINS] is the reason why modern aircraft with this equipment no longer carry navigators as members of the flight crew. No navigator is necessary. The aircraft navigates itself and with a degree of accuracy which a human navigator could seldom hope to attain.'[23]

This tells us everything.

Mahon also noted that Major Gumble in his Starlifter, the aircraft following the DC-10 south, when interviewed back in Christchurch the morning after the disaster — and this even appears in Chippindale's report[24] — stated: 'At the time we were navigating entirely by the INS [Inertial Navigation System]. We maintained 16,000 feet until McMurdo picked us up on radar; as I remember this was at about 38 miles.' In fact Gumble descended with his INS through cloud.

But Collins was descending visually. The transcript makes that perfectly clear. Collins was meticulous about it. The AINS was now secondary to his eyes. If he had been descending through cloud, his crew would most certainly have objected and, said transcriber Arthur Cooper, First Officer Graham Lucas would have made a most pronounced appearance on the flight deck.

But what Collins did not know was that in polar light conditions the normal conditions built into visual flight rules, and visual meteorological conditions, offered no protection if you were flying over a white surface underneath an overcast sky. Air New Zealand had made it a rule that Antarctic visual flight had to be 20 kilometres or more. But that meant nothing if you were flying towards a mountain in whiteout. Chippindale, knowing this about whiteout, gave it no weight at all in his determination of this accident.

What is dismaying now, 32 years on, reading the literature of the time, reading the evidence presented at the times, is how wide of the mark his report was. It is so incompetent that it has to have been wilfully so. That has to be the reason that even after Erebus, even after the Mahon Report, even after he was so completely exposed, Chippindale not only survived but did not retire from the Chief Inspectorate of Air Accidents for another 20 years.

We never found out who he consulted but after seven months of secret analysis behind closed doors and a few trips overseas, the great Chippindale pronounced.

The Chief Inspector did not have to tell anyone about whom he had spoken to in order to reach his determinations. What's more, apart from two from US Navy personnel, he took few statements. He had the statutory power to command anyone to deliver a statement to him under oath and he did not avail himself of the opportunity. The Chief Inspector, in those days, preferred the informal chat. That way, he told the inquiry, people would be frank with him.

Especially when it came to finding out about the Antarctic flights from the DC-10 pilots. He took statements under oath from none of them. In *Verdict on Erebus* Mahon speaks of his grave disquiet at this practice and says he asked counsel assisting the Commission to look into it. The Chief Inspector was in fact supposed to take such statements formally but that was not the way his work had evolved.[25]

Mahon wrote: 'I must admit that I thought it incomprehensible that the Chief Inspector could have published his conclusions on the cause of the disaster without the firm evidence which only a series of written and signed statements could provide.'[26]

In other words, his report was gossip. Hearsay.

What is more, sitting in on some, if not all, of the interviews Chippindale conducted with the Antarctic pilots was Captain Ian Gemmell, the man who would lead the Air New Zealand case at the Commission of Inquiry and the man whom Mahon called the chief pilot. In one interjection during the cross-examination of a witness, Mahon indicates his surprise that Captain Gemmell had been present at pilot interviews with the Chief Inspector.

Chippindale's findings were a travesty. His was a preposterous analysis. And in a nation searching for answers, it damned the good names of two highly competent, professional airmen who were amongst the best of the best, the two pilots of the DC-10 who had between them 19,085 flying hours, of which 4233 were on the flight decks of DC-10s. Chippindale had zero hours on passenger jet airliners.

His report was so incompetent it had to be dishonest. It was scurrilous. That his finding as to cause has been given a continued legitimacy in New Zealand is one of the great mysteries of New Zealand history. While no one disputes the validity of the technical information in Section 1 of his report, 'Factual Information', when it comes to Section 2, 'Analysis', the Chief Inspector goes seriously haywire. So that in paragraph 2.16 he writes, implying that Collins is flying at a mountain: 'Despite this and the aircraft's speed of 260 knots . . . the captain headed the aircraft toward the cloud covered island and no expression of doubt was made by the First Officer.'

Then, in paragraph 2.20: 'One explanation for his decision to continue on track toward McMurdo at this low altitude, was that it was the result of a misconception shared by himself, the first officer and the flight's official commentator that the approach path was over a sea level ice shelf to the west of Mt Erebus.'

In other words, McMurdo Sound. You don't say.

Then, again in paragraph 2.20: 'There were discussions on the flight deck indicating that some of the speakers believed they were to the west of Mt Erebus but the two flight engineers on the flight deck had voiced frequent queries about the procedure and expressed their mounting alarm as the approach continued on at low level toward the area of low cloud.'

No such protestations by either of the flight engineers were ever made.

Chippindale goes further. Collins and Cassin are being very bad boys indeed. Despite the pilots' demeanour being 'composed and confident' as the aircraft headed for impact, the 'apprehension expressed by the flight engineers indicated that these members of the crew were endeavouring to monitor the flight responsibly, but their suggestions of caution . . . were overtaken by the speed of the sequence of events' (paragraph 2.25).

Again, this is pure invention. There was no indication by the flight engineers until seconds from impact that they were bothered by anything at all.

Yet, Chippindale's public image was the envy of anyone in public life. As far as New Zealanders were concerned, this fine, upstanding ex-squadron leader, this military man, this investigator of great expertise, could not possibly twist, deform or misrepresent the truth. In fact, Ron Chippindale was very good at it.

So how did he decide the pilots were ultimately responsible for the crash of the DC-10, onto the glistening ice of Erebus that early afternoon of 28 November 1979?

For Ron Chippindale altitude was sacrosanct. Air New Zealand had agreed with Civil Aviation, apparently, that the DC-10s should fly no lower than 16,000 feet until they were over McMurdo Station. Then they could descend to 6000 feet in a confined arc. That was what the airline had agreed with Civil Aviation when the flights went over Erebus. They had not done so for 14 months.

But Jim Collins was flying into the safety of the flat sea and ice of McMurdo Sound. He was not going over a mountain. The briefing had made it clear he would be flying down McMurdo Sound with the flat sea and ice beneath him, the high ground all away to the east. And the coordinates had been changed and he had not been told. It meant nothing, apparently.

So the airline had agreed height restrictions with Civil Aviation; what it had agreed with its pilots, though, would become a matter of bitter and legendary debate.

However, for Chippindale, altitude was sacred if he was going to blame the pilots, even though he admitted in a 1989 article in *North and South* that he knew at the time about flights below 6000 feet in Antarctica, though Air New Zealand denied knowing anything about them.

The *North and South* article states: 'But he now acknowledges that the airline's altitude claims were made to try to minimise the cost of damages it faced in litigation from the relatives of the dead passengers.'[27] Chippindale is quoted as saying: 'We had a tape recording of the flight that went before, which we knew had been down to 1500 feet.' The airline and Civil Aviation, therefore, had no better friend than Chief Inspector Ron Chippindale. What Mahon found, however, was that all flights, after the first two, went down to between 1500 and 3000 feet. They were sightseeing trips, after all.

We know for a start that Ron Chippindale was going for pilot error very early. On 14 December, a fortnight after the disaster, he paid a call on the stricken Maria Collins. 'Jim was too low, Maria. He was far too low,' he said. In fact, the world would come to realise later, Jim was not too low and there is nothing dangerous whatsoever about any aircraft flying at 1500 feet as long as there is not a 13,000-foot mountain in front of it.

Chippindale's claim of low flying distressed Maria terribly. She says he was courteous in her home and conducted himself as a gentleman. Yet, she found that she detested him. It was the way he spoke to her, as the little woman. And it was the way he patronised her husband when he spoke of Jim Collins's flying. Jim Collins, a man of 11,000 hours, was being patronised by a man of 4000, none on passenger jet airliners.

The next absurdity springing from Chippindale's report is the support he claimed for it. In the letter to the Minister released with the press statement in which he claws away impotently at Mahon for 19 typed pages, he made claims of laughable pomposity and grandiloquence.

'The sadness is that [the Mahon Report] abounds in errors,' he pontificates, 'which indicates that it was not reviewed by any uninvolved technical assessor or the arguments tested by anyone familiar with this particular accident or the investigation of large aircraft accidents. Certainly it was not checked for accuracy by any of my investigators.'[28]

Never mind that Mr Chippindale himself had no experience with 'large aircraft accidents'. He goes on: 'I consider it manifestly misleading for [Mahon] to state as fact so many assumptions on the conduct of this flight which were deduced from the statements, not subject to the rules of evidence, made by so many interested parties, and information gathered in private but not tested by experiment or cross-examination'.[29]

It was Chippindale at his most absurd.

This was the same man whose entire investigation was conducted in secret and without formal statements taken down in writing which could be studied and to which reference could be made.

By contrast, the entire Royal Commission was not only conducted in public, with the judge allowing television cameras to film the proceedings, but all evidence was subject to cross-examination. There were more than 3000 pages of written evidence and nearly 300 exhibits. Witnesses were seen and eyeballed, their demeanour assessed.

As Stuart Macfarlane observed:

> The corresponding weakness of the Chippindale Report is the lack of all those features. That investigation was conducted in private, the evidence was not subject to cross-examination, with few exceptions (e.g. three statements from US Navy personnel returning to the States) it was not taken down in writing, and it is not available to independent observers. In short, it is not possible to make any internal scientific assessment of it, since the data on which it is based are not available to public scrutiny . . . Not even the names are revealed by the Inspector of those who are alleged to have provided stated information.[30]

In the 1982 press release Chippindale claimed support from 'some 18 highly qualified international experts and aircraft accident investigators'. And who were they? He never said. He did say he had the support of Air New Zealand and Civil Aviation and that he ran the interim report past Gemmell, Air New Zealand's chief pilot and technical adviser to the Chief Inspector, before he released it to those who were going to cop the blame. (Notwithstanding that Air New Zealand was the most interested party in the whole disaster.) He claimed support from McDonnell Douglas, General Electric, the NTSB, the FAA, the New Zealand Air Line Pilots' Association — which he most certainly did not have — and he implied he had the support of the deceased pilots' families, which, again, he most certainly did not.

'Mr Chippindale would not even reveal the names of those persons who he alleged provided him with the information which he used for his report. In any scientific sense,' says Macfarlane, 'the Chippindale Report represents nothing more than unverifiable claims made by Mr Chippindale.'[31]

When Chippindale's report was made public, each of his assertions appalled the public and convicted the pilots thoroughly of killing themselves and 255 others. Chippindale gave five reasons for the DC-10 disaster. They are all absurd. They are all, as Mahon would later say, in his speech in Sydney to the aviation lawyers, 'hearsay . . . and, they were all wrong'.[32]

After a helicopter crash into a black, stormy sea in Anaura Bay north of Gisborne while on assignment for TVNZ in June 1989, a crash in which one man died, I was interviewed by Ron Chippindale. By this time he was using a tape recorder. I do not remember if his hair had gone white. He wore a clipped military moustache and was every bit the military man, the squadron leader. No man ever looked as much like his job as Ron Chippindale did. I found him quiet, precise, focused and intelligent.

I mentioned this to Captain Arthur Cooper late one afternoon after a long day of talking as we walked around his tree-filled property. Arthur replied, 'Well, that's interesting, because his Erebus report was anything but that.'

It was, of course, not meant to be.

11

What Chippindale Said and Why He Was Wrong

When the world has got hold of a lie, it is astonishing how hard it is to kill it. You beat it over the head, till it seems to have given up the ghost, and behold! the next day it is as healthy as ever.

— Edward Bulwer-Lytton

If you wish to strengthen a lie, add a little truth.

— Zohar

So, let us catch up for a moment and go through the causes that Chippindale felt were important in the lead-up to the accident.

Firstly, claimed Chippindale, the crash was caused by the pilot descending beneath 16,000 feet on approach to McMurdo on the north side of the mountain in breach of company rules. This was Air New Zealand brainwashing the Chief Inspector. The Chief Inspector accepted what the airline told him. There was no such restriction *actually* applied.

After 10 weeks of counsel prising information from reluctant airline management witnesses at the Royal Commission, it emerged that the Antarctic pilots were briefed to approach McMurdo at whatever altitude MacCentre offered them. Around McMurdo Station itself there was an agreement between Air New Zealand and Civil Aviation that the minimum altitude at which the aircraft could fly was 6000 feet. But after the first two flights back in 1977, no pilot observed this. You flew at whatever altitude MacCentre gave you. That altitude was likely to be anywhere as low as 1500 feet and depended on what traffic MacCentre was already monitoring in the area. But Air New Zealand told Chippindale nothing of descents beneath 6000 feet at McMurdo Sound itself.

Nevertheless, as we've seen from the *North and South* article of November 1989, 10 years after the disaster, Chippindale knew all about the flights below 6000 feet. And he knew what Air New Zealand was up to with its constant denial of knowledge of flights below 6000 feet. It was trying to minimise compensation claims. All of which makes his finding that Collins had breached company altitude regulations even more preposterously hypocritical.

His entire report rests on altitude, the Air New Zealand line. There would have been no accident if Jim Collins had remained at 16,000 feet until overhead McMurdo Station. Yet, in two of three statements he actually took, from US Navy people, Chippindale was told about regular low flights.

The McMurdo ATC supervisor, Charles Priest, told Chippindale: 'On numerous previous Air New Zealand flights, I have observed VMC altitudes as 500 feet (estimation) in the McMurdo Sound.'[1] Another air traffic controller, Kenneth Kondewich, told Chippindale that previous flights had descended to about 1500 feet above sea level over the 1000-foot hills behind Scott Base, giving a terrain clearance of 500 feet.[2]

Yet knowing this, Chippindale still took the Air New Zealand line on altitude. Everyone kept quiet, including the Chief Inspector. Something was seriously wrong here.

Justice Mahon, later on, would observe that the 16,000 feet/6000 feet minimum altitudes only became important to both Civil Aviation and the airline after the accident.

> But because the flight levels of 16,000 feet and 6000 feet and the flight path over Mt Erebus still remained as part of the official approval of Civil Aviation Division as at 28 November 1979, both the airline and Civil Aviation Division immediately seized upon these official conditions as being the vital factor in the disaster. From the point of view of both organisations they could obtain, so they believed, absolution from their own numerous errors by merely ascribing the disaster to a failure by Captain Collins to observe a minimum flight level of 16,000 feet . . . it was in my view a basis without any justification whatsoever.[3]

Secondly, Chippindale said, the aircraft was flying towards an area of poor visibility. But visibility left and right of the aircraft was fine. Passenger photos make that clear right up to the very point of impact. What was ahead was sector whiteout. In the end, it is true, the weather destroyed the aircraft, but it was not cloud. It was the specific phenomenon of polar whiteout upon which none of the crew on the flight deck had been briefed.

Yet Chippindale knew very authoritatively about polar whiteout and wrote extensively about it in his report. He had come to understand through his own reading and from what the Americans told him at McMurdo that when you are flying over a uniform white surface with a low overcast with the sun low behind you, you would likely be flying in or into whiteout. In other words, you must never fly under cloud in Antarctica unless there are clear black objects like trucks and huts and rocks to be seen. Jim Collins was told nothing of this.

For neither Air New Zealand nor Civil Aviation to have bothered to brief the Antarctic pilots on whiteout was a very serious, life-threatening omission indeed. Yet Chippindale gave no weight to whiteout being a cause. It was incredible. But, of course, he could not attribute whiteout as a cause because he knew neither the airline nor Civil Aviation had conducted a thorough whiteout briefing. As Mahon would say, it was whiteout, ultimately, that destroyed the aircraft.

As I will repeat time and again in this narrative, none of the four experienced flight crew on the flight deck of the DC-10, neither the pilots nor the flight engineers, with 95,000 hours' flying time between them, with clear air all round them, ever saw the mountain. Nor did the experienced Antarctic explorer Peter Mulgrew. Not even in the last seconds. Never.

Thirdly, said Chippindale, 'The aircraft's radar would have depicted the mountainous terrain ahead.'[4] This implies that if Captain Collins had kept an eye on his radar, he would have seen a mountain ahead of him.

Of all of Chippindale's claims, this was the most monstrous. Yet it seemed so perfectly sensible to the public. Of course your radar would see the mountain. How careless of Captain Collins not to have kept an eye on his radar. Radar sees everything, doesn't it?

The *Auckland Star* shouted on the day the Chippindale Report was released, DC-10's RADAR SHOULD HAVE 'SEEN' MOUNTAIN. 'The report into the crash by the Chief Inspector of Air Accidents, Mr Ron Chippindale, said expert opinion from the radar makers held that the rising ground would have been clearly indicated.' On the day of his report's release, Chippindale's radar assertions made one of the most dramatic headlines.

The effect this had on public opinion of Captain Jim Collins was devastating. How could it not be?

If Ron Chippindale should have been fired in disgrace for nothing else, he should have been removed for this allegation alone. It was wrong. He was not only wrong, he was lying. He did not receive expert opinion from the 'radar makers'. He called someone at McDonnell Douglas — who manufactured the aircraft — and someone there told him the radar should have seen the mountain. The person at McDonnell Douglas, whom he never named, was wrong. McDonnell Douglas did not make the radar. The Bendix Corporation did. Bendix sold the radar to McDonnell Douglas.

Chippindale's radar allegation is one of the sorriest, most disgraceful episodes of the entire sorry saga of Erebus. When pilots expressed to Mahon during the inquiry doubt about the efficacy of using radar to detect high ground on the approach to Antarctica, Mahon became curious. On his investigative trip to the United States and the United Kingdom late in the inquiry, he went out of his way to visit the Bendix Corporation in Fort Lauderdale, Florida.

There, Mahon met the two most senior radar experts at the Bendix factory, Wayne Shear and Daryal Kuntman. To his astonishment, Mahon found out that there was no way the DC-10's radar, either in mapping mode or weather mode, could see an Antarctic mountain. Antarctica was dry, drier than the Sahara desert. The radar pulses would have been absorbed. There would have been no return to the aircraft. The radar would not have seen the mountain. In fact, the Bendix manual makes it clear that radar cannot be used for navigation in polar regions.

Air New Zealand DC-10 crews used their radar to detect moisture in cloud at night across the ocean in order to make altitude adjustments to avoid bad weather. The DC-10 radar looked for water.

What is more, Chippindale admitted at the Royal Commission that he knew Air New Zealand forbade its crews using the radar in its 'mapping mode' for navigation.[5]

Baragwanath: 'Now, you say that the radar is not approved as a navigation aid. Does that mean that it is disapproved or there is absence of positive approval. What do you mean by that?'

Chippindale: 'My interpretation of the information that I received would equate to your term "disapproved".'

Baragwanath: 'And by whom?'

Chippindale: 'I do not recall exactly who advised me but I do remember it was a member of the Air New Zealand briefing staff.'

Baragwanath: 'Was he speaking for himself or Air New Zealand or CAD [Civil Aviation]?'

Chippindale: 'Certainly not for CAD and I believe him to have been speaking for the company.'

Baragwanath: 'So you understood the matter [to be] company policy?'

Chippindale: 'Correct.'

In other words Collins would have been in breach of company policy using the radar as a navigation aid on his approach to McMurdo Station. He was required to be visual, looking out the window.

Then Roger Maclaren for Anne Cassin gave Chippindale a go.

Maclaren: 'Did I understand you to tell my learned friend Mr Baragwanath that in fact if the weather radar had been disapproved as a nav aid and the source of that information came from Air New Zealand briefing staff [sic]?'

Chippindale: 'That was my understanding.'

Maclaren: 'And you wouldn't contradict that, would you?'

Chippindale: 'I have no knowledge of this equipment or its capabilities.'

Chippindale later, under cross-examination, admitted that the airline was quite right to prohibit the use of the radar for navigation.[6] And it is common sense. No pilot flies along finding his way round the countryside by looking at a radar screen. He looks at a map. He looks out the window. He looks at his compass. He notes how long he has been flying and at what speed. What's more, Chippindale admitted under examination by Lloyd Brown QC that the main use of the radar in the DC-10s was for weather detection.[7]

Chippindale never revealed who told him the radar would have depicted the mountain ahead. In his infamous press release, he said, 'While I did not know the name of the radar expert, the Air New Zealand counsel, who was cross-examining me, did.' Macfarlane asked Lloyd Brown if he knew the name. In a letter to Macfarlane, Brown denied what Chippindale said. Chippindale was lying.

Stuart Macfarlane, way back in the eighties, wrote to Chippindale asking the expert's name. Chippindale replied, 'It is not our policy to release the names of our witnesses.'[8] What kind of secret squirrel game was this?

Macfarlane wrote to McDonnell Douglas, to various people there, asking for a name. No reply was ever received.

In his press release in February 1982, Chippindale said the name of the expert was known to Mahon because he, Chippindale, had given the name to David Baragwanath. Baragwanath told Macfarlane he could not recall if he ever knew the name. The other counsel assisting the Commission, Gary Harrison, told Macfarlane he had never heard the name.[9]

The Bendix people told Mahon that the radar was probably in the weather mode when Collins saw the gap in the cloud. During his descent he was flying visually. It wouldn't occur to Collins to switch his radar to the mapping mode. There was no point. He could see where he was going and what was in front of him. In any case, he would not navigate by a radar screen because not only was to do so dopey, it was against company rules.

But Mahon was also told by Bendix that at 1500 feet Collins was too low for the mapping mode to work for him no matter where he was in the world. Even 3000 feet, they told him, would be too low for the radar to show anything. But Chippindale knew better. In his press release he wrote, 'Our expert's view was that in the case of the aircraft approaching the solid 12,500 feet AMSL [above mean sea level] the crew would see a shadow on the radar that could be nothing other than high ground ahead.' In other words Mahon was a liar.

Who was right? Chippindale, who admitted knowing nothing about the capabilities of the radar[10] and was told about it by a bloke at McDonnell Douglas whom he never named? Chippindale, who had never read the Bendix manual?[11] Chippindale, who admitted at the Royal Commission that the radar was used for weather detection?[12] Chippindale, who agreed it was wise of the airline to prohibit the pilots' use of the radar for terrain detection and as a navigational aid?[13] Was Chippindale right about the radar being able to see the mountain ahead? Or was Mahon right, Mahon who went to Bendix in Florida and spoke to its two leading radar experts?

In fact, Chippindale lied about the evidence. In his report, at paragraph 1.8.9, he says that some pilots of previous Antarctic flights reported that 'radar indications of high ground correlated well with the contours they observed visually in VMC'.

Then came this extraordinary exchange between Chippindale and David Baragwanath at the Royal Commission.[14]

Baragwanath: 'Now can you tell us who the pilots were who reported this correlation of contours on the screen with what they'd seen visually?'

Chippindale: 'No. The discussions that we held with most of the crews who had participated in previous Air New Zealand Antarctic flights were specifically informal and designed to achieve a complete frankness between the investigators and the pilots concerned. Therefore no specific records were kept of much of the discussion that took place.'

Baragwanath: 'Do I take it from that that you do not have a record or recollection of who gave you this information?'

Chippindale: 'I have no recollection at this time whether or not in the brief note I took there is a record.'

Later he told the Commission that he believed it was Captain Simpson who told him he could see the high ground on his radar screen.[15] He took a written statement from Simpson. Simpson said no such thing. He told Chippindale that he could not recall what the radar was showing of Erebus.[16]

Yet the headlines about the radar, and the clear implication from Chippindale that Collins and Cassin had been remiss in not keeping an eye on the radar screen, did enormous damage to the public perception of the competence of the flight crew. It was dishonest. It should have finished Chippindale. It was a lie that did terrible damage to the good names of good dead men. But Chippindale had what he wanted, another nail in the coffin of poor Jim Collins.

Fourthly, Chippindale said his department found 'no evidence' that the crew had been misled by the 2 degrees of longitude change in the computer flight path from McMurdo Sound across to Lewis Bay.

In fact, as Mahon came very quickly to see, the unsignalled coordinate change was the fundamental, obvious and single most effective cause of the entire disaster. Of course the flight crew was deceived. It was obvious. Collins had been briefed on the McMurdo Sound route. That is where everyone went. As Mahon, in his Sydney speech, said of Chippindale's assertion: 'I need not comment further on this astounding statement.'[17]

Collins had been briefed down McMurdo Sound, the computer change sent him to the mountain and there was no evidence Collins was deceived. No, what Chippindale understood to be evidence was paperwork, a map upon which the pilot might have plotted the 'wrong' course, some documentation found at the crash site, with a course path plotted on a map. He always denied that Collins plotted his course the night before, as Elizabeth and Kathryn Collins told the Royal Commission. What's more he said Jim Collins could not have had the maps the girls described.

In fact Collins *did* have the maps. And Chippindale knew very well that

Collins had them. But he said nothing about it. It would have blown out of the water his assertion that the crew was not deceived. I shall explain later what Chippindale knew about Collins's maps and even how he knew it. It was all part of Chippindale's masterly cover-up.

Again, Mahon, to the intense annoyance of the government, would find completely the opposite of the Chief Inspector.

> It is really beyond dispute that Captain Collins plotted on a topographical map or maps the nav track of the proposed flight which would journey from Cape Hallett down to the destination coordinates located near the Dailey Islands at about the centre of the southern end of McMurdo Sound. This fact dominates the whole of the Inquiry. It is a fact which must always have been distinctly unpalatable to the management of Air New Zealand and to the Director of the Civil Aviation Division because it led to a conclusion which they strongly desired to avoid. But on the evidence, the conclusion is inescapable.[18]

Fifthly, Chippindale claimed that the crew were 'uncertain of their position'. This claim caused consternation in the land. The headlines were frightful, especially so for Maria Collins and her girls. Kathryn and Elizabeth remain tortured by the headlines that accompanied the release of Chippindale's report.

New Zealand Herald, Friday 20 June 1980: CRASH REPORT POINTS TO ERROR BY DC-10 CAPTAIN. CREW 'UNCERTAIN' AS PLANE NEARED SLOPE.

Here it was in a nutshell. 'The probable cause of the Air New Zealand DC-10 crash in which 257 people died last November on Mt Erebus was the decision of the captain to press on at low level in poor conditions when the crew were uncertain of their position,' wrote the *Herald*.

This claim was absurd. The crew was in no way 'uncertain' of their position. There is, on the CVR, no evidence or comment whatsoever between the two pilots that they did not know where they were. The crew were absolutely certain of their position. That is why towards the end of the second of his prudent, textbook descending orbits, Collins locked the aircraft back on to Nav Track and the big aircraft rolled round onto its programmed course towards what he thought, because of his briefing, was the top of McMurdo

Sound, but which was in fact the mountain, hidden in whiteout. He trusted implicitly his area inertial navigation system and, as Mahon said, such was its blinding accuracy, he was right to do so. And he trusted the integrity and competence of Air New Zealand's Navigation Section.

The notion that his course was anything other than that upon which he and First Officer Cassin had been briefed would never in a hundred years have occurred to either man. In fact, the evidence of the CVR makes it clear the pilots were certain they knew exactly where they were.

Mahon reported that even Mr G. W. Shannon, the expert Canadian polar pilot Mahon consulted in his investigations overseas, noted, after studying the CVR transcript, 'that neither the pilot nor the co-pilot entertained the slightest apprehension at any stage, and he drew the further conclusion that that each of them was perfectly satisfied as to the course and position of the aircraft.'[19]

In fact Mahon would observe that Collins and Cassin were flying perfectly professionally. The descent was normal. Both pilots constantly kept each other informed of what each was doing, and affirmed what the other had done. They kept MacCentre advised of their actions. There are 'no less than 13 references' on the tape to flying visually.[20] 'Neither before nor after the decision was made at 26 miles out to fly away is there any remark made by either pilot referring to worsening visibility.'[21] There was 'the non-committal discussion between the two pilots as to whether they would climb out to the left or to the right'. They had no sense of impending danger whatsoever.[22]

Mahon would remark, in fact, that the CVR transcript shows the crew was adhering to every detail of flight deck discipline. And there is not the slightest shred of evidence that either pilot 'took any notice of, or even heard, the running sequence of indistinct cross-talk between the various persons at the rear of the flight deck and in the galley'.[23]

Finally, Chippindale said the pilots disregarded the 'mounting alarm' of the flight engineers at conduct of the flight — disagreement in the cockpit, in other words. And that was all there in the newspapers too, on the day of the Chippindale release. COCKPIT CONFUSION MARKS FINAL MINUTES, cried the *Auckland Star* on 20 June 1980. There was no evidence of this whatsoever. No one else, not the Royal Commissioner, not the Chief British Air Accident Inspector, no one else, heard either of the flight engineers disputing with Collins and Cassin any aspect of the flight. It was a lie.

The Chippindale Report caused immense damage to the reputations of the dead pilots. It was meant to and it did the job beautifully. This was a dark period in the history of our public service. One man, working in secret, had the power to destroy so much.

Newspaper headlines right through to April 1981, when Mahon's report so completely countered and debunked Chippindale, must have been excruciatingly painful reading for the families of the dead aircrew. *New Zealand Herald*, 20 June 1980: FLIGHT THOUSANDS OF FEET TOO LOW. The *Auckland Star*, also 20 June 1980: PILOT ERROR 'MAJOR FACTOR' IN ANTARCTIC AIRCRASH. The effect on public opinion was deep. It was exactly what the government, Civil Aviation and the airline wanted.

The fact is, Chippindale's findings were perfect for Air New Zealand, for Civil Aviation and for the government. His inquiry was held in secret. He never said who he spoke to.

As Peter Mahon declared emphatically after it was all over, Chippindale's findings were all hearsay and they were all wrong. Nevertheless, he stayed in the job a long time. Even after his exposure by the brilliance of the Royal Commission of Inquiry, he held his job until his retirement in November 1998.

Ron Chippindale must have done something right.

12

Chippindale and the Cockpit Transcript

When more is meant than meets the ear.

— John Milton

Nowhere was Chippindale more deliberately and dishonestly lethal to the reputation of the pilots, and nowhere was he more influential in the formation of public opinion as to the cause of the accident, than in his treatment of the cockpit voice recorder.

The CVR is the device in the DC-10 cockpit that recorded the entire conversation between crew members and others on the flight deck for the last 30 minutes at any stage of the flight. And the DC-10 recorder worked right up to the point of impact into the mountain at 1.50 p.m. on 28 November 1979.

When, on 20 June 1980, Chippindale published with his report the transcript of conversation in the cockpit, it caused a sensation. Newspapers published it hungrily. It was riveting. It was the drama played out. There for everyone to see was a flight crew who had no idea where they were or what they were doing. This was major incompetence laid out in dramatised form, in the way we might read a play at school.

We can get some measure of the huge confirming impact of the CVR by recalling this, written by Auckland columnist Brian Rudman 25 years later in 2004.

> The cockpit transcript of the last few minutes of the flight indicates these guys had no idea where they were as they

> flew straight into the foothills of Mt Erebus. Everyone in the cockpit seemed to be throwing in their penny's worth. It was like the country cousins up from Eketahuna, mum with map book on her knee, lost on Spaghetti Junction. Cruising along at 480km/h in a whiteout looking for a volcano, the prudent thing would surely have been to ensure you were higher than the object you were seeking.[1]

This was such nonsense. But 25 years after the crash, a journalist as intelligent as Rudman could still hold that view, such was the impact of the release of the cockpit transcript.

This indeed was the impression the CVR transcript gave. But closer examination of the CVR and knowledge of the recording quality and the politics of its history would show a dramatically different picture, of course. What no one in the news media could have known at the time was that the published transcript was a ruthless manipulation by the Chief Inspector of Air Accidents, who was using the CVR transcript to shore up his case as to accident causation.

The impression given was, of course, that conversation on the flight deck happens as it does in the theatre or in television drama where actors speak on cue. John speaks, then David does, then Mary, then Andrew, then John again and it all happens in such a way that we can hear everything anyone says. This is the fundamental device of written drama. Things are said one after the other. But this is most certainly not the way of normal interaction between four or five people, as anyone can find out by taping a normal conversation round a dinner table. People speak hesitantly, they might overlap another speaker, they interrupt, they might pause to complete what they were saying after a dining companion has said something else. There will be the clunking of plates, the rustling of paper, perhaps, if someone were showing someone something in a newspaper, and other extraneous noises. And a listener to the tape later on, who was not at the dinner, might wonder what on earth was being talked about, what was being said and who actually said what. It might not be possible, necessarily, to assess the competence of the cook from the garbled noise on the tape.

Nevertheless, the impression from Chippindale's transcript was that everything said in the cockpit was clearly heard on the tape. In fact the CVR recording was a mess. It was of poor quality. Apart from the words of the two operating pilots, Jim Collins and Greg Cassin, and the words of the operating flight engineer, nothing else was even vaguely distinct.

When the tape was taken to Washington to be transcribed, everything written down as transcript, apart from the words of the pilots, was agreed to by consensus, by a committee of men appointed to do the job. It took half a day to write down what Collins and Cassin said in those last 30 minutes. It took another week for the group to work out what everyone else on the flight deck said — that is, what was said by the spare flight engineer, Nick Maloney, or the in-flight commentator Peter Mulgrew or whoever else was on the flight deck at the time. This transcript would become known as the Washington transcript.

The transcribing team selected to be sent to the United States was Milton Wylie, an air accident inspector from Chippindale's department; Air New Zealand DC-10 Fleet Captain Barney Wyatt; chief flight engineer Don Oliff; and DC-10 Captain Arthur Cooper, chosen to represent ALPA, the Air Line Pilots' Association. This was the same Barney Wyatt, friend of Jim Collins from air force days, who had told Maria Collins of the terrible computer error at Air New Zealand and that he, because of the seniority of his position, was not going to be able to see her again. Barney Wyatt therefore knew of the coordinate blunder before he went to Washington. He would say nothing to Don Oliff, Arthur Cooper or Milton Wylie.

With Wylie in charge of the CVR, the group travelled to Seattle, to the Sunstrand Corporation, manufacturers of the recorder. Here the box would be opened and the recording transferred from metal to magnetic tape.

'We walked out the back door and ended up in a little trailer,' says Arthur Cooper. 'And here in the trailer was this machine which was to play the tape. And that's when we heard it for the first time. And Milton Wylie and Barney and Don and I listened to it. That was one of the most horrendous occasions of my life. It was like going to the thriller movie and you knew there was going to be a horrible ending but you didn't know what it was. And it was for real. So, we all came out of that and we were shattered. So that's how it started off. We could only pick up odd words at that stage.'

Off they then flew to Washington DC, to the special listening equipment at the National Transportation Safety Board (NTSB), the American air accident investigators. And there they spent the week on the transcription. When Mahon heard the process took a week, he guessed correctly that the sound quality of the CVR was very bad.

Indeed, what Cooper and his team in Washington learnt, and what Mahon would come to understand too, was what any old sound man knows, any radio man who has been involved in sound recording for years. If your original recording is a dog, the tape will forever be a dog and no amount of fancy filtering devices will improve its quality much at all. You could employ the facilities at the NTSB and the FBI or you could go, as Chippindale did, to Farnborough in the UK, but in the end, if your original recording is incomprehensible, then incomprehensible it stays and even the aviation research giants do not have the equipment to clean up bad sound.

At this stage of his career, Arthur Cooper had over 13,000 hours of flying time in aircraft cockpits. He had started as a 'snotty-nosed' co-pilot in DC-3s with NAC, the National Airways Corporation, in 1957. Arthur Cooper was superbly trained. He was not only an accomplished and superior pilot. I would come to know Arthur during the research for this project, not only as a fair, decent and restrained man but a man who contemplates human nature with great shrewdness.

Supervising the New Zealanders in their work that week was Colonel Turner (retired) of the USAF. Colonel Turner told the team there were three fundamental requirements for the transcribers.

Firstly, they needed to be familiar with the persons whose voices they were listening to. Secondly, they needed to be familiar with the aircraft type, in this case the DC-10, and thirdly, they needed to be familiar with the airline's flight deck procedures and terminology. The terrible quality of the recording soon showed the importance of those requirements.

Colonel Turner went further. He said the team should only transcribe word by word those it could unanimously agree on. Credit words to a specific person only when there was unanimous agreement as to who was saying what on the tape. Be cautious about editorial judgements. Be cautious about interpreting what might have been said. Do not attempt to analyse, just do the words.

Cooper says the team worked well and at the end of the week they were united and happy with what they had done. 'We went through the whole thing again, everyone was satisfied that it was a true and accurate recording and that we'd picked it bloody well clean. There was no dissension whatsoever that there might be something of confusion that we'd come up with. So we came away believing that there wasn't anything left that could have been done.'

It is clear, however, as Mahon would make plain later, that the translation of the recording was diabolically difficult. Mahon wrote of this exercise:

> The gist of the whole exercise really was that many sections of the transcript dealing with conversation and remarks made by people other than the two pilots were the result of combined opinion on the part of the persons who were listening . . . In the end, a great many sections of the transcript merely represented an agreed joint opinion which might not be an opinion in all cases unanimous.[2]

Frankly, Mahon thought, anything but the conversation between the two pilots was 'difficult in the extreme' to understand. He was appalled by the quality of the recording. He believed that the quality was such that anyone could use the CVR to support whatever preconceived view they had for both the conduct of the flight and the destruction of the DC-10. In other words, sound emanating from anyone other than the pilots was, in any evidential sense, of extremely doubtful worth. In paragraph 121 of his accident report, Mahon makes it clear the he believes the Chief Inspector has entered into the transcript words which could not be heard with any certainty

> . . . and he was persuaded to adopt that course because of his firmly held opinion that the crew had been uncertain of its position. That is to say, the Chief Inspector had a natural inclination to ascribe to remarks of doubtful meaning an interpretation which favoured his own theory because, believing as he did in the validity of that theory, he also believed that members of the flight crew must from time to time have expressed apprehensions . . .

According to Arthur Cooper, air accident inspector Milton Wylie brought the tape back to New Zealand and the transcription was further copied and typewritten, and the rest of the team was approached individually to compare the tape with the typewritten copy.

Cooper: 'And if we were satisfied it was true and accurate then we would all sign to acknowledge that and that would become the official cockpit voice recorder transcript, the original handwritten one would go into the archives.'

Holmes: 'So it was agreed that if you all agreed that the typewritten transcript coincided with what had been agreed between all the parties in Washington then it would become the official transcript of record?'

Cooper: 'Correct. And it never happened.'

No, it did not. Because Ron Chippindale, Chief Inspector of Air Accidents, was about to execute a most dishonest act. Early in 1980, he set off with the CVR tape to the United Kingdom, to RAF Farnborough to firm up his findings.

Against all cockpit voice recorder interpretation protocols, Chippindale, a man on his *own*, would hear much more than the four senior airmen who laboured over the tape for an entire week in Washington DC. The CVR transcript he wrote after the trip to Farnborough was the transcript that would accompany both his interim and final reports. He would later claim, spuriously, that the sound equipment was superior at Farnborough to that available at the National Transportation Safety Board in Washington DC.

In March 1980, Chippindale, as was his statutory requirement, circulated his interim report to counsel for those he was likely to hold blameworthy for the accident. Those parties had a period of time in which to respond. There was intense national curiosity about who had received copies. It was not long before everyone knew that whilst Air New Zealand and Civil Aviation had received copies, so had the lawyers for Maria Collins and Anne Cassin. In other words, to a greater or lesser extent, Collins and Cassin were going to share the blame for the destruction of Flight 901.

At Farnborough, Chippindale was about to analyse the cockpit conversation of the last 30 minutes of the flight that ended in the fourth worst air crash in world aviation history. Of course, he possessed none of the requirements that Colonel Turner had impressed upon the Washington team as being essential for true and accurate CVR transcription. He did not know any of the crew on board the fatal DC-10. He was not familiar with the aircraft type and he was not familiar with Air New Zealand flight deck procedures. He knew nothing about flying a DC-10.

Arthur Cooper did not know of Chippindale's trip to Farnborough. He assumed there was an agreed CVR transcript and it was the Washington transcript and that this was the one Chippindale would honour in his report if he was going to publish the transcript at all.

When Chippindale released his infamous report with its absurd conclusions, he had rewritten the CVR transcript himself. It contained not less than 55 departures from what had been agreed in Washington. Some of the changes were minute. But some involved several lines that Arthur Cooper remains sure were never said by anyone on the aeroplane.

When the report was released with the dramatically altered CVR transcript, Cooper began, for the first time, to wonder seriously about what Chippindale was up to. He did not erupt. He tells me he was 'perplexed'. And right at the start of the Royal Commission hearings, Arthur Cooper and the Air Line Pilots' Association made their dissatisfaction and suspicions clear to the judge. Mahon noted the objection and stored it away. Mahon, like the rest of the country, thought the transcript and the CVR would be perfectly clear and reliable witnesses. They would be anything but.

Everything Chippindale added to the transcript was detrimental to the view an observer would have of Captain Collins's conduct of the flight. And none of the new material could be heard by anyone else. Chippindale made it all up. He used the chaos of the appalling sound recording to make it all up. Both Mahon and the Privy Council would deny that any of what Chippindale alleged was said was spoken at all. They would both declare him to be mistaken.

In fact, he was a liar. It was one good way he could shore up pilot error.

So Chippindale came back from Farnborough and he had the unknown voices uttering the following crucial lines at the time of 1.47.23 p.m.

'What's wrong?'

'Make up your mind soon or. . .'

1.47.43, Collins: 'We might have to pop down to 1500 here, I think.'

Cassin: 'Yes OK. Probably see further in anyway.'

In the Washington transcript Collins says they might have to 'drop' to 1500 feet. At Farnborough Chippindale has him saying 'pop' down to 1500 feet. The implication Chippindale is making is that Collins is regarding descent to 1500 feet too lightly. 'Pop' does not have the gravitas of 'drop'.

One aspect of the cockpit at this stage is that the door was probably open and there were probably passengers and staff in the galley right behind it. Who knew who was saying what?

Then, at 1.47.55, Chippindale adds this: (Unidentified person) 'Bit thick here eh Bert.'[3]

Mahon himself and counsel assisting the Commission, David

Baragwanath, went to Washington and to Farnborough and neither man could make out 'Bit thick here eh Bert?' Mahon says you could hear the word 'thick'. But who was Bert? There was no Bert on the flight deck. There was no flight engineer called Bert. There appears to be no passenger called Bert either, if one peruses the list of the dead. In Washington, Colonel Turner told Mahon he could not discern the word 'thick' at all. Both Mahon and David Baragwanath believed the phrase or sentence of whatever it was to be unintelligible. 'Bit thick here eh Bert' might in fact have been 'This is Cape Bird'. Either way, 'A bit thick here eh Bert' was never said.

At 1.48.05 p.m. the Washington team had flight engineer Maloney saying 'Spending a long while on bloody instruments at this (time/height) are you erh.' The brackets were inserted by the transcribers. The brackets mean 'questionable text'. They mean, 'We don't really know if this was said or not.'

Chippindale turned this into, 'You're really a long while on instruments this time are you?' The implication is clear. Collins is on instruments because he's in cloud. Or he doesn't know where he is. Mahon and Baragwanath both could hear the word 'instrument' but that was about all and it might be two speakers or two sentences but apart from that they agreed with Colonel Turner that it was unintelligible. At Farnborough their determinations were the same. Neither the 'spending a long time on instruments' quote nor 'bit thick here eh Bert' existed as intelligible speech.[4]

In any case, no native English speaker would use such a construction as 'you're a long while on instruments at this time'. The operations personnel on the flight deck were native English speakers. If the person who made that remark — if any one person did indeed make it — was a passenger, then their opinion did not matter at all.

The point was, neither remark was made and neither was made by a flight engineer trying to persuade the captain to come to his senses, as Chippindale maintained. He wrote at paragraph 3.24 of his report, 'The flight engineers endeavoured to monitor the progress of the flight and expressed their dissatisfaction with the descent toward a cloud covered area.' They did not. That just did not happen. Even in Chippindale's own transcript it did not happen.

Minutes earlier, at 1.41.40pm:

Captain Collins (to Cassin): Tell him we can make a visual descent, descending to the ah…

Unidentified: My God.
Collins: On a grid of one eight zero.
Cassin: Yep.
Collins: And make a visual approach to McMurdo.
Cassin: OK.

To Chippindale, 'My God' is gold. Presumably this is one of the flight engineers doing his best to bring Collins to his senses. The voice is not identified. Mahon was having none of it. In his driest tone he writes, 'I must say that I am at a loss to understand how the interjection "My God", presumably thought to have been uttered by a flight engineer, can be interpreted as an expression of alarm as to the decision of Captain Collins to advise McMurdo that he was able to make a visual descent.'[5]

There is no statement anywhere in the transcript in which a flight engineer or anyone else is bothered by the way in which Collins is flying the aircraft. If the flight engineers were warning the captain, they were doing it by mental telepathy. Both men, Brooks especially, were outspoken. They would have said it loud and clear. They did not. In the Washington transcript, what follows the above exchange is 'irrelevant conversation'. There is hardly Chippindale's 'mounting alarm'.

But that was the scene Chippindale had set out to portray. Chippindale was attempting to prove that the flight engineers were doing their best to correct the stupid and irresponsible behaviour of the pilots in taking the aircraft down into bad weather. It was false evidence. It was dishonest.

The first thing that has to be said was that the conditions were fine. It wasn't glorious blue sunshine but the weather was quite acceptable for visual flying as the passenger photographs showed. Not that Chippindale included any of them in his report. That alone invites questions about his fundamental honesty.

In his report, Chippindale asserted at paragraph 2.20: 'There were discussions on the flight deck indicating that some of the speakers believed they were to the west of Mt Erebus . . .' (in other words, they believed they were flying down McMurdo Sound) '. . . but the two flight engineers on the flight deck had voiced frequent queries about the procedure and expressed their mounting alarm as the approach continued on at low level toward the area of low cloud.'

In his conclusions, Chippindale summarises: 'The flight engineers endeavoured to monitor the progress of the flight and expressed their dissatisfaction with the descent toward a cloud covered area.'[6]

None of this was true. None of it happened. None of it was said. It was nonsense. At no stage in their entire transcript does either of the flight engineers express worry or concern, scepticism or any negativity whatsoever. Gordon Brooks is perfectly happy right up until 26 seconds before impact when he says, 'I don't like this,' at which point Captain Collins reacts immediately with his own concern.

Arthur Cooper says there was not one indication of concern from the flight engineers whatsoever.[7] Cooper, who knew both flight engineers, and Brooks especially well, says Brooks would definitely have made it clear to a captain if he thought he was behaving less than professionally. Brooks himself was an instructor in the crew loop procedure, the modern, fail-safe flying procedure that Chippindale was trying to suggest Captain Collins was ignoring.

Even by 1979, cockpits of commercial airliners throughout the world were run by the crew loop. A younger man feeling he could not override his commander was the reason for the world's worst air disaster, at Tenerife, in 1977 when two Boeing 747s collided on the ground. Essentially, if it were a two-person flight — captain and co-pilot — the captain had to listen to any concerns the co-pilot held about the captain's conduct of the flight. If it were a three-person team on the flight deck, the flight engineer could have his say as well. Eventually, the co-pilot or flight engineer can demand, 'Captain, you must listen to me.'

You can hear on the Erebus transcript that conversations and snatches of conversations are going on. This did not mean, however, that the captain had to listen to all of the conversations occurring behind him. It was common sense. The captain had to listen when it was clear that he had to listen and not before.

Air New Zealand cockpits were already abandoning their hierarchical structures by the early seventies, so Arthur Cooper tells me. Arthur Cooper says that if a co-pilot was afraid of telling him he was 'bullshitting' then he, Arthur, was not a good captain.

What Chippindale was now trying to say about Jim Collins was that he was refusing to listen to the concerns of his flight engineer. To make this assertion Chippindale made up words that no one else could hear. And he published them as part of the transcript of the CVR with his report as if they were fact — as if they were gospel — as if they were comments clearly made by crew members. It was disgraceful dishonesty by a senior New Zealand public servant.

It was all a malicious fantasy. Mahon realised it, of course.

Chippindale used the opportunity at Farnborough to shore up his bogus theory that the crew were 'uncertain of their position'. At the time of 1.45.36, just over three minutes from impact, the Washington transcript has Mulgrew saying, 'Taylor on the right now,' immediately after which someone says, 'Oh yeah.' Mulgrew is pointing to a valley which, if the aircraft had been entering McMurdo Sound, would be the Taylor Valley.

When Chippindale came back from Farnborough and the transcript was published, Mulgrew's remark had become 'The Taylor or the Wright now or do ya . . .?' In other words, a statement has become a question. More uncertainty is implied.

There was a curious omission. Not in the Washington transcript, but included in the CVR transcript in the Chief Inspector's interim report was the following exchange by unidentified parties on the flight deck roughly 15 minutes before impact.

'We're going down below cloud.'

'Where's Wilson?'

'Over to the right.'

In other words, the giant Wilson Piedmont glacier was over to the right. In other words the crew knew where they were. They were not correct about it but they believed on good grounds they knew where they were.

But, strangely, when Chippindale published his final report, this exchange was gone. So were others. Chippindale, asked about this at the inquiry, gave a bizarre answer.

> The purpose of the transcript in the final report is to, in my opinion, support the conclusions of the report itself, and in recognition of the sensitivity, particularly of the NZ Airline Pilots Association, I endeavoured to limit the extent of the transcript to the minimum which I consider necessary for that purpose. Therefore, I continued editing the transcript almost continuously until the time I presented it to the Government Printer for publishing.[8]

We can imagine he did.

Then counsel asked about the reference to Wilson: 'Would that be a reference to the dry valley area to the west of the aircraft?'

Chippindale: 'We were unable to identify any place with the single name of Wilson.'

It defied sense. The Wilson Piedmont glacier is one of the largest features of McMurdo Sound, stretching some 50 kilometres north to south. Leaving out the reference to Wilson does nothing for the credibility of the crew. It is to the crew's detriment. This doesn't gel with Chippindale's professed sensitivity to the pilots.

After Farnborough we have in the transcript, 'Bit thick here eh Bert', 'What's wrong?' and 'Make up your mind soon or...' none of which anyone but Chippindale ever heard. As Mahon wrote:

> I think I should make it clear, although perhaps the point is obvious, that it requires no expert skill to listen to a tape recording. The expertise in this area lies in being able to play the tapes through special filters so as to make certain words and phrases more audible, if possible, than they were before. We found, when we heard portions of the tapes played through filters, that the filter mechanism did not achieve any great improvement in what could be heard when the tape was played without the aid of these devices.[9]

Not so, cried the Chief Inspector in the hysterical press statement that Transport Minister George Gair allowed the humiliated Chippindale to release at the beginning of 1982.

> The judge is entirely wrong in his contention, 'it is now clear that neither of the remarks as set out in the transcript was in fact made.' We were aware there was no crew member on the flight deck called 'Bert'. But that is far from proof that no one called Bert was on the flight deck, neither is it in any way proof that the words were not spoken. I know they were from the many hours spent listening to this tape.[10]

'I know they were . . .' he pleaded. But no one in Washington, neither the New Zealanders nor the NTSB staff who heard the tapes; no one at Farnborough;

not Mahon, not David Baragwanath and not Mr W. H. Tench, the Chief British Air Accident Inspector; none of these men heard 'Bit thick here eh Bert.'

Chippindale continued in his 1982 rant, 'It was because many of the critical sections of the tape were not deciphered by the Washington team that I took the tape to Farnborough.' If they were not deciphered how did he know they were critical? What was Chippindale going to hear that Wyatt, Oliff, Cooper and Wylie could not? This was Chippindale's unspeakable arrogance and his determination to whitewash the state agencies.

It was absurd. There is an implication here that everyone else who listened to the tape was deaf. But, as Mahon says, no skill is needed to listen to a tape recording. The pilots were appalled by Chippindale and his Farnborough inventions. It was the first complaint they made about Chippindale to Justice Mahon as the inquiry began. Chippindale had doctored the transcript to make his case look better. It was as simple as that. He was a crook and they knew it.

This was a routine flight. As far as the entire flight deck was concerned, they were flying down the middle of McMurdo Sound. It was not the most perfect Antarctic day but neither was the weather bad. Passenger photographs show sun streaming through the cabin windows seconds before impact. The pilots affirmed 13 times in the last 30 minutes of the fatal flight that they were flying visually. Why would they do that if they were not? Collins even says at one point, after his first descending orbit, 'I have to stay VMC here.' He and his first officer continually affirm to each other that they are flying in clear air. It was professional, textbook flying.

Cooper, who spent a week in Washington listening to the CVR, is adamant there were no tensions on the flight deck of Flight 901 and the notion that Captain Jim Collins was dragging a flight crew down to 1500 feet kicking and screaming is false. 'That's utter crap. It's just ludicrous. And all the decisions made by Collins, all those operational decisions were accepted by the remainder of the operating crew, without question, the whole lot. There was never anywhere that I can recall in the whole transcript where anyone is querying a decision that Collins has decided to take.'

Chippindale, in the Washington DC court case in 1987 (when the families of the aircrew took action against the US Navy — we come to this later), harped on about a 'mounting atmosphere of concern' on the flight deck from the moment some unidentified person says, 'My God', at 1.45.45. This, Chippindale gravely told the court, came right on top of a previous comment. What comment was that? He said it was after Collins said quite calmly, 'Tell him we can make a visual descent.'

Someone in the US court suggested 'My God' might have been someone marvelling at the scenery. The judge suggested someone might have been praying. No, says Chippindale, 'I have listened to it carefully again. And it certainly doesn't seem to be a complacent observation. There was a certain stress on it.' He says, 'There was no reassuring event after that.'

Chippindale was making it up again.

Mahon, at the stage of writing his report, was still gracious towards Chippindale. He said he could not agree there was any deliberate attempt by the Chief Inspector to doctor 'the Washington transcript so as to conform, so far as possible, with his own opinion as to the state of mind of the flight crew'.[11] But then, in the same paragraph, he admitted that the Chief Inspector was inclined to take 'remarks of doubtful meaning' and make them match his own theory. That surely is dishonest. 'The inclination to hear what the listener expects to hear is a familiar feature of the ordinary judicial process.' Mahon knew exactly what Chippindale was up to.

So, on the flight deck there were still no concerns. Not until that last frightful minute when they all, Captain Collins, First Officer Cassin and Flight Engineer Brooks, realised at once that things were not right, that something was not right. This was the minute Arthur Cooper first heard in that little caravan in Seattle, the last frightful minute in which the aircraft had flown through the gates of hell guarded by the evil son of Chaos, never to be safe again, never to fly north again, never to see home again.

Up until then everything on the flight was absolutely normal. It was not a difficult flight. It was a flight into unfamiliar airspace and for any pilot this invited extra concentration. MacCentre had told Jim Collins they had heavy overcast but the cloud base was about 3000 feet, visibility beneath the cloud was 40 miles (in aviation terms, infinite). 'Within a range of 40 miles of McMurdo we have radar that will, if you desire, let you down to 1500 feet on radar vectors' (1.19.56 p.m.). Cassin says that is 'acceptable'. Collins says, 'Crikey, that's what we want to hear.'

But Jim Collins has seen a wide, gaping hole in the cloud all the way down to the sea ice. He makes his way down towards it. From the moment he begins his descent below FL160 he is flying visually, with the AINS as his backup. The AINS will always point him the right way. But through the windows, he is flying visually.

Now he is at 1500 feet approaching McMurdo. The crew could see the black cliffs of Cape Bernacchi on the right. On the left, they have passed Cape Bird and are approaching Cape Royds. Neither cape is what they think it is. In fact, on their right is Cape Bird and on their left is Cape Tennyson. The crew cannot know this. The navigation coordinates have tracked them 2 degrees left, 40 kilometres left of where they think they are. None of the operating crew is familiar with the air space. Only the Antarctic explorer and veteran of four of these DC-10 flights, Peter Mulgrew, has a hope of indentifying the mistake but even he is misled by the uncanny physical similarity between where they are and where they think they are. Even Mulgrew thinks they are in the middle of McMurdo Sound.

Everything is normal. Then suddenly, nothing is adding up.

1.48.46, Collins: (looking, probably, ahead of the aircraft.) 'Actually, those conditions don't look very good at all, do they?'

1.48.50, Mulgrew: 'You're down to one one four now are you?'

Note the reply to the Captain's observation comes from Mulgrew, the commentator. Not from a flight engineer and not from Cassin.

1.48.51, Collins: 'Fifteen hundred.'

Four seconds pass. Each man's head is filling with thoughts.

1.48.55, Collins: 'Have we got them on the tower?'

Arthur Cooper always believed that from his knowledge of the crew and from that long week of transcription that this was Jim Collins's first indication of concern. Arthur says, 'He knows bloody well they haven't got them on the tower but he's looking out. The tone of his voice showed he was puzzled not worried. It was asked as a question.'

In the way we might ask a question we know the answer to, in order to involve another interested party in the discussion, Jim Collins is inviting the crew to join him in his growing concern.

Gordon Vette, writing in *Impact Erebus*, would say that Collins was merely thinking that his passengers might not get the photographs they'd been looking for, but would have been thinking other things simultaneously: 'We're pretty close to the head of McMurdo and it's brilliantly clear air so why can't I see Shackleton's hut down there at Cape Royds? Why can't I see the penguin rookery there? Why don't they have me on radar? And where's Mount Discovery up ahead? Why am I not seeing Mount Discovery. It's all a bit odd. This isn't gelling. Why isn't it?'

Passenger photos taken at this time showed sunlight streaming into the cabin. Another four seconds passed.

1.48.59, Cassin: (returning Collin's vocal puzzlement with his own bemusement, says Arthur Cooper) 'No . . . I'll try them again.'

What else can he do? There is nothing he can do. Nothing is wrong, yet everything is wrong. Cassin has come into the crew loop.

1.49.04, Collins: 'Try 'em again.'

Cassin: 'OK.'

1.49.10: 'Mac Tower this is New Zealand nine zero one on one three four one, do you read?'

There is now no extraneous talk on the flight deck.

1.49.24, Brooks: 'I don't like this.'

Gordon Brooks has come firmly into the loop. This is an actual verbal concern, as opposed to a tonal concern, from a member of the operating flight crew. Something else has happened. Gordon Brooks is sitting between the pilots, about half a metre back from them. The engineering panel is on his right, blocking his view of the black rocks of what he thinks is Cape Bernacchi but is really Cape Bird. Mulgrew and Moloney are on his left, blocking his view of the black rocks of what he thinks is Cape Royds but is really Cape Tennyson. This means that as far as Brooks is concerned anything not white has disappeared from his sight. As he looks ahead through the windscreen of the aircraft he has gone into complete whiteout. There is no terrain to be seen. This is why he is suddenly alert. The pilots remain in sector whiteout, meaning that what they're seeing in front of them is in whiteout, they can still see topographical relief through the side windows of the cockpit.

Collins replies immediately, one second later.

1.49.25, Collins: 'Have you got anything from him?'

Cassin: 'No.'

Collins has made his command decision.

1.49.30, Collins: 'We're 26 miles north. We'll have to climb out of this.'

Arthur Cooper says that even at this point Collins's voice contained puzzlement, not worry or alarm. There was after all, nothing in front of him. He could see for miles ahead across unbroken flat white ice. None of them saw any obstruction of any kind. In whiteout, where overcast skies meet a snow-covered surface with the sun behind the pilot and with no rocks or man-made objects in view, even a mountain can disappear. Erebus, right in front of them, all 13,000 towering feet of it, had disappeared.

But neither Collins nor any of the crew knew this. There was nothing in front of the aircraft but daylight. This was very hard for the public to understand at the time of the Erebus inquiry. Now we accept the seriousness and power of whiteout. Mahon, when he went to Antarctica, found it the most extraordinary phenomenon. Jim Collins's lack of understanding of and familiarity with polar whiteout, the ultimate optical illusion, the failure of the airline and Civil Aviation to make sure he was briefed, was a recipe for human tragedy.

But there was nothing in front of him. Why, then, did Collins decide to climb out? Gordon Vette, in *Impact Erebus*, says Collins announced his decision to climb out 'casually but with regret'.[12] Casually and with regret, says Vette, because his passengers would not see McMurdo or Scott Base.

Mahon, in Canada, consulted one of the leading North American authorities on whiteout, Mr G. W. Shannon. Shannon was vice-president of an airline that flew in Northern Canada and the sub-arctic. He also knew the McMurdo area and had flown there extensively.[13] Mr Shannon's view was that Collins decided to climb out because he could see no terrain, especially the high ground that he ought to have been seeing some 30 miles ahead. Shannon told Mahon that the moment Captain Collins levelled out on Nav Track after his descending orbits, had he been an experienced Antarctic pilot, he would have got it straight away. But Shannon also told Mahon that, in fact, Collins realised after 'only a brief interval' that things were not hunky-dory, because 'he could not discern the clear visibility MacCentre had told him would be apparent once he had descended to 2000 feet'.[14]

'We're 26 miles north. We'll have to climb out of this.' Two words are important here, 'climb' and 'this'. With what Gordon Vette calls 'the natural caution of airmen', Jim Collins wants the safety of height because he cannot quite work out what 'this' is. 'This' might be nothing dangerous but, whatever it is, 'this' is weird. 'This' doesn't add up. No radar, no radio, no Shackleton hut, no penguins, no Mount Discovery. Something is not right.

It is interesting to wonder about Collins's decision to 'climb out'. He was convinced he was flying over flat sea ice. Why, therefore, would he want to climb? Captain Wilson, the briefing officer, suggested at the inquiry — before he came clean — that it might have been an indication that Collins knew the actual course he was on and that there was a mountain ahead.[15] This was a disgraceful suggestion. It was simply Captain Collins being cautious. Any trouble in front, any pilot wants altitude.

In paragraph 355 of his report, Mahon says that at no stage of the descent is there anything but 'a most careful adherence . . . to every detail of flight deck discipline and procedure'. At all times, each pilot acknowledges changes in instrument settings. 'There is not the slightest indication from the recorded communications between the pilot and co-pilot that either of them took any notice of, or even heard, the running sequence of indistinct cross-talk between the various persons at the rear of the flight deck and in the galley.'

But there is no real visibility crisis. The discussion between Collins and Cassin that follows is unhurried.

1.49.33, Cassin: 'It's clear on the right.'

Collins: 'Is it?'

Cassin: 'Yep.'

1.49.35: An indistinguishable remark from Moloney or Mulgrew, who had similar voices and who both mumbled, says Arthur Cooper.

1.49.38, Cassin: 'You're clear to turn right there's . . .'

Collins: 'No, negative.'

Super cautious Collins will not turn right because he can longer see terrain on the right so is unsure what turning circle is available to him. So much for Chippindale's irresponsible captain.

Cassin: 'No high ground if you do a one eighty.'

Cassin is saying two things here, that he can still see land and has assessed that the DC-10 has room in which to turn without any terrain issues and that if they fly back the way they flew in they know they will be in clear air.

Suddenly the aircraft's altimeter showed 700 feet. Then the 500 feet warning light illuminated. Then, out of the blue, the ground proximity warning sounded.

1.49:44. Whoop Whoop

Pull up.

Pull up.

Brooks: '500 feet.'

Pull up.

1.49.48, Brooks: '400 feet.'

Whoop Whoop

Pull up.

Whoop Whoop.

Pull up.

Gordon Vette says that the hands of Captain Jim Collins flew 'almost immediately' to the throttle controls as he called for 'Go round power, please'.

Go around power is pilot speak for 'Power up and get the hell out of here fast'. It is the command given generally to abort a landing approach for whatever reason may present itself. You power up and go round again.

Collins did not firewall the engines. When the flight data recorder was examined later, when it was all over and burnt out, the engines were just short of full thrust. Even with the ground proximity warning sounding, for no apparent reason, remember, for no reason whatsoever, Collins and Brooks avoided firewalling the engines and possibly damaging them. Even then, Captain Jim Collins was mindful that he needed his engines running perfectly for the long journey home to New Zealand.

1.49.50. Impact.

The men had all spoken their last words. The final word Jim Collins ever uttered is one of the greatest words of courtesy in the English language.

The aircraft collided with the 14-degree lower slope of Mount Erebus with its nose 10 degrees up. Impact was halfway along its belly. Its fuselage compressed a hole 2 metres deep in the ice and there were two shallower holes, one on each side of where the fuselage impacted, gouged by each of the wing engines.

Gordon Vette wrote in *Impact Erebus*: 'Death came to the 257 occupants in milliseconds — far quicker than turning off an electric light. Mercifully, they had no conscious inkling of its arrival. The human misery Erebus extracted was from those they left behind.'

And much of that misery would be caused by evidence falsification and absurd allegations by a Chief Inspector of Air Accidents who convinced the public that a careless, joyriding pilot had flown himself and 256 other people in a $40 million aircraft into the side of a mountain in cloud.

In the last seconds of his life, Jim Collins would still not have had a clue as to what had gone wrong.

13

Enter Justice Peter Mahon

I wanted you to see what real courage is, instead of getting the idea that courage is a man with a gun in his hand. It's when you know you're licked before you begin but you begin anyway and see it through no matter what. You rarely win, but sometimes you do.

— Atticus Finch in *To Kill a Mocking Bird*, Harper Lee

However I had to deal with the matter in hand, namely that I had agreed to an independent enquiry.

'Couldn't we,' I suggested thoughtfully, 'get an independent enquiry to find no evidence?'

'You mean rig it?' enquired Sir Humphrey coldly.

'Well. . .yes!'

'Minister!' he said, as if deeply shocked. Bloody hypocrite.

'What's wrong with rigging an independent enquiry if you can rig an internal one, I should like to know?'

Though I already knew the answer — you might get caught rigging an independent enquiry.

'No, Minister, in an independent enquiry, everything depends on who the chairman is. He absolutely has to be sound.'

'If he's sound,' I remarked, 'surely there's a danger he'll bring it all out into the open?'

Sir Humphrey was puzzled again. 'No, not if he's sound,' he explained.

'A sound man will understand what is required.'

— *Yes Minister*, Volume 2, 'The Compassionate Society'

The story goes like this. It was told to Erebus researcher Stuart Macfarlane by his old law school friend Roger Maclaren, who was counsel at the Commission for First Officer Greg Cassin's wife, Anne. Maclaren had chambers in the same building as Lloyd Brown QC, just down from the Intercontinental Hotel in Auckland, now the Hyatt.

It goes like this. Prime Minister Robert Muldoon knew he was going to have to hold a public inquiry into why the DC-10 flew into Mount Erebus. There was no way round it. It was a huge event of international importance. But who should run it? Muldoon was a passionate supporter of Air New Zealand. His office was full of model aeroplanes.

Muldoon's lawyer and friend was Des Dalgety. Dalgety was Deputy Chairman of Air New Zealand, Muldoon's man on the board. Dalgety persuaded Air New Zealand to instruct Lloyd Brown QC to represent Air New Zealand at the Royal Commission. Then Dalgety asked Brown whom he thought Muldoon should appoint as Royal Commissioner.

Justice Peter Mahon had lived in Auckland just under a decade. He was a reserved, formal man of the old school. His best legal friend in Auckland was Lloyd Brown QC. They shared a strong interest in the horses. Mahon loved a punt.

So Dalgety asked Brown whom he thought Muldoon should appoint as Royal Commissioner. Brown, thinking he was on to a good thing, suggested his friend Mahon, a good conservative fellow.

On 11 June 1980, just over half a year after the Erebus disaster, Attorney General Jim McLay appointed Justice Peter Mahon to conduct the Royal Commission of Inquiry into the destruction of the DC-10 and the loss of 257 lives on the Antarctic mountainside. But there were a couple of aspects to Mahon's character that Lloyd Brown and Des Dalgety failed to reckon with. Mahon was scrupulously honest. He had sympathy for the underdog. He was passionate about justice. He had an extraordinary command of detail and an ability to make sense of the most baffling minutia. He would demonstrate time and again during the Commission hearings an ability to understand the most daunting detail of flying and navigating a jet airliner.

Eleven days before the appointment of Mahon as Royal Commissioner, however, Ron Chippindale signed off his air accident report and sent it up to the Minister of Transport. The Attorney General, Jim McLay, requested and was given a copy. We may be sure that Muldoon saw the contents, too.

Debate ensued about whether, with a Royal Commission about to be held, the Chippindale Report should be published. Mahon, the lawyers for the estates of the dead pilots, lawyers for ALPA and counsel assisting the Commission were all deeply opposed. In *Verdict on Erebus*, Mahon says he even wrote to the Prime Minister imploring him not to publish the report before the Royal Commission hearings because its release could prejudice the integrity of the inquiry findings. But that, of course, was exactly what the government wanted it to do, just in case Mahon was a man who didn't play by the old boy network rules. Whatever happened, Muldoon was determined that the pilots would wear the blame.

So Mahon was appointed on 11 June 1980 and the following day the government approved the release to the public of the Chippindale Report. Mahon even learnt, he says in *Verdict on Erebus* (page 35), that the report was being given high priority by the Government Printer and that the government seemed intent on getting the Chippindale Report in front of public eyes before Mahon's own hearings were due to start in just a few weeks on 7 July 1980.

And that was the moment at which Mahon started asking himself questions. It was the first time in this whole sorry saga that Justice Mahon wondered what the government's motives were. It was obvious to Mahon that for the sake of the integrity of the Royal Commission the report of the Chief Inspector of Air Accidents should not be released before the hearings had begun. In Mahon's view of process, this was quite wrong. It undermined the Royal Commission. The government told Mahon that 'publication of the final report would assist the Royal Commissioner'.[1] Mahon no doubt saw the release of the Chippindale Report as contempt of the Commission.

But Mahon realised the government was hell-bent on publication for another reason. Chippindale's final report was likely to follow closely his interim report, in which everyone knew by that stage, through a series of leaks to the news media, the dead aircrew were held primarily responsible for the disaster. Mahon knew what the government priority would be. The airline was owned by the state, Muldoon as Finance Minister was the only shareholder, an election was looming the following year and Muldoon wanted to ensure that the government, the airline and he himself were safe.

And unless the government made the Chippindale Report public before the Royal Commission hearings, it would not be published at all. Counsel for the dead aircrew, for a start, would instantly object to the report being published because it would be second guessing the Royal Commission and

Greg Gilpin

The crash site from the air, taken by police disaster victim identification team member and the officer in charge on the mountain, Greg Gilpin. The photograph looks up the crash site. No one could believe the smudge had once been a DC-10. Taken with Gilpin's Instamatic camera at 21.30 hours on 5 December 1979.

Gordon Vette

The campsite for the body recovery teams. It has been positioned well away from the horror but for day after day, night after night, there was no respite.

Nigel Roberts

Nigel Roberts's iconic photograph, flashed to a shocked world. It was taken at 6 pm on 29 November, some 18 hours after the wreckage was sighted by the US Navy.

Antarctica New Zealand

In the midst of the nightmare, body recovery teams pick their way through the broken aircraft. The cabin section, upper centre, showed the effects of intense fire.

Chippindale Report

A forlorn section of the undercarriage and the remains of the aircraft's tail, which once held an engine.

Gordon Vette

ABOVE: The tangled wreck of the cockpit, in which two pilots and an engineer flew the majestic airliner.

Antarctica New Zealand

RIGHT: Part of the DC-10's cockpit instrument panel.

Antarctica New Zealand

A graphic illustration of the treachery of the terrain upon which the aircraft crashed. The red flags signify danger. The icicles were formed by fuel freezing.

RIGHT: Sergeant Greg Gilpin, 33, left, and Constable Stuart Leighton, 22, on the mountain during the body recovery process. Both men are now inspectors. It was a week that affected them deeply and forever.

Greg Gilpin

BELOW: The Antarctic skua, fiercely predatory, 'the raptor of the south', and the scourge of those recovering the bodies. The skuas were relentless and fearless in their quest.

Antarctica New Zealand/Phil Reid

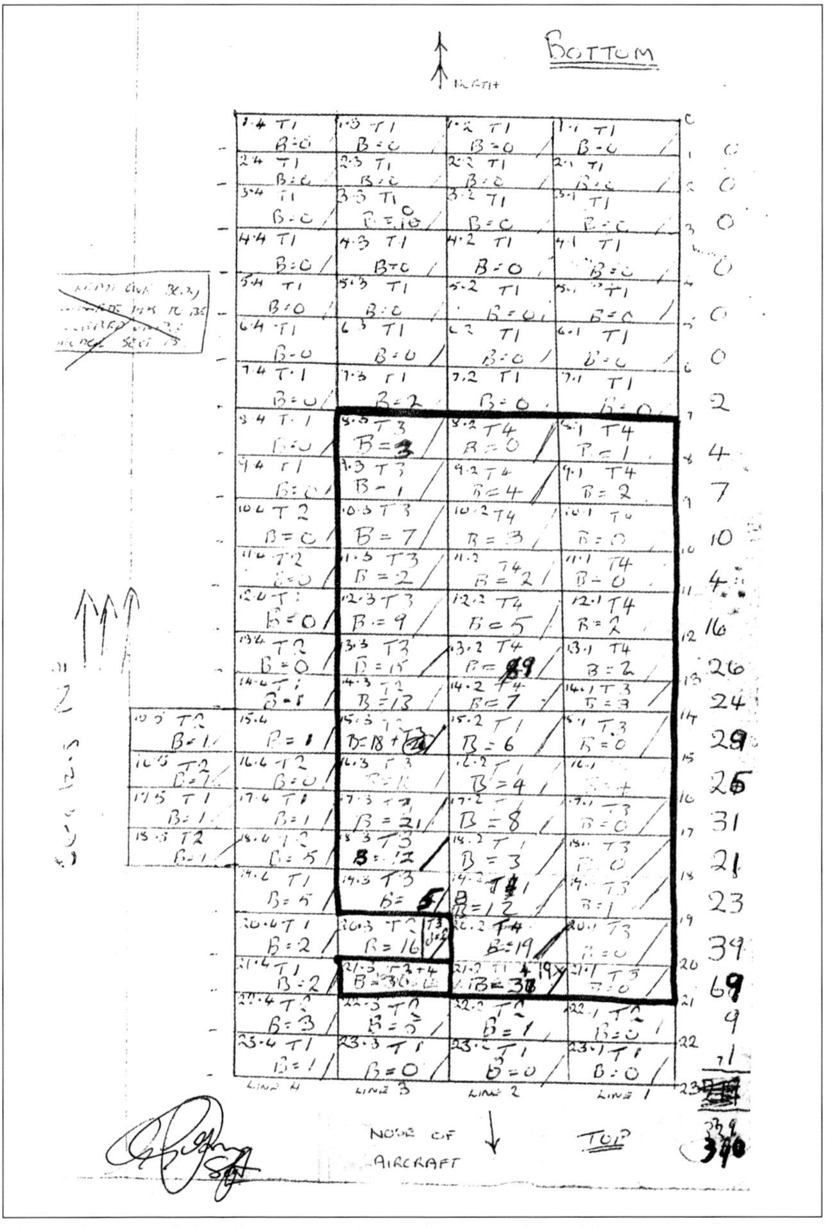

Greg Gilpin's grid showing where the bodies were found. The crash site was marked out in 30-metre squares, marked by black flags. The aircraft's point of impact is at the top of the page. The body count of each section of four squares is listed on the right, with the total at bottom right.

Nigel Roberts

The simple wooden cross made in the carpenters' workshop at Scott Base was erected above the crash site on December 20, 1979, three weeks after the accident. During its erection, cloud kept covering the site, then receding.

Nigel Roberts

The proud registration plate of DC-10 November Zulu Papa, which was later placed in the centre of the wooden cross.

Mahon would have no option but to comply with their request.

Reading Mahon's accident report, the work of his life, over 30 years on, one marvels not only at his mind and the brilliance of his investigative powers but at the way he wrote, the grace, elegance, the muscularity and the rhythmic balance of his prose. His accident report reads like a thriller and is no less authoritative for it. He can write with expected judicial loftiness and he can write the language of the man in the street.

Sam Mahon, in *My Father's Shadow: a portrait of Justice Peter Mahon*, his moving memoir of his father, believes the most important thing we have to know about Peter Mahon is that he was a returned serviceman who saw terrible action through the brutal, bitter Italian campaign. He went overseas a private soldier and returned a second lieutenant. There appears to have been at least one singular act of bravery for which he was offered the Military Medal or a commission. Mahon took the commission. His pay went up two shillings a day.

He understood men and he could speak to all men.

This is Peter Mahon: 'A judge is not entitled, as a matter of personal predilection or opinion, to consider as being wrongly decided a prior judgement given in conformity with established legal principle, merely because the judge entertains his own views as to the propriety of that principle.'[2]

Mahon could write a long and beautiful letter to his daughter Janet, discoursing upon Dante's *Inferno*. When Jana Wendt, whom Sam describes as 'the most beautiful woman in the Southern hemisphere', the host for many years of Channel Nine's *A Current Affair*, came to New Zealand to interview him at the height of the storm, she asked him for a voice test for the sound man before the interview started. Mahon started talking gobbledegook. The sound man asked what Mahon was saying. Jana Wendt laughed and explained that it was Dante in Italian.

There is the Peter Mahon who knew the language of the street, the language of the soldier. When Sam was shuffling the cards too long in a game with his father one day, Mahon said, 'Cut it out, Sam. You'll rub the tits off the queen.'

What intrigued me when I first started reading Mahon again in earnest — and I spent most of 2010 poring over Mahon, trying to understand Erebus and to understand him — is that there is a clear Mahon, and there is a Mahon who writes in the grey, a Mahon who lurks, a Mahon who can make himself invisible, a Mahon who can pull his punches, a Mahon who can say something while meaning something else, and there is a Mahon who can write with withering exactitude and certainty. I wondered early on if, with Mahon, one had sometimes to read between the lines.

Then I picked up Sam Mahon's book and found myself completely absorbed by Sam's attempt to come to know his father. In his introduction, he speaks of his father's letters being the true way to track the tendency of his father's heart. It is 'through his many letters in which he weaves language like a master of tapestry . . . and even then,' writes Sam to my amazement, 'it is a matter of reading between the lines, for apart from one or two letters written to colleagues at the time of Erebus, he never said anything plainly.'[3]

In fact — no disrespect to Sam — Mahon could be brutally plain. There is a speech he gave to aviation lawyers in Australia in August 1982, several months after Chippindale had tried vainly to pull Mahon's report apart in a long-winded, hysterical press release at the beginning of that year. If ever Mahon laid out how the Erebus disaster happened and how he was stymied in his researches into cause by every state agency he encountered, it was in this speech. It was the only occasion on which he ever publicly unleashed his generally restrained contempt for Ron Chippindale. The speech was lethal.

Mahon was no fool. And he knew that Chippindale was not one either. Yet Mahon knew Chippindale's report was foolish. That was one of the great questions, of course. If Chippindale was no fool, why were his findings so wide of the mark, so much so that through the inquiry Mahon was always asking himself what game was being played here. Here is a small section of the speech in Sydney.

> I only mention the attitude of the US Navy because it was characteristic of the position taken by every official agency involved in the inquiry. The three main participants in the events preceding the tragedy were Air New Zealand, which is wholly owned by the State, the Civil Aviation Division of the Ministry of Transport, and the United States Navy. Each of these agencies set out to establish that it had no responsibility for the disaster and that the aircrew of the DC-10 were wholly to blame.
>
> In addition to all this, my difficulties as investigator were compounded by the prior investigation conducted by the Chief Inspector of Air Accidents, who is an official employed by the Civil Aviation Division. The Chief Inspector is by statute

> rendered independent of his employers, but it was singularly unfortunate in the present case that Civil Aviation Division was and is believed responsible, and by many people primarily responsible, for the occurrence of the disaster.[4]

Mahon knew the game exquisitely. Then this, to the Sydney lawyers:

> In short, the Chief Inspector's report, produced by him with commendable diligence and effort, was based upon hearsay, and many people unfortunately told him whatever they thought might extricate themselves from responsibility. But when direct evidence was taken from the witness box a very different story emerged and long before the Royal Commission's hearings were complete, the Chief Inspector's report, valuable though it was for its maps and technical data, was tacitly put aside by everyone (except the airline) as having little relevance to the question of causation. But its publication prior to the Royal Commission hearings had certainly been of great value to Air New Zealand and to Civil Aviation Division because it white-washed them both.[5]

The key parts of Mahon's accident report are also brutally plain. The expression of his frustration at what he saw emphatically as a conspiracy by Air New Zealand to lie to him and to obscure from him the truth in 'an orchestrated litany of lies'[6] is one of the plainest and most rhythmically pleasing descriptions uttered by a New Zealander.

But Sam's reality is Sam's reality and is not to be dismissed. When I phoned him to compliment him on his book, Sam said, 'God knows, I'm the last person who should have written about him. I hardly knew him.' And I wondered if we don't all feel that, if we don't all have some of that sadness, those of us orphaned slightly by the war, by the death of parts of our fathers who saw action. I wondered if Sam knew any more or any less about his father than I knew of my own. And I wondered how much boys ever really know their fathers, and perhaps never really knowing our fathers is just part of the inevitable disappointment of life. Yet without question, as his letters show, Mahon loved his children and they, as Sam's book demonstrates, adored him back.

With Margarita at her home in Point Chevalier in Auckland, the first day I went to see her for this book, was Sam's only sister, Janet. Janet has managed to remain out of the limelight for 30 years. Janet missed most of the hell that broke loose when Mahon released his report and arrived home from living in Paris just as the Court of Appeal tore Mahon's heart out. Janet, herself already by then a lawyer, was appalled and deeply pained. It is Janet who put together the family's newspaper clipping file on the Court of Appeal. Her initials are on the cover. Janet took ownership of that job.

I asked if she would talk to me for this narrative. She declined. And I think she came along that day to see if I was sufficiently on top of things to begin a project such as this. And I think talking would have been too painful for her. 'You've got him, anyway, Paul. He's all there in his writing.'

But is he? Sam can't always find him. Mahon is not always easily to be seen in *Verdict on Erebus*, his story of the inquiry. In the engaging letters by which he may always have communicated best with his children, though, we see the essential decency of the man and the warmth of his heart.

There is a story Sam tells of Mahon's days at the bar in Christchurch. In the 1950s Peter Mahon was prosecuting counsel at the sensational trial of Pauline Parker and Juliet Hulme, who between them murdered Pauline Parker's mother by bashing her with a brick in a stocking. Towards the end of the trial the judge called both counsel into chambers and said he intended not to allow the defence of insanity and would instruct the jury so. Mahon informed the judge that if he did that then he, Mahon, would remove himself from the case. The defence of insanity was allowed. But round the legal fraternity in Christchurch, Mahon earned big points for fairness.[7]

There is another important aspect of Peter Mahon. He grew up poor but good. He won a scholarship to St Bede's, the Catholic private school in Christchurch. He was exceptionally bright and won all the prizes. But because he was a scholarship boy, the school would not make him dux.

But when it comes to *Verdict on Erebus*, there is one very sound and important reason he ducks in and out of sight. When he wrote his accident report, he did so with the full protections and privileges of a Justice of the High Court. He was unassailable. He could pretty much say what he liked. No one can sue a Royal Commissioner for defamation. When Morrie Davis and Air New Zealand erupted at being accused of conspiracy to perjure by Mahon in his report, they went to the Court of Appeal for a judicial review. This was the closest Davis could come to proceedings for defamation against a High Court judge.

But by the time Mahon came to write *Verdict on Erebus*, the story of how the truth came out despite the queer findings of Chippindale and the stalling and the obduracy of Air New Zealand at the Commission of Inquiry, Mahon had walked away from the bench. He was no longer a judge and no longer enjoyed anything more than the rights of an ordinary man. It is a testament to Mahon's certainty and to his courage, shown long before on battlefields in Italy, that he repeated exactly what he wrote in the accident report. There had been a 'predetermined plan of deception' by Air New Zealand at the inquiry and he had been 'forced . . . to listen to an orchestrated litany of lies'. He repeated his stunning assertions which New Zealanders found so hard to believe possible. This was the famous paragraph 377 of the accident report, reprinted unchanged on page 249 of *Verdict on Erebus*.

In other words, in *Verdict on Erebus*, Mahon was inviting those who had taken him to the Court of Appeal to now sue him in open court. No one did. No one made a peep. No one ever did. His allegations of perjury were deeply serious. They involved public officials conspiring to lie under oath to a Royal Commission of Inquiry. Those accused had to sue if they were innocent. None did. It was Mahon's ultimate put-down of two Court of Appeal judges for whom he had nothing but contempt, Sir Duncan McMullin and Sir Owen Woodhouse. And while it is true that, later, the Privy Council would 'reluctantly' support the New Zealand Court of Appeal in the matter of the conspiracy allegation, in no way whatsoever did they reverse Mahon's fundamental findings as to causation. Instead the Privy Council — and this is what ultimately matters — professed profound admiration for Mahon's 'brilliant' investigation.

But this is all in the future.

Now, in June 1980, with the Royal Commission hearings due to begin at the start of the second week in July, to Mahon's horror and the horror of most of the lawyers involved in the Royal Commission, at midnight on 20 June 1980, the government released the Chippindale Report. It sold out next morning in minutes. Another print run was ordered. Its effect on public opinion, fanned by the news media, as we have seen, was fundamental.

The CVR transcript the New Zealand public was reading as Mahon began his inquiry a few weeks later appeared to show a flight deck upon which no one knew too much of what was going on, a flight deck in disarray. The publication of the transcript, with its lashings of alarmist punctuation, read like a radio play. And it not only damaged terribly the reputation of the aircrew, but it undermined the hearings and probably the eventual findings of the Royal Commission. The release of the transcript was probably contempt of the Commission.

Later, Mahon would learn from a man he came to respect immensely — Mr William H Tench, the Chief Inspector of Air Accidents for the United Kingdom — as they sat round having a drink at the end of a day and listening to the Erebus CVR, that Tench sent his reports directly to the Secretary of the State for Trade. They were never released publicly. The Secretary of State then decided whether there should be a public inquiry. If so, the report was treated at the inquiry only as evidence, not as a pronouncement from the mouth of God, as Chippindale's had been.

As Mahon understood, nothing quite alarms the flying public as much as an allegation of low flying. That looked bad for the pilot. Despite the Chief Inspector acknowledging whiteout and having the most insidious form of it described to him at McMurdo; despite his acknowledging the last minute change in the aircraft coordinates without the pilots being told; the real cause of the DC-10 crash, according to Chippindale, was the decision of the pilot to descend below 16,000 feet on the north side of Erebus and to continue to fly towards dodgy weather in which he could not see the high ground.

Chippindale also said the crew didn't know where they were and, in any case, the aircraft's radar would have seen the mountain. What's more, the flight engineers were trying to bring the pilot to his senses. It was damning.

Chippindale's report seemed an entirely reasonable conclusion about an inexplicable accident. Mahon thought so. In the speech to the Australian lawyers, he said, 'The effect on the public . . . was clear and uncomplicated. The aircraft had been flying in cloud, and the crew did not know where they were, and they had not bothered to look at their radar screen.'[8]

The cockpit voice recorder transcript, when you glanced at it, did seem to show a great uncertainty about where the crew on the flight deck thought they were. The CVR did not look good for Captain Collins. As he read the report a few times before the Royal Commission hearings began, Mahon said he 'was naturally inclined to treat the Chief Inspector's conclusions as being quite correct. He seemed to have covered every aspect of the occurrence.'[9] Mahon did not expect the Commission to take very long.

Only a couple of questions nagged him. One was whether the Chief Inspector was right to say that the late change in the flight plan coordinates about which the crew had not been briefed had not misled the pilots. Mahon had seen the newspaper story that appeared in the *Weekend Star* of 1 January 1980, in which the DC-10 pilots apparently believed it did and that the change actually caused the crash. He says it occurred to him that the DC-10 pilots might know more about this than the Chief Inspector 'who had not flown a DC-10 with its sophisticated navigation equipment'.[10]

The second question was a human one. How could this highly experienced crew, led apparently by the most methodical man on the DC-10 fleet, fly at such a low level into cloud in an area where there were towering mountains everywhere you looked on the map. Mahon knew men. He had been in action with men and he had not only been the barrister of his generation but had been a judge for many years. And the captain of this accident flight was air force trained. So Mahon found himself wondering . . .

But there was something else that Mahon cottoned on to very quickly and it was a matter of crucial importance. There had been a revolution in aviation navigation in the early part of the 1970s and Mahon understood what it meant in terms of this inquiry. Airliners these days were computers. Correctly programmed, you could trust your computerised navigation computer greatly. It was why navigators had gone from the cockpits of airliners.

When the Germans sent their V1 and V2 rockets over the channel to rain down on London during World War Two, the deadly weapons were navigated by inertial navigation equipment developed by pioneering rocket scientist Werner von Braun. After von Braun surrendered his 500 scientists to the Americans in 1945 and brought them to the United States — the very scientists whose work would send astronauts of their adopted land to the moon just over 20 years later — they adapted their inertial navigation technology to rocket guidance. These days all navigation in deep space is inertial. The men went to and from the moon with inertial navigation guidance. It was not only a cheap system but it was tireless and did not make mistakes. People, navigators, make mistakes. Inertial navigation does not.

DC-10s made their way round the world every day of the week in 1979 using the area inertial navigation system. DC-10s would fly themselves, hour upon hour, 10 kilometres above the earth, the pilots checking off the waypoints as they flew, arriving effortlessly at their destination. And Mahon understood its significance immediately.

What the AINS meant, of course, was that the aircraft now navigated itself. If you were flying, say, from Auckland to Honolulu, you put a cassette of your flight plan, your waypoint coordinates, into the flight deck computer and the aircraft took you there. The AINS navigation system was state of the art. It was brilliant and Air New Zealand pilots found it 'completely accurate'.[11] They trusted it totally. The AINS meant flight decks need not contain plotting tables. The AINS was now fundamental to modern commercial aviation. 'The captain need not ask a human navigator where the aircraft is. The aircraft itself is telling him where it is.'[12]

How do we know that Mahon understood the importance of the modern pilot's reliance on the AINS and what it meant in assessing the worth of the Chippindale Report? We know it because in *Verdict on Erebus* he started his chapter 'The [Chippindale] Report is Published' with a full description of the AINS, and the quite sensible respect pilots had for it.

What he was saying to Chippindale was this. You cannot claim the pilots were uncertain of their position when they were flying on the Nav Track directed by their area inertial navigation system. You cannot say the change of coordinates did not deceive the pilots when they were navigating with the pre-programmed AINS down what they thought was the flat sea ice of McMurdo Sound, the route upon which they had been briefed. You cannot say a fellow is not going to be deceived when, after a briefing about the flight path, the navigation coordinates are changed and he is not told.

Navigation — the brilliance of the AINS — is also one of the first subjects Mahon addressed at length in his accident report.[13]

For Mahon, the inertial navigation system told him almost everything he needed to know about the fate of TE901. It told him that even if the pilots were flying the aircraft faithfully, visually, responsibly and with skill, a mistake at Head Office could cause the sudden destruction of an aircraft some 4000 kilometres away on the frozen continent.

In this way of thinking about an accident, Mahon was revolutionary. It was not until 1994, 13 years after Mahon was shelved, that ICAO, the International Civil Aviation Organization, recognised the Mahon Report. ICAO decided the report was valid. It had correctly identified the cause of the Erebus crash as management error, not pilot error, and, above all else, it had transformed the investigation of accidents. In its *Safety Digest on Human Factors No 10*, the ICAO said, 'The [Mahon] Report was, probably, ten years ahead of its time. After all, Chernobyl, Bhopal, Clapham Junction, Kings Cross and other major high technology systems catastrophes had yet to happen.' They need not have if Mahon had been listened to.

So you couldn't just declare pilot error when what the pilot was doing was exactly what Head Office had told him to do. These days, round the world, air accident investigators have to note relevant organisation and administrative factors that might have contributed to a disaster.

This is how you find your way through Mahon. It takes a while. It takes many readings. You get to know your man. I could not at first work out why Mahon in both his report and his book spent so much time and so many pages on the AINS. But Sam was right about reading between the lines. Janet was right. Mahon is all there in the writing.

14

Mahon Begins to Wonder

The greatest enemy of knowledge is not ignorance, it is the illusion of knowledge.

— Stephen Hawking

After Mahon's report was published, he saw one of the many documents he claims Air New Zealand kept to itself despite his order that all documents be produced. The document revealed that, shortly before the hearings began at the Royal Commission, management had decided 'that the case for the airline was to be founded upon the breach of the 16,000 feet minimum safe altitude, and that the report of the Chief Inspector was to be the foundation of their case'.[1] This affirmed a conspiracy, surely. And so much, thought Mahon, for the airline's senior counsel's assertion, during final submissions, 'that the airline had come to the inquiry with the devout and sincere intention of simply producing all the facts and not with the intention of advancing any specific case'.[2] In fact, the airline had only one view. The pilots were to blame.

What is a revelation, reading the transcripts of the Royal Commission and reading Mahon 32 years on, is how quickly the Air New Zealand case — that the airline was blameless and the pilots, regretfully, were to blame — against the pilots started to unravel.

Air New Zealand and Civil Aviation said the figure was 16,000 feet. Flight level 160, as pilots put it. That was the rule. No captain was to descend below flight level 160 until you'd flown over Erebus and was over Williams Field at McMurdo Base. Then for sightseeing purposes you could descend in a tight 'chimney' to 6000 feet but no one — no one — was to go below 6000 feet. If there was cloud above McMurdo, if it were no lower than 7000 feet, you could get a radar letdown from MacCentre to assist in the descent in a tight blind spiral.

The 16,000-feet altitude formed the very foundation of Chippindale's report. If Captain Collins had maintained the required altitude, there would have been no accident. Yes, the coordinates were changed or 'corrected' at the last minute without the pilots being told, but that did not matter to Chippindale. If Captain Collins had maintained the MSA, the minimum safe altitude, of flight level 160 on the northern side of the 13,000-foot mountain there would have been no accident.

The Commission knew right at the start about the coordinate change, of course, and the pilot not being told, because Chippindale had noted it in his report.

Chippindale was the first witness at the Royal Commission. He was unshaken in his stated belief that the failure of the crew to maintain the required altitude, the altitude both Air New Zealand and Civil Aviation stipulated that their pilots maintain until well over the top of the mountain, was a fatal and unforgiveable error.

Mahon found him impressive, yet was disturbed by the Chief Inspector's insistence that if Collins was not exactly flying in cloud then he was at least heading the DC-10 at 1500 feet towards an area of poor visibility. What disturbed Mahon about this was that Chippindale was asserting a kind of behaviour quite out of character with what was known about Jim Collins, especially given what Collins would have known about mountains all round him in that part of the world.

Mahon noted the passenger photos. They were his first shock at the inquiry. They showed an aircraft flying in clear air left and right. They showed sunshine throughout the cabin. There was no evidence whatsoever that Collins was flying in cloud or towards cloud, as Chippindale had apparently made up his mind he had.

And while Chippindale said on the stand that, if evidence showed he was wrong he would alter his views without hesitation, something about him told Mahon that this was a man who would not change his mind once he had formed an opinion. Politically he couldn't. His views of probable cause had been published right round the world. To concede that he had to change his mind would damage him badly.

And that was exactly how it turned out. Chippindale never changed his mind. Chippindale was always right, this clever man who played the dark hand. Had he been an honest man he could not have reached the conclusions he did. As Arthur Cooper told me, as we sat down in his garden to talk in the middle of 2010, 'If those pilots had been told about that coordinate change, Paul, you and I wouldn't be talking about this 30 years later. The cause of the accident was always very simple.'

But at this stage, Mahon assumed that Chippindale was more or less right. If Collins hadn't gone down to 1500 feet in front of the mountain and flown towards it, he would not have collided with it. There seemed no escaping this.

Then came another surprise. Air New Zealand's senior counsel, Lloyd Brown QC, the veteran trial lawyer, told his good friend Mahon, the veteran trial judge, that Air New Zealand would not be making an opening statement 'at this stage'. Brown reserved the right to make an opening statement 'at a later stage'.

Mahon said he began to wonder what the airline was up to. In *Verdict on Erebus* (page 68), he says he began to think Air New Zealand was acting like a defendant. 'When this occurs in the courtroom, as it does so frequently, the usual explanation is that counsel for the defendant, or counsel for the accused as the case may be, is not quite certain what his witnesses will say under cross-examination.'

And so it was for the Air New Zealand counsel. Mahon says they complained to the other lawyers that they sometimes did not know what the Air New Zealand position on a particular issue would be and that the airline changed its evidence at the last moment. He notes in *Verdict on Erebus* that the lead counsel for Air New Zealand complained to him of these difficulties on four occasions. This was Lloyd Brown. He and Mahon were still friends at that stage. By the time Mahon wrote *Verdict on Erebus*, they were not, and Mahon does not mention him by name once in the book.

Air New Zealand called its first witness, Captain Peter Grundy, a senior executive pilot. Grundy was Flight Operations Manager DC-10/DC-8. This would become another obscure aspect to a case in which there was so much deliberate obfuscation. Grundy and Jim Collins were friends. 'Tall, good looking and weak,' Kathryn Carter, Collins's eldest daughter, says of Grundy now. He was the perfectly courteous, intelligent and fluently spoken DC-10 captain any airline would love to have.

Grundy's first day on the stand went smoothly. He had commanded the second sightseeing flight to Antarctica. He said it was made clear to him at the briefing conducted by Captain Gemmell and 'a member' of the Navigation Section that his programmed route would be direct from Cape Hallett to McMurdo, in other words, straight over the top of Mount Erebus. Except, fancy this, Grundy never went over Erebus. The weather was clear so he headed the aircraft down the richly scenic coast of Victoria Land, that is to say, way to the west of the mountain, down the right-hand side of McMurdo Sound to McMurdo Base, at no time, of course, descending below 16,000 feet.

Yes, 16,000 feet was the magic number. It was the number upon which Air New Zealand was going to live or die at the inquiry.

A month before the fatal flight, Antarctic pilots received the following memo. The memo was headed, 'Descent to 6000 ft for cloud penetration at McMurdo'. It told pilots that 'permission has been given to descend to 6000 ft QNH [barometric] in VMC [visual] conditions or using the approved NDB procedure in IMC [instrument flying] conditions'. Flight at 6000 feet was to be restricted to a tight arc round McMurdo. Visibility had to be 20 kilometres or more. It was quite clear that the memo was to do with descent through cloud overhead McMurdo to 6000 with a cloud base no less than 7000 feet.

Then a couple of weeks later came a new memo: 'McMurdo NDB [non-directional beacon] not available.' It explained that, with the NDB out of action, there could be no descent through cloud over McMurdo. All descent now had to be visual and visibility had to be 20 kilometres or more. This explained why Jim Collins went down when he saw the gaping hole in the cloud. There was going to be no let-down possible if he arrived over McMurdo above the cloud. He knew his passengers wanted to see Scott Base and McMurdo. He was offered radar and he accepted radar but he saw clear air. He could fly visually and visually is always better than descent through cloud in mountainous country, he would have thought. What's more, his passengers had been looking at nothing for five hours. At last, here was a sight of Antarctica from the middle of McMurdo Sound. At last, they could take some photographs.

These two memos caused intense debate all the way through the inquiry. Were they altitude restrictions or were they simply cloud break procedures, that is to say, ways of getting down to the safe height of 6000 feet after which you could fly at whatever altitude McMurdo invited you to?

Nevertheless, almost all of the Antarctic pilots said that they considered the 6000 feet altitude to be merely a cloud break procedure, a procedure after which you could fly at an altitude nominated by McMurdo Control. But Chippindale at the inquiry claimed that only two pilots told him they believed this.

We cannot examine the veracity of this because Chippindale took no sworn statements, which seems an alarming way to conduct an investigation into the deaths of 257 people. At least he said he did not. He may have taken a few. We know he taped Captain Simpson. But by not producing any statements, he could say what he liked about what he had been told by the pilots and then accuse the pilots of not telling the truth to the Royal Commission.

In fact, the stream of pilots who presented at the Royal Commission said the exact opposite of what Chippindale claimed. Captain White (Antarctic flight 21 November 1979) believed he was permitted to descend below 6000 feet. His first officer, Barry Irvine, who attended the same briefing as Collins, said descent beneath 6000 feet was allowed. Captain Simpson (14 November 1979) believed the reference to 6000 feet was ambiguous but believed he could negotiate his altitude with the local air traffic controller. Captain Gabriel (14 November 1979), then a first officer on Simpson's flight, considered 6000 feet to be a cloud break altitude. Captain Gabriel said they went down to 2500 feet. Captain Dalziell (7 November 1979) actually said that the briefing officer, Captain Ross Johnson, led a discussion about going below 6000 feet. Captain Calder (14 November 1978) said he believed 6000 feet was a cloud break procedure and descent below 6000 feet was at the captain's discretion. Captain McWilliams (7 November 1978) understood 6000 feet as a cloud break procedure and that he was free to descend further. Captain Vette (15 November 1977) believed 6000 feet to be a cloud break procedure and you could go lower with McMurdo's approval. Captain Johnson, the briefing officer himself (8 November 1977), admitted that he went down to 3000 feet. He testified that 6000 feet was nevertheless an altitude minimum but the weather was so nice on the day . . .[3]

The majority of commanding officers on the Antarctic flights, therefore, believed descent below 6000 feet was permissible. It was a sightseeing flight, after all.

After the crash, 16,000/6000 feet became the airline's mantra, just as it was the mantra for the Chief Inspector and for Civil Aviation. It was absolute: 16,000 feet *was* 16,000 feet. The 16,000-feet platform allowed all responsibility to fall back on the aircrew. You stayed at 16,000 feet until you got to McMurdo Station itself then you could descend visually overhead.

Except . . . every flight since the second had flown well below 6000 feet. And every flight since 1978 had flown down the safe flat sea of McMurdo Sound. If that were so, what did it mean for the airline and for its so-called altitude restrictions?

Peter Grundy was impressive, but towards the end of his first day of testimony things started to go badly for him.

It turned out that Civil Aviation had passed on to Air New Zealand, just days before the fatal flight, a complaint from the US Navy at McMurdo that a commercial airliner had been seen flying over a glacier at 1000 feet. Now, leaving aside whether 16,000 feet was a real or manufactured requirement, general aviation rules round the world demand pilots maintain a clearance of 2000 feet above mountain terrain, and a glacier is regarded as mountainous. In New Zealand, this height is stipulated in the Civil Aviation Regulations of 1953. All pilots learn these during their flying training.

Chippindale mentioned the American complaint to Grundy during his investigation. Never mind that the Chief Inspector himself had taken the American complaint no further; Grundy had apparently done nothing about it either. He said he might have mentioned it to one or two pilots. The danger here for both Grundy and Chippindale, in Mahon's eyes, was that, in terms of this accident, both the Chief Inspector and Air New Zealand were adamant that 16,000 feet and 6000 feet were sacrosanct altitudes. For Chippindale, flight below 16,000 feet until you were over McMurdo Station, when you could descend to 6000 feet, was forbidden. He was reflecting the complete Air New Zealand line. You maintained 16,000 feet until overhead the NDB, checked your AINS, before descending with the help of the American radar.

Yet here was the Chief Inspector not appearing to care too much about a report of a civilian aircraft 1000 feet above a glacier in Antarctica and seemingly unbothered by both a complaint by the Americans and the fact that one of the most senior DC-10 pilots at Air New Zealand was showing no concern about it whatsoever.

Next morning Mahon received another shock. Grundy took the stand and read from a typed supplementary brief which explained the very serious action he took about the low flying allegation. He even had correspondence between him and Civil Aviation. He produced a letter he wrote to Civil Aviation on 11 January 1980 in reply to their letter of 24 December 1979, weeks after the disaster, in which they asked what action he had taken. So here was the production of correspondence about a serious incident of low flying for which he was responsible, yet the previous day he could not recall any of it. Next morning he remembers everything and even has the letters.

Very strange. Again, Mahon started to wonder what Air New Zealand was up to. Mahon was wondering if Air New Zealand was 'running the Inquiry as if it were a court case in which they were defendants. Admit nothing, unless compelled to do so. Do not volunteer evidence.'[4] Hardly the spirit of a Royal Commission of Inquiry in which everyone is expected to do their best to find out what happened.

But that is exactly how it went for the entire 75 sitting days of the inquiry. Air New Zealand admitted nothing. They volunteered nothing. The lack of documentation surrendered by the airline shocked Mahon. The key revealing documents, such as Exhibit 164 — to be discussed later — were discovered and presented by counsel opposing the airline. It took Gordon Vette, using his own money, to present the equally shocking research about polar whiteout. To read the evidence of the Air New Zealand witnesses today is to look at what had to have been a deliberate policy not to engage, and to marvel at the gall of the wall of denial.

And now on day two of Grundy's evidence came king hits that left Mahon reeling. Had Captain Grundy seen this article by any chance, published on 22 October 1977 in the *Auckland Star*? The article described the Antarctic flight of 18 October 1977, under the command of Captain Mayne Hawkins. The article spoke about flying over Scott Base at 2000 metres and then flying at 200 metres (about 600 feet). The article described the aircraft as being 'well below the towering volcano Erebus belching smoke only 50 kilometres away'.[5]

Captain Grundy had neither seen it nor heard of it. But, he was asked, wasn't the pilot in command of that flight, Captain Maynard Hawkins, the senior Air New Zealand training captain? Well, yes, he was. (Hawkins always denied flying below 6000 feet. He knew, he said, that 6000 feet was the minimum. Strangely enough, his co-pilot, Peter Mulgrew's brother Ken, said he had no knowledge of any 6000-feet limit.[6])

What came next was worse. Grundy was shown a copy of a brochure entitled *Travelling Times*, an Air New Zealand publicity brochure from

September 1978. In it was an article by John Brizindine, President of the McDonnell Douglas Corporation, manufacturer of the DC-10. Brizindine was a friend of Air New Zealand Chief Executive Morrie Davis and Davis had shouted him a trip on the last Antarctic flight of 1977, commanded by one of the most senior pilots of all, Captain Gordon Vette. Brizindine wrote of approaching Ross Island at 3000 feet. Naturally, Captain Grundy had not seen this article. No, he had heard nothing about Gordon Vette's flying at 3000 feet. Brizindine also wrote about flying over Scott Base at 'perhaps half a mile', in other words about 2500 feet. Grundy knew nothing whatsoever about that either.

It emerged later that Brizindine was so impressed he had gone back to the United States, written an article and sent it to Morrie Davis as an attachment to a letter of thanks for the flight. Morrie Davis never saw the attachment, of course. No, never saw that. Davis didn't read attachments, not even an article of praise from the president of McDonnell Douglas. Neither had he seen or read it when Air New Zealand, so proud of the Brizindine endorsement, sent his story as a pamphlet to 900,000 New Zealand homes — in other words, every home in the country. In fact, at the inquiry, no one in management at Air New Zealand ever knew anything about a pamphlet with Brizindine's account of his flight.

Grundy could also have been asked about an article by Christchurch Suburban Newspapers reporter Sue Neale, who was on her own Antarctic flight. She wrote of the staggering Antarctic sights. 'The aircraft cruised then at 12,000 ft, below the height of that Erebus monster, and it was indeed an amazing sight to see passengers on the floor, cocking their cameras at strange angles to cavture [sic] the close-up views of the snowy mass.'

Grundy was asked about an article by a Mr McGregor published in Auckland's *Central Leader* and later in the *Western Leader* in which he described a flight round Antarctica on 7 November 1978 at 2000 feet. No, Grundy had not seen it.

Then counsel for ALPA, Paul Davison, spoke up. He, too, was interested in that flight. It was commanded by Captain Ross McWilliams. Was Captain Grundy aware that a passenger on Captain McWilliams's flight was Air New Zealand's then Director of Flight Operations, Captain Doug Keesing, and that Captain Keesing had been quite happy about flying at 2000 feet? No, Grundy had heard nothing about that and Keesing had never said anything. The denials were becoming absurd.

Then he was asked, 'Would it be a difficult matter for a captain with the experience of Captain Keesing to determine at any stage whether the aircraft in which he was travelling was flying at 2000 as opposed to 6000 feet? Is that a difficult judgement?'

Grundy: 'If he was on the flight deck it would be very easy. Looking outside a passenger window, not as easy. Height estimation viewed from the cabin in the vastness of Antarctica would be considered to be difficult.'[7] In other words, it depended what window he was looking out of. Mahon knew this was ridiculous.

What's more, the entire so-called 16,000/6000 feet altitude stipulations seemed to have been continually violated with no one expressing any concern. When they were publicised, no action was taken. Yet, in the end, as far as Grundy was concerned, there would have been no accident if his friend had not dropped well below 16,000 feet on approach to Ross Island.

But, at the same time, Grundy also praised highly the flying skills of every one of the three operating crew on the fatal flight. He spoke of them, says Mahon, reverentially.[8] Again Mahon was wondering how to balance that apparently foolish act of descending way below the stipulated 16,000 feet and flying towards an area of bad weather against what were so widely attested to be the cautious and masterly flying skills of Captain Jim Collins.

Nevertheless, Peter Grundy made one significant concession. Mahon asked him if Captain Collins might have plotted his course on a topographical map he could have acquired. Grundy agreed to the possibility. Well then, asked Mahon, could Captain Grundy consider this hypothesis? If Collins had plotted the computer track he had been given at his briefing, he would have seen that his destination waypoint was right at the head of McMurdo Sound, still some 30 miles from McMurdo Station over on the left. And if this were the case and if Captain Collins kept the aircraft navigation system in nav mode, that is to say, on the course directed by the computerised flight plan, then he could at all times be confident that he was flying right up the middle of McMurdo Sound. That being the case, Captain Collins could be sure that as he passed Ross Island that Erebus was well out of the way to his left, about 30 miles well out of the way. Captain Grundy agreed with Mahon.

But, said Mahon to Grundy, 'if that hypothesis were correct, and the computer track had been changed a matter of hours before the departure of the aircraft, then would not that be the major originating cause of the disaster?'

Grundy replied, 'On that hypothesis, I would have to agree.'[9]

And there it was. A week into the hearing, Mahon had the guts of it. The causation. It was very, very simple. It was a major concession from Peter Grundy and Mahon said that he observed a great ruffling of feathers amongst the management team at the Air New Zealand table as Grundy made it.

But there remained the altitude question, though this was not looking too secure for Air New Zealand after the newspaper articles had been produced in evidence, and there remained the question of why a man flew a jet airliner at 1500 feet into cloud with a mountain higher than Mount Cook in his way.

But Mahon would get no concession from the next Air New Zealand witness.

Captain Ian Harding Gemmell held the title Flight Manager, Technical. He had been recently promoted. He was the architect of the Antarctic flights. Gemmell's career was on the line. He could also be in trouble legally if anything other than pilot error were found to have caused the disaster. The Antarctic flights were Gemmell's babies.

Sam Mahon, in *My Father's Shadow*, in one of his reading-his-father-between-the-lines moments, tells us his father wanted us to 'take note of this character with special reference to his previous observation that someone was modifying the company's evidence'. In *Verdict On Erebus*, Mahon starts the Gemmell chapter thus:

> I had heard something of Captain Gemmell before he gave evidence. He was one of the most senior members of Flight Operations Division and one of the most dominant figures in the airline. He was said to be a close friend of Mr Davis. I knew that he had been the airline's accident investigator and had accompanied the first party of officials to the scene of the accident. He was said to have been the principal adviser — perhaps the only adviser — to the Chief Inspector in relation to the technicalities of jet flight and of the inertial navigation system. He had accompanied the Chief Inspector when he visited the McDonnell-Douglas Corporation in California in the course of his inquiries.[10]

In other words, getting between the lines, Gemmell was too clever by half and as a senior staffer at Air New Zealand — the principal interested party in all of this — far too close to the interdepartmental inquiry of Ron Chippindale. In other words, immediately the aircraft wreck was sighted, Gemmell was at Chippindale's side. And that was where he stayed. Mahon spent a great deal of this chapter observing Gemmell and while he admired his simplicity and the raw nerve with which he held to his story, he did not warm to him.

Paul Davison QC told me Gemmell was a 'stern, authoritarian figure within Air New Zealand'. 'Imperious' is a word Davison used in our conversation.

Gemmell explained to Mahon the long history of the Antarctic flights going back to 1969 when they were first talked about. In January 1977, with the DC-10 rated suitable, Air New Zealand applied to Civil Aviation for permission to conduct two flights to Antarctica the following month. Civil Aviation had insisted the captain of each flight make at least one supervised flight to the ice before assuming a command of an Antarctic flight. Captain Gemmell even seemed to have agreed minimum safe altitudes with Civil Aviation. There was an agreement to fly over Erebus at 16,000 feet — with 6000 feet overhead McMurdo added later — though only the first two flights ever flew over Erebus.

Gemmell commanded the first flight to McMurdo. He maintained, he said, 16,000 feet over Erebus and overhead McMurdo, circled round for 40 minutes or so and then, still maintaining flight level 160, headed up the Victoria Land coast, climbed to the cruise and returned to Christchurch — with a couple of nice low passes over Invercargill and Dunedin, so one of his passengers tells me.

The trouble with 16,000 feet, of course, was that passengers saw nothing but great expanses of ice and no detail. You do not fly passengers at 16,000 on a sightseeing flight. Mahon realised that an altitude of 16,000 feet for a sightseeing trip was pointless. There were no good photos at 16,000 feet. And it seems, Mahon tells us, that these reservations reached the Flight Operations Division, because Gemmell then went back to Civil Aviation and asked to be able to descend over McMurdo to 6000 feet.

Now the cross-examination started and the questions came thick and fast. But Gemmell was tough. Gemmell was not Grundy, which is why, Mahon observed, the airline called Grundy first. Again, thought Mahon, the old trial trick. Bring your nicest witness out first, make a nice impression on the jury.

Gemmell never flinched. He was 'unhesitating and positive'. He didn't use one word he didn't have to.

> When possible, his answers were monosyllabic and he seemed to treat the various counsel with thinly veiled contempt . . . His answers were given with almost military precision . . . Everything he said was clear and brief. If he considered a question repetitive, he did not hesitate to say so. After he was asked a question, he would immediately lean forward towards the microphone, pronounce his answer, then lean backwards and regain his former posture.[11]

Mahon looked at the man. He, the returned serviceman, reminded Mahon of someone. Then he realised who. Gemmell, with his 'bronzed, immobile aquiline features, and his close cut grey hair', seemed to Mahon to bear an uncanny resemblance to the World War Two German commander, Field Marshal von Manstein, a man Mahon described as the finest army commander of the twentieth century. Von Manstein was a brilliant and ruthless operator. He had to slow his advance on Leningrad because other German units could not keep up with him. He came close to relieving the Sixth Army, surrounded and dying at Stalingrad. Field Marshal von Manstein's daring plan to attack France in a fast and narrow corridor through the Ardennes is a matter of military legend.

He was sacked by Hitler in 1944 and after the war was sentenced by a court in Hamburg to 18 years' prison for the war crime of 'neglecting to protect civilian lives'. He did four years, came out, and became a military adviser to the West German government. There you go.

What Mahon was noting there, however, was the intelligence and perceived arrogance of a senior German commanding officer. Mahon knew he was up against it with Gemmell. As he was, it has to be said, with many of the senior Air New Zealand people. On several occasions Mahon noted their attitude to him. He said they spoke to him as if only they, not he, could understand the intricacies of navigation and the operation of a large jet airliner.[12] On one occasion he complained that they spoke to him as if he were obliged by law to believe them.[13]

Gemmell was asked about the wisdom of programming a jet airliner full of people 2000 feet over an active volcano. Mahon was ahead of his time in his concerns about this. This was two years before all four engines of the British Airways 747 failed on a night flight from Singapore to Melbourne in 1982 when they became clogged with volcanic ash from a Javanese volcano. The aircraft's radar didn't see the volcanic cloud because the ash was dry and the aircraft's weather radar was designed to detect moisture.

The first Air New Zealand flight track took the DC-10s just to the east of the mountain peak with 3000 feet of clearance. That's where the winds swept most of the volcano's emissions. Mahon thought it an odd thing that you would expose an aircraft to such danger.

No worries there, said Gemmell. If the mountain were erupting, he was sure the airline would receive adequate notice it was happening. Why, Gemmell was asked, did the airline not use the military track up the centre of McMurdo Sound. This might have been better scenically, and it was obviously safer because American radar could pick the aircraft up 40 miles out and guide it in if need be.

No, said Captain Gemmell. The scenic advantages were negligible. And really, it was better to fly directly from Cape Hallett to McMurdo Station in order to fly over the NDB, the non-directional beacon, in order to check the accuracy of the aircraft's inertial navigation system. This was nonsense, of course. Pilots could just as easily fly up to the head of McMurdo Sound, turn left and fly straight over the NDB and do the same checks. The beacon didn't care which direction you came from.

In any case, the checks were academic. Everyone knew that the AINS was brilliantly accurate and if you could see McMurdo Station below you, then, well, McMurdo Station was below you. What was the problem? There was no other town for thousands of kilometres so it had to be McMurdo Station. Well, said Gemmell, going up the Sound would have used too much fuel. Never mind that all of the 1978 and 1979 flights had done exactly this with safety, success and very happy passengers. Mahon got his ruler out and did some arithmetic. Mahon was a thorough barrister. He worked things out and did the numbers himself. Gemmell's concerns about fuel were silly.

And what about whiteout? Chippindale had described the kind of whiteout relevant to this accident in his report. This was the pernicious whiteout that causes so many accidents in polar regions, 'solid, pale low overcast coupled with white forward terrain, and the consequent inability to perceive that the apparently flat terrain is in fact rising'.[14] The problem is made worse if the sun is low behind you, as it was about the time of day Jim

Collins's DC-10 arrived at Lewis Bay, Erebus ahead of him.

But Gemmell seemed only to think of whiteout as cloud.[15] In fact, Gemmell had to know about whiteout but he wasn't about to tell Mahon. What he said was that he didn't tell the pilots about whiteout because that would have encouraged them to go below the minimum safe altitudes and they were sacrosanct. What was he saying? Were they children?

Look, in the end, if Jim Collins had stayed at the MSA of 16,000 feet north of Mount Erebus there would have been no whiteout problem and this accident would never have happened.

Months later, in a second appearance at the Royal Commission, Gemmell continued to assert the Chippindale line that the crew were uncertain of their position, that they were trying to 'establish their position'. Mahon simply refused to wear this.

> How could the crew ever have been 'uncertain' as to where they were without one single word on that topic having been exchanged between the pilot in command and the co-pilot? That was the single question. And of course, it was the stumbling block against which the Chief Pilot's theory and the Chief Inspector's theory inevitably had to collapse.[16]

There was one final area counsel were curious about. Why had he, Captain Gemmell, requested and got the dispensation from Civil Aviation to do away with the requirement that no Air New Zealand pilot should captain an aircraft to Antarctica without having first undergone one flight under supervision? The US Navy, the USAF, the RAAF and the RNZAF each insisted upon three initial flights under supervision. Well, it wasn't necessary, said Captain Gemmell, without hesitation. A previous flight over the area wasn't necessary because of the quality of the briefing the Air New Zealand pilots received prior to departure.

Mahon said, however, that at that stage he thought Gemmell might be right about a full briefing in advance of a polar flight being sufficient to keep a pilot safe. It was not until he went to Antarctica himself later on that he saw how wrong Gemmell was. 'There was simply no substitute for having flown in the area before.'[17]

Shrewdly, Gemmell was asked by one of the counsel at the hearing if the Americans had been advised that the Air New Zealand flight plan took the

DC-10s overhead Erebus. Such a flight plan meant that the big DC-10s did not appear on radar until they were 20 miles away, and were the Americans happy to provide radar assistance overhead McMurdo for the aircraft to descend to 6000 feet through cloud? No, the American Navy had been given no formal notice.[18]

In fact, the Americans were later adamant that the Erebus flight plan was bizarre. In an affidavit sworn at the Naval Air Station at Memphis, Tennessee on 10 December 1980, Chief Warrant Officer Priest, the chief air traffic controller at McMurdo at the time the DC-10 crashed, said:

> We were not aware at the time, of the sector within which the Air New Zealand DC-10 flights were said to be required to fly. This required sector . . . would in my opinion have been absurd. Any radar controls . . . for the purposes of assisting in descent maneuvers [sic] would have been virtually impossible since Ice Tower radar does not function above thirty degrees . . . there could be no adequate ground-based control should it have been required . . . I would have regarded such a plan as extremely ill advised . . .

Priest went on to state that if the US Navy had been asked to comment on a flight path overhead Mount Erebus, 'we would have nonconcurred'.

In other words, MacCentre could not assist with the bizarre tight spiral let-down through cloud over McMurdo that Air New Zealand was telling its pilots they could perform, as long as the cloud base was not lower than 7000 feet. The radar was set to monitor American traffic at too low an angle. It couldn't handle aircraft popping over the top of Erebus at 16,000 feet and wanting to come to 6000 feet through cloud without losing contact with its own aircraft. What the pilots were being told was nonsense. In fact no Air New Zealand DC-10 ever descended this way.

And finally, David Baragwanath, counsel assisting the Commission, put to the chief pilot the same published articles Captain Grundy had been presented with. No, the chief pilot had never seen any of these accounts before and had heard nothing of them. 'He said he had never heard, prior to the disaster, of any Air New Zealand DC-10 descending below 6000 feet in the McMurdo area.'[19]

Paul Davison made an astute observation to me. Gemmell, he said, 'was the architect of the flights, [in charge of] the operational requirements of the Antarctic flights and therefore if there was a failure in the operation structure . . . he was the person who was going to be looked at. And he took a very offensive [attacking] position.

'I think the most remarkable thing about this investigation — this really relates to Chippindale — we have an accident and we don't know why it has occurred and what do we do? We allow people who have vested interests to clamber all over the scene. Compare that to a crime scene conducted by the police. Do they let people who are close to the events walk all round it, take things away or conduct the investigation on the police's behalf? I mean, it's bizarre. And yet that's what happened with Air New Zealand having Ian Gemmell seconded to assisting Chippindale.'

In fact, Air New Zealand controlled Chippindale's inquiry. Brilliantly.

And then Gemmell was gone. He would be back much later, as we've seen, in December, when the inquiry was much older and the Chippindale findings had been obliterated. But he had his story and he was sticking to it. He had to.

But nevertheless, if there had been a deliberate or mistaken change — whichever it was — in the flight path so that it followed the centre of McMurdo Sound to McMurdo Base, and an acceptance of this in the middle of 1978, then given that Gemmell was the overseer of the Antarctic flights, then it takes no great leap of faith to believe that he must have known about it.

No one had touched him. No one landed a punch. No one hurt him. He never deviated from his course: the Air New Zealand flight planning was in all ways 'impeccable'.[20] Mahon says Gemmell went straight to the back of the courtroom each day and sat with the Air New Zealand counsel. 'Whereas at one time Captain Gemmell had been technical adviser to the Chief Inspector, he was now the technical adviser to the airline counsel.'[21] And he sat there with counsel day after day, except when he was off in Australia completing a conversion course to fly 747s, which Air New Zealand was acquiring and which might be less the bad luck bitch that the poor old DC-10 had turned out to be.

Then, as the weeks went by, one after another they came forward, the senior pilots, those Mahon called the executive pilots, the senior company men, management men, men who mixed their flying responsibilities with administrative duties, ambitious men. Every single one of them denied knowing anything about flights below 16,000 feet on approach to McMurdo or below 6000 feet around McMurdo and south off Ross Island.

What's more they remained, to a man, emphatic that no authority to descend below 16,000 feet and 6000 feet had ever been given. This had all been agreed in writing between Air New Zealand and Civil Aviation. It was open and shut.

But two witnesses would soon tear the entire airline case about minimum altitudes apart. The fact was that, in practice, those minimum altitudes simply did not exist. Especially after the sixth flight, when the flight plan was changed to avoid the madness of overflying Mount Erebus, an active volcano, before the plane would wind down in a weird spiral descent above Williams Field through cloud with radar assistance that would never be available.

After which, actually, when it broke out of the cloud, it might well be in whiteout.

15

Captain Keesing Shows Up

He who does not feel his friends to be the world to him, does not deserve that the world should hear of him.

— Johann Wolfgang von Goethe

One morning Captain Arthur Cooper, the ALPA representative, was sitting at the Royal Commission waiting for proceedings to start. Arthur by now was becoming the captain of record for the other pilots in terms of what was going on at the Royal Commission. The company was letting Arthur Cooper attend the Royal Commission through the week and then on Friday afternoons, in order to let him keep his flying hand in, they rostered him to take a DC-10 full of passengers to Tahiti and to bring the flight back on Sundays.

When Arthur ran into other pilots at the airport, or at Air New Zealand House or at Flight Despatch, they all wanted to know what was going on. Arthur told me that when he explained what seemed to have happened was that Jim was fooled by a combination of the flight plan being changed, not being told, and polar whiteout, the pilots to a man would say, 'Well, Arthur, if that caught Jim Collins, it would have caught me.'

So Arthur had taken his seat waiting for the hearings to start when he noticed his old boss Captain Doug Keesing about to take the stand. Arthur wondered what was going on and what Doug Keesing was doing there. Captain Keesing had been, until early 1979, Flight Operations Director (International) of Air New Zealand. And he had been involved with the negotiations with Civil Aviation regarding the Antarctic flights. Keesing was old school. Keesing joined the RNZAF in 1943 and every cell in his body was aviation.

In April 1979, Captain Keesing retired and spent the rest of the year as a consultant to Air New Zealand. He told the inquiry that since the accident no one from Air New Zealand had asked his opinion as to the cause of it. He seemed, in his last year, to have been treated rather shabbily and given nothing to do, with Gemmell pushing him out.

But Captain Keesing had featured in one of the many articles published about the Antarctic flights. In the 30 November 1978 edition of the airline's in-house magazine, *Air New Zealand News*, he — 'the boss' — is described as having a great time cruising past Mount Erebus at 2000 feet, in dire contravention, apparently, of his own flight rules on a flight commanded by Captain Ross McWilliams. Yes, he had seen the article and what's more he said, he had approved it as accurate and fit for publication.

Since the end of 1979, Doug Keesing had been working for Polynesian Airlines in Western Samoa. He had not been keeping tabs on what was being said at the Royal Commission until someone told him he had been mentioned as having condoned low flying in breach of the MSA. What's more, he'd got hold of a copy of the Chippindale Report and he thought there were a few things the Royal Commission should be told. So he climbed on an aircraft to Auckland and went to see counsel assisting the commission. And, says Mahon, 'Captain Keesing had a curious tale to tell'.[1]

Doug Keesing produced much correspondence between himself and Civil Aviation. In January 1977 he wrote to the Director of Civil Aviation requesting a flight route from Auckland to McMurdo returning to Christchurch. Keesing made it clear in the letter he imagined some low altitude flying round McMurdo. No altitude was specified.

Then he wrote to Civil Aviation on 2 February 1977 with a specific outline of sightseeing altitudes. He proposed flying at 2000 feet terrain clearance, which is the regulatory altitude with mountain flying, the altitude chosen to be at the captain's discretion. There never seemed to be a formal reply to this and the first flight took off under the command of Captain Gemmell, on 15 February 1977, with a Civil Aviation inspector on board.

It wasn't until the Royal Commission that he read there had been some correspondence between Gemmell and Civil Aviation whilst he, Keesing, was still the head of Flight Operations. A letter signed by Gemmell asked for a special descent to 6000 feet over McMurdo and noted that Air New Zealand had already imposed a restriction of 16,000 feet everywhere else. Keesing told Mahon this was the first time Gemmell had altered conditions that he, Keesing, had settled with Civil Aviation. Gemmell had done this without the approval of Keesing, his superior, and without telling Keesing. In other words, he had done it unilaterally behind his boss's very experienced back. Keesing had no idea, even upon his retirement from the airline in April 1979, that there were anything more than the standard regulatory altitude restrictions for the flights to Antarctica.

Keesing, an aviator of vast experience, thought he had made a perfectly sensible arrangement with Civil Aviation based on the normal mountain flying regulations. Then one of his subordinates had come along and made 'some other arrangement involving a minimum safe altitude of 16,000 feet, and in certain conditions, 6000 feet'.[2]

No one ever found the answer to why Ian Gemmell made his own arrangement with Civil Aviation only a couple of weeks after his boss had made his. 'The answer to this enigma was never given,' says Mahon.[3]

Keesing's evidence showed that the airline's planning of flights to Antarctica was a mess. There had been, said Mahon, 'the most consummate confusion in the planning by Air New Zealand and Civil Aviation over the altitude factors which should control the Antarctic flights'.[4]

The result of it all was to show that if there ever had been formally decided MSAs of 16,000 feet and 6000 feet, there was no clear correspondence to show that such an agreement had been formalised.

As for the flight at 2000 feet written about in the *Air New Zealand News*, Keesing was clear he had given permission for the article to be published and he declared it to be accurate. 'Therefore,' said Captain Keesing, 'his own experience on that flight had merely confirmed that the aircraft was being operated in accordance with requirements imposed by himself and Civil Aviation.'[5]

As for Captain Collins, Keesing was effusive in his praise of 'the meticulous care with which Captain Collins had always carried out his duties'. If Captain Collins had flown his DC-10 into a mountain in broad daylight, something was very badly wrong. Captain Keesing believed it 'probable' that if Captain Collins thought that the flight plan his crew inserted into the inertial navigation system was taking them right down the middle of McMurdo Sound 'that at the point of impact Captain Collins thought they were in fact over pack ice with flat areas on each side running for many miles'.[6]

It was a shrewd assessment. Keesing was ruthlessly telling the Royal

Commissioner the cause of the accident — obvious to Keesing — right there in front of senior Air New Zealand people who had schemed behind his back.

Mahon liked Keesing. His evidence was 'clear and concise'. He comes off Mahon's pages as decent. And I suppose, by that time, Mahon appreciated the novelty of a precise memory.

Arthur Cooper watched his old boss with admiration. Keesing was frightened of no one. As he left the stand he was obliged to walk past Arthur. Arthur said quietly, with a grin, 'That was very impressive, DK.'

Equally quietly, Keesing replied, 'They're not going to fuck my boys over, Arthur.'

So that was Keesing. He was there. He lashed the room like an ace high diamond flush and was gone.

So altitude increasingly seemed not to be set in stone on these flights, as Air New Zealand and Civil Aviation and the Chief Inspector all emphatically — and together — asserted. But what ultimately destroyed altitude as an Air New Zealand defence, and as a tool to be used against the dead pilots, was the evidence of Captain J. P. 'Johnny' Wilson, one of the two officers who briefed Collins and Cassin in the Route Clearance Unit (RCU) three weeks before their flight.

Again with Mahon, we have to read between the lines. The first thing he tells us about Wilson is that he had flown for the RNZAF in the Pacific theatre in World War Two. He was awarded the Air Force Cross. It is awarded to junior officers for courage and devotion to duty while flying on operations not in contact with the enemy. The Air Force Cross was a very good medal. To Mahon it meant a lot, and that is why he tells us all of this before discussing the evidence of Captain J. P. Wilson in *Verdict on Erebus*.

Captain Wilson had flown nearly every route in the world for various airlines. Gordon Vette describes him as 'a lean, alert man with the command captain's knack of engaging attention'.[7] Unfortunately, of the many routes John Wilson had flown, Antarctica was not one of them.

Wilson and Captain Ross Johnson briefed Jim Collins and Greg Cassin on 9 November 1979, some three weeks before their Antarctic flight. Also at the briefing were Captain Simpson, First Officer Gabriel and First Officer Irvine. Irvine would make captain by the time of the Royal Commission. The airline was short of one.

Wilson presented a lengthy brief of evidence. He said he told the pilots that 'I'm sure it goes without saying, but during this phase of the operation at least one pilot must be nominated to monitor the instruments as all eyes outside enjoying the view is a very big temptation and a dangerous practice. What I'm trying to get across is: "Have someone minding the shop".'[8]

If that statement is true, and if indeed Wilson, a former DC-10 captain himself, said that, then it was a peculiar thing to say to DC-10 crews. You might give that advice to a 19-year-old with 150 hours who was about to fly into difficult territory. But Wilson was briefing DC-10 pilots, men with many thousands of hours of flying. He was not talking to low-timers. This is not something a DC-10 captain would say to a DC-10 captain. Captain Les Simpson, who was at the same briefing, would later say, 'I certainly cannot remember Captain Wilson warning us to ensure that one pilot be nominated to monitor instruments. This sort of comment would be entirely unnecessary for professional pilots.'[9]

If Wilson had not flown to Antarctica, it was not his fault. He had applied time and again to go on an Antarctic flight. Finally, two days before his briefing to Collins, his request had been granted but Captain Wilson's flight was the only one so far that failed to get to McMurdo. Bad weather had the crew divert to the alternative route, which was always the South Magnetic Pole. So despite his best attempts, Johnny Wilson had never made it to McMurdo.

Wilson went through his briefing. The court was transfixed. Mahon noticed the news media was wholly attentive. What had the accident crew been told? And where did the crew think they were going to fly? Down the centre of McMurdo Sound before turning left under guidance from McMurdo Control or directly overhead Erebus?

Then, Wilson pulled out a chart at the briefing. He said, 'I said you are coming from Cape Hallett over Erebus to McMurdo. At that point I was using my pen and running it down the page.'[10] This was devastating to the case of the dead crew.

Captain Wilson said he got for the crews copies of the computer flight plan of his own flight two days before. This was, of course, a flight plan showing the latitude and longitude coordinates of the route down the centre of McMurdo Sound, not over Erebus at all. He placed the four copies on the tables in front of the pilots and left them there for some considerable time. In the end, he said, he picked up the flight plans and took them with him.

But Captain Wilson was emphatic. The crews knew that the route took them over Erebus, and the MSA was 16,000 feet until you passed overhead Mount Erebus and then you could drop down to 6000 feet over McMurdo Station.

But the crew were shown the 7 November McMurdo Sound flight plan — with the destination waypoint right at the head of McMurdo Sound. There seems little doubt that the thorough and industrious Jim Collins had a good look at the flight plan in front of him and took one home with him. He may have made notes about the last couple of waypoints in the small black ring binder he carried with him and in which he made notes, the same ring binder that would be found by Greg Gilpin and Stu Leighton in perfect condition near the smashed flight deck on the mountain weeks later. It was the obvious thing for an inveterate note taker to do.

Either way, being a very experienced airline pilot and being a trained navigator himself, as was Simpson, the other captain at the briefing, he would have noted the latitude and longitude of the final waypoint in relation to the previous waypoint. In fact, as Captain Gabriel would testify, the destination waypoint had been highlighted in some way. This would have given Collins an immediate idea of the track. And he would have noted the longitude of the final, or destination, waypoint, because this would have told him where he was going.

And these men can do this in their heads. Pilots at this level are trained to read navigation coordinates and picture where they're taking them. And the crucial 164 line of longitude would have been easy to see in the atlas Collins had with him because it ran straight over blue water down the centre of McMurdo Sound. With what Gordon Vette calls 'the natural caution of the airman', Collins and Simpson would have noticed immediately that the high ground, Erebus, was a good 40 kilometres away to the left — exactly where the mountain appeared to be in Captain Wilson's audio-visual presentation minutes before.

It seems clear Jim Collins did take one of the 7 November computer flight plans home with him and used it to plot his flight track on a chart. A few days after the accident Captain Dave Eden asked Captain Ross Gordon, Jim Collins's good friend who, with his wife Marg, was helping Maria cope with everything in those first days, to have a look through the flying documents at Maria's house.

Ross Gordon was told by Captain Eden that Jim Collins had taken a copy of the flight plan with him when he left the briefing on 9 November.[11]

There was, however, no flight plan to be found at the Collins home. It is a fairly safe assumption to make that Jim Collins, tidy, methodical Jim, would have replaced his copy in his black flight bag in the absence of a better place to put it. Why would he not?

Captain Johnson handed in his briefing documents to the Air New Zealand investigating committee set up in the days after the crash to compile — and destroy — airline documents on the Antarctic flights. These were never seen again. And First Officer Cassin's Antarctic documents and briefing notes, which he had forgotten to take with him on the flight, were acquired by Captain Bruce Crosbie the day after the flight when he went to the Cassin home. Anne Cassin's brother-in-law simply handed them over upon request. They, too, were never seen again.

So directly overhead Erebus it was. Wilson was adamant. That's what those crews had been told the day of the briefing.

But something inflammatory, something mighty, a seismic upheaval, was about to shake the Royal Commission. As Captain Wilson rambled on with his brief of evidence in his engaging way, every now and then he would go off the written brief to emphasise how much he and Captain Johnson had insisted the crews were to fly directly overhead Erebus. The news media were watching and listening intently.

But Mahon had noticed something, though its importance was not yet apparent. The last page and a half of evidence in Wilson's 35 pages of evidence had been typed with a different typewriter from the one that had typed the rest of it. Mahon had an impression of a last minute decision.

Suddenly the courtroom heard Wilson declare that he had become aware in 1978 that flights were descending beneath 6000 feet. His office was on the seventeenth floor of Air New Zealand House within the Flight Operations Division and that is where he heard comments to this effect, right inside the mother ship, right inside Flight Ops. He thought he had also read the story of Captain Keesing's day out at 2000 feet underneath Erebus. Wilson says he wasn't worried because he assumed the flights had taken place with the consent of McMurdo ATC. That was his belief. What's more, his own briefing materials appeared to imply to him, he said, that the airline had given permission to McMurdo ATC to bring the DC-10s down to whatever altitude they felt was safe or suitable.

What is more, Wilson went on, as the court listened, dead still, everyone present understanding the ramifications of this:

> I remember remarking in passing at some of my Antarctic briefings that I was aware that some flights had been below 6000 feet. I cannot recall at precisely which briefings I made the comment nor can I recall whether I made such a comment during the briefing of November 9, 1979 [Collins's briefing]. When I made such a comment to crews it was not with any tone of criticism for the reason I have just given, namely that I assumed it had been done with the prior authority of air traffic control at McMurdo.[12]

He said he believed the 6000-feet restriction had been laid down by McMurdo ATC and that McMurdo ATC had reserved 'the ability' to give consent to descent below 6000 feet. He said that all the descents below 6000 feet that he heard of had been effected with McMurdo ATC. Mahon said that under cross-examination Wilson made it clear that aircrews understood from this information that they could fly at whatever altitude McMurdo ATC gave them.[13]

At the same time, it emerged that, during conversations he had with Chippindale, Wilson had apparently never told him about telling the crews they could descend below 6000 feet if invited by McMurdo ATC.

It was a dramatic revelation. Suddenly, said Mahon, 'the airline's implacable and persistent "altitude defence" had now disintegrated'.[14] Wilson's admission was completely contrary to what the airline had been asserting at the Royal Commission for 10 long weeks. The entire Air New Zealand case and the entire Civil Aviation case, which Chippindale had bought into, was that Jim Collins was too low, that he had descended below 16,000 feet and 6000 feet in violation of clearly stipulated altitude minimums.

Chippindale knew that Collins had been invited down to 1500 feet by a relaxed McMurdo controller — it was in the cockpit voice transcript — but he gave no weight to the clearance at all. Collins would have had faith in McMurdo's call because McMurdo told him visibility was 40 miles in all directions.

The entire Chippindale case was predicated on Collins having flagrantly abused the Air New Zealand altitude restrictions as if this, said Mahon in his report, 'obliterated each and every error that might have previously been made by the airline or by Civil Aviation Division. But as from the time of Captain Wilson's admission, the MSA defence, if I may call it that, could not prevail against Captain Collins.'[15]

That was that. Mahon went on in his report to say, 'When Captain Collins decided to descend to 1500 feet in VMC conditions, with the specific authority of McMurdo Air Traffic Control, he was in fact acting in accordance with the authority given to him at his RCU briefing. . . This allegation of pilot error must accordingly fail.'[16]

Mahon now said he believed the airline insistence that Collins had breached regulations was worthless.

And now, at the Royal Commission, Chippindale's report ceased to matter. It, too, was worthless. Chippindale had accepted hearsay altitude evidence, probably provided by his technical adviser from Air New Zealand, Captain Ian Gemmell, and was prepared to assert that Collins was bound by two MSAs, 16,000 feet and 6000 feet. He was wrong. Collins was not.

Chippindale had apparently accepted a senior company man's word and the man had not been straight with him. Air New Zealand had not told Chippindale 'of the authority given to aircrews by Air New Zealand to operate into McMurdo [Sound] at whatever altitude was suggested by American Air Traffic Control'.[17]

It was another instance in which Chippindale should have used his statutory power to take written statements under oath from people he was interviewing. If he had done so, Captain Wilson might have come clean earlier. It was certainly a further example of the dubious and gullible investigative skills of Ron Chippindale. Mahon had no respect for dull, incompetent investigation. He is very strict about this in his foreword to Gordon Vette's book *Impact Erebus*, in which Gordon Vette, one of the several heroes of the entire Erebus affair, explains how he could simply not believe the findings of the Chief Inspector of Air Accidents that the pilots were to blame and that the findings did not make any sense at all.

Mahon regarded Vette as a superior investigator. He wrote:

> There are two golden rules for an investigator, and they become well-known to people like trial lawyers and police officers who spend most of their time inquiring into the disputed facts of accidents and crimes. The first is, eliminate the impossible. If something could not have occurred, however attractive its possibility may be, then forget it. The second rule is, and it applies especially to judges along with lawyers and police officers, do not enter upon any inquiry with a pre-conceived

> view. Find out all the facts first, and then construct your conclusion. In my time as a trial lawyer I investigated many accidents and occurrences of which a great number, if I may say so, were far more complicated than the Mt Erebus inquiry, and I came to respect these two fundamental rules more and more as the years went by.[18]

And with the collapse of the 16,000-feet evidence Mahon realised something else. How were passengers supposed to sightsee from 16,000 feet, anyway? It was a foolish proposition. How were they expected to get even halfway decent photographs from 16,000 feet or even 6000 feet for that matter? They were sightseeing trips, for heaven's sake. Surely, said Mahon, you would need to be round 2000 feet to see with your average camera any significant detail of this historic place where Captain Scott's heart was broken, where the hopes of an empire were shattered in that brief but golden age of Antarctic heroism.

So what were 16,000 feet and 6000 feet, anyway? What did they ever actually mean to Antarctic aircrews? Did they ever exist as minimum safe altitudes? Certainly after the second flight, that of Captain Grundy, which might also have gone well below 16,000 feet, no one paid any attention to those altitudes. You flew down and you conducted the flight as you would approach any foreign port. You liaised with air traffic control, the people who knew the weather, the professionals who knew the area. You can tell from the cockpit voice recorder transcription of the fatal flight that there was an easy relationship between MacCentre and the Air New Zealand crews. What's more, Mahon had come to understand how much the flights overhead by the big roaring jet airliners had come to mean to the people on the ice. They wanted a nice view too. Whilst monitored by the American air traffic control there was no danger whatsoever from these altitudes.

I spent a great deal of time in my research for this book trying to figure out when exactly the 16,000 feet and the 6000 feet altitudes appeared and became important. The answer, I came to realise, is after the crash. The fact is that after the abandonment of the insane planned route over the active volcano by design or by accident, crews knew they were approaching McMurdo Base and Scott Base straight up the safety of the flat sea ice. They were briefed that they could do whatever McMurdo ATC invited them to do. When they got to the top of the Sound at West Dailey Island, they turned an easy left and Bob's your uncle, there was McMurdo Station 30 miles in front of you.

Jim Collins, during his descending orbits, could see the 'ground', meaning the sea and the coasts, at all times.

Yes, there was that bizarre, confusing and indefinite correspondence between Keesing and Gemmell and Johnson and Civil Aviation in 1977, but it established nothing. What it provided, though, was just enough evidence to try to hang a case on, in the desperate situation the airline had blundered into so catastrophically — just enough evidence to confuse and to cast more than a doubt in the mind of a layperson about the performance of Captain Jim Collins that fateful day.

The balance of power at the inquiry had now changed dramatically. The ballast had been thrown to the other side of the ship in the developing storm. There was venom and hostility in the courtroom now. Things were turning nasty. The cover-up was being torn apart by a storm of new revelation.

The Air Line Pilots' Association, represented by Alister MacAlister and the brilliant, carefully researched and tactically savvy young barrister who would make his name at the Royal Commission, and who still had a lethal card to play, Paul Davison, now flooded the Commission with a succession of pilots describing what exactly they had been told at the Antarctic briefings. Naturally, Davison called the surviving pilots from the Collins briefing, Captain Simpson and First Officers Gabriel and Irvine.

For a start, not one of the line pilots agreed with Captain Wilson and Johnson that they had been told verbally they would be flying overhead Erebus. The computer track would take them down McMurdo Sound, right down the centre and Erebus would be away to the left of them. In fact, as we have noted, the audio-visual display actually showed Erebus way to the left of track.

But then enter Simpson, Gabriel and Irvine, who attended the 9 November briefing with Collins and Cassin and were alive to describe it, and had since flown to Antarctica themselves. Simpson went through what was told them with what Mahon describes as 'meticulous care . . . He was forthright, clear and quite unshakeable'.[19] Captain Simpson said he could recall no comments whatsoever that headed the aircraft over the summit of Erebus and he was positive that no remarks were made at the audio-visual briefing or at the simulator briefing about any flight directly overhead Erebus. What's more, if he thought he was being asked to take an aircraft full of passengers over the top of an active volcano, he would have 'objected immediately'.[20] And he made it clear that he could not believe what he was hearing regarding what comments were said to have been made about the flight plan at the briefing.

Simpson said he knew exactly where the flight path lay. He cast an eye over the flight plan coordinates of the flight that had taken off two days before the briefing and saw that it took him to a destination waypoint south and west of what the Americans call the Byrd Reporting Point to the head of McMurdo Sound, a few miles to the west of McMurdo Station. It took him straight down McMurdo Sound, which was the entirely predictable and safe place for the track to lie.[21]

Simpson was damaging badly the airline evidence as to the flight briefing. Lloyd Brown QC, for Air New Zealand, made the mistake of taking him on.

Brown: 'Captain Simpson, my instructions enable me to say to you that so far as my client company is concerned your integrity and veracity is [sic] beyond any question. For your part do you accept a similar position so far as Captains Ross Johnson and John Wilson are concerned?'

Simpson: 'Yes.'

Mahon: 'Does it matter what he thinks? It's what I think.'

Brown: 'And you would accept no doubt that there are areas where your recollection diverges from that of Captains Johnson and Wilson?'

Simpson: 'Yes.'

Brown: 'Would you accept that they and yours [sic] could be at fault in certain areas of personal recollection?'

Simpson: 'I make no claim to having an impeccable memory. I heard and saw the briefing once so I have had no other experience of a briefing to confuse my general recollection . . . Captain Wilson's evidence in general I have no great conflict with. It's just the extreme fine detail that he appears to have included for the Commission that I don't recall. In Captain Johnson's case, however, the description I heard in this court was so different to my recollection that I wondered if in fact I had attended the same briefing.'[22]

There was no gap whatsoever between the evidence of Simpson and that of Gabriel and Irvine. There was no suggestion whatsoever of a track over the volcano. The track lay down the centre of McMurdo Sound.

So the altitude violation contribution to causation of the destruction of Jim Collins's DC-10 had disintegrated. But the admission that pilots were told they could accept altitude invitations from McMurdo ATC had come in the tenth week of hearings from the twenty-fourth witness.

'No better illustration could be given of the implacable opposition of the airline management to any suggestion of organisational fault on its part. I could only wonder how it was that Captain Wilson had dared to brave the storm which now had arisen in consequence of this last minute addition to his evidence,' Mahon would later write.[23]

Wilson might have toed the party line under oath. But in the end, he did the right thing. He made a late decision about what he should say and he typed it up himself. He breached the dam. Mahon knew why. Captain Wilson had done something very courageous once, something that earned him the Air Force Cross. Now he had done something brave again.

Davison is not so generous.

'There was a lot of dialogue going on outside the Commission and the pilots were saying to some of their colleagues, "Listen, you come along to the Commission with some half-baked story and the lawyers are going to turn you upside down." The '78 pilots had their briefings in their papers. There was enormous pressure on someone like Wilson, who had given a statement to Chippindale initially, but by the time he came along to give evidence he knew that Jim Collins's defence team had all the paperwork, not Jim's, but paperwork we thought would be pretty much like it.'

In other words the briefing papers of the 1978 pilots, all of whom had been briefed to fly down McMurdo. 'So Mahon was right to give him some credit but he didn't tell the truth in my view,' says Davison. 'Wilson had a lot to be defensive about. He briefed the crew. He briefed the crew to fly down the Sound. End of story. He handed out a computer flight plan that had 164 [degrees east] on it. You know, just end of story.'

So now Mahon had a vast gulf in the evidence with regards to the briefing. Now he was going to have to decide whom he believed.

It went through Mahon's mind that the line pilots, the pilots called by counsel for ALPA, might simply be acting as loyal members of a union, sticking up for a dead mate who made a terrible mistake. Yet, the risks were high for them. Air New Zealand had plenty of pilots. Half the world wanted to fly DC-10s. Half the world wanted to live the glamorous and dashing life of the DC-10 pilot. The pilots' testimony was making their employer very angry. Mahon knew this.

So there was not a lot in it for the ALPA pilots to dump on the airline approach or to question so emphatically the testimony of the briefing pilots. There were, after all, not a lot of outfits round here that hired DC-10 pilots.

Shortly after Mahon's report was released to a conflagration of objection and outrage in April 1981, he received an amiable and most interesting letter which Margarita, Justice Mahon's wife, showed to me. It came from an Auckland lawyer with an old legal name of some prominence. The letter is dated 30 April 1981.

> Your Honour,
>
> I was on the first flight to Antarctica. That was a pretty jolly flight because all of us on board knew the whole thing was risky.
>
> Anyway, we were wined and dined in the DC-10, and shown a film we never saw the end of because icebergs came into sight long before we reached Antarctica, and all the blinds were put up.
>
> At some point in the middle of the ocean, still north of Antarctica, the Americans at McMurdo did a sort of countdown of seconds, for our pilot [Gemmell] to make a left hand turn. We were flying above cloud at about 33,000 feet, then we went down through the cloud, and nobody could see anything.
>
> . . . All of this 'count-down' had come over the PA system, and as we went down through the cloud we couldn't see anything, I thought about navigation quite seriously. I well remembered from youthful studies of Scott's expeditions in the Antarctic that Erebus was quite close to Ross Base [sic], also that it was about 13,000 feet, also that we were going down to about 9,000 feet, to get out of the cloud cover, though we couldn't see where we were as we went.
>
> When we did come out under the cloud, at about 9,000 feet, there was this huge mountain just off the right wing tip. It was damned close. But we had missed it. Then Gemmell did some extremely skilful figure of 8 turns beside the mountain then we flew lower to Ross Base [sic], did the same there and a couple of other excursions and set out for home.

The writer says he has eight reels of 'unspliced film' which he will put together someday.

In a descending aeroplane with cloud all round and nothing visible, one can only think, or hope, that the guys flying the thing, who can't see any more than I can, know what they are doing. Although the Antarctic trip was dangerous and all of us on board knew that, we also knew that modern navigation aids gave us a reasonable chance of getting home again.

. . . Your report is a delight to me. You got to the bottom of the whole thing, despite efforts to divert you. That must have been a hard, tiring, late night thing to do. Personally I am delighted you told the government that various witnesses had been flatly lying. They plainly were. I am glad to see that friends at the Bar brought this out, because it's the sort of thing we lawyers are supposed to do.

Now, the press and the politicians are 'fluffing about'. They find your findings too hard to accept. Well, I've had quite enough of dealing with politicians, in tax reform matters and so, privately, I'll say they are a pack of pricks. The Erebus disaster should never have happened.

I don't expect any reply. I just wish that somebody else would take some of that work off my desk.

Yours sincerely,
Bruce Grierson

Could it be that what the writer claimed about the altitude was true?

16

Mahon in Wonderland

Read the directions and directly you will be directed in the right direction.

— The Doorknob in *Alice in Wonderland*, Lewis Carroll

Q. So, in your view then, the phrase 'as the DC 10 cruised at 2000 ft past the Antarctic Mt Erebus', properly translated, means ' as the DC 10 cruised at 16,000 ft over Mt Erebus'?

A. I would have to assume that.

— Cross-examination of Captain Tony Lawson by David Baragwanath at the Royal Commission.

Now we come to the deliberate and fundamental error made by the New Zealand Chief Inspector of Air Accidents, Ron Chippindale, the deliberate misstatement of fact. Chippindale said that the late change in the coordinates of the flight plan without the crew's being told had no effect on the fate of Flight 901. It was an impossible conclusion.

At 2.16 in the morning of 28 November 1979, the day of Jim Collins's flight to the ice, the flight track to McMurdo Sound, the track upon which Jim Collins and Greg Cassin had been briefed by Captain Wilson, was changed. The pilots were not informed. Someone, somehow, forgot to tell Jim Collins. Given the flying patterns the Antarctic pilots had established, nice and low for sightseeing down the middle of McMurdo Sound before turning left for the final few miles to McMurdo Station and Scott Base, the change was disastrous.

Whichever two crew members performed the task of programming the flight plan into the navigation computer — a task, incidentally, that they performed correctly — they were, as Captain Gordon Vette would later write in *Impact Erebus*, programming the deaths of 257 people.

But the reader has to understand the big mistake that led to the bigger mistake that killed 257 people.

The original flight plan of 1977 took the aircraft slightly to the left of the summit of Erebus, directly from Cape Hallett to McMurdo Station. In mid-1978 the flight path changed. We never found out why. It was a safer route of course. Whether the change was deliberate or a mistake, we shall never know. In the hours before Jim Collins reported to Flight Despatch on 28 November 1979, it changed back to the original flight path.

What happened was very simple. We shall have to go a little more into complicated territory but we need not linger. There is no need. The reader should not be intimidated. This book is written for everyone in the room.

Men who did not want to reveal the truth of what happened, that is to say, the sheer ordinary incompetence of it, wanted us to believe it was complicated. It was to the benefit of these men to make us believe that it was a series of errors that could only be made by a superior race of men.

Ordinarily, on a scheduled route, an Air New Zealand flight crew received from Flight Despatch a cassette which contained the navigational coordinates for the track to their destination. The crew simply inserted the cassette and the computer read its information. It was foolproof.

But the Antarctic flights were considered non-scheduled, said Air New Zealand. So a flight plan was printed out on paper from the computer and given to the crew before each departure. There was no cassette. On it were also fuel weights that should be expected at each point along the journey. This enabled the crew to monitor their fuel to distance ratio, according to the obvious requirement that they make it safely back to Christchurch with an hour's fuel left in case Christchurch was fogged in.

The waypoints, or geographical positions, by which the DC-10 would make its way to Antarctica, were listed on the printed flight plan and it was these numbers of longitude and latitude that the crew punched manually into their onboard computer.

In mid-1978, Air New Zealand's information systems were moving into the computer age and all flight plans were to be entered into and stored within a ground computer. As in many firms at the time, when so many staff were intimidated by computers and resisted having anything to do with the baffling new machines, when it came to navigation, Air New Zealand had one man who embraced the computers and made himself indispensable with his command of them. He was the Chief Navigator, Brian Hewitt. So, in 1978 Brian Hewitt entered into Air New Zealand's ground computer the coordinates for the standard Antarctic flight plan. In doing so he made his first mistake of several.

The first mistake seems a small detail. It was not the mistake of the century. We can debate what that was. Hitler's invasion of Russia? Decca turning down the Beatles? The Great Leap Forward? Holmes going to Prime? (This small indulgence I hope the reader will forgive.)

It was no big deal. But it was a mistake nevertheless by Nav Section and a careless error for a Chief Navigator to make. Hewitt, instead of typing into the computer the coordinates of the McMurdo non-directional beacon (the NDB), typed in the original coordinates for Williams Field, the ice airfield at McMurdo Station. It was distance of a mile, nothing much.

The Williams Field coordinates had been the original McMurdo Station coordinates when the Antarctic flights began in early 1977. But in mid-1977, Captain Gemmell, the reader will recall, while subordinate to Captain Doug Keesing, the Director of Flight Operations, had begun his own insubordinate correspondence with Civil Aviation in order to establish a set of flight rules for the DC-10 overhead McMurdo Station. You could descend visually overhead McMurdo Station if the weather was fine — and on all but two of the Antarctic flights it was beautifully so — but Gemmell would always say, and he has never wavered on this, that he established a minimum safe altitude of 6000 feet for flight round McMurdo Station. As long as the cloud base was 7000 feet over McMurdo Station, then by using the NDB, the non-directional beacon, a pilot could descend by instruments in a tight spiral through the cloud, avoiding the high ground of Black Island and White Island just south of McMurdo Station. This descent was in the area of five major mountains. Of course, it meant flying under cloud, perfect conditions for whiteout to occur.

Air New Zealand's entire altitude evidence was bizarre and incongruous. Why did you have to maintain 6000 feet over the flat McMurdo Base area but maintain only a 2000-foot clearance over erupting Mount Erebus itself? Why did you have to maintain 16,000 feet down McMurdo Sound over flat sea ice? When you left, you climbed to 10,000 feet and you could fly at that altitude north along the coast of Victoria Land where the highest terrain was over 11,000 feet.[1]

Mahon believed, however, that every flight apart from the first two — Gemmell's and Grundy's — went to McMurdo Station well below the so-called minimum safe altitude of 16,000 feet. The 16,000 feet and 6000 feet altitudes 'had no relation whatever to the realities of sightseeing flights in Antarctica'.[2] The 16,000/6000 feet figures

> . . . continued to be the officially approved levels between Civil Aviation and the airline from February 1977 right to the date of the disaster. But in practice the airline disregarded those minimum altitudes and in my opinion were justified in doing so. . . . Contrary to what I think has been a public misconception over this altitude question, there was at no time on 28 November 1979 any unauthorised 'low flying' by the crew of TE901.[3]

In other words, Jim Collins was only doing what everyone else did and what the company condoned.

Anyway, as we've seen, for the aircraft to fly to the NDB, for the sake of Gemmell's IFR (instrument flight rules) descent, the coordinates Hewitt should have typed in were 77:51 degrees latitude south and 166:41 degrees longitude east. Instead, the coordinates he typed in were the old Williams Field coordinates of 77:53 south and 166:48 east. It was a small detail. It was two minutes of difference, less than two nautical miles from the NDB. The Chief Navigator had failed to notice that the coordinates had been changed from Williams Field to the NDB to enable Gemmell's bizarre idea of descent through cloud over McMurdo Station to 6000 feet and below.

As I say, not the mistake of the century, but one which would itself contribute in no small way to a frightful mistake being made later.

But in attempting to type in those mistaken coordinates the Chief Navigator made what the airline always insisted was another 'mistake', a mistake that would contribute so catastrophically to the disaster of November 1979. It was the mistake that made it two digits wrong out of five, an unbelievable mistake for a chief navigator programming the last leg of a flight to mountainous Antarctica.

Again, this is mid-1978. Instead of typing in 166:41 degrees east, the longitudinal coordinate for the McMurdo NDB, Hewitt typed in 164:48 degrees east. Despite his checks, he failed to notice the errors. This was a 2-degree navigational shift, 166 to 164 degrees longitude east.

What it did was send all of the 1978 aircraft and all of the 1979 aircraft before Captain Collins's flight, not to Williams Field or to the NDB but to West Dailey Island at the head of McMurdo Sound, some 30 miles to the west of McMurdo.

So when the aircraft rolled right at Cape Hallett on its destination leg to the south, it headed not towards the towering Mount Erebus just to the north of McMurdo Station and Scott Base but straight down the middle of McMurdo Sound.

A 'mistake', said the airline. A 'mistake'. But look at it. What a beautiful, fortuitous 'mistake'. Instead of flying over an active, erupting volcano belching steam constantly, eternally, thousands of feet into the air — both a dangerous and incomprehensible track — the aircraft would now track safely right up the middle of the flat sea and the flat sea ice of McMurdo Sound, the way the military boys did, well away from high ground, miles of empty sea on each side of the aircraft. Having reached the new destination waypoint at West Dailey Island, the captain would turn left and McMurdo was straight ahead on the nose. Easy. No worries.

It was such a wonderful mistake, of course, that the question was always asked whether 164 degrees was a mistake at all. Whether 164 degrees was a genuine mistake, or a deliberate course alteration, was one of the great debates at the Royal Commission. We will never know the truth.

There was a great deal of scepticism at the Royal Commission.[4] What luck to have a 'mistake' that now took the DC-10s right down the middle, not the right side or the left side of McMurdo Sound, but down the very middle, close to the same safe flight path used by most Antarctic aircrew to an easily identifiable turning point that enabled an approach to McMurdo Station from the west across to the east and a little to the south in a wide, gentle curve that allowed great viewing of Erebus out of the left side of the aircraft, after which, no doubt, the captain would turn and retrace the line to enable those on the right to take their photographs as well.

But Brian Hewitt was adamant under oath that he made a mistake. The Air New Zealand position was always unshakeable. It was a mistake. No Air New Zealand management witness would accept any other suggestion.

But the curious — and for Mahon, impossible — assertion was this.

None of the executive pilots and none of the navigation people said they ever knew about the 'mistake' before the fatal flight, even though 164 degrees longitude east had been the McMurdo destination waypoint for 14 months. None of them admitted knowing that since November 1978 all Antarctic flights — seven of them — had flown down the middle of McMurdo Sound before turning left to McMurdo and Scott Bases. No one in the airline's management knew about it at all, in all that time. The flight plan was over Erebus and that was that.

That is what the Royal Commission was asked to believe, that no one at Air New Zealand had noticed Brian Hewitt's finger trouble for over a year. Mahon thought it was a lack of knowledge that was incredible in the true meaning of the word. It involved the airline making far too many mistakes. The airline was too professional.

Why did the airline hang on so fiercely to their insistence that 164 degrees longitude east was a 'mistake'?

There was one fundamental reason.

The Air New Zealand position that the McMurdo Sound flight plan was a 'mistake' enabled the airline to justify the coordinate change in the early morning of 28 November 1979 as being a 'correction'. So that when, at the end of January 1980, a newspaper published a report that the coordinates for the Collins flight had been changed without the pilots being told and that other DC-10 pilots believed this had caused the crash,[5] Morrie Davis was able to the assert that the programmed coordinates had been 'correct'.[6]

It was wonderfully, ruthlessly, clever. The claim that the navigational coordinates for the flight were 'correct' went to the heart of the airline's defence. If the coordinates were 'correct' then the airline could not be blamed — it was pilot error. Jim Collins should have known there was a mountain in front of him if he had examined his coordinates. While the failure to inform the flight crew was most unfortunate, nevertheless — and here was the crunch — if Jim Collins had kept to the stipulated minimum safe altitudes and if he had been mindful that he was headed towards a mountain upon which he had been briefed, then he and his aircraft and passengers would have returned safely to Christchurch. That was the airline case.

To put it more brutally, if Collins had maintained 16,000 feet as he was told to, there would have been no accident, coordinate change or no coordinate change. It didn't matter. Altitude was the essence of the Air New Zealand case. It was the essence of Chippindale's approach — as it was Civil

Aviation's. It was the case Muldoon backed, and possibly even engineered. The navigational data on board the aircraft were correct. The pilot broke the rules on altitude, entertained some low flying in dodgy weather, ignored the mountain in front of him and flew into it, killing everyone. That would let everyone alive off the hook, because sure as night follows day, no one alive was going to take responsibility for the crash.

And yet it didn't make sense. The argument turned itself on its own head. If you were briefed that you were flying over Erebus, as the briefing officers said Collins was, why would you fly towards it at 1500 feet and fly into it?

One of the most bizarre moments at the inquiry, one of the most famous, involved the evidence of the Director of Civil Aviation, the rotund Captain E. T. Kippenberger, with the compulsory air force moustache. He knew about whiteout but was emphatic that whiteout was not a factor in this case.

But if whiteout was not a factor, then why did both pilots make the same 'gross visual error'?[7] Mahon wrote, 'He [the Director] suggested that each may have become afflicted by some mental or psychological defect which controlled their actions. This involved the startling proposition that a combination of physical and psychological malfunctions occurred simultaneously to each pilot.'[8] And to the other three on the flight deck, of course. Mahon was appalled that such a senior man as the Director could utter such nonsense.[9]

Why was the airline so intent on blaming the dead aircrew? As always, we must follow the money. If the pilots were proven to have caused the accident through their own negligence, the airline's insurers were protected in terms of the amount of damages for everyone on board by the Warsaw Convention — replaced in 1999 by the Montreal Convention — which would limit the airline's liability to $US42,000 per dead passenger. If the airline itself were proven to have been grossly negligent, however, then the claims for damages would be unlimited and would have filled the New Zealand courts for a long time. The costs to the airline and the country could have reached several hundred million dollars in compensation awards. Juries in courts, in the United States particularly, had been lavish in their awards against negligent airlines. It could well happen here. So the pilots had to be blamed. The airline could not be found to be culpable. The situation would be intolerable. Davis knew it. So, of course, did the Prime Minister and Finance Minister and sole shareholder in state-owned Air New Zealand, Robert Muldoon, who had a difficult election looming at the end of the following year.

As we have established, Alan Dorday and David Greenwood at Flight Despatch had already discovered the crucial 2-degree change in the Collins flight plan late in the evening on the day of the disaster. It struck them like thunder. They knew what it meant. That is why neither man told the air accident inspector Milton Wylie when he was there at Flight Despatch the night they made their discovery. Everyone in Flight Operations who knew of the coordinate change knew what it meant. This is why the information was kept so tight. That is why Dave Greenwood went into Air New Zealand House early next morning to inform Ian Gemmell before Gemmell went to the crash site.

The other reason Air New Zealand had to maintain that Hewitt's initial 1978 change of the longitude was a mistake was that, in making the original change, the airline had not informed or sought clearance to do so from Civil Aviation. Civil Aviation would have rubber stamped it, of course. That was one aspect of Air New Zealand's relationship with Civil Aviation that emerged during the hearing. What Air New Zealand wanted, Air New Zealand got.

Having said that, Civil Aviation had, at that point, no reason to doubt the competence of Flight Operations at Air New Zealand. McMurdo Sound was actually a sensible and much safer flight path and Civil Aviation would have been right to approve it. These were sightseeing trips after all.

However, Captain Arthur Cooper believes the change from 166 to 164 was genuinely a mistake. He believes it, simply because he knew Brian Hewitt, and Brian Hewitt, says Arthur, made mistakes.

'Brian was one of these guys who wanted to get respect. He's coming to the end of his time as a navigator and he wanted to have a position within the company. So he went after the job of Chief Navigator, which he got. Now Brian was not a very good navigator, he just wasn't. Navigators are a bit like golfers, sportsmen. Some are natural, just natural at it, and others, they're bloody hopeless. I mean, they get from A to B but it doesn't come easily to them. And he was one of those. He navigated for me on the Electras a few times and on DC-8s but I'd always keep an eye on him just because I didn't have that confidence in him. He was prone to making mistakes. And yet he was a senior guy at that stage.

'What I believe happened,' says Cooper, 'is that in the Navigation Section, with the introduction of the computer systems, he made himself an expert on that and he made himself indispensable so that when he finished flying they couldn't do without him. But to me, when he made the mistake of 166 to 164, I could quite believe it was Brian. And he'd set it up so that there was no cross-check of it. And the same again when they changed it back; there were no checking systems in the system they had.

'When he gave evidence it was quite clear to me that he knew exactly where the blame lay and who was responsible. He knew he was responsible. I felt very sorry for him because he knew he'd made that mistake, in fact two mistakes. And the second one [the "correction"], he didn't Notam [Notice to Airmen] it.'

Civil Aviation's contribution to the disaster was a very real one, however. In mid-1978 Air New Zealand simply did away with the original Civil Aviation requirement that no pilot should command a flight to the ice unless he had flown there at least once before under the supervision of an experienced Antarctic pilot. Remember that the US Navy, the RAAF and the RNZAF all insisted that even a senior command pilot make up to at least three trips to the ice under supervision before commanding their own flight, so weird, unusual and deceptive are the flying conditions in Antarctica. Jim Collins and Greg Cassin were fine, respected pilots, but neither had flown in Antarctica before.

Since the first two flights, Air New Zealand had simply failed to comply with this provision. In October 1979, it applied for an exemption. On 5 December 1979, a week after the Erebus disaster, Civil Aviation granted it. Civil Aviation decided that the airline's RCU briefing was of such quality that a pilot didn't need to fly to the ice first under supervision, never mind that no inspector from Civil Aviation had ever seen a complete RCU briefing. Mahon, however, decided that Civil Aviation, in failing to monitor 'the flight under supervision requirement' and in issuing this dispensation to Gemmell, contributed significantly to the disaster and had committed 'a serious breach of its duty'.[10] This was one area in which he agreed with Ron Chippindale. He believed in this area alone, Civil Aviation was up for millions in compensation claims.

In the entire world of aviation, the navigation section of an airline never changes the coordinates of an automated flight track without informing the pilot in command of the aircraft. Had Collins been so warned, he would most certainly have squared this change off on his topographical chart and have seen that the principal effect of the course alteration was to place some very high ground between Cape Hallett and McMurdo Base. Simple. In which case, he might still have chosen to avoid that cloud-covered high ground and dropped down early into the safety of McMurdo Sound in order to approach McMurdo visually over flat ground in clear air.

Retired DC-10 captain Arthur Cooper told me: 'It was simply inconceivable for a flight plan waypoint/reporting point to be changed without affected crew being notified and I would suggest that virtually 100 per cent of Air New Zealand line pilots at that time, i.e., not those required to represent the company line, would concur with that view. For Ron Chippindale to suggest that . . . Hewitt neglect[ing] to ops flash the change that he had made to the McMurdo coordinates was irrelevant/immaterial to the final outcome of the flight is quite plainly ludicrous.'

In the end, Mahon decided it didn't matter whether 166 degrees becoming 164 was a mistake or a deliberate change. But he was convinced that if it had been a mistake, then senior Flight Operations people must have noticed it and accepted the longitude, because it was 'uncorrected' for 14 months of flying. It was impossible for such trained, professional people to have made the number of mistakes required for them not to have known.

What mattered was that Jim Collins and Greg Cassin had been briefed on the flight path straight down McMurdo Sound with a flight plan showing that route, that Jim Collins plotted this route, that Jim Collins had no reason to believe that flight path would change but that it did at the last minute, and that all of the Antarctic pilots since November 1977 had flown down McMurdo Sound at whatever altitude suited both them and McMurdo Control.

Mahon leaned more to the idea that the navigation alteration of 166 to 164 degrees of longitude was, however, deliberate, and that the airline was not telling the truth when it claimed the Erebus coordinates given to Captain Collins were correct. McMurdo Sound made operational sense and the sightseeing was better. He believed Air New Zealand should have squared away the original alteration of the course with Civil Aviation, who would have been quite happy with the change because it was a much safer route and did not take an aircraft full of passengers over an active volcano. The new flight track ran roughly down the military route and the Americans had no qualms. The McMurdo route also enabled good quality, unimpeded radio communications between the DC-10s and the American controllers and enabled the American radar to see the aircraft early and guide them in to McMurdo.

What's more — and this is crucially important — Air New Zealand based its publicity material on the McMurdo Sound approach to the American and New Zealand bases. The brochure *Travelling Times*, distributed by Air New Zealand to over 900,000 homes, contained the article by John Brizindine, President of McDonnell Douglas, lauding his fabulous flight with Gordon Vette approaching Ross Island at 3000 feet.

One airline publicist, Vern Mitchell, wrote of the Antarctic flights in August 1979: 'Then they fly for nearly an hour down the Ross Sea, with the Victoria Land mountains on the right, to reach McMurdo Sound.'[11] (Note: no mention of flying over Erebus.) Mitchell continues, 'At that stage they are at relatively low altitude and they spend about 45 minutes "touring" the McMurdo area — winging over Scott's hut on Ross Island and on over the Great Ice Shelf . . . The flights make a low level circuit of steaming Mount Erebus, sweep over the existing McMurdo bases, the airfield and the New Zealand dog lines . . .'[12]

There was the clear and graphic map given to the passengers and shown to pilots that showed the route to be down the middle of McMurdo Sound and back up over the Sound to cruise altitude back to New Zealand.

But at the inquiry, under oath, no one, not one executive from Air New Zealand, knew before the crash about the original computer 'error' that placed the southbound aircraft in the middle of McMurdo Sound. Not one of them had known anything about an 'error' in the flight plan. As far as they knew, all flights had flown overhead Erebus. And it was only in the last days before the Collins flight that the 'mistake' was discovered and the coordinates 'corrected'. It was mind-bendingly absurd.

But why was the 'mistake' suddenly 'corrected' early in the morning of Jim Collins's departure from Auckland? And why was Collins not told? We shall examine this in the next chapter. Mahon's own chapter in the accident report, 'THE CREATION OF THE FALSE MCMURDO WAYPOINT AND HOW IT CAME TO BE CHANGED WITHOUT THE KNOWLEDGE OF CAPTAIN COLLINS', contains some of the most complicated reading of the entire report. You can pore over this chapter for a very long time.

To get to the bottom of it, Mahon demonstrated a Machiavellian capacity as profound as those Machiavellian, highly intelligent men whose actions he was called upon to assess. He was just as tricky as they were. Paul Davison QC told me that Mahon loved investigation, loved subterfuge, loved finding out, while keeping his thoughts private.

Sam Mahon said of his father in his memoir:

> For the most part my father pleased himself and he was at no one's behest. He was an individual who moved easily amongst his fellow men while keeping his thoughts to himself and it seemed to me that he was most at one with the world when he was alone with a glass of old malt and his books communing with the thoughts of men most of whom were long dead. There's a comment by Cicero, 'I am never less lonely than when I am by myself.'[13]

He also wrote:

> Someone, a female lawyer, said to him once at a bar dinner that judges were not suited to understand the ordinary man. 'Judges live in a refined world,' she said. 'A shadow lands.' But Peter had spent more than two years in huts and tents with his fellow man, sleeping in broken *case* [houses] and ditches and digging shit-holes in orchards and ruined vineyards with a trenching tool. My father said nothing in reply, he just took another glass of wine.[14]

Peter Mahon knew good men. He knew Jim Collins was a good and honest man who was happily married with four daughters and he knew Jim Collins's reputation as a pilot. He knew that Jim Collins's voice had been silenced forever. Dead men could not defend themselves. He made it clear in his report that he would examine carefully Collins's performance as a pilot on 28 November 1979, as he was required to do. But it became clear that if he was lied to, and attempts were made to deceive him and hoodwink him, he would say that, too.

Peter Mahon, we would soon learn, as the legal professional already knew well, was not afraid to speak the truth to powerful men.

And Peter Mahon missed nothing.

17

The 'Mistake' is Corrected

I think I should understand that better if I had it written down: but I can't quite follow it as you say it.

— Alice in *Alice in Wonderland,* Lewis Carroll

The clever young counsel for ALPA, who was also Maria Collins's lawyer, was 29-year-old Paul Davison. His was one of the several brilliant minds to emerge at this inquiry. I asked Maria how she came to have such a young barrister representing her. Indeed, she told me, her father, himself a successful lawyer in Vienna before fleeing the Nazis in 1939, wondered what she was doing employing 'that boy'. Maria says she accepted the advice of her solicitor, Michael Friedlander. He told her she would do no better than use his own firm's barrister, Paul Davison. Maria has always, it seems, taken good advice. Paul Davison QC has carved a career as one of our most successful criminal defence and prosecution counsel. He is one of the most respected men in the New Zealand courts.

Davison had a most unpleasant surprise up his sleeve for a Navigation Section that continued to maintain that the original change in the 1978 McMurdo destination waypoint had been a mistake.

He waited patiently through the evidence of the executive pilots and he waited through much of the Navigation Section evidence. Then he pounced. One afternoon, he produced for Keith Amies, of the Navigation Section, a piece of paper that became Exhibit 164, and one of the most important pieces of evidence to be presented at the Royal Commission. It was not a map, exactly. It was rather what navigators call a track and distance diagram, a primitive chart. The untrained eye would not make much of it but to pilots of the authority and experience of the DC-10 crews, it was quite clear that it depicted a flight track to the head of McMurdo Sound, well to the west of Mount Erebus. There was a semicircle drawn round the south side of Ross Island, that is, round McMurdo and Scott Bases, and then there was a line with a little arrowhead drawn upon it pointing north up the eastern or right-hand side of the Sound.

Mahon noticed that Keith Amies became very 'disconcerted' by the sight of Exhibit 164.[1] The airline could not allow this to be proven in any way as a chart down McMurdo Sound.

This track and distance chart corresponded with the map the passengers received, incidentally, which showed the aircraft flying up and down McMurdo Sound. What is more, Exhibit 164 appeared in existence roughly at the time the change was made, or the 'mistake' was committed. In other words, it seemed that the 'mistake' might not have been a 'mistake' at all. And if it was not a 'mistake', then what happened in the early hours of 28 November 1979 must have been the mistake.

This track and distance diagram was issued to all of the 1978 Antarctic pilots. Davison knew this because he was in touch with all the 1978 pilots. Mahon came to believe, on the basis of the evidence, that 'Exhibit 164 was included in the flight documents taken by aircraft crews to Antarctica'.[2]

This was another slap at Chippindale. Chippindale insisted a document called 'Annex J' was taken on the flight decks. Annex J indicated a route over Mount Erebus.

Mahon noted:

> But in my opinion, on the totality of the evidence, Annex J never formed part of the 1979 flight documents and was not on the fatal flight. Consequently there was no track and distance guide carried on the fatal flight which indicated that the nav track lay on a direct course with Mount Erebus. On the contrary, there were three charts (four, if I include Exhibit 164), which all showed a track down McMurdo Sound.[3]

It remains extraordinary that the airline had still not managed or bothered to provide their flight crews with a topographical map with the flight plan route printed over it. The passengers got such a map, the flight crew did not. Captain Arthur Cooper would wonder, in his evidence, if in the airline, 'the order of economic priorities was allowed to become a little distorted'.[4]

So important, obviously, was this track and distance document that Mahon noted that there was 'an angry confrontation' between counsel for ALPA and counsel for Air New Zealand at the end of the day's proceedings. Air New Zealand's junior counsel, Richard McGrane, claimed that the ALPA counsel should have given notice to Air New Zealand that this document was coming. Davison told McGrane it was very interesting that Exhibit 164 had not been produced by the airline itself.

I have located a brief written exchange between Davison and McGrane. Davison wrote, on 16 September 1980: 'Richard, I recall during our "discussion" following the production of Ex 164 you mentioned that you were aware of its existence relative to the 1978 flight briefings — is that correct?'

McGrane replied, also by hand: 'Paul, Yes that is correct. The matter was canvassed with everybody in Flight Operations who I thought may be able to cast some light on the matter. I recall approaching Navigation Section . . . Mr Amies cannot have been there since he had not seen the chart before it was produced in evidence.'

In other words, the airline knew about the diagram chart but did not produce it.

Chippindale had been given Annex J by none other than his technical adviser, Ian Gemmell.[5] He was given it after he asked Gemmell what documents the crew were given at Flight Despatch. Captain Gemmell handed him Annex J and claimed the document had been part of the sheaf of documents carried by the crew of the fatal flight. Gemmell may have told Chippindale that the actual document had been recovered from the crash site. It is not clear.

Once again, Chippindale believed what he was told. He accepted the document he got from the airline and inquired no further. Annex J allowed Chippindale to assert that Captain Jim Collins flew carelessly and deliberately at a ridiculously low altitude into the mountain on his way to the McMurdo TACAN (tactical air navigation aid), which was now being used instead of the NDB.

Richard McGrane, the young counsel who flared up at Davison, was Air New Zealand's junior counsel. Like Davison, he was 29 years old. In at least one respect during the hearings of the Royal Commission his behaviour remains questionable if not inappropriate.

Kathryn Carter, by the time of the inquiry, had turned 16. Maria Collins mentioned to me one day that McGrane used to come round to the Collins's of an evening and take Kathryn for driving lessons in his Mini. Maria says she thought at the time that the young man, by doing so, was putting his head in the lion's mouth.

In the middle of a discussion with Kathryn about the Chief Inspector, Kathryn spoke to me of how 'pathetic and inadequate' she found Ron Chippindale as a person and an investigator, a man who, she noted, avoided looking people in the eye. 'He never once said anything to us during the inquiry. Even during the breaks when you could have a cup of tea. He never once said, "I'm sorry for your loss".'

Holmes: 'Did any of the other people at the inquiry do that?'

Kathryn: 'Richard McGrane. He came to our home sometime during 1980 during the weekend to visit us. He said he was professionally representing Air New Zealand's case at the inquiry, but that in a private capacity he wanted to offer to help us out in any way he could. He was kind and empathetic and Maria suggested that he finish the driving lessons that I had been in the middle of when Dad had died.

H: 'The other interpretation of that, Kathryn, is this. You were 16, he was 29. He's working all day to destroy the reputation of your father and at night he's coming round to teach you to drive.'

Kathryn: 'That's what Mum thought, but he wasn't.'

H: 'It's what I think, too.'

Kathryn: 'I asked him that at the time. I said to him, "What are you doing here? Why are you doing this?" He said, "I feel for your family".'

H: 'He was attracted to you. Your mother could see it.'

Kathryn: 'She said that. She always said that to me. It wasn't the case. He never once laid a finger on me. He said to me, "I'm here because I'm concerned about you, about what's happened to your family."

'It's about the fact that he knew he was representing the wrong side. He was kind, funny and entertaining and never showed impropriety towards me. He had a dilemma. That's what it was. My mother sees it rather simplistically.'

H: 'So do I. Forgive me.'

Kathryn: 'He felt morally conflicted and he couldn't say that.'

Maria, looking back, shakes her head. 'I was probably naive. I was just trying to hold it together, and teaching Kathryn to drive was one less job I had to do.'

So why did Air New Zealand decide suddenly to change or 'correct' the coordinates of the destination waypoint the night before Jim Collins departed for the ice? This is where the story gets strange and murky. Here, the orchestration becomes symphonic. Was the change to the destination waypoint deliberate or was it the result of a series of cock-ups? Whichever it was, no paperwork was ever produced.

On 14 November 1979, a fortnight before the fatal flight, Captain Les Simpson, like Jim Collins also rated a most methodical airman and one of the pilots who attended the same briefing as Collins, commanded the flight to Antarctica. At the briefing Simpson had noted in his head, while perusing the flight plans handed round, that the destination waypoint would be taking him west of McMurdo Station itself. 'It seemed to me to be a logical position in that it was at the head of the Sound clear of high terrain and a good position to start sightseeing from in the McMurdo [Station] area.'[6]

Under examination, Simpson acknowledged that it was clear to him that the destination waypoint 'was further south and slightly west of the Byrd Reporting Point'. He said he understood the track took him well clear of the high ground of Ross Island. Which, of course, it did, and had done since 1978. He noted this mentally from the flight plan handed out at his briefing. Pilots of his calibre, experience and training can read coordinates instantly.[7]

Nevertheless, when Simpson got to the head of McMurdo Sound at Dailey Islands, he found he was still some 30 miles west of McMurdo Station and the distance surprised him. He wasn't bothered by it. He saw, obviously, that he needed to turn left and when he did so McMurdo Station was in front of him. But the waypoint was further from McMurdo Station than he expected.

So the day after his flight, Captain Simpson said, he phoned the Director of Line Operations, Captain Ross Johnson, who had also briefed Simpson and Collins in the simulator.

'During this conversation which was fairly brief, and as an entirely secondary matter, I told him that I had been surprised at seeing approximately 27 miles across track distance . . . I suggested it would probably be a good idea to advise all other crews doing Antarctic flights of this distance between the flight plan McMurdo position and the TACAN position, so that they would not be surprised as I had been.'[8]

In other words, so that crews did not become alarmed at finding that, although they had reached their destination, McMurdo Station was still 20 miles away to the left, the boys should probably be given a heads-up that once they reached the top of McMurdo Sound, they still had to turn left and drive a few miles further to McMurdo Station and that there was nothing wrong with their navigation gear.

Then, said Captain Simpson crucially, 'I did not report this matter to Captain R. T. Johnson as an error in position as I had no reason to believe the McMurdo position on the flight plan was other than a logical place to terminate the southern point of the flight plan track.'[9]

But that is how Johnson said he took it, that Simpson was reporting an error in the position of the destination waypoint.

After Simpson's call to Johnson, we get the first of the mistakes that will lead to the late night coordinate change a fortnight later.

It is important to note that Simpson's evidence never changed. Johnson's evidence changed three times. He made an original statement to Air New Zealand's in-house committee on 10 December 1979. His evidence was different at the Royal Commission and was different again later on at the Court of Appeal.[10]

He told Air New Zealand's Investigating Committee that 'Captain Simpson rang me and said that the McMurdo position was in error and should be 166 degrees and 58 minutes'.[11] To the Royal Commission he said, 'Captain Simpson also asked me to get the Navigation Section to look at the position of the McMurdo waypoint on the computerised flight plan which he said would be better positioned at the TACAN.' In other words, overhead Mount Erebus. At the Court of Appeal, Johnson objected to Mahon's accusing the senior pilots of lying when they said they had no idea flights flew below 6000 feet round McMurdo. This was unbelievable. Johnson himself flew at 3000 feet.

Mahon, perplexed, wrote: 'Captain Simpson strongly disagreed with this evidence, and in particular disagreed with the suggestion that he told Captain Johnson that the McMurdo waypoint would be better positioned at the TACAN. But it appears that it was decided by someone, I am not sure whom, that the McMurdo position should be moved to the TACAN.'[12] And we never found out why.

But, if the flight path were changed to this course, and if you laid a straight edge over a direct course from Cape Hallett to Williams Field, you would be flying directly over Mount Erebus. In other words, the course would now be more or less the original course for the Antarctic flights, whereas for 14 months the course had been safely down McMurdo Sound.

The mix-ups and confusions that then occurred were unfathomable. They involved a serious breakdown in communication between Flight Operations and the Navigation Section. Johnson told Laurence Lawton, the Superintendent of Navigation Section, that 'something is wrong with the McMurdo position'. That is all Lawton said he was told by Ross Johnson.

So Lawton pulled the Antarctic flight plan out of a computer, but it was not the flight plan the flight crews had been using since November 1978. He did not at any stage retrieve from the computer the actual flight plan used by Captain Simpson. He could have done so, he admitted under cross-examination, but he did not. The flight plan he was now examining, which he had pulled up on the computer, had the McMurdo waypoint as 77:53 latitude south and 166:48 longitude east, the original longitude coordinates.

Captain Collins had by now, the reader will remember, been shown the flight plan used on the flight of 7 November 1979, the McMurdo Sound flight plan with the destination waypoint at the top of McMurdo Sound. Captain Gabriel who was at the same briefing, stated: 'I remember that the McMurdo waypoint was either underlined or highlighted in some way . . . These flight plans . . . were passed around amongst those of us present.'[13]

Then Lawton and Brian Hewitt consulted the latest American information and found that the TACAN was actually at 166 degrees 58 minutes longitude east. Hewitt was still apparently unaware of his original mistake that had put the aircraft down the 164 line of longitude — down McMurdo Sound — for 14 months. Right then, neither man appeared to have any idea of the 164 figure. They were looking at the old flight plan and they saw that the flight plan was now out by 10 minutes of longitude. The difference between 48 minutes and 58 minutes at that latitude is about 2 miles. So the change was ordered to 166.58 degrees longitude east.

At the Royal Commission, Brian Hewitt endured a ruthless cross-examination from Paul Davison, acting for ALPA. It ended thus, after Davison recited error and omission after error and omission as the Navigation Section owned up to a whole series of unbelievable mistakes.

Davison: 'All these errors, and in a company which in its Nav Section, tells us we are dealing with people and check, and cross check, and never assume anything. It is a woeful story, isn't it?'

Hewitt: 'It is not a good story.'[14]

It was a famous moment of Royal Commission cross-examination. It was one of the breakthroughs.

So, after Lawton and Brian Hewitt had noticed the 10 minute differential — neither apparently still knowing anything about the 2-degree differential — Lawton went back to Ross Johnson and informed him of the minor navigational error. Oh well, said Johnson, let's fix it.

It was to be Jim Collins's fate that the safe 164 became the dangerous 166 at 2.16 a.m. on 28 November 1979 and first appeared in the paperwork at Flight Despatch as Collins and his crew arrived for what should have been a spectacular day's flying in one of the world's finest aircraft at low sightseeing altitudes round what is said to be one of the most breathtaking parts of the world. The destination coordinates for Jim Collins were now the McMurdo TACAN, with a longitude of 166 degrees 58 minutes.

Just like that. And no one said a thing to Jim Collins.

The process had taken a fortnight and in that time no one thought to mention to Jim Collins that there was to be even a slight change in his flight path. And the Chief Navigator, Brian Hewitt, still did not realise, even late on the night the computer flight plan was amended, that 166 degrees became 164 degrees long ago and Collins was briefed on 164 degrees. Now 164 degrees had, overnight, without anyone telling Collins, become 166 degrees again. The Chief Navigator had no idea.

I hope the reader's eyes are not rolling.

But what was the reason given for not informing Collins? The difference in destination was only 2.1 nautical miles, was the answer. That's what Navigation Section and Captain Ross Johnson claimed they thought had been effected, a relatively insignificant destination variation between the old flight plan and the new. Two miles was nothing to bother a captain about.

The reason Johnson thought the shift was only 2 miles, he said in evidence,[15] was that he thought, essentially, that when Captain Simpson told him to shift the waypoint to the TACAN he was telling him to shift it from the NDB. The NDB, it was believed, had become unavailable and Johnson issued a memo to the Antarctic pilots accordingly which said any descent to 6000 feet now had to be visual: 'Descent to be coordinated with local radar control as they may have other traffic in the area.'[16] In other words, after 6000 feet, liaise with air traffic control on altitude.

Johnson's own flight — which he had taken down to 3000 feet, he told the inquiry — had taken him over Erebus to the NDB in November 1977. Of course, he had no idea there had been a 2-degree destination variance since 1978. He was one of the bosses and the bosses knew nothing.

But there is something wrong here. Johnson was one of the two briefing officers for the Antarctic flights. He was also Flight Manager, Line Operations for the airline. He was emphatic in his evidence that crews were briefed to fly overhead Erebus. His assertion that the change in the destination waypoint to the TACAN was only 2.1 miles required Ross Johnson not to have known that for 14 months Antarctic flights had been descending to low levels for sightseeing straight down McMurdo Sound and that the destination waypoint was West Dailey Island.

Mahon wasn't having a bar of it. In the tone he adopted when he knew he was being lied to (his code words for lies were 'elaborate', 'detailed' and 'ingenious'), Mahon wrote: 'Now this was certainly a most detailed and elaborate explanation for the fatal decision not to notify Captain Collins of the alteration in the McMurdo waypoint. But is the explanation true?'[17] Mahon decided it was most certainly not, mainly because Les Simpson had been such a credible witness with what he says he told Johnson about the destination waypoint.

Arthur Cooper was full of admiration for the way Simpson emphatically held his ground. 'The effect . . . was genuine and it was very powerful. I would say that overall Les was not a union guy, he was more a company man. But his evidence absolutely rang of sincerity and honesty and it was crucial to the final outcome.'

Mahon decided that both Johnson and the Navigation Section knew that the McMurdo waypoint had, for a long time, been 27 miles to the west of the McMurdo Station beacon, and because Civil Aviation had never been told, someone decided the waypoint should be put back to where it was and somewhere along the line, someone forgot to tell Captain Jim Collins. 'Such an interpretation means that the evidence as to the alleged belief of a displacement of only 2.1 miles is untrue.'[18]

Mahon decided that it was all lies. The likeliest explanation was that both Johnson and the Navigation Section knew that the track they were using lay 27 miles to the west of McMurdo Station and, while it had its obvious advantages, nevertheless, the company had never told Civil Aviation.

There was a letter Johnson wrote to the Director of Civil Aviation in October 1979 in which he expected that the next edition of the Ross Sea chart, NZ RNC4, would print the Air New Zealand flight path. He may therefore, suggested Mahon, have decided the safest course was to put the Air New Zealand flight path back where it was.[19]

There was one other little 'deception' or 'mistake'. The computer operator typed up the flight plan that the airline sent to MacCentre after Collins departed. In doing so he pressed a key that removed the latitude and longitude of the destination waypoint and printed instead 'McMurdo'. Mahon understood that MacCentre had plotted the coordinates of the first of the 1979 flights and assumed each subsequent flight would follow the same course and fly down the centre of the Sound and turn in towards MacCentre. If the navigational digits had been printed on the flight plan sent to MacCentre on the day of Collins's flight, MacCentre might well have noted that the course had changed and queried and opposed it. Instead, they saw 'McMurdo' and assumed the usual.[20]

Then we have the matter of the briefing and what the pilots were told of their route.

Not only was Captain Les Simpson at the briefing for the Antarctic flight attended by Jim Collins and Greg Cassin, but so was Captain John Gabriel, who was Simpson's first officer on the 14 November flight.

Gabriel was sitting next to ALPA's Captain Arthur Cooper at the Royal Commission when Johnson gave his evidence about what he told the crews in the DC-10 simulator briefing. Johnson was in full swing with what he showed them about Erebus. At frequent points during Johnson's testimony, Gabriel said quietly to Cooper, 'That never happened. That just didn't happen, there was no chart there. All we did was get in and did the procedure for the let-down. We were just doing procedure. None of that happened.' Says Arthur Cooper: 'Here was Johnson saying this is what he did and it was all bullshit.' Johnson stood up at the Royal Commission and was emphatic that he had told the crews the flight plan took them over Erebus.

Captain Les Simpson never wavered from his evidence that what Wilson and Johnson told the Commission was nonsense. Simpson told the Commission that much of what Wilson and Johnson claimed they told the pilots he had no recollection of. He was backed up in this by two others who attended the same briefing, Captain John Gabriel and First Officer Irvine.

Which pretty much said it all. None of it added up. It never did. But if we stay out of the torturous dissembling that Mahon had to listen to, if we keep it simple, then comprehension of this disaster is not difficult to obtain.

For whatever reason — and no satisfactory reason ever emerged — there was a crucial change of the original destination waypoint to the nice, safe waypoint, that may have been a mistake or may have been adopted by design, when flight plans were being entered into the ground computer in 1978. What mattered was that, when Jim Collins took off, there was programmed into his flight computer a different flight plan from that upon which he had been briefed. It was heading him directly to a 13,000-foot erupting volcano over which, apparently, an aircraft full of trusting people would have to fly. It was also true that Jim Collins would adopt the usual, reasonable and acceptable option of trusting his AINS to faithfully take him down the route upon which he had been briefed. As Arthur Cooper says, 'Jim was a guy who used every available navigational aid.'

Mahon had no doubt that every flight except the first two, and there had been 11 between the second flight and Jim Collins's flight, had descended perfectly safely well below the so-called MSAs of 16,000/6000 feet. The specific Antarctic altitudes were never enforced, even though senior airline management and Civil Aviation had to have known about the low altitudes pilots used flying down McMurdo Sound. There had been so much prominent publicity for them not to have. A brochure had gone nationwide mentioning specific altitudes below 6000 feet.

Mahon's inquiry established clearly, beyond doubt, that Jim Collins had been briefed to fly down McMurdo Sound and that he had been briefed to descend lower than 6000 feet in visual conditions if MacCentre invited him down. And, indeed, the CVR transcript showed the American controllers to have been happy with Collins all the way.

What he had not been briefed on were the malevolent peculiarities of polar light, specifically whiteout, which a newcomer could never detect and which would ultimately destroy Collins's aircraft and all on board. He had no reason whatsoever to believe that he was anywhere but slap in the middle of McMurdo Sound.

And with the NDB withdrawn, as Jim Collins had been told, he knew that in the clear but less than perfect weather he was meeting on his approach to McMurdo Sound, with visibility still at 40 miles, he should use the earliest opportunity to descend. With the NDB withdrawn from service, he knew he would not be able to drop down through cloud at McMurdo Station. But McMurdo and Scott Bases were very much part of what Collins's passengers had paid good money to see.

But no one could ever explain why the waypoint was changed on 28 November 1979. Probably we will never know. Somebody, someday, may cough before they croak.

A complete lack of documentation did not help. Mahon despaired of and was alarmed by the 'almost total lack of documents' recording computer programming decisions of the Antarctic flights between October 1977 and November 1979.

'There is not one memorandum from the Flight Operations Division to the Navigation Section giving instructions for any change, nor is there any written report from the Navigation Section notifying Flight Operations of changes which had been made.'[21] This is a recurring theme in his report: where was the paperwork?

But Mahon noticed something else. This man who knew men deduced from Johnson's reaction to what Captain Simpson told him in his phone call that the notion the McMurdo waypoint was 27 miles out in the Sound had not surprised Johnson.[22] Nowhere, in anything Johnson said and claimed, was there any element of surprise at what Simpson told him.

But Johnson and the Navigation Section had decided a fortnight before Collins took off for the ice, for whatever reason, to redirect the flight path to its original waypoint to Williams Field and somehow someone forgot one important and crucial thing, to inform Captain Collins. As Mahon wrote in his report:

> I have reviewed the evidence in support of the allegation that the Navigation Section believed, by reason of a mistaken verbal communication, that the altered McMurdo waypoint only involved a change of 2.1 nautical miles. I am obliged to say that I do not accept that explanation. There were certainly grave deficiencies in communication within the Navigation Section, but the high professional skills of the Navigation Section's staff entirely preclude the possibility of such an error. In my opinion this explanation that the change in the waypoint was thought to be minimal in terms of distance is a concocted story designed to explain away the fundamental mistake, made by someone, in failing to ensure that Captain Collins was notified that his aircraft was now programmed to fly on a collision course with Mt Erebus.[23]

The indomitable Erebus researcher Stuart Macfarlane, who discreetly wrote both the epilogue and notes on the text in Gordon Vette's *Impact Erebus*, published in 1983 and never questioned, calculated that for management to have not known about the McMurdo Sound flight path required the airline to have made 54 mistakes or omissions. It was too many for a professional airline to make. Therefore what Mahon was told were lies.

One aspect of the entire Erebus disaster that never failed to confound Mahon was that the Chief Executive never wrote a report on the accident to the airline's board of directors. However, on page 255 of *The Erebus Papers*, Macfarlane mentions an Air New Zealand board meeting held on 5 December 1979, just days after the disaster. We can only imagine the mood of despair and even panic that infused this meeting. But Macfarlane had seen notes marked 'Strictly confid. Not to be used'. The notes referred to the wreckage as 'off track (considerably) . . . Aeroplane . . . was left of centre.'

As Macfarlane observed: 'These comments seem to invite the assumption that the Board believed that the airline's flight path ran considerably to the right of the crash site (in other words, up the middle of McMurdo Sound) and had not been told that it had been shifted to cross Erebus.'

Without the pilot being told.

18

Life Carries On

We have to be willing to let go of the life we have planned, in order to live the life that is waiting for us.

— E. M. Forster

Maria does not remember if she slept that first night, the night of Dave Eden's phone call, the night of Jim's death, when Elizabeth crawled into bed with her and asked her if she would marry again and she began to make her little plans. You must always make your plans. A day should always go as you plan it.

But they all, Maria, Kathryn, Elizabeth, Pip and Adrienne, speak of the house being full of people in those first weeks after Erebus. Maria says the fridge and the freezer filled up with food. Friends and colleagues brought endless meals. Every jar, every vase, every container that could be used, held massive bunches of gypsophila, carnations and chrysanthemums.

It is a wan smile that crosses Maria Collins's face when she recalls those first shocking weeks and the swirling waves of people. 'It was fantastic because it was anaesthetic, it was a perpetual party. We had parties without my having to do anything, nothing was expected of me. I could, well, I didn't weep and wail in public but nothing was expected of me and these people came. And they kept coming and coming.

'And on the table here we had this stack of mail and eventually I got some thank you cards made and as the mail came in somebody sorted out the mail, kept all the addresses and stacked them in alphabetical order. And when everybody would go at the end of the day, I would read them. There were hundreds and hundreds of them. People were fantastic. There were many I didn't know. People I didn't know brought food. We tried to keep a list of who brought what because that was the thing you did.'

Kathryn remembers the people, the cakes, the sausage rolls and the freezer piling up. 'People were sitting in the living room, people sitting in the kitchen, there were people on duty to make cups of tea for the more people that were coming and going and we were like guests in our own house. It gave you a break from your own life, from the reality of being alone.'

But Elizabeth remembers too some Air New Zealand types who came, stood round and didn't say much, men who appeared more interested in looking round.

Morrie Davis never came. He never went to see Maria Collins. A few days after the crash, he sent his wife. She was nicely dressed, very much the well-to-do eastern suburbs corporate wife. Mrs Davis told Maria, 'Morrie sent me round to do women's stuff.'

The only Air New Zealand Chief Executive ever to cross Maria Collins's threshold was the current man, Rob Fyfe. He went to Maria's for dinner at the time of the thirtieth anniversary of the accident. Maria appreciated this. She was touched by his gesture. He remained guarded in everything he told her. Maria expected nothing less.

It was at the thirtieth commemorations that Rob Fyfe, on behalf of the airline, said sorry to those affected by the accident. What was never clear was what he was saying sorry for, and while they appreciate that he did this, Maria, Kathryn and Elizabeth all tell me that Rob Fyfe's 'sorry' is not enough. They have no negative attitude to Rob Fyfe. But that simple 'sorry' will never be enough. Not for what happened. Not for what Kathryn calls 'the systemic abuse' they endured in those first years and at every anniversary since, when the inevitable articles appear in the newspapers and magazines and the eternal debate about causation rages again and Air New Zealand runs a mile and allows the debate to continue when the company could, as Justice Peter Mahon said years ago, have laid its cards on the table. Mahon was always sure, as he wrote in his Royal Commission report in 1981, that there were still one or two cards in the pack.

Holmes, to Maria: 'How were the kids during this period?'

Maria: 'Well, a lot of the time, I've no idea. They were swept up in the . . .'

H: 'Well, would Kathryn and Elizabeth have looked after Pip and Adrienne?'

Maria: 'Oh yeah. Nobody was neglected as such. I don't know, to be quite honest, because I was really absorbed in my own grief. And I knew that as a mother I just had to keep the domestic ship afloat here, and that the older two were that much older and therefore I probably didn't tune in to their grief enough. I can say that now, looking back on it. But at the time I had this dogged attitude. We had to survive. I had to survive. I had to survive to keep these kids going. Even if people are going to say, "Do you realise your husband is responsible for the deaths of 257 people?"'

H: 'Did anyone say that to you?'

Maria: 'Nobody said it to me but I'd fantasised that that's what they'd say because when you hear that the aircraft has gone down, that they're all dead, well, who was flying the aircraft? Therefore, they're going to hold Jim responsible regardless.'

The day after the accident, Pip and Adrienne were kept out of school. 'The house started filling up with people and the phone rang,' Pip says. 'And flowers, huge, ornate bunches of white and green, accompanied by sympathy cards with great swirls of embossed silver writing. A close family friend took Adrienne and me to Pizza Hut for lunch. Wow! Pizza Hut! On a school day! I'm not sure where it was — Royal Oak? It was empty except for the three of us.'

For Kathryn, the eldest and 15 years old, it was as if the greatest hole in the world had opened up and swallowed her. Somehow she too survived those first torn and painful weeks and months after the death of her father. Somehow she got through. 'Your heart keeps beating, doesn't it? You get up in the morning and you do your thing and you come home and youth, to a degree, is quite an advantage because you don't have a full picture of your life ahead of you. You innocently continue with your life in a way because you think that's what you do. I don't think it's as hard as when you get older and see what you've missed out on perhaps . . .'

There is a great weight in the room as Kathryn says this. And there is the simmering anger that sometimes consumes her. 'He couldn't be there for me. It killed me.'

Holmes: 'Does it still feel like that? Part of you is dead? Part of you is gone?'

Kathryn: 'It still guts me. I'm still gutted. I know that Elizabeth is too, in a different way. I know that she is and that's partly why she has the pain still. We lost 30 years of our lives. Our lives have been partial. They haven't been complete. We're emotionally scarred. I don't want to sound indulgent in saying that. Of course we've had full lives in terms of going to university and I got married and had children but it's all against the background of a half picture, a half life that you experience when you lose a parent.'

Kathryn is talking to me in my high-rise apartment overlooking Auckland, sprawling away forever beneath us. It is one of those grey and mournful late Sunday afternoons in winter at the dying of the day. There may have been a shower. There may be a shot of yellow in the haze but it doesn't lift the spirit much. It is the kind of day that could get a person down if a person were to let it. She is looking to her left, away from me through the window across the harbour to the Gulf islands in the distance. Apart from the gentle humming of the little recording machine winding its tape from one spindle to the other, there is silence.

She turns back, away from the day. Her eyes are burning. Her honesty is raw.

Kathryn: 'I'm a passionate person, you see. I loved my father more than anything. I love my mother as well and they were so symbiotic in their relationship and the tragedy was that they were happy. It always tore me apart that they were torn apart by forces greater than themselves.'

Silence. Life suspended.

Holmes: 'Do you really feel you've lost 30 years?'

Kathryn: 'Emotionally, I've had a hard time of it. I don't think I've lost 30 years obviously in terms of the paths my life has taken. I think I've had a good path but at times it's been very lonely. At times it's been very hard. At times I've felt very alone.'

H: 'How often do you feel alone?'

Kathryn: 'Much less so now, since I've had my own children and my own family. I'm the chief bottle washer.'

When I met Kathryn Collins, more years ago than either of us wants to calculate, she was in her early twenties. She didn't seem to be alone or unhappy at all. She was charming. She had a famously radiant smile. She says all of this was outward stuff, not what was inside her. She was always good at rocking up and talking to people.

H: 'Was Dad like that?'

Kathryn: 'Yeah.'

H: 'Could Dad talk to anyone?'

Kathryn: 'Yeah. I've got the same interest in people.'

Silence. The afternoon drifts on.

H: 'Is part of you still 15? Is part of Elizabeth still 13?'

Kathryn: 'Yes.'

H: 'Are parts of you locked in there?'

Kathryn: 'But I've had children and moved in the direction of having a family. I feel I've had to become an adult.'

H: 'And Pip and Adrienne. I observed that first day, remember when I came to Maria's for lunch and you got them there to have a look at me, that only one of you has married.'

Kathryn: 'I was thinking, actually...'

H: 'You don't have to get married, of course.'

Kathryn: 'I was thinking years ago of not getting married. I was thinking, I could make a choice here and not ever get married. Nothing is ever perfect. You learn that early. I learnt that with the accident. Nothing's ever perfect so why even take the risk of exposing yourself to more potential imperfection? Then I thought, life's a risk. Why not take one and see what happens? Especially if you meet someone you really like.'

Nineteen years on, Kathryn Carter is still married to Luke and they have four children.

They were all hit, of course, hit badly in the core of their souls, all of them. Both Maria and her friend Kathryn Schollum believe it was Elizabeth who took Jim Collins's death the hardest of them all.

Holmes: 'Did it break your heart?'

Elizabeth: 'Definitely.'

H: 'Did it ever mend?'

Elizabeth: 'Probably not. Not fully.'

H: 'Has it stopped you being able to love people?'

Elizabeth: (thoughtfully) 'Maybe. Maybe. Yeah. Maybe.'

Elizabeth is dedicated to her many animals. She is dedicated to finding homes for them. These are cats people have found under hedges, in rubbish bins. She calls this her rescue, rehabilitation and rehousing work. She is also dedicated to helping care for elderly neighbours with their food needs and matters of hygiene. Elizabeth is not only a brilliant organiser, she is a carer. Elizabeth deals with problems immediately.

In the days after the accident, Elizabeth took over Jim's role as the person of action round the house. She changed the light bulbs. She replaced fuses. She unblocked the sink. She organised the dishes roster.

Holmes: 'Did the accident cause you to find it easier to love animals?'

Elizabeth: 'Is this a psychologist's visit? Maybe. Don't know.'

H: 'What do you think?'

Elizabeth: 'Or maybe I didn't want to love anyone else because the cats are so adorable. There are lots and lots of dorks round. There are lots of people of unsuitability around.'

But we are moving ahead too quickly and far too far. Jim Collins had just been killed flying an aircraft with 257 people on board into an icy mountain. The tears of a nation were a flood. They were ceaseless. The grief was everywhere and relentless. Every town had lost someone. The Collins house had been full of people.

But the weeks went by and eventually, for such is life, the people, with their company, their cheer and comfort, began to withdraw. They stopped coming round.

Christmas, the first Christmas without Jim, was approaching.

Elizabeth: 'I felt alone. I think I felt alone. We appreciated the closeness of immediate family and genuine friends. Absolutely. But only I knew what it was like to be in my shoes. There was nobody else, there were my sisters, but everyone was dealing with it in a different way.'

Maria: 'Adrienne was in my bed for months and months and months. She would just get into Jim's side of the bed. For months. But she was six. And she'd ask me, "You're not going to die too, Mummy, are you?" Which is a normal thing for a six-year-old to do.'

This was the time during which Maria first heard the words 'pilot error'. This was the period in which the Collins girls would first come to understand the simple, invaluable and vital human virtues of loyalty, honesty, decency and the beauty of genuine friendship. This is the time when they would learn that men who had known their father since his teenage years in the Royal New Zealand Air Force, men he trained with, who were friends, suddenly were not around any more.

'There were a few people who stayed with us but there was a vast disappearance of a lot of people,' says Kathryn. 'Apparently, the word was that the pilots couldn't support us because they would risk their own reputation within the airline in terms of their own jobs. The only person who knew Dad who didn't do that was [Captain] Gordon Vette because he didn't care and he was interested in finding out what actually happened. He believed that any pilot could have had that happen to him that day. The likes of Ross Gordon and other family friends stuck round but a lot of them disappeared.'

Maria Collins might have been wrapped in her own soaring grief, but the girls watched her carefully. They are full of admiration for the courage and resilience their mother showed in those first days and months after the death of their father.

Kathryn: 'Mum was very focused on getting on with her life on a daily basis, getting on with her life for us so we had some degree of normality with regard to what we were doing in those days. So we had a routine. The routine got us through. Getting up in the morning, having breakfast, brushing your teeth, brushing your hair, going to school, so the same routine kept going. If she'd actually gone, "I can't do this any more," and had been in her room 24 hours a day, seven days a week, we would have lost not only him but her as well. I think she felt we needed her to show some fortitude and she did. She was there.

'Emotionally she was under huge stress so we didn't have huge dinnertime conversations any more, we didn't have time for that. Elizabeth's and my issues tended to be . . . she had to focus on Pip and Adrienne and make sure they were dealt with. Elizabeth's and my discussions about whatever we wanted to talk about came second because you didn't have . . . effectively, we just got on with the process of living and she had to do it any way she could and to her credit she did a really, really good job. What she showed us was that you can't give up. Despite the fact that you want to wallow, and she used to joke about ending up in Sunnyside, she said, "I could never allow myself to because I had you guys to live for and that was much more important than anything self-indulgent that I could have considered doing".'

Maria would say that she still had Jim. She just had to think of each of her girls as a quarter of Jim and the four of them made up the whole.

Kathryn looks back and marvels at her mother. What had occurred was not just the loss of a beloved family member who had died suddenly or had died quietly after a long illness. This was the loss of a vital husband, a key energetic force within a marriage and within a family of four very smart and very creative girls, in frightful circumstances. He had flown his aeroplane into the side of a mountain, possibly in cloud and he and 256 other people were killed. The accident was not only a national catastrophe and a national trauma, it was receiving massive attention right round the world. It was the fourth largest air accident of all time in terms of loss of life. Her late husband, the loss of whom had swept away the foundations of her world, was the focus of a very serious investigation.

'She was stressed. She'd lost Dad in terrible circumstances and she was very depressed by that, I think. I think she described herself as being like a taut rubber band. Strung out. She was strung in this tight, pin-droppy situation. We were all in a stress situation for a long time, which meant you couldn't sit back and smell the roses, you couldn't sit back and have a chat about this or that and those little in-between things, the minutiae of life because the minutiae didn't matter any more — what mattered was existing.'

Elizabeth: 'Mum is pretty sure of her own needs. And they include her sanity time. For as long as I can remember she's been to yoga class twice a week, if not more, and her yoghurt time, as Dad used to call it, her yoghurt time is her sanctuary. That's where she does her physical strengthening and also her spiritual renewal. I think that's been invaluable for her, just to have time out from the rat race of life. She walks regularly. She walks every morning, she's well read, she has a wide circle of friends, she's in touch with a lot of people, so she's a pretty together kind of person.'

But it was tough. The two younger girls had to be managed and brought through, as unscathed as possible, the huge event the family had suffered. Christmas was approaching. This was going to be a heartbreaker.

And on 14 December, just over a fortnight after the accident on the mountain, Ron Chippindale, the Chief Inspector of Air Accidents, came to visit. That's when Maria knew from what he said and from his tone that he'd already made his mind up as to the cause of the loss of the DC-10. He was already reciting his mantra, 'Jim was too low, Maria. Jim was too low.'

Maria was not entirely downcast by her realisation of where Chippindale's mind was heading in terms of causation. Just before his visit, one of Air New Zealand's most senior pilots had come to see her. This man, during the course of the next year, would make history with his convincing research into polar whiteout, the curse of polar fliers, the polar ocular phenomenon that finally doomed Flight 901. He was Gordon Vette, one of the most senior DC-10 captains of all.

He told Maria: 'This is not Jim Collins's behaviour. I trained him and I know what he was like. It would not have been a scenario where Jim said, "Right, well chaps, let's go just a bit lower and see what we can do down there", with the rest of them on the flight deck saying, "No, no, no" and he's saying, "Let's do it".' Vette told Maria that Jim Collins was simply not like that.

And he told Maria he was going to find out what happened. Captain Barney Wyatt, remember, had already told Maria about some serious misadventure in the computer section. Strange claims were being made.

Strange things were being said. People who should have been there were not. In the meantime, there was a home to maintain. There were grieving, desperately sad children.

Elizabeth: 'I probably let her down. I think it was pretty hard for her to have teenagers, four young girls in the house with no father and being a solo mother all the time. And I was a right little shit, absolutely. Get her to tell you about that.'

I did not. And Maria would not have told me anyway.

Elizabeth: 'I didn't understand. I think Mum spent ages trying to work out what that was all about and I think she concluded that I felt it was her fault that Dad was no longer round. And I just don't think that was the right interpretation. I didn't for a moment blame Mum. But I just . . . I was going through hormonal stress as a teenager and just hating who I was and all that sort of stuff, you know. You go through stages of being awkward in your skin as a teenager.'

Holmes: 'Well, I suppose you *were* angry. Why would you not have been?'

Elizabeth: 'Yeah. Angry. But probably also felt like a fish out of water at school because my whole circumstances had changed and I was in a different space to teenagers of my own age at school. They had different areas of focus and priorities and stuff whereas my thoughts had changed to Commissions of Inquiry and counsel and witnesses and maps and I wasn't thinking about history or reading *To Kill a Mockingbird.* I mean, I did it for my schooling but my concentration was somewhere else.'

H: 'By being a shit do you mean slamming doors, bad tempered . . .?'

Elizabeth: 'No, I was just rude to Mum. She would irritate me. We can still irritate each other. And we're both very practically minded but if we're working in the kitchen together, which I find is quite a good place to work out a dynamic, often you can coordinate well with someone without speaking. But Mum and I always bang into each other, we're always going for the same place at the same time, you know how irritating that can be. It's just a small example. But then, we can travel together really well, we think similarly in many ways, too.'

Maria survived those first crazy, life-changing, cyclonic months. She was the bamboo in the storm. She could yield and bend to the changes in the weather. She managed, through it all, with the children torn apart at the loss of their father, to stay rooted and intact in the torrential forces that now began to bear down upon her.

But both Kathryn and Elizabeth paint a picture of a grim and grieving home. Kathryn told me several times that when her father died, the fun stopped. She wrote this in the notebook I gave her to write thoughts and memories in. The fun stopped. And I can imagine, from the fun we all had at our first meeting together, what fun there had been before Jim Collins was killed. They are fun women. Their humour is fast and sharp.

Kathryn: 'The jokes disappeared because a lot of the things we'd had as a family together revolved around being a group and the joker in the family was Dad. Dad was conservative but he had a great sense of humour and he made light of things in a way that was funny. Not having him there any more meant that disappeared. There was no levity.'

Holmes: 'Suddenly, too, you were a house full of women and the big presence, this strong male presence of your father, was gone.'

Kathryn: 'Say, for example, one of us was having an argument with another over something probably unimportant, he would intervene to stop the escalation of the argument because it was women arguing about women's things and he'd go, "Whatever, just don't worry about this and don't worry about that."

'In later years I often used to think that maybe if he'd been round while we were teenagers . . . as I got older Mum used to worry about my whereabouts and where I was at night. There was the toga party incident and I was reliant on a ride home from someone so I didn't get home till 1 a.m. and Mum had been waiting for me in the garden since midnight and she said, "What was I going to tell the police, you're wearing a sheet?" If Dad had been there he would have said, "Maria, don't worry," and I'm sure he would have helped Mum deal with stuff she was dealing with on her own. In many circumstances she had to deal with stuff on her own and he wasn't around to be her companion. The dynamics of how he integrated with the whole family at our different levels wasn't there any more, so it was like a big part of the jigsaw puzzle — if you regard a family as a jigsaw puzzle of people and personalities — a large part of that infrastructure had just vanished, been uprooted, removed.'

If both Maria and Kathryn Schollum believe that the two older girls took the brunt of their father's death and that, of the two, Elizabeth was affected the most, Pip believes Kathryn took the brunt, that she is closest to her mother in her experience of the tragedy. 'Kathryn's kind of the head of the family. I see her and Mum as having borne the brunt of the impact on the family when the accident happened and then all that happened in the years that followed. And she's outgoing and she likes to have input into the lives of the rest of us. And from my point of view that's welcomed. We know more about each other's lives than other families I know. We rely on each other.'

I'm sitting talking to Elizabeth one Sunday evening, also in the winter of 2010. The passion and admiration both of the older girls feel for their father had become apparent to me. Elizabeth is a fine conversationalist. She speaks well. She does not lack a barb in her wit and is not without a talent for a finely turned line. She has a fine contralto voice, the loveliest voice of all the Collins girls.

Holmes: 'He was good looking, wasn't he?'

Elizabeth: 'Absolutely. He was tall, dark and handsome.'

H: 'Sometimes I think you're both, you and Kathryn, half in love with him.' I am teasing.

Elizabeth: 'I think any psychologist would say to you that that's typical for daughters to fathers, and typical of a deceased father because they tend to be idolised by their daughters anyway. But I remember at the time, when he was alive, it was great to take him along to school because he was just the father that everybody loved. He was great.'

H: 'Could you tell he was handsome?'

Elizabeth: 'Absolutely. And he always smelt good, he always wore lovely aftershave. Yeah, he wore his uniform well. He had a very striking physique and being tall and slender and particular about wearing his uniform smartly, he just always looked crisp. And you know, I still watch captains come off aircraft now with their four stripes and very few of them have that same air of charisma, few if any.'

H: 'Have you thought about this a lot?'

Elizabeth: 'Yeah, I have. I'm very happy to admit that I was in love with Dad but as a daughter would be towards a father she has great affection for.'

I tell her that I think Kathryn feels the same way about their father. Their father was, says Elizabeth, a great buddy. And she and her father understood each other well. Elizabeth feels she was the closest to her father of the four sisters. Kathryn believes *she* was.

Jim Collins must have been doing something right.

The rivalry between Kathryn and Elizabeth is legendary within the family. Maria rolls her eyes. 'Talk about sibling rivalry, it was unbelievable. They could have scratched each other's eyes out at times. It was vicious. I was quite horrified. I'm an only child for a start so I never experienced that.

But how could they be so angry with each other?'

Or, as Elizabeth says, 'Kathryn was the beautiful, glamorous, attractive elder sister and I was very much the quiet ugly duckling.'

H: 'Why do you say that?'

Elizabeth: 'Because I was. I wasn't an extrovert. I was more of an observer.'

The 'ugly duckling' blossomed, of course, but she would do so later and she would do it a long way from New Zealand and a long way from Erebus.

The rivalry went both ways. I ask Maria what Kathryn would have envied about Elizabeth. 'Oh, the playing of musical instruments, by sheer hard work but, of course, Kathryn didn't acknowledge that. She practises, she worked at it. She got there.'

However, the watcher, Adrienne, has studied this too.

Adrienne: 'Well, Elizabeth's always thought Kathryn was the glamorous one who went to parties and never had to carry any responsibility or whatever and got bulimic and Kathryn will say that she was only doing that because she saw how stressed Mum was and she had to carry the can, or whatever. And Elizabeth felt like she was the ugly duckling and in her shadow. But, when Kathryn's first kid was born, Elizabeth came immediately from London and there are the two of them in tears, hugging each other in tears of happiness. So go figure.'

Both Kathryn and Elizabeth tell me directly that they felt Maria ceased having the time for them that she had before the accident. Kathryn tells me that Maria's conversation to her at dinner was reduced to 'Finish your dinner.' But again, they do not judge their mother harshly for this. It occurred in a barren landscape of sadness and grieving in which they had to live and observe each other, each finding their own grief worsened by the grief of their mother and siblings.

Both Kathryn and Elizabeth will tell you that Maria never let the side down. They both speak of her strength, her determination to keep busy, to keep moving ahead. Says Elizabeth, 'I've seen her weeping, and I've felt so protective of her at those times because that's when she's at her most vulnerable and tired. There's nobody there for her except us.'

I tell Maria about Kathryn's having written that the fun in the family stopped.

Maria sighs . . . and spends some moments thinking. 'Yeah. Because I could get through the day with the jobs, the meals, getting the girls to do this, this and this but I couldn't play with them as well as Jim could. Or read to them as well, or act the goat. I hadn't got enough energy or imagination, and I didn't feel like it anyway. But I hadn't anything left to give them.'

Jim Collins seems, by the accounts of people who knew him as a family man and who saw him as a father, to have been genuinely gifted in his dealing with children.

Maria: 'He was a wonderful father. And having had three younger siblings himself, two of whom were considerably younger than him, he was very good at being a calming influence when I was anything but, because when they were little, I'd had the children all day and one may have been fractious and I was probably doubting my own mothering skills. And he'd just pick that baby up and start humming away and that baby would be quieted. And I used to get angry, thinking: "He can do it. Why can't I?"'

Holmes: 'You've described your marriage as bliss.'

Maria: 'I know that for the few years we had together, I was very fortunate to have Jim as a husband. I know it from my friends who said to me, "What a gorgeous guy he is. You're so lucky. He listens to you when you're talking, you can have a proper conversation. He takes his part in dealing with the kids. He reads to them. He makes use of time that he might not have next week because he's away, by doing it today. He's nice to everybody." He was. Even the postman who walked up and down here would be talking to Jim as he built the fence outside and came to me later saying, "What a nice guy".'

But now, as Christmas 1979 approached, a month after the late night call that told her of the loss of the DC-10 on Mount Erebus, Maria felt the frightful hollowness, hopelessness and emptiness of her loss.

Kathryn recalls the bleakness of life then. The laughter had ceased. 'But I think it's come back. We can still laugh about things but at the time Pip and Adrienne were young, Elizabeth and I were stressed and Mum was completely just trying to cope. There wasn't a lot to laugh about. Life was all grey, serious. It was a treadmill.'

But on Friday nights, there she was. Kathryn Schollum would show up like sunshine at night. Kathryn Schollum threw love and life at them all. She would arrive with sweets for the girls, Jaffas or Snifters, or whatever had taken her fancy at the dairy up the road and she would say, 'Come on, Maria. Let's have a drink.' And she would go outside for a few cigarettes. In those days, Schollum tells me, at the time of the accident, her tipple was whisky and soda. Later it became sherry. Over time she abandoned the sherry, she chuckles, because she became 'ensconced' in it. Now she drinks a wine.

Kathryn Schollum's voice is one she has earned. Her manner of speaking is delightfully theatrical. She is full of humour and life and she uses language exactly. At the Collinses she laughed and talked and listened and got the girls to discuss their days. Kathryn Carter says there was no one round to do that then.

Kathryn Schollum watched them all closely, these daughters of Erebus.

And Christmas came. Jim had been dead a month. Maria did what she had always done and celebrated Christmas with a Christmas Eve dinner, in the European tradition.

'It was, I think, very bad for Maria that Christmas. I think that that was probably when it hit her more than any other time, because, you know, for a month, she was buoyed up by friends coming and making sure everything was all right,' Kathryn Schollum says. 'And I have to say, I think the girls, the girls were starting to feel the absence of their father. I think Kathryn said to me on one occasion, "I don't know how we would have survived without you." Which was really rather wonderful.'

She says she greatly admired Maria's insistence that Christmas should carry on as usual. 'She was determined that the girls should, as much as possible, put sadness and confusion aside and have a happy Christmas. Gifts were opened with great excitement before the meal. That lifted spirits considerably. There were 15 or 20 people gathered round the table all very conscious of the poignancy of the occasion. Our warm and generous host was conspicuously absent. We said grace and we toasted absent friends. And that was that.'

But it was not a happy place. As Kathryn Carter said: 'We knew that the Christmas magic Mum and Dad made together for us wouldn't work without Dad, even though Mum made a big effort as did our grandparents. And although there were Christmases when Dad was away working and he wasn't there, we always knew he wasn't far away from us in thought. Being dead is different from being away. We proposed the toast to absent friends and I thought then that his absence had probably broken many hearts round the table because his smile and kindness to others used to light the room. You could see the sadness in people's eyes that Christmas.'

Pip tells a story from round this time. She went to stay for the weekend with her friend Gillian. On Sunday morning, Gillian took Pip with her to Sunday school. The Sunday school teacher was Mrs Albrecht. She asked Pip what her father did.

Pip replied as she had heard her mother respond: 'My father was involved in the Erebus incident.'

'Oh,' said Mrs Albrecht, kindly. 'And what does he do now?'

19

Josef and Annemarie

Play the Marseillaise . . . Play it!

— Victor Lazlo, *Casablanca*

The parents of Maria Collins, Josef and Annemarie Tretter, were Viennese of a Jewish background. It was 1938. Hitler's Germany had taken Austria. Maria was three years old.

Until then, life for Josef and Annemarie had been elegant and gracious. Annemarie grew up with a governess and maids. She would not learn to cook until she came to New Zealand. She was amazed when she learnt that water to make tea had to be boiling. Her father, an industrial chemist — so Elizabeth Collins wrote in the story of her family background — travelled regularly on business. He was devoted to opera, he sang with a warm baritone and he was a keen violinist. He wrote to Annemarie once when she was staying in Prague, advising her to attend the theatre and to read the score or the play first. Whenever he got back to Vienna, the father and daughter gorged themselves on concerts. One summer, when Annemarie was 18, she and her father went to 74 concerts.

Vienna in summer is one of the world's loveliest cities. In spring the air is thick and warm after the bleak, endless mid-continental winters that seem to last forever. When Vienna throws off the desolate gloom of winter and explodes into spring, it is a city of romance, elegance and seduction. Suddenly the avenues and the parks are lush with an eruption of brilliant young green. In the wine villages and in the ancient Nineteenth District, revellers laugh the evening away with food and young wine from the hillsides, the trees above them flickering in the soft light of the lamps.

Annemarie loved the balls and the dance parties that filled the evenings in the summers of pre-war Vienna. The Austrian Empire might have been a thing of the past, torn apart in 1918 and its aristocracy banned, but it had been one of the greatest empires ever and the city's design and architecture reflected the might and power of imperial glory. Vienna is a grand city and a city steeped in a tradition of old families, grand apartments, beautiful women in beautiful gowns and the genius of the great composers. It is a city of glittering chandeliers and gorgeous parks and pavilions. It is a melting pot of people. The magnificent Gothic cathedral of St Stephen shares the skyline with the grand copper dome of Karlskirche, either side of which are two tall towers that resemble minarets. As the early nineteenth century Austrian Foreign Minister, Prince Otto Metternich said, 'Asia starts in the Landstrasse' — one of Vienna's inner-city districts.

As a girl, Annemarie danced her way through those sensuous, dreaming summer nights. Her regular dance partner was Franz Strauss, the son of Richard Strauss.

Josef and Annemarie met on a Sunday morning in 1923 when a group of friends assembled for a day's hiking in the mountains to picnic amongst the brilliant blue of the gentian flowers. Annemarie's father, Arnold, liked Josef. And like Arnold, Josef loved music.

Arnold, who managed cosmetics factories in Berlin and Krakow as well as in Vienna, was often away. In the late 1920s he became increasingly depressed. One day in 1929, possibly in response to the sudden economic collapse sweeping the world, he took a room at a hotel in Vienna and shot himself. A maid found him dead two hours later. Annemarie would always say that she never got over the shock and the sadness of losing the father she loved — in the same way her granddaughters would never get over the shock and heartbreak of losing their father as suddenly almost exactly 50 years later.

Annemarie and Josef married quietly in 1930. Her firstborn, a son, died of pneumonia at three weeks. She never recovered entirely from the death of little Franz either. Then, in 1935, Maria Tretter was born.

But now it is 1938, swastikas hung from all of the public buildings and the Imperial Hotel. The city was crawling with Nazis, the world expected war and the Jews were wondering what in God's name the Nazis were going to do. Austrian Chancellor Kurt von Schuschnigg resigned in a broken-hearted speech on radio because, he said, he wanted no bloodshed and the Germans wanted Austria. When his speech finished, the ORF, the Austrian state broadcaster, played the third movement of the Emperor Quartet by Haydn.

Elizabeth wrote in her family story that her grandmother cried copiously all the way through the quartet. Annemarie's mother could not understand her reaction. She thought nothing would change, not really, and that life would more or less go on as before. One simply should try and keep out of the Nazis' way. Josef and Annemarie, however, could sense the world was going to change forever.

Josef was a successful commercial lawyer. He was company solicitor for a confectionary firm, G & W Heller, in Vienna. He managed their export division and spoke English and Italian. The Nazis arrived in Vienna and Josef was sacked for being a Jew. He had served the company for 10 years. The letter of dismissal spelt it out. You have to go, Herr Tretter, because you are a Jew.

Both Josef and Annemarie, known to writers of anti-Nazi literature, were arrested by the Gestapo. Josef disappeared first. When Annemarie went to Gestapo headquarters to inquire if he was, by any chance, in their custody, she too was hauled in and locked up. Annemarie's mother, Paula, looked after Maria back in her vast apartment and feared the worst. The Gestapo denied knowing where Josef was.

Annemarie shared a cell for a while with a Czech girl, Tonicka. Tonicka greeted Annemarie with a big hug. They slept with the light on. Tonicka caught fleas and stuck them in the soap to frame her achievement. Annemarie received from the League of Human Rights half an ounce of butter and two ounces of cheese. Paula was able to send her daughter 10 marks every week for coffee, soap and cigarettes. And it was one day, when she was signing for her 10 marks — the Nazis loved record keeping — that Annemarie saw Josef's signature.

Still she knew nothing of where he was, but in the exercise yard one day, she realised he was alive and he was there in the men's section of the same prison. Annemarie and Josef had a little ritual from their hiking days. When they walked through thick woodland they kept in touch with a three tone whistle. Annemarie whistled the tune in the exercise yard. The same three tone whistle was returned. It had to be Josef.

Paula meanwhile told little Maria that mother and father had gone to the mountains to pick her some pretty gentian flowers and would be back soon. At the same time, she went to work with lawyers to negotiate for the couple's release. After 17 days, Annemarie was told she was about to be released and Josef would be released soon after. Annemarie went back to her cell and told a delighted Tonicka. Shortly afterwards Tonicka was called from the cell. When she came back, she was downcast. She collected her belongings and left. Annemarie never heard of her again.

It was all enough for anyone. It was time to get out. Paula suggested Prague. No, said Josef, out, away, far away from Europe. Josef applied for visas to the United States, Australia and New Zealand. The New Zealand visa for Josef, Annemarie and Maria, for which one of the New Zealand sponsors was the Christchurch-based philosopher Karl (later Sir Karl) Popper, arrived first. That would do.

Josef and Annemarie still lived in Paula's large apartment in Vienna's Fourth District. Paula, who was born a Czech, near Prague, knew that she too had to go, but New Zealand was not an option for this sophisticated Central European. She did not want to go, says Maria, to a country where the inhabitants were 'uncultured and wore grass skirts'.

She would go to Prague. Prague would be safe. Josef and Annemarie pleaded with her to come with them to the other side of the world but to no avail. So Annemarie helped Paula pack her belongings, got them insured, and saw her on the train to Prague just days before she, Josef and Maria left Vienna themselves. None of them would see Paula again. No one could imagine the historic monstrosities to come.

The Tretters left Vienna in mid-November 1938. They would never see family or friends again. They holed up in Albania for six weeks. They were out of Vienna and safe. Their possessions were packed and sent to Hamburg for transport to New Zealand by ship.

Annemarie maintained contact with Paula by letters for the next three years, until 1941. Her letters from Europe appeared to be censored. In her last letter, a postcard dated November 1941, Paula wrote that she had moved to Poland to a small town called Lodz where she was being well looked after. Then, a few months later, in February, Annemarie was informed by the Red Cross that Paula had died of typhus. She was 60 years old.

Annemarie made some inquiries over the years, after the war. They found out that there had been several transports of Jews in railway trucks from Prague to various concentration camps. Some went to Terezin camp in Czechoslovakia itself, others went to Auschwitz and others to the Jewish ghetto at Lodz, just north of Krakow. Maria says, 'Whether she died of typhus, or sheer cold, starvation or extreme stress, who knows?' An information bank in Jerusalem, Yad Vastem, holds the immaculate German records that show Paula was taken to Lodz.

In 2009, Maria and Kathryn went to Prague. They visited the main synagogue. The synagogue has on its walls the names of the Jews deported from Prague during the war. They found Paula's name. She was deported on 31 October 1941. She died four months later on 28 February 1942. What she endured in those four months haunted Annemarie forever. It haunts Maria, too.

Josef sailed to New Zealand first. He arrived in Wellington on the good ship *Arawa* in March 1939. He went to Christchurch where he got a job in a bakery. In the months during which he was no longer a practising lawyer in Vienna he had learnt some baking. Unfortunately Christchurch people didn't want Apfelstrudel and Sachertorte and Kugelhupf and Josef didn't do lamingtons or scones. Josef was fired. He moved to Auckland.

Annemarie and Maria had meanwhile made it to London to stay with a cousin. Then they sailed to New York and travelled by train to San Francisco, which they left on the *Mariposa* in April 1939, bound for Auckland. When they arrived in Hawaii they were greeted with sweet frangipani leis. Annemarie would never forget the smell of the exotic, tropical flowers. They thrilled her. Then it was on to New Zealand and the challenge of a new world and a new life in the safety of a land far from the unprecedented carnage, the destruction and heinous cruelty that was about to engulf not only Vienna but all of Europe and Russia.

Josef found work. He couldn't practise law without studying New Zealand law. And he wasn't allowed to study because he was an enemy alien, for which he reported twice weekly to the police. He worked in a factory during the week and as a photographer on Waiheke Island at weekends. Later, because he missed the family at weekends, he secured a job as a cleaner at the Bycroft biscuit factory. Then he went to Astley's leather tannery. They allowed him to take home second-grade leather. Then a friend, a Mr Dexter, who had seen a little niche in the market when it came to leather, suggested that Josef should set up a business making leather watchstraps. They weren't manufactured here. Supply was erratic, apparently. His business, J. K. Tretter, became a success.

And they developed their new life. They continued their tramping and their hiking. They loved Coromandel, Lake Waikaremoana and National

Park. Through this they met new friends. Josef went to the synagogue in Auckland's Greys Avenue. He formed many friendships there.

And Maria went to school. At Epsom Normal Primary, she was deemed very bright. She refused to speak German because her friends found it strange. And probably, one supposes, because there was a war on against Germany. Maria asked her mother not to send her to school with rye bread and cottage cheese but with white bread and jam instead.

Maria went off to Otago University. She wanted to study medicine. Josef said he believed it would be a waste of the resources of their adoptive country to train her to be a doctor, only to have her leave the profession to have children. She graduated Bachelor of Science in biochemistry and went to work as a biochemist in the laboratory at Auckland Hospital, where she met her lifelong friend, the charming, kind and irrepressible Kathryn Schollum.

Then she went to London, and whilst there met a young man she agreed to marry. But she must have been unsure. She came home to Auckland to think about it. She was invited one night with a friend to a flat of five young men in Remuera. She knew the boys from before she went to Europe. Now she was back with slides of her tours round Europe. The boys suggested she come round and show her slides.

'This is what we did then. This was how New Zealanders saw the rest of the world then. I already felt dubious because, you know, other people's slides are pretty boring.'

But go she did. One of the flatmates was new. She had not seen him before and he caught her eye immediately. Jim Collins was a pilot, she learnt. He flew the four engine turbo prop Electras for Air New Zealand. He had taken a night off from studying for a move into the right-hand seat of the DC-6. Maria noted that it was Jim Collins who had developed the flat's roster to keep the household clean and tidy. Jim ran the music on the turntable. It started with Mozart.

Kathryn Schollum says that Maria knew the minute she met him that she loved Jim Collins. But Jim was with another girl.

'I thought at the time, Oh what a shame, he looks and sounds really nice,' Maria says. She noticed his physical looks. 'He was a nice-looking guy. Not a hunk. He was a very slight build, always. But he was also caring. Instead of just swilling beer, everybody got coffee, everybody got something to eat. "Oh, I haven't met you before," you know. He played the gracious host without having to. And I thought that was nice.'

This was 1960. Jim was 26. He had big bushy eyebrows. Jim's eyebrows were famous.

Holmes: 'Did you think he was attracted to you?'

Maria: 'I wasn't thinking about what he thought of me. I was thinking more of what I thought about him. I was only home for a short time. I was going back to the UK to marry somebody else. I was just home for the summer.'

H: 'So you weren't expecting this at all, really?'

Maria: 'Not at all. I wasn't looking for it. But isn't that the way? When you're not looking?'

H: 'Couple of weeks go by, he rings you?'

Maria: 'Not a couple of weeks. Months went by, months went by. Would have been five, six months. And he invited me to go with him — one of his flatmates was getting married and they were having a party for him. And we were going to a dine and dance place in the Waitakeres called The Back of the Moon. I don't know, you're not an Auckland boy are you, Paul? This was a very trendy place in the Waitakeres.'

H: 'Why did he wait five months?'

Maria: 'I don't know. Yeah. I don't . . .'

H: 'I'll have to ask him.'

Maria: 'You'd have to ask him. I think he had other issues to deal with before he got to me. I can only guess.'

H: 'What was it like seeing him for the second time, then?'

Maria: 'It was great. We had a lovely time. He loved dancing and so did I. I don't remember much about anybody else. We just seemed to dance all night. And it was great.'

To dance. Just as Annemarie danced on those gorgeous, swirling, Viennese nights with the son of the great composer.

H: 'Was that the night you fell in love with him?'

Maria: 'Oh, falling in love with him? I felt very comfortable with him. He was a very pleasant, comfortable sort of person to be with. He was mindful of the needs of others. I don't mean he was servile but he was mindful there were other people in the environment apart from himself.'

Which would, of course, make him an excellent airline captain. I asked Maria to describe his intelligence.

Maria: 'Oh, he always said he wasn't brainy. He had to sit School Cert twice. He always considered himself not very bright because everybody got it the first time except him.'

This surprises me, because the boys who do well flying aircraft in the air force and who go on to captain great airliners are very good at sums. But, Maria says, maths is not the only subject in School Cert. True.

H: 'Did he really believe he was dumb or did he just say that?'

Maria: 'No, I don't think he thought he was dumb but he felt that because he was associating with me and I had a BSc, so I had tertiary education, that somehow his qualifications were not the same as mine.'

H: 'You were European, sophisticated, cultured, your parents spoke with foreign accents, learning meant a lot in your family. What was his background?'

Maria: 'He was totally different. I used to agonise as I thought, "I'm going to be marrying someone who has no tertiary qualification, who's got no degree. Does that matter?" And then I decided that he's got a far deeper wisdom. And in the end that's what matters. It's the wisdom, it's not the bits of paper that you accumulate as the only arbiter of the degree of your intellectual ability. He was wiser than me because he'd learnt it through his upbringing and his work. And his sense of responsibility, because he was the first of his siblings to earn a salary he might be able to help his parents financially, which he did. I soon realised that it's wisdom and the way you treat other people and the way you behave in your community which in the end matters more than the university degrees.'

H: 'The flying ever bother you?'

Maria: 'It bothered me hugely. The irregular hours, that he mightn't be here for certain birthdays, that there might be a concert the kids were performing in at school and he might miss it. Particularly if there wasn't much notice given. If there was notice, you know a month's notice given, he could ask for the time off.'

H: 'I suppose most people, if you were to ask them about their husband's flying, might think more about the thing hitting the ground.'

Maria: 'That was my first question to him. And he said that chances of him doing that were far less than me in my car every day. And he could quote statistics, about the number of people who got damaged in cars versus the number of people damaged in aeroplanes.'

H: 'What did you make of the other pilots?'

Maria: 'They were all great gentlemen on the surface. Many of them drank far too much, as soon as you got beneath the veneer. But Jim wasn't like that. He didn't need to drink in order to be laughing and jolly and sociable, he was naturally like that.'

H: 'I was just asking because despite all of that, were you ever surprised by anything about them, namely that they are actually, beneath it all, quite cautious people?'

Maria: 'Absolutely cautious people. I mean, they know, they knew not only was their own life on the line but on the line were the passengers who went with them. Of course they were cautious.'

It took Jim Collins a mere six years from when he joined Air New Zealand to be promoted to captain, to gain his own command. It is wrong to make the assumption that because you are a very good pilot that you will necessarily make captain. The captain is a commander and he must be able to command men and women and make responsible decisions in sometimes appallingly adverse conditions in sometimes appallingly short time frames.

Maria was proud when he made captain. 'Of course, because we'd just had a baby daughter as well. So it was a nice coincidence that in 1964 when he became captain, he became a father, virtually within days of each other. The two almost went together, so that was pretty nice.'

H: 'What were the things you had in common. I take it he didn't rush off to the Auckland Philharmonia?'

Maria: 'He didn't rush off to the Auckland Philharmonia. He would never have said, "I think this would be a wonderful concert, let's go." But if I said, "I think this might be a wonderful concert, let's go," he'd say, "Yeah I'm home that night. Yeah, let's, good idea." So we did all those things. We shared the child rearing, he was a wonderful father.'

Maria has described her marriage to Jim Collins as bliss. They had 17 years together. Their daughters are shrewd observers, I have observed. I have a feeling he was too.

H: 'Was he down to earth?'

Maria: 'He was really down to earth. But, look, he had to be because he dealt with the public. In those days, remember, the captain would get the aircraft set up at the top of the climb and then walk right back through the cabin when everything was fine and he would talk to everybody. And, you know, that was part of it, you hobnobbed with the passengers and made everyone feel secure. And you put your hat on when you walked through to the passengers so you looked the part and people felt secure. And he was nice to everybody and if someone was sitting by themselves looking a bit frightened, he would talk to them and put them at ease. That was part of their job in those days. So he was good at talking to everybody.'

H: 'How seriously did he take the responsibility of having passengers behind him?'

Maria: 'Hugely. Hugely. He loved it. I always said there were three of us in the marriage. There were him and me and the job. And I came second after the job. He loved it. He left school to go to the air force and he signed up for 25 years as an airframe mechanic because he thought that was the nearest he was going to get to flying and he would at least be in the air force as an airframe mechanic, that he might service the aircraft even if he didn't fly them because his parents were never going to be able to afford to give him flying lessons. Then he was selected for flight training. Suddenly the air force discovered it had too many pilots and at the same time, Air New Zealand, or TEAL as it was then, was looking for more pilots and so Jim was allowed an honourable discharge and applied for a job with Air New Zealand and that's how he became a commercial airline pilot.'

And that is how Jim Collins came to be flying TE901 to Antarctica on 28 November 1979 and that is how he came to be a dead commercial airline pilot. And now, he'd been blamed for the disaster, a blame that suited the government and the airline perfectly, even though the appropriate words of respect for the dead captain's flying ability had been voiced. But the initial findings did not ring true with the public, did not match what all his colleagues said about Jim Collins as an airman. Now there was a Royal Commission of Inquiry to investigate the accident further, an inquiry directed specifically to find out what and who caused the accident.

And representing Maria at this inquiry was the young barrister, Paul Davison QC. Maria knew nothing of barristers but she was starting to realise that Paul Davison was immensely capable. He worked hard, he was sharp and his skills as an interrogator and a cross-examiner were emerging as solidly backed by research and comprehension.

When she could, she attended the hearings of the Royal Commission and watched — and tried to understand. And to hope, for her late husband's sake that there was something in what Barney Wyatt had told her in those first days. Paul Davison, says Maria, certainly thought so. In fact Davison knew that, in the coordinate change, combined with the pilots not being told, they had the obvious accident cause.

But it was a time of profound despair for Maria Collins. Away from the children and the world, for whom she erected a brave and dignified facade, she knew only despair as the Royal Commission wended its alluvial, mercurial way through a seemingly unrelieved landscape of incomprehensible detail.

H: 'You've told me before you used to sit in a crumpled heap in Davison's office.'

Maria: 'I did. When the headlines were bad, when the headlines were shouting "Pilot Error". I mean, I know a little bit more about journalism and the media and so on now, but listen, I'm at that stage a 44-year-old mother of four and suddenly I'm dealing with headlines like this.'

H: 'Yes.'

Maria: 'About my husband. And I don't know how to behave. I don't know what to do. And I can see Michael and Paul in the office there with me in a crumpled heap. I'd just taken one of the kids to get her teeth straightened at the orthodontist who was in the building up the road and sent her off, got her off to school and now I'm sitting in Paul's office, you know, reading these awful headlines. Awful headlines.'

H: 'Were Friedlander and Davison encouraging?'

Maria: 'Oh yes, always. Paul told me, very early on, "You've got to be patient, Maria. The judge can see through what's going on." And I said, "See through what? See through what?" He said, "This is a huge can of worms and you've just got to be patient and trust us." And I thought, "Well, it's looking terrible for us." And he would say, "You've just got to trust us." I can remember it. Paul will remember it too.'

The Mahon Report was released in April 1981 and as a result of his inquiries the two pilots, Captain Jim Collins and First Officer Greg Cassin, were 'convincingly' cleared of all blame.

Maria: 'I said it then and I'll say it now. It was a hollow victory. Yeah, great, fantastic. So no more feeling that I was married to a man who irresponsibly killed 257 people through his mismanagement but through the mismanagement of the airline. Doesn't bring him back. So, it was bittersweet. It was a hell of a lot better than how I felt before. But nothing changed, Paul.'

Of course, as we shall discover further on in our narrative, when the report was released the Prime Minister of the day, Robert Muldoon, dumped on it for entirely cynical reasons and the report was never tabled at the time and would not be tabled in Parliament for nearly 20 years. The Chippindale Report remained the legitimate accident verdict. Collins was responsible.

Maria: 'I didn't know [then] that prime ministers do that sort of thing, that they connive with others, that people tell lies at inquiries. I, you know, I was wide-eyed. "I've got to tell the judge, I've got to tell Justice Mahon the truth and everybody else will too".'

H: 'Yes, everyone will tell the truth.'

Maria: 'But I'm intimidated. I'm a child of that time where authority meant something. So, I'm an idiot, a naive one, the one that's thinking, well, everybody else will do as I do. I mean, you tell the judge the truth, you wouldn't dare do anything else. I've got no idea that mates get together like that.'

H: 'Do you remember that line in Sam Mahon's book? Mahon's been made a judge and he's appointed to Auckland and he writes to an old mate in Christchurch, "No Old Boy network up here, every man for himself." He didn't understand Auckland at that stage, did he?'

Maria: 'No, he didn't. Well, Mahon knew about the networks but I didn't. Or should I say I knew we had old girls' and old boys' networks but I didn't think it would extend to crime —'

H: 'And dishonesty.'

Maria: 'And dishonesty. And jacking things up so they looked okay and here's another trip round the world for you and your wife. I didn't dream about that. I truly didn't.'

Maria is referring, of course, to the lavish hospitality extended to the Chief Inspector of Air Accidents over the years after Erebus in order for him to attend those very important air accident conferences in northern hemisphere summers.

Chippindale was killed instantly by a runaway car when he stepped off a curb on his morning walk at 7.25 on 12 February 2008. Like Jim Collins, he never knew a thing.

H: 'It has occurred to me that the manner of his death had a kind of poetic justice.'

Maria: 'Perhaps. But that's nonsense. He was going for a walk minding his own business early one morning and he was in the wrong place at the wrong moment and that guy hit him. I realised it could have been me.'

H: 'But he couldn't say goodbye to his family either.'

Maria: 'No.'

The Friday afternoon is drawing out. We have been talking for a long time.

H: 'Do you ever get over it?'

Maria: 'No. You get round it.'

H: 'How real is Jim Collins to you still?'

Maria: 'Well, after 31 years, I think I wonder what he'd think about this or that, or that he'd be growling about this or that. But he's here as part of the background of our lives.'

Maria then remarks that it has only occurred to her recently that many people might think that the Collins family might regard the Erebus disaster as being only about the Collinses. 'I know there were 256 other families who were equally bereaved as we were. It's just that our name comes up when the word Erebus comes up. I mean, their grief is just as intense and tragic as ours.'

H: 'What do you think of it all, looking back. Was it meant to test you . . .?'

Maria: 'Oh, I don't think so.'

H: 'No.'

Maria: 'It was an accident.'

H: 'Yes.'

Maria: 'You know, we had everything to live for. We were truly blessed, Jim and me. We had lovely kids, we didn't have financial worries, we travelled together, we had time together, we always had the odd weekend away together, even when the children were small.'

H: 'Is life cruel?'

Maria: 'Well if I start going into a poor me mode, yes it is. But it's been pretty fantastic as well. And look, now I've got my family, my friends and my health. What more? Jim coming back would be the final crowning glory.'

H: 'The fish would be off.'

Maria smiles. 'Never mind.'

Josef Tretter, who so successfully got his family away from Vienna and the Nazi plague in November 1938, and who, the girls agree, adored Jim Collins, watched his only daughter face the grief of his loss and the burden of bringing up four girls alone.

It broke his heart. Annemarie's mother had died at the hands of Nazi criminals somewhere in the freezing ghetto of Lodz, in Poland, in 1942. Now, decades later, the husband of his only daughter had died violently with 256 others on a frozen Antarctic mountain through a simple act of administrative carelessness, and she was a girl alone. In her heart was a pain as big as the world and he knew she would have a long, hard journey ahead of her.

Jo Tretter's heart broke. He died within 14 months of Erebus.

The other most important man in Maria Collins's life was gone.

20

What Becomes of the Broken-Hearted?

Give sorrow words: the grief that does not speak
Whispers the o'er fraught heart and bids it break.
— William Shakespeare, *Macbeth*, Act 4, Scene 3

1980. It was a time of desolate bleakness.

The Chippindale Report was released in June 1980 against the advice of anyone who had seen the interim report and was about to have anything to do with the Royal Commission, whose hearings would start in a couple of weeks, in early July 1980. It was brutal in its determination that ultimately the pilots were too low and if they weren't flying in cloud then they were headed towards it and there was a mountain inside it. The newspaper headlines punished the pilots badly.

The older girls, Kathryn and Elizabeth, felt bewilderment and indignation. Something was wrong. Something didn't add up. Their father had told them where he was going and it was nowhere near where he crashed. How could he have got over there to that mountain? Maria, for her part, hoped there truly was something in what Barney Wyatt had told her when he disappeared from her life forever, that there was a computer botch-up.

The Royal Commission got under way, Justice Peter Mahon presiding. Maria went almost every day to the Commission. She watched as the most senior airmen in the airline, people who had known Jim since their air force days, simply abandoned him.

If the anger towards the airline of Maria and Kathryn and Elizabeth and

Pip remains real to this day, it is because of that betrayal. Air New Zealand was, and is, a family. It employs several generations of the same family. Sons of pilots become pilots. It is not unusual. So the Collinses' grievance is fundamentally that they were betrayed by family. Is any betrayal worse?

A couple of months after Jim Collins died, Kathryn had a dream. Her father appeared and told her he didn't understand what had happened to him, 'why he was where he was. As if he hadn't quite yet understood that he was actually dead. It was as if he was saying to me that he needed help to understand where he was. He was confused and disoriented and incredulous that he was in this state of being, kind of like a limbo, because he didn't know how he got there.'

Then, about July 1980, just after the Royal Commission had begun: 'I had a dream one night in which he appeared again but he told me that he couldn't begin to describe how wonderful it was where he was. I saw a bright light with lots of colour in it and it exuded a sense of great happiness and wellbeing and he was somewhere in the light but I couldn't actually see his body. He was just talking to me. He told me that he'd met some very interesting, fascinating people including St Francis of Assisi. And he seemed happy to be telling me that he was okay and having a great time. I remember waking up feeling very happy and at peace but then I remember telling myself that I shouldn't be feeling happy, I should be feeling sad because Dad had died. He wasn't alive, and yet the sense of wellbeing stayed with me all day.'

Kathryn has given much thought to death, and its relation to life. 'The difference between the living and the dead is indistinct. Death exists as a physical reality but where emotion is concerned, the dead aren't that far away from us.' She has thought much about this over the years, 'trying to understand the barrier/separation/distinction between the living and the dead when great love exists between the dead and the living'.

The dreams. Jim Collins came home in the dreams. Kathryn: 'One night he sat in the car at the bottom of our old house. He can never hang out with us. He just visits, looks at us, tells us he knows we are here and that he is there and unable entirely to bridge the gap and be with us because he is not now on the same "plane". In the same way he seems less concerned with everyday issues and problems. He just wants us to know he is still there and hasn't forgotten us.'

In the long months after the disaster, to the dismay of their mother, Kathryn and Elizabeth had terrible fights. They were intense. There appears, while their father was alive, to have been a rivalry between them for his affection and attention. Kathryn, the oldest, believes it came more from Elizabeth than from her.

'I'd get mad with her and whack her or something because she was driving me nuts because she'd pick away at me. She'd torment me, Elizabeth. She tormented me. Once, I threw a marble at her. We were playing marbles. It was before Dad died. And we were playing marbles against a plate glass window and she tormented me so much that I threw a marble at her and it smashed the window. I was so angry. I think Dad picked up on that. I think he knew she'd made me angry.'

He might also have been contemplating whether insurance would cover all of a plate glass window.

And in those first early years after Jim Collins was killed, Maria and the two older girls were devastated, bereft. Elizabeth calls it 'personal devastation'. She calls it frightful, empty, as the bottom falls out of your world. Kathryn speaks of them all being lost in a sea of self, everyone trying desperately to survive.

I wonder to Elizabeth if one of the hardest parts of it all was not being able to say goodbye to her father.

'I don't know because I think I equate saying goodbye to knowing what his fate would be. And that would be terrible. To say goodbye and then know he was going to crash into a mountain? In this situation it was better not to know.'

The girls were, and are, quite different. Kathryn lives life more easily, one senses. For Kathryn, the invitations and the flowers poured in.

When beginning an MBA course some years back, Elizabeth wrote about her life. In one chapter she is planning for her fourteenth birthday party which she wants to be a simple picnic. In the story, Dad is still alive, of course. They'll all go out in the boat. Maria won't go in the boat. She likes her two feet on firm ground. Some friends will come, including the boy she likes. Elizabeth knows the little girls, whom she admits she bosses round a lot, will irritate her by playing with their toys until the last minute and will hold them up. Dad and Elizabeth, she tells us, are in the middle of staining the fence round their property. Dad made the special mixture up, Elizabeth stirred it and it's sitting in the garage in a 44-gallon drum.

Then she writes: 'Kathryn is my big sister. And will probably sleep in until the last minute. She takes ages crimping her hair and holds us up. I think fussing over her hair is a waste of time when we are all going to be wind-blown in the boat. I am the practical one and she is the artistic one, family friends tell us. Kathryn has just finished a modelling course so she can earn good pocket money while she is at university the year after next. I think she wants to study architecture. She is beautiful. The only problem is that she thinks she is the bee's knees. The Grammar boys all seem to, too. She does not eat much food these days and is really skinny. She is always admiring herself in the mirror and sucking in her cheeks.'

Kathryn did indeed go on to complete a bachelor's degree in architecture at Auckland University.

Elizabeth is more reserved than Kathryn. She is more formal. She is very articulate, her speech fluent and structured. She dresses very conservatively, as if she does not want to be noticed. She is, as we have said, the planner. Like Adrienne, she watches.

She was probably always going to resent Kathryn's beauty although she is beautiful herself. But it is a different kind of beauty.

They were both highly intelligent, both intense and with the loss of their father things would get very hard between them. Maria says there were times they could have scratched each other's eyes out.

Elizabeth has had an extraordinary career in the world of classical music and has played flute with the Auckland Philharmonia and successfully auditioned for the New Zealand Symphony Orchestra. Her music has taken her to top management jobs in London. She was offered the artistic directorship of Symphony Australia, which was at the time the governing body of the six professional Australian orchestras. But that is to get ahead of ourselves.

Through 1980, as the months dragged on through the first winter after the crash and the loss of her father, Kathryn was having great difficulty. 'In the sixth form we had accrediting, so we were under a lot of stress at school with exams, ongoing exams, and regular assessments. There was this constant assessment of how well you were doing at school. I just found it very difficult to be coping with my own internal stuff, plus all of the stress of school and all of the stress of home. I went from one stressful environment to another, to another. School was stressful, exams were stressful, studying was stressful.'

Holmes: 'Why was home life stressful?'

Kathryn: 'Because Mum had no time to talk about anything other than, "Eat your dinner".'

H: 'Why did she have no time?'

Kathryn: 'She just wasn't in the right space.'

H: 'Did you try and discuss this with her?'

Kathryn: 'I think I did but she also had a concern for Elizabeth. I had a social life too because I had friends and I had boyfriends and I went to parties and stuff and Elizabeth didn't. I was put in this framework of being the lucky one who was attractive and had the boyfriends and Elizabeth needed more consideration from her and more concern.'

This is Kathryn's view, of course. Elizabeth believes it to be quite wrong.

H: 'You didn't need looking after?'

Kathryn: 'I didn't need it, apparently. In a way. I can understand that. I can understand how parents do that. They go, one kid's better off than the other so I'll put my eggs into the basket that needs me more, as a result, emotionally, she was probably a bit shorter with me and didn't really have time to . . . to some extent she is still a bit like that . . .'

H: 'You felt emotionally deprived?'

Kathryn: 'Emotionally probably, yeah.'

H: 'You were the beautiful one?'

Kathryn: 'That's what she used to say to me. That's what she used to tell me. I didn't feel that. I don't think that of myself. When you look out from your own face you don't see anything other than what you see, you don't see yourself. I saw myself as needy as everybody else.'

So, far from getting easier as time passed through 1980, Kathryn's sense of personal loss only worsened. 'Because of the stress of the exams, and my own personal loss, I stopped eating because I couldn't eat because it made me feel sick because I was so stressed. And probably by October [1980] in the sixth form, I was quite thin.'

H: 'So Dad's been dead nearly a year, and you've stopped eating?'

Kathryn: 'Well, I ate but I was stressed a lot so I just didn't . . . I think somehow bulimia crept in because then if I did eat something I'd feel bad about it and I'd feel a bit sick and I made myself sick. The being sick thing was a way of exorcising the poison I had inside me, I suppose.'

H: 'The poison?'

Kathryn: 'The emotional pain. Then it physically exhausted me and then I'd sleep better. It was a way of getting rid of the pain inside me.'

H: 'To throw up.'

Kathryn: 'I had anorexia at first, then I think it was bulimia after that.

You could hide it more.'

H: 'Were you aware that you were becoming thin?'

Kathryn: 'No, not really. I was also doing some modelling as well, so there's a bit of pressure there to try and be a bit slim so I was seesawing in terms of my self-image — my perception of myself from the family point of view and also my perception of myself emotionally. I was seesawing. Plus the situation I was in with losing Dad. I had all this baggage I was trying to deal with emotionally. I didn't know how to handle it.'

H: 'Did you like yourself?'

Kathryn: 'Not particularly. I probably saw myself as a person in pain, really. I don't think I particularly liked myself but I didn't really hate myself. I just existed. Bulimia. Getting rid of the poison. All the anxiety that I had about all the issues that I was dealing with, it was a way of exorcising it and then I'd be tired and then I'd sleep. It was a way of being thin, so that was okay. Being thin, not having that feeling of psychological . . . it was relaxing, you're tired, your body's physically tired, it physically tires you out. What I should have done was gone for runs and had a physical training programme. In hindsight, a training programme would've fixed it instead of having Mum saying to me, "Eat your dinner" . . .'

H: 'So how long did this go on for?'

Kathryn: 'Off and on for a number of years. When I met Luke I was 23. I went to architecture school and I was okay. On and off I was bulimic but not on a daily basis. It would go on for a very few months. As soon as I felt the emotional stress building up in my body and I couldn't cope with something, then I'd be bulimic. It was my way out. Suddenly everything builds up in your mind and you've got no one to go to. Now I probably have a glass of wine or go to the gym. I know how to deal with it. I've learnt.'

Maria knew what was going on. She was horrified the effect that Jim's death, and his being blamed for the disaster, were having on her sunny eldest daughter.

'Your firstborn is always the cleverest thing that ever was, the most beautiful baby you ever saw. She enjoyed all the things she did, she had a nice circle of friends, and was competent at school without being ultra brilliant. She could laugh and enjoy life. I was horrified at the effect Jim's death had on her. She became anorexic and did all sorts of terrible things in that line which were a huge concern to me. Because I didn't know what I . . . how I could help her.'

Of course, in those days, no one really knew how to deal with eating disorders. Maria tried to play it cool. To encourage. To love. Says Maria, 'It was actually thanks to Luke that it stopped.'

Kathryn and Elizabeth are fundamentally close. Kathryn speaks lovingly of her sister. 'Elizabeth is a gorgeous person. She's like the big bouquet of flowers that she would never consider buying for herself. She's very kind. She's happy to give away her time to others because her own needs matter less to her than those of others. Her generosity of spirit is humbling. She is there to help me if I need her. I know that. She was there for me when I had my miscarriage.

'We fought childish fights. We were "tinkling cymbals" in the words of St Paul to the Corinthians. We were 18 months apart. It was sibling rivalry. My first memory of her was this cute, dark-haired, big, blue-eyed, fat baby sitting in white on the carpet and me, being three, she really annoyed me, just because she was there and she probably took Mum's attention away from me.'

Kathryn felt guilty about the bulimia but couldn't do anything. 'I felt guilty about it but it wasn't my fault. Again, it was all something thrown upon me. I had counselling . . . they had a bulimia support group at Auckland University that I belonged to. Apparently, bulimia dulled intelligence.'

Kathryn means it made things easier, it dulled your sensitivities. Certainly, she says, it made her tired and she slept better.

There they were, tossed in the storm in heavy seas of seething grief, rising and falling in the endless swells of emotion, trying to stay with each other for safety, losing each other, finding each other again, only just hanging on, misunderstanding what each of them was doing in order to survive, Maria, Kathryn and Elizabeth. As Kathryn says, they are all strongly bonded, the four daughters and their mother, but 'Elizabeth's way of dealing with things and my way of dealing with things are different'.

Even Kathryn's decision to have children — and perhaps unconsciously to have four — is tied in with the death of her father. 'One of the reasons Luke and I decided to have four children was so that I had some ongoing continuity in my life and I was thrilled when I did. They were forward momentum for me. I could look forward to seeing the next generation come forward, rather than defining myself only by death and destruction.'

H: 'Four deliberately?'

Kathryn: 'Well, four just happened that way. I suppose it was a little bit . . .

immersive. I wanted to be immersed in something that provided me with an opportunity to be all about busying myself with new life as opposed to making it sanitary and only having one or two, and still have gaps to think about how things could have been. In a way I think four immersed me in the process of the new lives rather than me having gaps in between to think about the past too much. Of course, I regret that Dad isn't round to see his grandchildren but it's busy with four.'

H: 'So you had to be busy to fill up the life?'

Kathryn: 'Yeah, and I think Mum did that at the time too. She was busy. When we were going through agony, she kept herself busy. She'd been a marriage guidance counsellor, she continued with yoga. She always immersed herself in doing things because being busy stops you falling into a pit of grief.'

H: 'It helps the grieving process?'

Kathryn: 'I think you continue to grieve all your life, honestly. I hate to say that but I don't think it stops. People talk about closure but I think that's bullshit. Closure doesn't exist. You just learn to live with things.'

It is the end of a long afternoon of talking, of Kathryn's reaching into her soul. Her sapphire eyes are grey now, like the day outside, tired and lifeless. There are burdens we all carry that are too heavy to bear and there are burdens which no one can lift from us no matter how great their love may be or how great their willingness of heart.

In Elizabeth, the still water runs deep. Maria replied one day when I asked her about Elizabeth, 'I wish you could answer the question for me, "Who is Elizabeth"?'

After November 1979, her third form year, Elizabeth says her entire school life was punctuated by Erebus-related events. The Royal Commission into the crash seemed endless. In the fourth form, the year of the Commission, her history lessons about various world revolutions didn't interest her.

'I was concerned about Mum attending the Royal Commission. Would she be cross-examined today? Would Justice Mahon be kind to her? Would the Air New Zealand administrators who told lies about Dad make her cry?

'I often spent Friday nights at home, fixing light bulbs and unblocking the sink or vacuuming the cars — doing the sorts of jobs Dad would have done. He would have liked me to do those things because it made life easier for Mum. My girlfriends usually went out to parties or to the pub on Fridays and spent hours looking at themselves in the mirror to make sure their lipstick was on straight. I wasn't interested in those things any more. We had grown-ups at our place crying a lot of the time, and Mum was trying to make decisions about lawyers and the house maintenance and selling the boat, *Sarasee*. Those things were important to me. Pubs and driving fast with boys in their parents' cars were not.'

There might be just the slightest element of the Methodist in the daughter of the methodical man.

But this little girl had grown up 'instantly', late on the night of 28 November 1979. 'I was 14 yet my concerns were of the adult world.'

But the same girl who stayed home on Friday nights was frantically busy with all kinds of activities at and outside school and must have been popular. During her fifth, sixth and seventh form years, Elizabeth was chair of the school's Young Enterprise company, chair of the School Committee, secretary of the Music Committee. She passed Grade VIII in the Royal Schools of Music — flute, Trinity College flute and began studying with the principal flautist at the Auckland Philharmonia. Somewhere along the line she passed nearly every badge Girl Guides had to offer. She passed School Certificate, University Entrance and Bursary and numerous dance exams.

Elizabeth remembers that in seventh form, all her peers seemed to know where they were headed. 'I was busy asking myself questions like, who knows what lies round the corner? What if someone else in the family dies tomorrow?' She was accepted into both nursing and teachers' college. Neither excited her. She chose to do the three-year teaching course and to combine it with a Bachelor of Arts in Italian and English. She wasn't happy. One night, during a flute practice, a friend said she was wasting her time and she ought to apply for an international youth exchange programme and head overseas. During the next few weeks she both applied for that and qualified LTCL in flute. This licentiate, with Trinity College in London, was the professional flute qualification.

The exchange committee sent her to Denmark. Elizabeth would therefore learn Danish. Maria wanted her to go to Austria to learn German. 'At that stage, I didn't mind where I went. I was looking forward to getting away from New Zealand, constant Erebus associations and absorbing fresh experiences on the other side of the world.'

Elizabeth left Auckland the day after the *Rainbow Warrior* was bombed in July 1985. 'Ross Gordon came to wish me all the best and pressed a one hundred dollar US bill into my hand. There were tears in Mum's and

Annemarie's eyes as they farewelled me. I felt sad for them having to cry again. I cried as the plane took off towards Los Angeles and then fell asleep. I was alone, but sensed that I would be alright. Dad would look after me, wherever he may be.'

In Denmark, Elizabeth flourished. There was no Erebus. No one knew a thing about her. She was a fresh canvas.

She was billeted with a farming family of four children, the Frandsens, Arne and Lise. Lise's sister, 38, had been blind, deaf and paralysed since contracting meningitis at the age of six. She often came to stay. On the first night, Lise's parents were there. So were two little boys, Andreas and Peter, who had been abandoned by their mother and adopted by Arne and Lise six months previously. The Frandsens were that kind of family. But, exhausting though it was for her at the start, Elizabeth says that 'their strong family values, honesty, compassion, sense of fun, themed parties, hospitality and kindness to everyone in need would have a lasting and positive influence on my future thoughts and behaviour'.

The language school she went to she felt was not helping her. She moved to the cookery school in Aarhus for two months. Aarhus is the second city of Denmark and the country's main port. It has been a port since the days of the Vikings. It is surrounded by beautiful lush countryside. Elizabeth says that at the college they 'prepared feasts during the day and danced and drank wine with the guys from the agricultural college next door most evenings. We had midnight adventure walks in the woods during silent snowfalls and graduated just before Christmas with a banquet of venison, pheasant, apple tarts and home-made chocolates.' Suddenly it wasn't such a bad thing drinking wine with the boys at night.

Soon she was fluent in Danish. She enrolled at a residential graduate school where you could pursue all sorts of interests before your life got too serious and confined. She describes the next six months of her life at the college as 'wonderful'. Some of her closest friendships were formed in these six months. She met physios, nurses, engineers, lab technicians, teachers, theologians and Henning, a policeman. Henning had spent six months touring New Zealand a few years earlier. Henning is now married to Greta and they have three children; their eldest is Elizabeth. The main thrust of the six-month course was the value of teams and leadership. This was perfect for the planner, the event organiser. This is pure Elizabeth.

She was told by one of her tutors that she had not taught someone so motivated and creative for a long time. 'Me? Motivated? Me? Creative? I thought Kathryn was the creative person in our family.'

In a party of others she travelled to Israel and Jordan in April 1986. Then it was back to Denmark for a summer of 'picnics on beaches, on cliff tops and on islands in the grounds of castles'.

Elizabeth was soaring high, loving her freedom, discovering the wonders of 'freedom from . . . New Zealand, freedom from comparison with Kathryn, freedom to be myself in new and challenging circumstances'. And free, at last, to some extent at least, from Erebus. She celebrated her twenty-first birthday in a golden wheat field, whose long, dry ears were about to be cut, 'listening to ducks on a pond and crickets in the grass'. She seems to have been, for the first time since her father was killed, deeply content.

She came home to Auckland in May 1988, after nearly three years away. She was greatly changed. Auckland was not. She spent the rest of the year teaching flute at schools, to 32 students at home, and set about deciding where she wanted to undertake a performance degree in the flute. By the end of the year she had been accepted by the smartest people at Victoria University in Wellington, at Auckland University, and by Thomas Pinchof, at the Victorian College of the Arts (VCA) in Melbourne.

The VCA was the score. 'At my audition, the head of the woodwind department welcomed me coldly by saying, "I hope you don't intend to play the Mozart because we've heard it 12 times already today." Such frank arrogance towards an apprehensive candidate prompted me to play Debussy's *Syrinx* better than they were likely to have heard it for a long time.' Now it was off to Melbourne. Her final recital, at the end of her third year, a duet with a soprano, two birds singing to each other from their separate trees, brought the house down. Elizabeth came back to Auckland with a distinction pass to a Bachelor of Music.

But suddenly, she knew she did not want to be an orchestral performer for the rest of her life. She did not want to teach music for the rest of her life.

Elizabeth took herself off to the British and American consulates. She accumulated addresses. She wrote to an astonishing 180 orchestras, managers and artists in London and the United States. She was offered an assistant manager's job at Haydn Rawstron International Management in London. She flew to London, via Denmark — for a school reunion — the following week. Her job was to manage young Scandinavian musicians. Haydn Rawstron represented such New Zealand greats as Dame Malvina

Major, Christopher Doig and Sir William Southgate.

In the summer of 1991 Elizabeth came back to New Zealand for Kathryn's wedding to Luke Carter, a young man who represented New Zealand in yachting at the Los Angeles Olympics. There was 'a lavish reception at the Northern Club. It was inevitable that I would compare my current existence with hers. She was a beautiful bride with a successful husband and a promised life of wedded bliss. I was living with relatives in London, attending wonderful concerts, meeting stimulating people and single. We each considered the other to have the ideal lifestyle.'

Back in London, at the start of 1992, Elizabeth was headhunted by the International Management Group (IMG), which manages the world's most famous musicians and opera stars, and the world's finest and most valuable sportsmen and women. She told Rawstron. Rawstron was furious and told her to get out immediately. Elizabeth went on holiday to Spain while Rawstron and IMG fought for her. Rawstron surrendered.

Elizabeth was now in the heady world of the management of the greatest musicians in the world. She was at the office by 7.30 in the morning. She grabbed a sandwich at some stage of the day. Then she went off to the Royal Festival Hall or the Royal Albert Hall or wherever her star was performing that night. After which, IMG would shout dinner 'at which we would give the artist due audience and feedback on his/her performance if requested. I would usually be home to turn out my lights at around 2 a.m.'

It was a glorious, heady existence for a young woman for whom classical music and classical performance were the centre of her life.

In her second year, IMG gave her the management job for their six leading orchestral conductors. She was 28 years old. IMG secured her a residency visa. They told the British government they needed Elizabeth to manage James Galway and their Norwegian flautists.

Elizabeth's job was to do everything for the artist. She was to be repertoire adviser, fee negotiator, confidante, companion, conflict resolver, mother, assistant financial controller, immigration consultant, PR and media guru as well as restaurant guide. She was particular to be friendly but not friends with the artists. It was a perfect job for the planner, the organiser, Jim Collins's little helper, and the girl who liked to keep her distance, just a little.

But Elizabeth needed to come home again, needed her family again. During the funeral of Princess Diana, while she and her friends — like the rest of the world — stopped breathing and watched the television in continuing disbelief — one of her great conductors called from Hamburg. 'He rang to advise that his concert the previous evening had gone very well and he had decided he wanted to conduct the Shostakovich Symphony No. 1 on 3 December in New York.'

Elizabeth could not believe the man's solipsism. 'He hadn't considered the needs of anyone else that morning before he picked up the phone to call me.'

She decided to leave that world behind. I find myself wondering just how far Elizabeth Collins could have risen in the dazzling world of the business of classical music. She had it all. She could talk to anyone. Handling the aftermath of Erebus had taught her that. She could play. She was steeped in the classics and she was a natural manager.

There was a whirl of farewell parties, letters, kisses, cards and flowers. Her boss, at her farewell at the company lunch on her last day, said, 'You have provided our highest profile clients with a Rolls-Royce level of service which is, simply, second to none. You have been to us a shining example of loyalty, diligence and fun and we will miss you greatly.'

Before she left, having given her notice, she received eight job offers managing artists and international orchestras. She wanted to come home. Back home, she turned down the offer to become artistic director of the Symphony Australia, six state orchestras.

It is hard to know why she did that. Elizabeth needed her mother and her sisters again.

21

What Gemmell Knew and Oldfield Did Not

All truth passes through three stages. First, it is ridiculed. Second, it is violently opposed. Third, it is accepted as being self evident.
— Arthur Schopenhauer

If what flight despatcher Dave Greenwood says is true, Captain Ian Harding Gemmell did know about the late 2-degree coordinate change before he left for Antarctica. Following Greenwood's revelation, it is safe to assume that Gemmell made inquiries as to what flight path the pilots had been briefed on. He would surely have made a phone call to clarify this before he departed Whenuapai on the RNZAF Hercules that afternoon, 29 November 1979.

If Collins had been told, then Collins was to blame for the accident. If Collins had not been told, then the airline was to blame. Whether Collins had been told was crucial.

Chippindale said he was not told of the coordinate change until he came back from the crash site, a fortnight after the crash, on or about 11 December, Mahon reported.[1] And if Captain Gemmell did know the coordinates had been changed and Jim Collins had not been told, then he also knew the company — and Gemmell himself — were in serious trouble.

As Mahon says, given that the airline Chief Executive Morrie Davis had issued instructions that all documents relevant to the fatal flight 'wherever they might be found' should be handed over to the airline management 'it was therefore a singular mischance that Captain Gemmell . . . was to be the arbiter [on the mountain] of which documents were relevant'.

In the end, of course, the coordinate change evidence never meant anything to Chippindale because he decided that there was a minimum safe altitude of 16,000 feet until you were overhead McMurdo Station and Collins had violated it. If Collins had maintained 16,000 feet on the 'corrected' coordinates, then there would have been no accident. And that, logically, is true. Never mind that Chippindale knew very well that nearly every flight had descended below 16,000 feet before reaching McMurdo Station.

But in that fortnight he spent on the ice, before he was told about the coordinate change, Chippindale was able to firm up in his mind his early theory — which would suit everyone — that Jim Collins was flying in cloud or towards it and far too low. For God's sake, how could you fly into this mountain? And look, by God, those coordinates were quite clear. They took you direct from Cape Hallett to McMurdo Station over the top of Erebus. Collins should have known that. The coordinates had been 'corrected'.

Captain Ian Gemmell's testimony at the Royal Commission on his finding out that the coordinates had been changed without the pilots being advised remains deeply unsatisfactory.

He was cross-examined by David Baragwanath, counsel assisting the commission, about what he knew before he left for Antarctica with Ron Chippindale on the RNZAF Hercules.[2]

Baragwanath: 'And when was it you left for Antarctica?'

Gemmell: 'The following day [29 November 1979] on the Hercules . . . accompanying Mr Chippindale and the police party.'

Baragwanath: 'Now before you left Auckland, what was the state of your knowledge as to problems with the coordinates?'

Gemmell: 'I don't recall having any knowledge of an error in the coordinates at that time.'

Baragwanath: 'Well, we've heard it was during the night that the Navigation Section came to realise what happened.'

Gemmell: 'Yes.'

Baragwanath: 'Do you say that that information was not conveyed to you before midday when you left Auckland?'

Gemmell: 'I don't recall it, sir.'

Baragwanath: 'When it did come to your notice, was it a bombshell?'

Gemmell: 'It certainly was.'

Baragwanath: 'Can you not tell us when that bombshell burst?'

Gemmell: 'What I imagine . . . it was the day after I returned from McMurdo approximately.'

Baragwanath: 'What was your point in going to the ice?'

Gemmell: 'It was appreciated that some members of Air New Zealand would need to be there and on an advisory capacity, both from operations and engineering. And in my position I would be the logical operations choice. And I believe Mr Eden would have made the approach to Mr Chippindale.'

Baragwanath: 'If part of your function [at Antarctica] was to assist with technical input [in] the investigation [on] the ice, wouldn't one have expected you to take down to the ice an up to date picture of what was known in Auckland about the technical operations, particularly in reference to the computer route?'

Gemmell: 'Yes. That would be a reasonable assumption.'

Baragwanath: 'Well, if it was known to the Navigation Section well before you left, that there was a spot of bother relative to the computer, isn't it probable that you really did know this before you went to the ice?'

Gemmell: 'As I recall, I left the rescue coordination centre in the early hours of the 29th morning, returned home and, anticipating going down to the ice, made arrangements in that direction, returned to the company offices later that morning, and I just imagine that the Navigation Section may have assumed I knew. I had no reason to know it, and I had little time in the office before proceeding to Whenuapai.'

Baragwanath: 'So who was it that told you, when you first were told of the fact that the computer route had been altered at 2 in the morning of the 28th?'

Gemmell: 'I don't believe I said that I was told on the morning of the twenty-eighth.'

Baragwanath: [Rephrases question]

Gemmell: 'You say the 28th, that's the day of the accident. I understood the coordinates were changed on the night of the 27th.'

Baragwanath: [Rephrases question]

Gemmell: 'It would have been after I returned from McMurdo, and I don't recall the date exactly. I can't recall who I heard it from.'

So we have a 'bombshell' and we remember neither when it hit us nor who delivered it. Two hundred and fifty-seven people are dead and we do not remember when we heard such a vital piece of information as that of the 2-degree coordinate change at Cape Hallett and the captain's not being told? It is impossible to believe that Gemmell could not recall when he found out and who told him. Mahon certainly believed that Gemmell knew of the coordinate change and the pilot not being told before he went to the ice.

In fact, David Greenwood, the flight despatcher, clearly told Paul Davison QC in November 2009 that he informed Gemmell of the coordinate change in the early morning after the accident.

It is unclear when Ian Gemmell left the crash site and arrived back in Auckland. The CVR and the DFDR (digital flight data reorder) had both been found quickly. He flew back to New Zealand with the black boxes and spent some time briefing Civil Aviation in Wellington. It seems likely he returned to Auckland on Friday 7 December and went straight to a meeting of the airline's investigating committee.

The relationship between Air New Zealand and Civil Aviation was cosy before the accident. There was always a suspicion — Mahon asked the odd question about it from time to time but got nowhere — that it remained more than cosy during the entire Royal Commission. Gemmell's relationship with Chippindale and his free access to the crash site would, these days, be regarded as highly inappropriate. Chippindale's office, although statutorily independent of the Ministry of Transport, was nevertheless part of the ministry, as was Civil Aviation. So, indeed, was the Meteorological Service.

When David Greenwood was suddenly summoned to the office of Director of Flight Operations Captain Dave Eden to be asked to take over the Navigation Section, in Eden's office was Captain Kippenberger, the Director of Civil Aviation.[3]

Morrie Davis had set up an investigating committee immediately after the crash and appointed the airline's Chief Safety Officer, George Oldfield, its secretary. George Oldfield's job was to collect and compile every company document relating to Antarctic flights. It was also Oldfield's job to determine their fate. George Oldfield was very busy at the shredder. Oldfield testified that during that meeting on 7 December, after Gemmell's return from the ice, 'Captain Gemmell was called from the room for a phone call and when returned he informed us of the error [in the coordinates], and I presume it came from that phone call'.[4]

Oldfield — the Chief Safety Officer — never asked who Ian Gemmell spoke to. And, of course, he didn't hear what was said during the call. Oldfield was also asked at the Royal Commission if he knew that Keith Amies had known of the coordinate change on the night of the crash, nine days previously. Oldfield said he did not know that, even though he conceded that Amies knew of the internal investigation at the airline.[5]

George Oldfield is not often spoken of by students of Erebus. Yet he makes a brief and dramatic appearance at the Royal Commission.

He was appointed Safety Officer in August 1977, a few months after the first two Antarctic flights. He admitted at the Royal Commission that he still had no full job description. His testimony actually reads, 'We have recently reorganised within the safety department and the full spec has yet to be wrote [sic].'[6]

Oldfield tells the inquiry he has never seen the safety briefing given to Antarctic pilots. He did not see it before the accident and he has not seen it since. He asked Captain J. P. Wilson for a copy of the written material but there must have been a mix-up and he still had not received it. He had never examined the briefing documents. He had no idea until after the accident that the flights were directed on a course over the top of Erebus.

Mahon asked Oldfield if, in the interests of safety, he had evaluated the feasibility of a DC-10 making an emergency landing at McMurdo Station.[7] 'Yes,' was Oldfield's reply. Captain Gemmell had told him it could be done.

'What type of runway is it?' asked Mahon.

'Ice, if I remember correctly,' said Oldfield.

'Well, do you know how thick the ice would have been?' asked Mahon.

Oldfield replied, 'No, I do not.'

'Well,' Mahon asked, 'what was the all-up weight of the DC-10 when it got to McMurdo Station?'

Oldfield would have to look at the file.

'It was just short of 200 tonnes,' Mahon told him.

How did Oldfield therefore evaluate the chances of the DC-10 not going through the ice?

It depends, said Oldfield, on how you define a successful landing.

'Perhaps you weren't aware,' Mahon told him, 'that at the end of November, the ice was only 6 or 7 feet thick. Would that have sustained the weight of a 200 tonne DC-10?'

Oldfield had to admit he couldn't answer that.

Oldfield, himself an ex-RNZAF pilot, had never flown to the ice and had never flown jet aircraft. He, the Safety Officer, did not know that Captain Wilson, the Antarctic briefing officer, had never flown there either.

Oh, and was Mr Oldfield aware of the 30 November 1978 edition of the company magazine *Air New Zealand News*, in which the Director of

Flight Operations, Captain Doug Keesing, flew round Antarctica at 2000 feet? No, he could not recall that. What about the brochure that Air New Zealand printed 900,000 copies of and distributed all round New Zealand, the brochure which contained an extremely complimentary article by the President of McDonnell Douglas himself, Mr Brizindine, who had a ball flying at 2000 feet, nice and low, over McMurdo with Captain Gordon Vette? No, Mr Oldfield could not recall that at all.

It is all there in his testimony to the Royal Commission.

George Oldfield was the document shredder. Oldfield used the shredder on Davis's orders. He said he shredded only 'extra or spare or duplicate' copies of Antarctic flight documents. Later, in evidence, Morrie Davis called them 'surplus' documents. At the end of each day he shredded his own notes. The Hon Maurice Williamson MP, then a young man working at Air New Zealand House, speaks of boxes of documents being poured into the shredder.

Mahon was scathing of Davis ordering the document shredding, describing it as a 'grave error'.[8] It meant anyone could cover anything up, responsibility could be hidden and it caused bitterness amongst the pilots and the families of the dead aircrew.

> This was at the time the fourth worst disaster in aviation history, and it follows that this direction on the part of the chief executive for the destruction of 'irrelevant documents' was one of the most remarkable executive decisions ever to have been made in the corporate affairs of a large New Zealand company. There were personnel in the Flight Operations Division and in the Navigation Section who anxiously desired to be acquitted of any responsibility for the disaster. And yet . . . it seems to have been left to these very same officials to determine what documents they would hand over to the Investigating Committee.[9]

In other words, it was quite disgracefully crooked. All documents should simply have been handed over to the Chief Inspector of Air Accidents.

It is worth noting at this point that Chief Executive Morrie Davis had never sent up to his board of directors a report into the Erebus disaster. Mahon wrote in paragraph 366(d) of his report: 'It seemed to me an extraordinary thing that the circumstances of an aircraft disaster of this magnitude were not reported to the company's board in writing by its chief executive.'

There is an extraordinary exchange at the end of the cross-examination of George Oldfield by Gary Harrison, counsel assisting the Commission. Harrison asked Oldfield to examine again the file of documents Oldfield put together.[10]

Harrison: 'Is that the file of the internal investigation you have been describing and as compiled by you?'

Oldfield: 'Yes.'

Harrison: 'In your index at the front of it you referred to page J14 which, I think, is a copy of the Antarctic brief.'

Oldfield: 'That is correct.'

Harrison: 'When I looked for it I couldn't find it on the file, can you tell us if it's there?

Oldfield: 'I'm just checking the index to see what was before and after it. No, it appears not to be here.'

Harrison: 'Do you have any idea where it might be?'

Oldfield: 'No.'

Harrison: 'I ask you to produce that file.'

J14 never appeared. It was never produced. It may have been the briefing notes Captain Ross Johnson sent to the committee which were never seen again. No briefing documents indicating exactly where the aircraft were being sent were ever produced.

The shredding of paper led to the paucity of documents the airline produced at the Royal Commission. As mentioned, the absence of paperwork was a sustained theme at the Royal Commission. The absence of any coherent paper trail in a modern international airline bewildered Mahon, especially in relation to the final changing of the coordinates in late November 1979, hours before Jim Collins took off.

This is another extraordinary thing. Every document that came up to the Royal Commission was a copy. All of the documents on Oldfield's file were copies. The Oldfield committee never found out anything. There was nothing in the file giving a clue as to how the crews had been briefed. '... and seeing that all pre-accident documents assembled on the file were copies, then where were the originals?' wrote Mahon.[11]

As for the shredding, Mahon was very quick indeed to see the importance of this. This kind of corporate behaviour was not supposed to happen in New Zealand. It happened in banana republics. It happened in the dodgy countries of Africa and South America. Mahon went to town about it in his accident report which shook the nation in April 1981.

> By 30 November the occurrence of this mistake over the coordinates was known not only to the Flight Operations Division but also to the management of the airline, and in particular, had been reported to the Chief Executive of Air New Zealand, Mr M.R. Davis. The chief executive saw at once what would happen if the story of the changed coordinates became public. Within a day or two that story would be carried by the world's newspapers, and indeed it would be a dramatic tale . . . A computer mistake had sent 257 people to a violent death on the distant frozen wasteland of Antarctica . . . This might be the worst publicity to which any airline had ever been exposed.
>
> The reaction of the chief executive was immediate. He determined that no word of this incredible blunder was to become publicly known. He directed that all documents relating to Antarctic flights, and to this flight in particular, were to be collected and impounded. They were all to be put on one single file, which would remain in strict custody. Of these documents all those which were not directly relevant were to be destroyed. They were to be put forthwith through the company's shredder.[12]

Davis, at the Royal Commission, in his contorted, rambling testimony said that only 'surplus copies' of documents were destroyed, declaring he didn't want any surplus documents hanging round that might fall into the hands of the news media. Davis detested the news media. He feared someone on the staff might seek an 'allegiance' with the press by leaking a document.

It is worth noting that Greg McGee remarks in his story of the production of the docudrama *Erebus: The Aftermath* ('Dancing on the Coffins of the Dead') that Ian Mune, playing Morrie Davis, rang McGee one evening and said he simply couldn't do that speech by Morrie Davis at the Royal Commission as it was written because it was gibberish, it made no sense. McGee wrote, 'I told him I'd actually edited down that speech by a third from its original length in order to give it whatever coherence it now had.'

And as long as he stuck to every word of the script 'he would be covered by TVNZ in any resulting defamation action'. From Morrie Davis presumably. 'The speech was word perfect on the day,' says McGee. They were dark, nasty, litigious times.[13]

According to Mahon, Ron Chippindale eventually discovered, on about 11 December, the facts of the last minute coordinate change,[14] which he mentions in his report released seven months after the accident. He had been on the ice for more than a week and Gemmell had not told him of the computer change, it seems. That is because Gemmell knew what a 'bombshell' the coordinate change revelation was going to be. Chippindale, in any case, gave no weight to the coordinate change in his report, despite having six months in which to think about it.

Mahon was usually pleasantly cordial to Chippindale. But in his accident report he slammed Chippindale for his attitude to the coordinates and the tricky way he wrote about them. Mahon wrote: 'In his report, which was published in June 1980, the chief inspector referred to what he termed the "error" in the McMurdo destination point, and the fact that it had been corrected a matter of hours before the flight left Auckland.'[15] Chippindale was as bland as that.

In fact, Chippindale was playing dirty. Mahon, seeing it for what it was, and possibly beginning to have serious worries about the Chief Inspector of Air Accidents, lashed the man.

> The chief inspector did not make it clear, however, that the computer flight path of TE901 had been altered before the flight, and that the alteration had not been notified to the air crew. Had that fact been disclosed in the chief inspector's report then the publicity attending the report would undoubtedly have been differently aligned. Instead of newspaper headlines featuring only allegations of pilot error, the headlines might well have been dominated by the disclosure that the aircraft had been programmed to fly on a collision course with Mt Erebus, and that the crew had not been told of the change. As will be seen, the news blackout imposed by the chief executive was very successful. It was not until the hearings of this Commission that the real magnitude of the mistake made by Flight Operations was publicly revealed.[16]

No wonder Morrie Davis detested Peter Mahon so vehemently. Davis said of Mahon's Erebus report in *North and South* in November 1989, 'I get pissed off when people lord the gentleman, who, in terms of that determination, was incompetent.' Mahon continued:

> [The chief executive] maintained the view that the [coordinates] mistake was not an operative factor, and that total culpability remained with the flight crew. This indeed was the case for the airline as presented before the Commission. It was based upon the proposition that the mistake over the coordinates had no significance. The silence over the changing of the coordinates and the failure to tell the aircrew was a strategy which succeeded to a very considerable degree.[17]

The failure by Davis and the Air New Zealand board to fess up to the public, and the grieving families and loved ones, both here and round the world, and admit the truth, even now, nearly 32 years later, remains a disgrace. Davis, at the Royal Commission, made it clear that the strategy of keeping the coordinate change quiet was driven by him. He saw it as a strategy of keeping the information away from the news media.

Listen to the sourness and paranoia of Davis's reply to Alister MacAlister, counsel for ALPA at the Commission.

> Generally throughout the country at the moment is that people have sought to make a name for themselves by passing the relevant and sometimes immaterial but also provocative documents to the media. Having experienced this I could recognise that it would be in fact distressing to all concerned. Matters taken out of context, considerations given that were erroneous. I required one single file authenticated and unadulterated.[18]

But, says MacAlister to Davis, 'Did you not consider it more prudent, and take the initiative and disclose the matter in its correct context, bearing in mind information would come to light in a subsequent inquiry?'[19]

Davis: 'I didn't really feel that that I needed to explain myself to the press.'

MacAlister: 'We're talking about the public not the press.'

Davis didn't get it.

Davis: 'The media by which the public are informed. I didn't see that under the circumstances that existed at the time I was under a significant obligation to make disclosures to the press.'

MacAlister: 'Or to the travelling public?'

Davis: 'I didn't consider it to be relevant to make a public statement in respect of the transposition error which had existed in the computer prior to the accident flight to the public via the media.'

In other words, he felt no obligation to be honest and forthright with the loved ones of the passengers who had trusted their lives to his airline, to the New Zealanders who hurt for those who died and those who were left behind, or to the public who owned his airline.

His remarks at the Commission make a grotesque lie of his letter to airline staff in *Air New Zealand News*, the in-house newspaper, a few days after the accident: 'In days to come the airline will be the subject of detailed examination as to the precise circumstances of the flight and all conceivable causes of the accident. That is only right and proper, and I have publicly declared my dedication for an early announcement of any probable cause.'

Then his paranoia surfaces.

'Before that can happen, however, it is inevitable we must suffer the illusions of those who would speculate as to the imagined background to the crash. In many instances these unsupportable claims will go unchallenged. As is proper at this time the investigation of the crash rests with the appropriate authorities and we must certainly not attempt to pre-empt their considerations by counter claims of our own, even in response to the irresponsibility of others.'[20]

It was florid, vindictive nonsense. As for being dedicated to an 'early announcement of any probable cause', Davis was anything but. He knew the reason the aircraft had crashed and he managed to keep it quiet for nearly a year. Throughout the hearings of the Royal Commission of Inquiry, the Flight Operations management team did everything it could, in concert, to obstruct public understanding of how the DC-10 collided with the Antarctic mountain.

Public officials lied and perjured in the biggest cover-up ever conducted in New Zealand corporate life, a cover-up that started the night of Dorday's discovery of the coordinate change when he failed to explain his discovery to an inspector of air accidents who was right there in the office with him. It carried on. It never stopped. The airline's senior flight operations management of 1979 was exposed in the end by a brilliant, honest judge and some relentlessly hard-working lawyers who believed in justice.

What's more, it would have been unthinkable for Davis not to let Muldoon know the truth. Muldoon, for his part, must have decided to protect the country's economy from the tens of millions of dollars worth of claims and to save the airline. It was a hard political choice. And in the end, for Davis and for Muldoon, justice could go to hell.

And in St Heliers, in Auckland, New Zealand, a grieving, broken-hearted family, a mother and four daughters, the Collins girls, endured their husband and father being blamed for the deaths of 257 people. The complete loyalty the dead captain had given the company, hundreds of thousands of whose passengers he had delivered safely across the oceans, was repaid with betrayal, lies and deceit.

The more one studies the material of the time, the more staggering is the cynical gall Davis and his henchmen displayed. Justice Peter Mahon saw through it all.

But what of Ian Gemmell, Mahon's 'chief pilot'? Mahon made it clear Gemmell was a formidable character. Indeed, to read the transcripts of the hours he spent under cross-examination is to read a man who, under sustained pressure, managed to say little.

Gemmell has been accused by many of removing documents from the crash site and causing them to disappear. There is no evidence that he did so and he always emphatically denied any improper behaviour. And none has ever been proven.

In the view of Paul Davison, in a conversation with me, in the end, Gemmell was simply not a likeable character. His attitude was hardline on the pilot error causation theory of the Erebus disaster. Gemmell accepted, he said, that the crew should have had a topographical chart with the flight path printed on it. In the end, though, 16,000/6000 feet were the airline's prescribed Antarctic altitudes and that was that. Nothing else mattered. Never mind that Collins and Cassin must have had a sound and rational reason for believing they were entering McMurdo Sound. Never mind that Collins was flying visually and none of five highly trained men on the flight deck ever saw the mountain.

Davison took Ian Gemmell on in an intense cross-examination journey at the Royal Commission that still reads grippingly today. Gemmell conceded that having a DC-10 descend beneath cloud cover over McMurdo to 6000 feet, which is what the airline recommended, could put the pilot into whiteout conditions: 'There could be some probability.'

Davison suggested to him: 'Page 54 of Mr Chippindale's report. The company has claimed the whole philosophy behind the Air New Zealand Antarctic flights was for crews to avoid a whiteout situation by remaining strictly VMC [visual] throughout the sightseeing part of the flight. I suggest to you that this philosophy is based upon a fallacy because of course we know a whiteout situation is insidious and the viewer may be in a situation where he believes he has visibility, he may believe that he has VMC conditions, when indeed that's not the case. Do you accept that philosophy is ill-conceived?'[21]

Gemmell: 'No.'

He could be insolent, Gemmell. If Davison offered a statement that didn't quite become a question Gemmell would reply, 'Was that a question?' Or if he needed to play for time he would steal a second with a patronising 'Help me out?', or 'I don't know what you're getting at' or a brief 'Correct' or 'I understand so'. He stepped carefully through the minefield as Davison questioned him on the inadequacies of the pre-flight briefings given to the Antarctic pilots, with the photograph of Erebus way to the left of the aircraft as it flew south in the audio-visual presentation; pilots being briefed to fly down McMurdo Sound when the airline insisted they were told to fly above Mount Erebus; pilots thinking there was no 6000 feet MSA; and pilots being provided with inadequate photocopied maps when the passengers' maps were beautifully simple and clear.

Rarely did the carapace crack. Sometimes it did.

Davison asked him where he first heard the CVR.[22]

Gemmell: 'Mr Chippindale's residence in Wellington.'

Davison: 'When was that?'

Gemmell: 'Early this year [1980]. I can't recall exactly.'

Davison: 'Please be more specific.'

Gemmell: 'I'd have to refer to my records and consult with Mr Chippindale.'

Davison: 'Perhaps we could just say was it before the release of the public report?'

Gemmell: 'I would think so, but I'm not sure.'

In other words Captain Ian Gemmell, the chief pilot of Air New Zealand, and Mr Chippindale, the Chief Inspector of Air Accidents, were very cosy.

When asked why he heard the tape at Chippindale's home, Gemmell's answer was suddenly abstruse. 'There was some discussion apparently that there was some attention evidenced on the flight deck during the descent and it was from this view that I asked him if I could listen to the CVR to determine if I believed if there was any basis for this.'[23]

In other words, to translate, the Chief Inspector is allowing his opinion of the performance on the flight deck to be informed by the judgement of the chief pilot of the airline that sent the aircraft into the mountain.

And no, Captain Gemmell had most certainly not seen any publication of the Director of Flight Operations having a jolly time cruising at 2000 feet above McMurdo or any other such publicity. He had no knowledge of any flights below 6000 feet until the accident. Absolutely none.[24] 'I'm still unable to believe that it wasn't spoken of in more general terms.' Nine-hundred thousand copies of a brochure distributed? To every home in the country? And he did not know?

He did concede, however, under examination by David Baragwanath, that under Air New Zealand's own operating instructions, when it came to checking the flight plan on the flight deck before departure, there was no requirement upon Captain Jim Collins and First Officer Greg Cassin to do anything other than check what they had put into their flight deck computer with what was printed on the flight plan itself. In other words, they were simply to check themselves against themselves.[25]

Lloyd Brown QC, senior counsel for the airline, intervened at last to ask Gemmell one direct and friendly question. Had Gemmell removed anything from the crash site and failed to hand it to the accident investigator. Gemmell replied simply, 'No.'

Then Mahon intervened.[26] He reminded Gemmell that the evidence suggested that the company, or at least the Navigation Section, was aware before the wreckage was discovered that the coordinates had been changed without Captain Collins knowing.

This was the bombshell, remember.

Gemmell: 'I believe so.'

Mahon: 'You remember, I assume, that in the New Year [January 1980] one of the newspapers alleged that the wrong coordinate had been entered into the aircraft's computer system.'

Gemmell: 'I remember something of that nature.'

Mahon: 'Do you remember that the Chief Executive made a public statement to the effect that the right coordinates were in the aircraft system before then?'

Gemmell: 'Yes, I do.'

Mahon: 'Now at the time he said nothing, did he, about Captain Collins being unaware that the coordinates had been changed?'

Gemmell: 'I don't believe he did, sir.'

Of course, Davis most certainly did not. This was the great Davis cover-up, brilliant in its simplicity. The coordinates were 'correct'.

But Mahon was not finished with Ian Gemmell. 'And was it not a matter of very considerable anxiety to the company when it was found on the night of 28 November or early morning twenty-ninth that the nav track had been changed without the Captain being told?'

Gemmell got straight back onto script.

'I'm not so sure that that would be the way to express it, Your Honour. I believe, as I understand it, from the people that were in the area of discovery of the information that they knew it had been corrected and therefore it couldn't be a factor in the accident. In other words, the aircraft was going to the correct position.'

But, said Mahon, the captain didn't know that.

But if there was a ruthless Ian Gemmell, who completely embraced the company line that no senior management ever knew that flights went down McMurdo for 14 months, or that pilots were descending round McMurdo to below 6000 feet, there was also the Gemmell the mountaineers saw while he was up at the crash site. Hugh Logan, one of the first onto the crash site, described Gemmell in a letter to Air New Zealand, which the company took to appeal, as being in a very emotional state during his time on Erebus. Logan told me that, at the time, he wondered if Gemmell was in a fit state to be on the mountain, so upset was he by the sight of the carnage.

And another of the mountaineers, Keith Woodford, made a statement also taken to appeal by Air New Zealand — in reaction to Mahon's statements about Gemmell in his report — that Gemmell's behaviour on the mountain was impeccable.

Woodford wrote:

> Captain Gemmell was on the crash site for approximately six hours. During that time he was never more than eight metres distant from me and for much of this time he was roped to me. He was in the vicinity of the flight deck for somewhat less than two hours and during this time he was always within five

> metres of me. At all times, the three mountaineers observed the investigators extremely closely as our safety and theirs depended on our monitoring their every movement.

At no time, says Woodford, was Captain Gemmell the arbiter of which documents were collected.

> His actions were also consistent with his being unaware that the computer coordinates had been changed. The search of the crash site was obviously a very painful experience for Captain Gemmell and it was a period of great stress. It was clear at this time that Captain Gemmell was completely bewildered as to the cause of the crash. To conceal the stated information about the changed coordinates would have required a masterly piece of acting which I am confident did not occur.

Indeed, the mass of bodies and body parts was a horrendous sight. But Ian Gemmell was not bewildered as to cause at all. He knew what he was looking at. He knew he was standing amongst the human and engineering carnage caused quite simply by the coordinates being changed without the captain being told.

22

Gordon Vette Shows Up

In a whiteout condition a dark object is visible for many miles while a snow covered object, even a mountain, next to the observer is invisible.

— US Navy Weather Research Facility,
quoted by Gordon Vette in *Impact Erebus* (1983)

But one part of the jigsaw was missing. The picture still was not quite right. There remained another great question.

Given that the passenger photos showed Captain Jim Collins was flying within the visual flying rules and as McMurdo had insisted, why did he fly himself, his aircraft and 256 other people into the side of a mountain in broad daylight?

One day there appeared at the inquiry Captain Alwyn Gordon Vette. Gordon Vette was one of the most senior Air New Zealand training captains. Gordon was a masterful flyer and a superb navigator. Whilst flying across the Pacific, he had saved a lost American aviator using only his radio, his thumb and the height of the sun. He worked out in his head where the American must be.

Since the Erebus disaster Gordon Vette had applied his formidable abilities to working out how it happened. Since telling Maria shortly after the accident that low flying and skylarking with passengers on board was not Jim's style, and that he was going to get to the bottom of it, he had spent a lot of time and his own money.

He had done a lot of work. As he wrote in his highly successful book, *Impact Erebus*, in 1983, he approached the problem on the assumption that this was a good crew, a crew which would not have taken any action which he could attribute to poor airmanship. And he was a realist. He knew the Chief Inspector of Air Accidents 'would, naturally, have less regard for this assumption'.[1]

However, he admitted, things were starting to emerge that did not look good for the crew. Collins and Cassin seemed a long way off the usual course when they impacted the mountain. They were far to the left of the track Vette assumed they were programmed to follow. And if Jim Collins was flying in cloud at 1500 feet, he was demonstrating very poor airmanship indeed. If he was doing so, then Chippindale was right. Collins was lost and flying in cloud in mountainous terrain, and to do so was a special kind of insanity.

But Vette knew Jim Collins — he taught Collins to fly in the air force — and he knew Greg Cassin. And he knew the spare first officer on the flight, too, Graham 'Brick' Lucas. Lucas, he says, was a very outspoken fellow. And like Captain Arthur Cooper, Vette knew that if Jim Collins and Greg Cassin were flying foolishly that Lucas would have been straight up on the flight deck demanding to know what the hell they thought they were doing.

For Captain Arthur Cooper, the role of 'Brick' Lucas in the accident is constantly underestimated, not so much for what he did but for what he didn't do. At no point in that final 30 minutes of the cockpit voice recorder is the voice of First Officer Lucas to be heard. In other words, he was back in the cabin, chatting to passengers or resting, without a doubt as fascinated as everyone else was with the Antarctic scenes below them through the cabin windows, and not at all concerned.

The passenger photos showed that Jim Collins seemed to have flown into that mountain in clear air. But that was impossible, surely. Vette says he asked himself two questions. 'Was it possible that the crew of Flight 901 had positively identified what they believed was their position before descent — and were deceived? And was it possible that they flew into a mountain in perfectly clear weather without ever seeing it?'[2]

The release of the Chippindale Report and the cockpit voice recorder transcript confirmed the first question for Vette. His own research would confirm the second.

As mentioned, because of the crew loop procedure, sometimes called the challenge procedure, any member of the flight crew may question the actions or omissions of another. Modern jet aircraft, if they carry a flight engineer, are essentially flown by three people, the two pilots and the flight engineer.

The old days of the commander above reproach were long gone. And the nub of the matter here was that in those last minutes of the Erebus flight there were on the DC-10 flight deck two pilots, two flight engineers and an experienced Antarctic explorer, Peter Mulgrew. And contrary to the erroneous and invented assertions of Ron Chippindale, not one man on that flight deck objected to Collins's flight path as he flew ever closer to the mountain.

The lack of concern by either pilot and the failure of anyone to mention a mountain in front of them confirmed to Vette that the crew must have flown into what Mahon would later call 'a total optical illusion'.[3]

We have established clearly that the crew was convinced the landmarks they were looking at were exactly what they expected to see at the entrance to McMurdo Sound. And the cockpit voice recorder established clearly that the crew believed they were entering McMurdo Sound. In any case, Jim Collins and Greg Cassin knew exactly where they were because of the confirmation of AINS, which was never wrong. It could not be wrong. And if the coordinates of the last leg of the flight to McMurdo had not been changed in the early morning before they departed Auckland, without anyone telling Jim Collins, then that indeed is where they would have been.

But how, if Collins was flying visually, could he have flown into a mountain? Gordon Vette asked round and was surprised to learn of the power and extent of a visual polar phenomenon that even experienced ice pilots treated with great respect: whiteout, the loss of surface definition. As the American Navy Weather Research Facility, quoted by Gordon Vette, says, 'In a whiteout condition a dark object is visible for many miles, while a snow covered object, even a mountain, next to the observer, is invisible.'

If there is a clear sky, we can still figure the relief of snow-covered terrain with accuracy because of shadows of the terrain. Remember, whiteout occurs when the viewer is looking at an area that is completely white, when there is a light-coloured cloud cover above and if the sun is low behind the viewer. The effect is that terrain flattens out ahead of you forever, even if the terrain is a mountain. 'This freak of polar weather,' wrote Mahon, 'is known and feared by every polar flier.'[4]

But the double jeopardy of whiteout, Vette learnt, is that the pilot has no idea he or she is in whiteout. Not an inexperienced pilot, anyway. The experienced polar pilot gets to be able to read certain warnings.

Mahon, in his accident report, stated damningly that he did not believe that either the airline or Civil Aviation ever understood the true danger of whiteout or thought it to be anything other than some loss of visibility in snow showers.[5]

In fact, Gemmell knew about the complexities of whiteout but elected that the pilots receive no briefing on the danger of whiteout below 6000 feet because that would encourage them to descend below that altitude. David Baragwanath asked the sensible question: 'But isn't it the case, that any human being, even a child, is more likely to act in accordance with a direction, if he can see the reasons for it, and that those reasons are sensible ones?'

Gemmell's answer was extraordinary. 'Possibly true. But I still feel that [if] the pilots [were given] that sort of instructions and qualification, it would seem to give them some latitude in interpreting the minimum level they could fly at.'[6] This, despite Gemmell's having to have known, from pilot talk and newspaper articles and wide publicity given the flights, that pilots were flying on average between 1500 feet and 3000 feet, possibly as low as 500 feet, according to American evidence given to Chippindale. Despite this, there was no instruction in the perfidies of polar whiteout given to the crews, the great majority of whom, when they flew to the ice, had never been there before.

It turned out that between 1946 and 1973, there were 50 aircraft losses in Antarctica. Whiteout was blamed for a 'large proportion' of the losses.[7] Many other aircraft were badly damaged over the years, again through lack of visual depth perception.

Civil Aviation particularly could not seem to get a handle on the true insidiousness of whiteout. At the Royal Commission, the Director of Civil Aviation was shown up badly on whiteout, as he was on almost everything. He was examined by MacAlister.[8]

Kippenberger: 'Speaking as a pilot, your visibility only extends as far as you can see, for whatever reason you cannot see. And if there are objects within that distance that could not be seen, then in [my] mind the flight visibility would not extend that far.'

Whatever that all meant.

MacAlister: 'We again get to the problem as to how a pilot would be aware of this.'

Kippenberger: 'I would have expected him to be aware of it, because he could not see, and he should have been able to.'

MacAlister: 'Rather, could he not think he was looking into infinity, or the distance?'

Kippenberger: 'I wouldn't have thought so, because objects could be seen from either side of the aircraft.'

MacAlister: 'But that's what you're basing your statement on, when you say visibility was not 20 km [the minimum visibility required by Air New Zealand for a flight to be in visual meteorological conditions (VMC) in Antarctica]?'

Kippenberger: 'That is correct. That he flew into, and towards, and eventually flew across, Ross Island, without seeing what was before him.'

MacAlister: 'You say that, even though he might have been quite unaware and incapable of appreciating that?'

Kippenberger: 'I can't see that he would be incapable of appreciating it. I would have expected a pilot looking ahead to see something, not just a white mass. And then, if he couldn't distinguish something, to become concerned.'

That seemed to be the level of the ignorance of whiteout at Civil Aviation. But it was a lie. It was all bluster. Kippenberger was very informed about the perception difficulties of whiteout, as opposed to simple snow showers, because he had been to the ice in 1969, come back and written a report about whiteout conditions, a report known about within Civil Aviation, as the evidence of Mr Omundsen, the Controller of Airline Operations at Civil Aviation, made clear. Civil Aviation had a wealth of knowledge of whiteout. Negligently, they chose not to pass it on. Kippenberger wrote in November 1969 of 'whiteout conditions caused by difficulty of depth perception and evident particularly in overcast no shadow conditions with ceiling 3000 feet or below'.[9]

In his investigation, Chippindale looked into whiteout in some depth and it is clear from his report he knew about the kind of whiteout that occurs in clear air in calm conditions, the most insidious of all types. Nevertheless, and despite quoting a serious expert on whiteout in his report, Chippindale gave the whiteout depth perception phenomenon no weight in his finding of causation and, incredibly, continued to talk about 'poor visibility'.

Collins was not flying in cloud. It was not poor visibility the crew was flying towards. It was perfect visibility and the crew were seeing exactly what they expected to see, flat sea ice all the way up McMurdo Sound ahead of them. But the visibility was a lie. No one on the flight deck, in broad daylight, ever saw the mountain.

Could Jim Collins, asked Vette, have been flying visually towards a mountain hidden in what seemed like crystal clear air but was in fact sinister whiteout on a massive scale without him, or any of his colleagues on the flight deck, realising it, none of them having been warned about the pitfalls of this polar visual phenomenon, knowing only the very limited properties of whiteout that Civil Aviation passed on?

So this must be a gargantuan and terrifyingly dangerous phenomenon. A mountain could disappear? It was hard for anyone at the time in New Zealand to believe this. How could a mountain disappear when all round it was broad daylight? Yet even Chippindale himself was left in no doubt about the perniciousness of whiteout when he was on the ice in the days after the accident and in conversation with the Americans there. The American airmen, all the old hands there, could not believe Collins had been allowed to command an aircraft to Antarctica without ever having flown there before.

And we have to remember the double jeopardy of whiteout. You cannot see it. You do not know you are entering whiteout and you never know when you are in it. What Jim Collins and Greg Cassin, and Gordon Brooks and Nick Moloney, saw as flat white sea ice stretching a hundred miles ahead of them, exactly what they expected to see, was whiteout. And, as the DC-10's CVR showed, not one of those experienced airmen on the flight deck that day ever saw the mountain. Not one of them. Not even in the last seconds. That was the most extraordinary thing.

The crew had a mindset to which they were entirely entitled, that they were flying down McMurdo Sound. They had every reason to believe they were 30 miles to the west of the mountain. That was the brief. And you never changed the brief without telling the pilots. It just didn't happen. Jim Collins had plotted the route on his charts from the digitised flight plan he took home with him from the briefing.

It was simple. There was no mountain in front of them on the route they were briefed on. There was no mountain in front of them when they looked out the cockpit window. Everything fitted. The mountain was well away to the east in the cloud. Everything looked safe and flat below and ahead of them. Collins and Cassin may even have seen a line of flat horizon in the distance, such are the deceptive twists of whiteout.

Vette made contact with American ice pilots. He began to read and to contact visual perception specialists at universities round the world. Yes, they told him, it was possible for Captain Collins and his entire crew to have been looking at the mountain and to have not seen it.

So for Vette, short of the accident being the mass suicide of four experienced airmen and an Antarctic explorer, there was no other explanation possible. The crew had been sent on a course of which they had not been made aware and whiteout had killed them.

As he came to understand whiteout more comprehensively, Gordon Vette started to get angry. He too, commanding the flight that won such praise from John Brizindine, had taken a DC-10 full of passengers to Antarctica knowing nothing about whiteout.

Vette wrote: 'I have been flying for 34 years, and like to think I have never exposed my passengers to unnecessary danger. I know the same can be said for all my colleagues in the airline, and in other airlines, who have flown passengers around the sights of Antarctica — and below the height of its snow-covered mountains.'[10]

In this, Vette makes the legitimacy of Jim Collins's altitude perfectly clear. 'All of our flights would have descended below the altitude of the surrounding terrain, confident that because they had full visual conditions, and plenty of space in which to manoeuvre, they were safe. This was the impression clearly conveyed at the airline's Antarctic briefings . . . [that] if they maintained visual flight conditions [they could] fly exactly as they were cleared to do by McMurdo air traffic control. It was the same procedure as would be followed at any airport in the world.'[11]

So, you flew below the mountains. That was part of the thrill of the Antarctic flights, of course. Everyone knew that. Flying past mountains is great fun. But even Gordon Vette himself had known nothing about the malevolence of whiteout. With Air New Zealand and Civil Aviation telling the pilots nothing, Vette concluded, some 2500 people on some 13 flights to Antarctica had potentially been in danger. Vette wrote of the Collins flight, 'And had the crew been alerted to the visual traps inherent in polar conditions, they would never have flown in clear conditions beneath a light, but solid overcast.'[12]

So when we add together the uncanny similarity of the entrance to Lewis Bay to the entrance to McMurdo, the meticulousness of Jim Collins as a pilot in plotting a course of the brief he was given and the deception of sector whiteout we can see that a trap had been set that could have taken any pilot. Jim Collins was headed straight into the trap and he and everyone with him was going to die.

As to Collins's navigational position, Vette believed he had to have been sure he was on a track other than the one he was actually on. There was no other possibility. Vette's instinct proved to be correct. It was now revealed that the coordinates had been changed and Collins had not been told.

Gordon Vette brought to the Royal Commission, at his own expense, Professor R. H. Day, the Foundation Professor of Psychology at Monash University. He was 'an expert on perception studies and it was accepted by all counsel present that he was a world authority in his field. He had special qualifications with regard to human factors in aviation'.[13] Professor Day testified to the Royal Commission, supporting fully everything Gordon Vette claimed.

Mahon wrote later, when it was all over, that he looked across the courtroom at Captain Vette and the Australian professor and began to wonder.

> I could not help but reflect that, in spite of the worldwide resources of the airline and of Civil Aviation and their access to all information on this topic, neither of the two organisations had proposed to bring forward one word of evidence on this vital point. It had been left to the untiring industry of Captain Vette to unearth all this literature and detail, and to produce from Australia a world authority in the person of Professor Day.[14]

They did not, of course, because both organisations had been found badly wanting in their education of the Antarctic pilots on the unique and treacherous conditions into which they were being sent to fly.

Later, in his final appearance at the Royal Commission in early December 1980, Gemmell was asked when he last had studied whiteout. He replied that he had become more familiar with whiteout at the time of the application for the approval of Antarctic flights. 'Obviously, the attention that it's received at this commission has shown me very clearly there's been extensive development in the knowledge of this subject.'[15]

The failure of Air New Zealand to warn its Antarctic pilots about the full dangers of polar whiteout was egregious, and was, according to the retired law lecturer Stuart Macfarlane, probably criminal.

The airline always thought in terms of visual flight rules and, what they understood on all of their other routes, as visual meteorological conditions. So for Antarctic flying the normal visibility requirement that you had to be able to see an object at least eight kilometres ahead was extended to 20 kilometres.

An Air New Zealand pilot was quoted by the *Auckland Star* on 30 November 1979. He was asked about whiteout a mere two days after the accident. Asked if the Antarctic was inherently more dangerous than flying elsewhere, he said, 'If you are eyeballing the situation, you are eyeballing the situation whether it's ice you are looking at or the Sahara Desert. The flight is conducted within the confines of normal visual flight rules, the same as you would flying round New Zealand — you look out the bloody window.'

This pilot had obviously received the airline's Antarctic briefing. His remark to the *Star* was nonsense.

In fact, as Erebus showed us and as Gordon Vette would discover, visual flight rules — and eight kilometres out to 20 kilometres — meant nothing in Antarctica. In Antarctica you could be flying in clear air and fly straight into a mountain right there in front of you. You simply wouldn't see it. Visual flight rules meant nothing.

According to Stuart Macfarlane, who knew Captain Vette well, and who wrote sections of Vette's book, Vette was horrified when he learnt about whiteout and what could happen should you descend under cloud in Antarctica. You may have to descend through cloud but you would do so only over McMurdo Sound and under radar guidance. Gemmell's answer to the Commission that he did not brief the New Zealand pilots on whiteout was farcical. He said to have done so would have encouraged them to go below the [non-existent] altitude requirements. It was as if he were treating lifelong, careful professional pilots as boy racers on drugs. In fact it was a serious, unforgiveable failure not to warn captains of giant airliners carrying hundreds of people of clear and present danger. If the punctilious Collins had been informed of what could happen to your spatial awareness if you flew under cloud in Antarctica, he would never have done so.

The whiteout evidence that so disturbed Peter Mahon as he listened to Gordon Vette at the inquiry and which so shocked him when he experienced the phenomenon for himself down at the ice, and Vette's expressed concerns about the negligence on the part of Air New Zealand and Civil Aviation in not instructing the pilots about the dangers of whiteout in polar regions, angered the airline badly.

Morrie Davis gave Vette a serious beating about the damage his evidence was doing to the airline. Because of the stand he took, Vette was to lose the flying career he loved. But he remains one of the great heroes of the Erebus saga. He became a scientist, effectively, and was honoured as such with an

Honorary Doctorate in Engineering at Glasgow University, such was the intensity and the extent of his study into the way the eye and the brain work together, the eye being, in fact and effectively, part of the brain, an extension of the brain through the eye socket in the skull.

After the Royal Commission, with the Erebus controversy still painfully raw but essentially put to one side of the official national life, and with Muldoon stubbornly refusing to acknowledge the findings of Justice Mahon, Gordon Vette went back on the flying roster. They all did. And on the long hauls Gordon Vette was subject, as are all airline pilots with regularity, to check flights in which a senior captain sits on the flight from start up to shut down. So on a long haul the check captain was there all the way for hours on end, the aircraft hanging endlessly in the skies across the Pacific. And Gemmell checked Vette. Gemmell sat stonily silent behind him and his co-pilot, all the way, saying nothing. Essentially, Vette was edged out of the airline. The Erebus researcher, Stuart Macfarlane, says that these days we would call that constructive dismissal.

In the end it got to Gordon Vette and he retired. He went to run a motel. It was very successful. But Gordon was not meant to run motels. Gordon was born to play amongst the stars. And as Gordon Vette says in *Impact Erebus*, in terms of human life, an airline pilot has greater responsibility than an astronaut. And as Arthur Cooper says of Gordon, Gordon had a huge ego but then Gordon had a lot to have an ego about.

Gordon Vette has a special place in the history of New Zealand aviation. His health is poor but the ALPA continues to support him where they can. Pilots know the importance to airline safety of Alwyn Gordon Vette. Gordon had a stroke in 2003, which removed much of his movement and removed his ability to speak. In the 2007 Queen's Birthday Honours, Gordon was made an Officer of the New Zealand Order of Merit. His mind continues to be sharp as a tack.

Peter Mahon, who knew there was nothing like going out and seeing for yourself, decided he wanted to see Antarctica, in order to examine this whiteout phenomenon for himself. He retained, probably, although he does not say so in either *Verdict on Erebus* or the accident report, a decent judicial and judicious scepticism about what he had been told.

He left for the ice three days short of a year after the Erebus disaster, on 26 November 1980, flying through the night on an RNZAF Hercules. On board was the Deputy Chief of Defence Staff and a radio journalist, Carmel

Friedlander, who would note over the next few days the respect Mahon would be shown on his visit. Margarita Mahon tells me that after the sound and fury of the release of the accident report, and the savaging he received at the hands of the New Zealand Court of Appeal, the respect continued. She says it was unspoken but it was always there, silently offered wherever he went, right to his painful end. The public at every level of society sensed his intelligence, his decency and, I have always suspected, some innate loneliness.

At some stage the aircraft crossed 60 degrees of latitude and one of the crew came back to tell them they had crossed the point of no return and that McMurdo Control was reporting clear weather. The US Navy was most certainly aware of who was on board this flight. The US Navy was going to watch Mahon like a hawk. They were right to. Mahon's magnificent head for detail had already begun to calculate that McMurdo radar may have identified and seen the aircraft's track for at least 30 seconds as Captain Collins conducted his first, right-hand descending orbit, before disappearing behind the mountain. Mahon had let them know that he thought that. Of course, like Air New Zealand and Civil Aviation, the US Navy was not going to wear responsibility for the loss of a New Zealand DC-10 full of passengers in their controlled airspace.

Then as dawn approached and as Antarctica began to emerge, Mahon was invited up to the flight deck, under the command of Wing Commander Ken Gayfer. Mahon sat behind the pilot, Flight Lieutenant Russell. The aircraft flew on at 31,000 feet. Below them was the northern point of Victoria Land.

Mahon stared ahead of him, falling under the spell of his first sight of the continent that has tempted men for hundreds of years. For a man of Mahon's deep sense of poetry and his intellectual curiosity, for a man who had survived the horrors of war, this might have been a little akin, perhaps, to finding Atlantis.

> Below us there were patches of cloud but, as we flew on, the clouds receded backwards, the view below became as clear as the view ahead, and I found myself looking at one of the most striking panoramic scenes the world can provide.
>
> On our right was a long sequence of mountain peaks stretching far away to the south, dwindling unbroken into the horizon towards the South Pole. The sun was shining on the

> snow and ice of the mountain tops, and the peaks glittered and shone as if touched with white fire. Far away to the west were further ranges and valleys, forming a white tableau which extended in clear air to the very limit of vision. Over to our left was the dark blue expanse of the Ross Sea, and straight ahead on the horizon I could just see the vague white haze which marked the coast where the Ross Sea ice-shelf began. The sheer immensity of this limitless expanse of sea and snow seemed almost unreal.[16]

Pip Collins, as we shall soon see, will have a similar response to Antarctica's vast grandeur 30 years later when she too was invited onto the flight deck on the approach to Antarctica in her pilgrimage to the place where her father, and everyone with him, perished. Pip will experience the same sense of wonder at the vastness of it all, mixed, of course, with the old emotional complexity of the grown-up version of the little girl who lost her father in the savage wilderness of this, the harshest, the most inhospitable, the most unforgiving place on earth.

As the aircraft approached the entrance to McMurdo Sound, about 150 miles north of McMurdo, Wing Commander Gayfer strapped himself into the co-pilot's seat and told Mahon what he would like to do. Mahon approved. Gayfer radioed McMurdo for clearance. Mahon could see Erebus clearly in brilliant early morning sunshine. He could see the steam at its summit, he could see its long, gentle slopes and he could see the black rocks at the base of the 300-foot ice cliffs that marked Ross Island's emergence from the sea of Lewis Bay.

As the aircraft flew abeam Cape Bird, rolled left, flew over the saddle between Mount Bird and Mount Erebus and across the lower slopes of Erebus itself, Mahon could see a snow-dusted piece of the remains of the DC-10.

Then Gayfer, about to recreate the final minutes of Jim Collins's fatal flight into Erebus, instructed the pilot to fly north over Lewis Bay. Having flown north for some distance, the Hercules turned south again, on track to the mountain, 11 miles ahead. Mahon could see the crash site clearly. Gayfer was using a topographical map on which he had written the exact details of the DC-10's flight path, planning to replicate the DC-10's speed and altitude.

As they approached the mountain, Gayfer began by repeating Jim Collins's wide right-hand descending orbit from 17,000 feet down to 10,000 feet before beginning the left-hand orbit with its long arm to the north, then the final turn back towards the mountain and the descent to 2000 feet. Then as the Hercules flew towards the impact point, Gayfer instructed the young pilot to drop down another 500 feet, as Collins had done.

The wing commander then told the pilot that upon his command he was to execute a very smart and very sharp 180-degree turn. They flew on. Mahon did a quick calculation. When Collins said, 'We're twenty-six miles north, we'll have to climb out of this,' he was two miles from impact. Then of course he began his brief discussion with Cassin about whether to turn right or left. This was not indecision, but rather the normal way captains and first officers worked, by agreement. Their discussion took about 15 seconds. If the two airmen had not had that discussion, there might have been a very close call, people in the back might have been thrown about and injured by the sudden nose-up climb but there might have been no collision. 'That quarter-minute delay was fatal. Such are the inequalities of chance,' Mahon wrote.[17]

Gayfer gave the order, 'Turn now,' and the Hercules rolled away to the left and headed north. They had been 25 seconds from impact.

Mahon took three important lessons from this demonstration.[18] Firstly, he was satisfied that he was right at Farnborough to conclude that Mulgrew, as the DC-10 entered Lewis Bay, said, 'This is Cape Bird,' and that Chippindale was quite wrong to think that what was said was 'Bit thick here eh Bert?' Mahon was staggered by the similarity between the coastline of Cape Tennyson and that of Cape Bird. They looked just the same. Even Mulgrew was fooled on the fateful day.

Secondly, as Collins and Cassin approached the mountain, with Collins continually locking the DC-10 onto Nav Track, they must have not been able to see the mountain. If Collins had seen the mountain he would not have locked the aircraft into a collision course with it. Therefore, if no one on the flight deck had seen the mountain and remarked upon it, there had to be a very good reason.

Thirdly, Mahon began to understand how the crew did not recognise Beaufort Island, a rocky outcrop which sits clearly marked on the charts well to the north of Cape Bird in the Ross Sea. It is rather a sprawling feature, bearing a striking similarity to Australia's Ayers Rock. It rises to 2500 feet out of the water.

The failure of the TE901 flight crew to see Beaufort Island, to recognise it and to wonder why it was on the right-hand side of the aircraft instead of miles away to the west of it, gave strength to those who argued that the Erebus accident was pilot error. Those of the pilot error view claimed that if Collins had noted the island and then examined the chart upon which he had so conscientiously plotted his flight path, he would have realised in horror that he was on track to catastrophe and would have taken the aircraft immediately away to the right towards the centre of McMurdo. He would have also gained some height in order to have space to do some serious thinking and discussing.

But on the CVR there is no mention at all of Beaufort Island. No one, including Mulgrew, identified the island either as being there or being on the wrong side of the aircraft. Mahon lay on his bunk back at Scott Base, he told us, and realised why. The main reason, he believed, was the recurring power of the mindset of Collins and Cassin. They knew where they were. They had been briefed to fly down McMurdo Sound, and that was where the AINS had to be taking them. 'The suggestion of error on the part of the flight crew in not identifying Beaufort Island will therefore be seen to be the result of an apparent confusion of mind on the part of its proponents,' Mahon would write.[19]

In any case, as Arthur Cooper reminded us, the DC-10 in straight and level flight flies with a nose-up attitude of 5 degrees. The crew looked over the top of the instrument panel not at what was below them, which was no threat, but what was coming at them 50 miles ahead as they streaked towards it at 460 kilometres per hour.

This is one of the basic rules of flying and aircrew learn it very early. The faster the aircraft you are flying, the further ahead you need to be looking, and the sooner you need to be making your plans. Jim Collins and Greg Cassin were looking ahead, way up ahead across that perfectly flat ice shelf, planning their turn to the left and thinking about handling the aircraft over McMurdo and Scott Bases.

Lastly, none of the crew might have seen Beaufort Island. Two of the passenger photographs show why. Antarctic islands are not lush green set in tropical blue water. They are black rock in black sea. Such islands can look, in the distance, like flat breaks in the sea ice, just like other breaks in the sea ice. Antarctica is a continent of visual deceit and deception.

And Collins flew on to destruction.

23

The Malevolent Trick of the Polar Light

I looked out the window, and far away in the night sky . . . I saw an arresting sight. In the distance the sky was lit with long pale green streaks of fire. 'The Aurora Australia,' said the pilot laconically.

— Peter Mahon on the RAAF Hercules,
climbing out of Antarctica

There were two further dramatic displays that affected Mahon deeply on the ice in November 1980, one year after the Erebus disaster.

On 28 November 1980, the fateful date one year on, the American Navy provided a helicopter for Mahon and his party. The American pilot negotiated the aircraft over the saddle between Mount Bird and Mount Erebus, through a gap between the ice and the cloud that Mahon appeared to be saying was about exactly the height of the helicopter itself.[1]

This was precision flying by a highly trained military airman. The aircraft headed north over the crash site and out into Lewis Bay, a good way north. Then the pilot turned it south towards the mountain, again on the same track as the DC-10 and at the same altitude Collins had selected, 1500 feet.

There was no fog coming off the sea obscuring the black rocks beneath the 300-foot-high ice cliff that marked the edge of Ross Island and the start of the climb towards Mount Erebus. On the day of the disaster, however, one year to the day before this, those black rocks were covered with fog rising from the sea. Remember, the DC-10 flies 5 degrees nose up when straight and level, so objects in front of the pilot disappear from sight underneath the aircraft when they are still quite a way ahead.

Suddenly Mahon was about to become witness to the weather phenomenon that Captain Vette believed had killed Collins and his people. All around them was bright sunlight but what Mahon saw now staggered him: '. . . the mountain itself was becoming enveloped in pale cloud, and in a minute or so it totally disappeared from sight. Even though the mountain slope began only some two or three miles ahead of the crash site, no part of the mountain could be seen.'[2]

A mountain had completely disappeared. Upped and walked. Over to the left, Mahon could still see the black coast of Cape Tennyson. Over to the right he could clearly see the black rocks of Cape Bird. In front of the helicopter, approaching the mountain at 130 miles an hour, there was nothing but clear air for a hundred miles.

This very weather event that Mahon described, exactly one year to the day from the date of the accident itself, was caught on film. There were three photographs taken by the DSIR's Antarctica Director, Bob Thomson, taken at 30-second intervals through the windows of the helicopter as the aircraft approached the lower slopes of Erebus.

The navy pilot was experienced in polar conditions, of course. He knew, as they all did, there was most certainly a mountain right there in front of them and not a hundred miles of flat ice as the novice might have thought. He negotiated the aircraft up to a rocky area about 4000 feet up the mountain, close to the small wooden cross the men at Scott Base had constructed in the carpentry shop in the days following the catastrophe. Mahon stood there examining the sprawling mountain slope down to the broad blue-grey expanse of Lewis Bay.

> The pale cloud kept drifting towards us from the direction of Cape Bird [across to his left]. Sometimes it was thick enough and high enough to blot out the sun. When this happened, the even white slope which ran down from where we were standing [above the wreckage] towards Cape Bird imperceptibly became almost level. It was hard to tell that the ground was sloping away before us.[3]

Mahon later wrote of his experience that day:

> We had been only onlookers at a dangerous peaceful scene, but for a polar aviator it was something else again. With a pale overcast above him obscuring the sun, and with clear air all around, the sloping contours of the snow would disappear. In every drifting bank of cloud lay the presence of death, silent and unseen. Such was the environment into which the airline management had arranged, so it seemed, for its airliners to fly, not only at low altitude but piloted by crews who had never flown in polar regions before.[4]

Some weeks before he went to Antarctica, Mahon and Baragwanath journeyed to the United States and Canada to consult three acknowledged world experts in the perception difficulties for the human eye and brain in polar flying in whiteout.[5] They all concurred that Jim Collins and the entire flight deck crew had been deluded by a combination of their lack of familiarity with polar flying and a major whiteout event. Every one of them.

Mahon and Baragwanath undertook this trip because the Director of Civil Aviation claimed he did not believe in the existence of the kind of whiteout being described by Captain Vette and Professor Day.[6]

While on this trip, Mahon was to encounter more of the US Navy mystery that pervades the entire Erebus story; the central mystery being the question of whether MacCentre did, in fact, capture TE901 on radar even for half a minute during Collins's right-hand orbit, which would have had him in line of sight above Cape Bird.

It was one of the terms of reference under which Mahon was to conduct his Royal Commission. Had there been an act or omission on the part of those controlling the aircraft in the McMurdo airspace that might have contributed to the accident?

So the question for Mahon, therefore, was, if MacCentre had the DC-10 on its radar, could and should MacCentre have warned Captain Collins he was going behind a large hill? While the US Navy had not allowed their air traffic control staff to come to New Zealand to give evidence, Mahon and Baragwanath were told they could interview some of them in California. It remains significant that two of the staff Mahon did not get to meet were the man on duty in the control tower and the man on duty at the radar screen at MacCentre at the time of the disaster.

What the US Navy staff all did in Mahon's visit to California in late 1980 was to confirm to Mahon the perniciousness of the polar light and whiteout itself as a major concern in polar flying. All expressed to Mahon their consternation that the captain of the DC-10 had been sent to Antarctica in command of an airliner without having flown under supervision in Antarctica before.[7]

But there was another little matter that Mahon wanted to bring up with the US Navy. He interviewed Lieutenant Commander Fessler from the Judge Advocate General's branch of the US Navy. The last four minutes and 42 seconds of fully recorded MacCentre tape was silent. Mahon tells the Lieutenant Commander this. Mahon said that this was apparently because MacCentre said nothing to the DC-10 in the last four minutes and 42 seconds. The Lieutenant Commander said that that was his understanding too. Yes, however, said Mahon — no doubt irked he had been denied access to the air traffic controller and the radar operator — there was at one time another explanation. 'What would that be?' asked the Lieutenant Commander.

So Mahon told him how in those very first days after the crash, First Officer Peter Rhodes, in his capacity of secondee to the Chief Inspector of Air Accidents, had gone over to MacCentre from Scott Base and asked to hear the tape of the last minutes of communication between the DC-10 and air traffic control. MacCentre obliged him but told Rhodes that four minutes and 42 seconds at the end of the fully recorded tape had accidentally been erased.[8] 'Lieutenant Commander Fessler,' said Mahon, 'was astounded at this revelation.'

And, again, being the old radio man that I am, having spent half my working life looking after tapes, I'm sure he was. In all my years in radio I have not ever, and I can recall no colleague in any of the five countries in which I worked ever, wiped or erased any part of a master tape. Even if you had, as you once did, to move tapes from one machine to another during difficult edits, you never messed with your master tape. The master tape, after all, is all you have. It is your base, it is your rock.

The Erebus air traffic control tape was not only what the military called a 'guard' tape, it was also a legal document that had suddenly become extremely important. What's more, to wipe part of such a tape, a man would have to go out of his way. I find it incredible that a manual recording function would have been available on the recorder the air traffic control tape was connected to. Therefore the tape would have to have been accidently taken some distance to another machine for it to be wiped, again accidentally, there. Some real effort had gone into the accidental erasure of four minutes 42 seconds of magnetic recording tape. The effect of this great accident was to obliterate any sound record of the performance of the ground controllers during the last few minutes of Flight 901.

Well, asked Lieutenant Commander Fessler out loud to Mahon — skirting Mahon and feeling Mahon out — supposing it had happened, what inference was one to take from it?

Well, said Mahon, it wasn't uncommon in air crash litigation for ground controllers to report that sections of the recording were accidentally erased. In this case, a case could be made that the radar operator captured the DC-10 going from right to left from out behind Mount Bird, before disappearing back behind the mountain again. He could have told the radio operator to tell the DC-10 captain that he was about 30 miles off course to the east on a collision course with a mountain.

Again, I do not want to get too complicated, but one of the curiosities of the radio set-up at McMurdo was this. The only frequency available to the control tower was VHF. VHF contact requires line of sight. This made it perfect for aircraft arriving at McMurdo down the centre of McMurdo Sound.

If an aircraft was behind a mountain, then HF (high frequency) was required. McMurdo's own helicopter traffic went in and out of VHF and HF all day every day of the week. Cassin, towards the end of the flight, found HF increasingly to be the only means of communicating with McMurdo.

The HF controller was about a mile across Williams Field in the massive McMurdo radio room. He monitored the VHF transmissions to and from the tower. If he heard that the VHF was not working, he intervened on HF and repeated on HF what the tower was trying to tell a pilot. Everyone, says Mahon, understood this.

By the time Mahon was at McMurdo, developing a theory prompted by the four minutes 42 seconds of tape loss, and at Scott Base, standing on his own looking away to the north across that famous saddle between Mount Bird and Mount Erebus, he had become convinced that as Collins began his first, right-hand descending orbit from 18,000 feet and turned west in a wide arc which took him round to the north, there had to have been a significant time period in which he was captured on radar. During this period, the radar had to have seen Collins tracking west, then tracking north, then, descending all the time, tracking east again before disappearing behind Erebus at 12,000 feet. Surely, during that time, thought Mahon, the

American radar must have seen the DC-10 and wondered what on earth was going on.

In fact, Mahon eventually asked the Department of Lands and Survey to plot Collins's height and position in relation to the radar during that right-hand orbit according to the flight data recorder. Lands and Survey concluded that Mahon was right and that Flight 901 had to have been visible to McMurdo radar for one minute of flying time through and above that saddle between Mount Bird and Mount Erebus.

Therefore, said Mahon to the Lieutenant Commander, what if the radar operator, noticing that the DC-10 was 30 miles east of where it should have been, told the tower to warn the DC-10 captain that he was going behind a mountain and, if he was coming this way, there was a mountain in between? And what if the control tower operator had tried warning Captain Collins on VHF that he was headed for a mountain and was getting no response? And what if the HF controller, hearing that the VHF controller was getting no response, failed to pass on to the aircraft a warning on HF — the frequency which had been communicating successfully with the aircraft throughout its approach?

That failure could be seen as an omission that may have contributed to the disaster. What if, Mahon put to the Lieutenant Commander, in listening to the last stages of the tape later, after the crash, this had been realised? Might that not have been a reason to wipe a portion of the tape that demonstrated that omission — the omission that McMurdo's radar had in fact captured the DC-10 and nothing effective was done to warn the captain he was in grave danger? Had they done so, Collins would immediately have climbed out to safety. Perhaps this was a valid reason for certain individuals to panic and wipe an entire four minutes and 42 seconds of tape. Mahon told Fessler he had no evidence with which to take this matter further and he probably never would have. He was just alerting the Lieutenant Commander to the 'sinister' litigation possibilities. Nevertheless, as he farewelled Mahon and Baragwanath outside the Pentagon in Washington DC, the agitated Lieutenant Commander told Mahon he was determined to get to the bottom of it all.[9]

So by the time Mahon got to Antarctica, the US Navy was ready for him. Fessler had told Mahon he could visit the radio room at MacCentre but he could not interview anyone naval without him, Fessler, flying to McMurdo and being present. Mahon wondered if that was because Chief

Warrant Officer Choyce Prewitt was still there. Prewitt had been in charge of MacCentre on the day of the crash.

Mahon spent pages on this American Navy matter. For a time, I wondered why. After all, it goes nowhere, really. In the end, as Mahon wrote in paragraph 317(6) of his accident report, the United States Department of Defence publication regarding civilian use of the American Antarctic navigation aids made it clear that civilians used them at their own risk.

But I went back several times to read and re-read this section of *Verdict on Erebus*. By then I had learnt that Mahon didn't waste time on what didn't matter. I had learnt, as Sam Mahon advised, to read his father between the lines. Mahon was writing carefully, of course, so as not to be sued by anyone. For Mahon to spend so much time on a particular matter meant, I understood, that he had to know something. And what he had realised once and for all whilst at McMurdo was that 'the line of sight between tower and aircraft had been uninterrupted'.[10] In other words, Mahon was saying radar could easily have seen the DC-10. That is why the tape was wiped.

By the time Mahon made it to the radio room at MacCentre in November 1980, the legal department of the United States Navy was well aware of the wiliness of the investigative abilities of the New Zealand Royal Commission judge. But the judge had agreed to Fessler's terms. He could not ask questions. He had to simply listen.

> I had been taken for a tour through McMurdo Centre shortly after arrival in Antarctica and had been impressed by the singular brevity of the technical descriptions given to me, Baragwanath, Harrison and Air Marshal Sir Rochford Hughes [technical adviser to the Royal Commission] by a senior warrant officer who had conducted us through this big radio communication complex. I had also been impressed by his courteous hostility. I knew that this would have stemmed from a long signal from Washington warning the warrant officer of the possibility, which I had revealed in Washington, that the last few minutes of the ground tape might have been erased.[11]

At one point, the warrant officer pointed to the recording tape and looking pointedly at Mahon said the tape recorded 'each and every word' of all radio transmissions. Mind you, said Mahon, the previous evening in the canteen he had been given a heads-up about the American attitude to him.[12] A young American serviceman, obviously the worse for drink, sat down at the table opposite Mahon.

> He was loquacious and confidential and alluded in humorous terms to a very long signal which he said had been received from Washington prior to my arrival. The warrant officer in charge of McMurdo Centre knew more about me, so my informant reported, than I did myself . . . 'They told us loud and clear, sir,' he said. 'They told us — don't tell him nothing.'[13]

I mention this whole US Navy affair reluctantly because it takes up space and remains inconclusive. But it does lead to a most interesting development. In 1987 the families of the 20 Erebus aircrew, including the Collins family, took a suit for negligence against the US Navy to a federal court in Washington DC, claiming that Collins's DC-10 had to have been seen on radar and MacCentre had failed to warn him that he was 30 miles to the west of where he ought to have been and where he thought he was.

The year 1987 was probably a bad time for a New Zealand class action against the United States Navy. The US Navy was in reaction at the time, feeling that New Zealand had rewarded decades of American protection and friendship towards the people of New Zealand with what it saw as treachery, namely the banning of its ships from our harbours.

And, I must say, that I have mixed feelings about the action the New Zealanders took. The Americans threw everything they had at helping the New Zealanders when the DC-10 crashed, firstly finding the downed aircraft, then assisting at the wreck site with the recovery of bodies and property, then with storage of the bodies. This was a disaster of the first magnitude and the Americans were unstinting. Without the Americans, several of the New Zealanders who were on the ice at that hectic, painful time have told me, they could not have done the job adequately. I wonder if we ever really repaid their generosity. What we did, of course, was turf that same US Navy out of our harbours just a few years later. And, after all, it was an 'appalling blunder' in Auckland that set the aircraft up for destruction, and the weather finished it off.

At the same time, all the Collins girls have ever wanted, any way it can be achieved, is the removal of the stain from their father's name. The case in Washington might have been a way to achieve it.

Nevertheless, there is a bizarre twist in the 1987 American case. The litigating families of the dead aircrew needed the testimony of Ron Chippindale. They needed him to prove that an Air New Zealand DC-10 had crashed on the lower slopes of Mt Erebus and for him to relate sundry facts about the accident. American lawyers arrived in Auckland to have him swear evidence before them. This he did on Thursday 16 October 1986 on Floor 11, 70 Shortland Street in Auckland at 9.20 a.m.

But when the case opened in Washington DC, to the consternation of the plaintiffs — the families of the dead aircrew, the Collins family and Captain Arthur Cooper — who should show up out of the blue at the court as a witness for the US Navy? None other than the New Zealand Chief Inspector of Air Accidents, Ron Chippindale. There he was, six years after his report had been shown by evidence presented to the Royal Commission to be silly and wrong.

And there was Ron Chippindale in 1987, still spouting his conclusions as if they were gospel from on high. It was yet another example of Chippindale's preposterous self-regard, his unfathomable arrogance and his dangerous intellectual rigidity. Appearance, in law, supersedes deposition. The lawyers had to call him. The US Navy attorneys could ask him anything. Chippindale obliged.

By this time, the Privy Council of five Law Lords had complimented Justice Mahon on the meticulous brilliance of his investigation. The Privy Council made it absolutely clear that Mahon's findings as to causation of the Erebus disaster could not be challenged. Yet here was Chippindale in Washington, as outrageously confident as ever, as if the Delphic wisdom of his report could never be, and never had been, challenged or overturned. Justice Mahon, by now, was dead.

In fact, Chippindale's findings had become irrelevant. They became so before the Royal Commission hearings had even concluded. But there were two most surprising and baffling revelations from Chippindale on the witness stand in that United States federal court. He was asked why he was there.

Chippindale: 'I am on duty at the direction of the New Zealand government.'

Question: 'The New Zealand government directed you to come here to this trial?'

Chippindale: 'That's correct.'

Question: 'Did the New Zealand government provide for your transportation?'

Chippindale: 'They did not.'

Question: 'Do you know who is providing for your transportation?'

Chippindale: 'The US Navy — the United States Government.'

If this were true, and there is no reason to suspect that in this case Chippindale was lying, it was nothing less than a conspiracy between the New Zealand government and the US Navy against a group of New Zealand's own citizens.

Judge Green threw the case out. Chippindale had executed a beautiful double cross.

But that was 1987. Back in late 1980, on his visit to Antarctica as Royal Commissioner, Mahon had one more graphic lesson to be taught before he left the ice.

At the end of the day of his visit to the crash site, Bob Thomson told him they could hitch a ride home on an RAAF Hercules leaving that evening at about 6.30 p.m. As Mahon boarded the flight, the Australian pilot in command invited him onto the flight deck for the take-off. There was something the crew wanted Mahon to see.[14]

There was cloud overhead McMurdo, a low overcast of about 3000 feet, and the Australian navigator told Mahon that he had been there at McMurdo on the day of the DC-10 crash the previous year and that conditions were almost the same then as they were today.

The pilot in command explained to Mahon that he was going to take off to the east, climb to about 1000 feet, turn 180 degrees back towards Scott Base, flying west, descending to 500 feet as he did so. He wanted Mahon to keep an eye out for a snow ridge they would pass over as they approached Scott Base. Mahon knew this snow ridge. He had seen it from Scott Base. At the end of the snow ridge was a rocky outcrop upon which there was no snow. The ridge was 3000 feet high. The lads were going to make sure Justice Mahon understood whiteout once and for all. The lads were also going to show the old boy some flying.

Mahon said he remembered what one of the world experts, a Captain Ginzburg, consultant to the US Air Force on visual phenomena, had told him in the States — that whiteout doesn't exist if there is still 'a single dark point of reference in the snow [which] can relay to the brain a slope or a contour which the eye cannot distinguish'.[15]

In other words if you can see some black rock, for example, it will keep you real. Ginzburg was adamant to Mahon that given everything he knew about the Erebus accident, the overcast, the pure white of the ice, the low angle of the sun, Collins would have thought he was looking ahead through clear air for miles and would fly on into it.[16] Mahon noted to Ginzburg that it was undisputed that no one on the flight deck saw the mountain. Ginzburg told Mahon he would expect that. He said that only pilots who had flown in polar regions before would know that something was up. Such pilots wouldn't see the mountain either, he said, but they would note the overcast and be aware there might be something in front of them they could not see. Collins had never been briefed that you must never fly under cloud in Antarctica.

Now Mahon was about to have his true epiphany. As the Hercules bore down on the snow ridge, Mahon put his hand across his left eye to block the black rock from his vision. To his consternation, 'the top of the snow ridge disappeared instantly and I was now looking at a flat expanse of snow'.[17] Like the mountain earlier, the ridge had simply disappeared. 'All that could be seen was a flat expanse of snow-covered ground running on for many miles ahead, and in the distance I could see the mountains of Victoria Land.'[18]

As the crew flew out into the middle on McMurdo, turned right and climbed out for New Zealand, Mahon noted that they entered cloud at 3000 feet and flew out the top of it at 5000 feet. It was the kind of thin but solid layer of cloud that caused the specific trouble that destroyed Captain Jim Collins and his DC-10. As the aircraft climbed towards the night, Mahon could see, out to his right, the majestic beauty of the top 7000 feet of Erebus. Probably he realised that he would never see this again in his life. But he knew that he had seen, that day, the exact visual delusion that had so deceived Captain Collins.

Mahon was deeply touched by the actions of the RAAF flight crew. He thanked them in *Verdict on Erebus*, as he thanked them in his original Royal Commission accident report.[19]

I imagine the crew kept him up there on the flight deck all the way to Christchurch. Pilots are intelligent men, curious about many things, and night flights can be long. Mahon loved the boys on the Australian flight deck. He became the officer again, the leader of men. He wrote in the Royal Commission accident report:

Here are their names and ranks:

Captain — Flight Lieutenant J. R. Howie
Co-pilot — Flight Lieutenant J. G. Thyer
Navigator — Flying Officer C. J. McHugh
Flight Engineer — Sergeant J. P. Vellacott
Loadmaster — Flight Sergeant G. I. Pollard.

They are members of No. 36 Squadron, Royal Australian Air Force.

As the son of a returned World War Two soldier, the son of a stretcher bearer who saw service at Alamein and, like Mahon, lived the monstrosity that was Cassino, I cannot read the above without being moved at what it tells us about Mahon. Mahon was looking after his men. Mahon loved the truth, and he liked people who showed it to him. He so appreciated what those young men did for him that afternoon that he gave them all a mention by name in his official accident report. He knew their inclusion would tickle them when they heard. He was also a father and he knew it would make them proud. I can imagine their saying to him at the end of the flight in Christchurch, 'Give us a mention, Judge.' He may have laughed and said he would. If he did so, he kept his word.

It is interesting to note that when Mahon published this story of clearing that Scott Base snow ridge by a mere 200 feet, there was no denunciation of him for having flown too low and there is no evidence the Australian boys got into trouble for showing the whiteout phenomenon to the judge so graphically.

It had to be done. They did it. They did it for the dead aircrew.

And in doing so they showed once and for all that 1500 feet was, by no means on earth, 'low flying'.

24

The Wise Mr Tench and the Clever Mr Martin

If you judge, investigate.

— Lucius Annaeus Seneca

Just a few weeks before Mahon boarded the Hercules for his epiphanous journey to Antarctica, he and David Baragwanath had travelled to the United States, Canada and the United Kingdom.

Air New Zealand Chief Executive Morrie Davis and both the Chief Inspector and the Prime Minister were no doubt greatly irritated by the infinite curiosity, diligence and obvious investigative prowess Mahon was demonstrating. Why could the man not simply accept what Chippindale said? Then everyone could keep their dignity. The aircraft had crashed. Behind the scenes we knew why. It was a monumental cock-up. Well, damn it, no one could put the plane or the lives back together. Let's move on. Jim Collins and Greg Cassin were dead and it was a hell of a thing but nothing could bring them back.

Before — this is very important — before he adjourned the Royal Commission for his overseas inquiries, Mahon had become deeply concerned about the disbelief with which the Air New Zealand evidence was being greeted in the courtroom, sometimes to laughing derision by counsel opposing the airline and from the news media.

Mahon was not the only one worried about how the airline was looking. Captain Arthur Cooper and First Officer Peter Rhodes, watching the inquiry closely, decided, out of loyalty to the airline, that they had to tell

Morrie Davis how badly the airline's case was starting to look. Every line pilot was by now coming forth and speaking about the altitudes they flew at over McMurdo at the invitation of McMurdo Control. They were not dangerous altitudes. They were the altitudes that the professional controllers at McMurdo knew were safe to fly at for sightseeing.

They arranged to meet Morrie Davis in his office at 4 o'clock on Thursday afternoon, 11 September 1980, Arthur remembers. Morrie was at his desk. Next to him was Alan Kenning. He was virtually the company deputy. He is barely mentioned in the Erebus literature.

Mahon wrote of this meeting in *Verdict on Erebus*. His account of it is quite at variance with Cooper's own account to me. Mahon described it as an ill-tempered affair with Davis lashing at people verbally left and right. But both accounts agree on one thing. The meeting lasted 40 minutes. Arthur Cooper spoke for five minutes and Morrie Davis spoke for the remaining 35.

'And it was quite extraordinary,' Cooper tells me. 'But the gist of his approach, and he was very friendly, there's no animosity or anything like that. He said, "Look, don't worry. Don't worry about it. Don't worry about these little things that are happening in there, there're bigger things going on." So we could interpret that any way we liked. With the benefit of hindsight, it seems to me clearly what he was saying was, "Look, there's a game being played, the outcome has been ordained from the top and that's what will happen. Don't worry".'

Holmes: 'What do you mean "the top"?'

Cooper: 'Muldoon. But clearly this is speculation on my part. I can't prove anything. We left Morrie's office after 40 minutes and outside the office Alan Kenning came out and he said, "Oh Arthur, I'd like to have a chat sometime if it's convenient for you, if you could find time to come and see me".'

A week later Cooper went to see Alan Kenning. 'I went in and the first thing he said to me was, "Oh yes, what did you want to see me about?" I said, "No, Captain, you wanted to see me." So I told him where things were going and that I thought the company was not looking good and that I was concerned. And he asked me what could be done about it and I said, for instance, [Captain] Pete Grundy gave evidence and it just didn't come across, as if he was reciting the hymn tune or the same bible everyone from the company has spoken from and it just doesn't add up and it doesn't look good.'

Cooper went on to express misgivings about Air New Zealand's legal team. Lloyd Brown, he said, was more often absent than present at the Royal Commission. Said Cooper to Kenning, 'I can see them losing the plot and I'm just concerned about it.' The meeting ended. Cooper left Kenning's office and right there in the hallway was Morrie Davis. Davis said to Arthur Cooper, 'Oh Arthur, I hope you didn't feel I was being too abrupt the other night?' Cooper replied, 'No, Morrie, that's fine.'

'So I told him everything I was concerned about. I went on for about five minutes I suppose. So, I finally got my message across.'

Cooper says Davis thanked him.

Holmes: 'But he was dismissive of Mahon, wasn't he?'

Cooper: 'Well, only in the sense of, "Mahon's not an aviation guy, he's not like you and me. We know what aviation's all about." That sort of thing. Yes, dismissive. But it was this, the big thing was, the bigger picture . . . Don't worry about down there [the Royal Commission courtroom], it's the bigger picture going on.'

Mahon, who seemed to have an ear finely tuned to what was being said away from the main stage, heard of the meeting. He heard that Davis was furious at the way 'that whippersnapper' Davison had cross-examined the hapless Chief Navigator, Brian Hewitt.

But it was the suggestion that the Royal Commission didn't matter that haunted Mahon. In *Verdict on Erebus*, Mahon wrote: 'He [Davis] described me as an "amateur" who did not know what he was talking about. He further went on to say that I was "incompetent" to decide these major issues and he hinted darkly that there was far more involved in this inquiry than the deputation from ALPA could ever realise. He did not elucidate this latter point.'[1]

Mahon went on to write that it was not unknown for Davis to say to pilots in quite public places, '. . . "and I would like you fellows to know that I have the government right behind me on this." It was evidently thought by Mr Davis that this was a decisive factor.'[2]

Nevertheless Mahon felt he needed to let Air New Zealand know that their case was crumbling and that his findings could be very severe. How to do that without experiencing the troubles of Justice Taylor?

Justice Taylor was the no-nonsense retired New South Wales Supreme Court judge hearing the Arthur Allan Thomas Royal Commission in Auckland at the same time as Mahon was hearing Erebus. Taylor accused one of the police witnesses of being a liar. The police lawyers took Taylor straight up to the High Court to enjoin him and to seek an order of prohibition. They wanted the High Court to shut down the Thomas Royal Commission on the basis of the judge being biased. Mahon wanted no such development to undermine the Erebus investigation.

Mahon had already received two signals that Air New Zealand, in the person of Morrie Davis, might be ready to take the same action against the Erebus Commissioner. Morrie Davis, said Mahon, 'had expressed an adverse view about the way in which counsel assisting the Commission and counsel for ALPA were conducting the proceedings'.[3] Mahon knew that from Arthur Cooper's meeting with Davis.

When, at one point, Mahon asked a question during the cross-examination of Bob Thomson, the New Zealand Antarctic Director, Lloyd Brown, counsel for Air New Zealand, had 'launched a trenchant and carefully prepared criticism against my asking questions during cross-examination'.[4] In other words, Mahon feared that the airline was setting him up.

One afternoon in October 1980, with the navigation evidence all in, Mahon called Air New Zealand counsel into his room. Only David Williams, one of the Air New Zealand counsel, was still there. He also asked one of the counsel assisting the Commission to come in as well.

> When he arrived, I said that I felt I was under an obligation to tell him that I was concerned at the possibility that he and the airline witnesses might think I had made up my mind against them on the issue of credibility. I referred to the executive pilots who had given evidence on the altitude question. I said that at this juncture, and especially having regard to the unexpected evidence of Captain Wilson, I had no option but to have doubts as to the credibility of those witnesses, or at least as to some of them. As to the navigation section witnesses, I again had no alternative but to maintain at the present time a considerable degree of doubt as to whether they were telling the truth.[5]

Mahon made it clear that despite the 'air of profound disbelief' in the courtroom about the navigation, or flight path, evidence, he assured counsel that he had not made up his mind and would not, until all of the evidence had been heard.[6]

With all of this developing, Mahon adjourned the Royal Commission and, taking David Baragwanath with him, headed off on his research trip to the United States, Canada and the United Kingdom.

Their purpose in the United States and Canada was threefold. They interviewed the navy air traffic control witnesses. That was when Chief Warrant Officer Priest told them the US Navy had no idea Air New Zealand ever had, what he regarded as, the daft idea of approaching McMurdo overhead the active volcano, Erebus. If it had been proposed to them, and it never was, then the US Navy would have sent them packing. The radar let-down from 16,000 feet through cloud overhead McMurdo was fantasy in the US Navy's view and it knew nothing of it. The Americans could not and would not have done it.

Mahon then headed to the headquarters of the Bendix Corporation in Fort Lauderdale, Florida, the designers and manufacturers of the DC-10's radar. There, he spent a day with the top two Bendix experts, Wayne Shear and Daryal Kuntman, who made it absolutely clear to Mahon that the Chief Inspector was quite wrong. There was no way the aircraft's radar could, with any meaningful definition, have seen the mountain and displayed it for the crew. The DC-10's radar was weather radar. It was designed to look for cloud. Cloud causes turbulence. Pilots try to avoid turbulence for the sake of the comfort of their passengers. As mentioned, what the radar is picking up in cloud is moisture. The experts asked if there was any moisture in Antarctica. Mahon was able to tell them that the Antarctic ice was completely dry and that Antarctica is drier than the Sahara desert. In that case, said the experts, radar signals from the DC-10 radar would elicit no return. In terms of detection of a mountain, the DC-10 radar would be useless.[7]

The experts had read Chippindale's report. Mahon showed them some of the passenger photos, taken right to the point of impact, showing the aircraft was in clear air at all times. 'When they saw the passengers' photographs I showed them, they were astounded,' he said.[8] The experts had assumed from Chippindale's report, as all New Zealanders had, that the aircraft was flying in cloud. They asked Mahon why Chippindale hadn't included at least one of the passenger photographs in the release of his report. Then people could have seen that the aircraft was in clear air. 'I could only reply by saying that I had frequently asked myself the same question.'[9]

So Chippindale was flat wrong. However, his assertion that the DC-10 radar would have picked up the mountain had been, as Mahon said, reported very prominently in the news in New Zealand, its implication being that the pilots had been negligent in not monitoring their radar. 'But now, as was painfully clear, this was a complete fallacy.'[10]

Mahon wrote on page 125 of his accident report:

> It was also ascertained at a later stage that the chief inspector had also been appraised of this information. I also found, again at a later stage, that the airline had been made aware by McDonnell Douglas of the same information.
>
> While I did not expect the airline to produce evidence from Bendix which tended to absolve the aircrew from any degree of fault . . . nevertheless it was unfortunate, in my opinion, that the chief inspector did not disclose those special features of the DC-10 radar in his report. He should not have said . . . 'The aircraft radar would have depicted the mountainous terrain ahead'.

Mahon wrote later, in *Verdict on Erebus*:

> This was another example of the results which had been obtained by the Chief Inspector by virtue of a verbal discussion which he had used as the basis of a very serious finding in his report. I remembered that when he had been asked by counsel to identify the 'expert' from whom he had received this information, he had said that he did not recall his name. Such are the dangers of relying upon second hand hearsay.[11]

And such, one might also add, are the advantages of not taking a statement. Chippindale knew all about the radar and lied.

Mahon and Baragwanath then had long discussions with three experienced and highly qualified polar visual phenomena specialists, two of them American and one of them a Canadian with vast experience of flying in the far north of Canada. They all confirmed the insidious perils of the tricks that polar light can play on the eyes and minds of polar aviators. Their three professional polar airmen each told Mahon they detected no fault on the part of Captain Collins. His and his crew's inexperience in the Antarctic and their failure to be adequately briefed had caused them all to fly straight into perfect whiteout. One of the experts, Captain A. P. Ginzburg, stationed in Dayton, Ohio and a PhD on the subject of visual phenomena, also insisted that the similarities of appearance between the entrance to Lewis Bay and the entrance to McMurdo Sound had to be taken into account.

To Washington they went. There, at the National Transportation Safety Board, Mahon and Baragwanath listened to the CVR tape for themselves. Mahon was dismayed at its terrible sound quality. And he began to understand why it took Arthur Cooper and the transcribing team an entire week to decipher everything said on the flight deck apart from the words of the two pilots.

You will remember that, against established and agreed post-accident protocols, Chippindale had released his interim report to those he was going to find blameworthy, and had then quietly headed to Farnborough in the UK to listen to the tapes on his own there. And when he came back, the CVR transcript had many extra comments in it that no one had picked up from the tape when transcribing it in Washington DC, all of them comments detrimental to the reputation of the flying crew. So the published transcript the New Zealand public was reading now included comments like 'Bit thick here eh Bert' and 'Yeah my . . . oath'.

Chippindale asserted that this sequence of speech occurred on the flight deck just after 1.47.55, less than two minutes from impact.

Maloney: 'It's not right.'

Unidentified: 'Bit thick here eh Bert?'

Unidentified: 'Yeah, my . . . oath.'

Maloney: 'You're really a long while on . . . instruments at this time are you.'

These remarks gave the impression of a pilot flying in cloud. Remember, the passenger photos gave the lie to that. And we know that Captain Collins was adamant he was flying visually. The crew assured McMurdo and each other they were visual 13 times in 30 minutes.

Mahon listened but simply could not hear 'a bit thick here eh Bert?' He believed, as did Colonel Turner at the NTSB. that what was being said was, 'This is Cape Bird.' And 'Yeah, my oath,' is not necessarily a response to 'This is Cape Bird'. There was none of what Chippindale called 'mounting alarm' from the flight engineers. It was a figment of Chippindale's imagination. Mahon realised that the CVR could, in fact, be used to support whatever theory one chose to form in one's mind. As simple and as dangerous as that is the CVR.

Then it was off to the UK to do what Chippindale had done in his desperate attempt to shore up his theory as to the cause of an accident he simply did not or refused to understand — to listen to the cockpit voice recorder at RAF Farnborough, outside London.

And we are about to meet one of the most interesting characters in our entire story of honest people and scallywags, the legendary Chief Inspector of Air Accidents at the Department of Trade of the United Kingdom, Mr W. H. Tench. William Tench had an extraordinary career. He flew first as a military pilot, then for KLM Royal Dutch Airlines and became an air accident inspector in 1955. It was now 1980 and Tench was the boss. Tench had seen it all.

And he was up to speed on the Erebus crash. He had actually testified a few weeks before at the Royal Commission, having been in New Zealand for a conference. Baragwanath heard about him and roped him in. And since his appearance, the Commission had as a matter of courtesy supplied him every night with the day's evidence.

Tench took Mahon and Baragwanath to Farnborough.[12] Mahon once again marvelled at the 'truly appalling' quality of the sound recording. Once again Mahon heard nothing of the new material Chippindale claimed to have heard. He could not hear 'Bit thick here eh Bert?' at Farnborough either. Neither did Baragwanath. Nor did the Farnborough technician. Nor did Tench. The Farnborough technician expressed surprise when Mahon pointed out to him that there was no one on the flight deck called Bert. Chippindale, it seems, had not mentioned that to the technician.

Later in the day, all the listening done, Tench invited Mahon and Baragwanath back to his office at the Department of Trade. This was early November in London, late autumn. It may well have been grey outside and, in the air, a damp chill. Lights would have been coming on over London. Tench would already have turned them on in his office. I see the three of them settling into armchairs. I see Bill Tench walking to a cabinet, withdrawing a bottle of scotch and three glasses. I see them settling in as he begins the eloquent discourse of a senior British public servant.

Bill Tench had not only been receiving the daily evidence of the Erebus Royal Commission but had obviously been reading it closely. Mahon wrote in *Verdict on Erebus*:

> Mr Tench said there were some observations he would like to make. He said he was not referring to any specific air disaster in what he had to say and would only speak in general terms.

> Mr Tench then developed his thesis. His experience of air accident investigation both in the United Kingdom and on the Continent had been very wide and, of course he was familiar, as one might expect, with the detailed aspects of all serious air disasters in the world over previous years. He said that it had often been a matter for regret that aircraft operators and aircraft manufacturers had frequently thought it advisable to make an attempt to conceal some fact or occurrence which it was thought might be damaging to the particular company concerned.[13]

Tench explained that these 'misguided attempts were nearly always unsuccessful'. He said that in the UK, the US and in Europe the process of the gathering of evidence, and the questioning and cross-examination, inevitably uncovered the fact the airline or the manufacturer were trying to hide. 'In the result, the final determination reached by the inquiry tribunal was almost always highly critical of the vain attempt to conceal damaging evidence.'[14]

I can see Mahon sitting in that office with this senior British public servant. I can see the light fading outside. I can see the long still face of Mahon listening intently, clearly understanding what Bill Tench was telling him.

> Mr Tench said . . . he believed that airline operators . . . were now convinced that the best policy was to admit at the outset some error or malfunction which might have been a contributing cause to the accident under inquiry. He said that his branch [these days] seldom encountered these evasive tactics which were sometimes fairly common in aircraft disasters. He went on to say, however, that there had been recent incidents of such tactics being employed overseas. He did not refer to specific cases. Neither did I, but I knew to what he was referring. He had in mind the Windsor Incident of 1972, the Turkish Airlines disaster at Paris in 1974, and I suspect he was well informed about the American Airlines disaster at Chicago in May, 1979 . . .[15]

Each of these disasters, as Mahon well knew, involved a DC-10 aircraft. Mahon knew what he was being told.

Mahon wondered aloud whether airlines might attempt to conceal the real cause of failure under pressure from their insurers. Tench agreed that was 'conceivable' but added that he felt that, these days, even insurance companies had cottoned on that it was much better for an airline to open the books straight away, to front up and be honest. Better to tell the truth right at the start. Juries would be more forgiving when it came to deciding awards for damages if an airline had owned up straight after they knew why the accident happened.

Mahon wrote, 'I carefully noted these opinions which certainly came from an expert source. Mr Tench was closely familiar, as I knew, with the transcript of evidence so far given at the Commission hearings. But he had been speaking only in general terms.'[16]

What the Chief Inspector of Air Accidents of the United Kingdom was telling Mahon, of course, was that Air New Zealand was having him on.

Later, back at his hotel, Mahon took a call from a man who said he was calling on behalf of an insurer who needed to see him urgently before he left London. Next morning, deeply curious, Mahon, taking Baragwanath with him as a precaution, met Peter Martin, an aviation law expert at Lloyds, the Air New Zealand underwriters. They met at Lloyds and Martin took them straight to the famous Lloyds Coffee House, quite the place to be in London if you're an aviation insurance lawyer meeting a Royal Commission judge.

They took coffee. There was small talk and great cordiality. Mahon didn't push it. He waited for Martin to make his play. Suddenly, busy-beaver Peter Martin was all business. Like Bill Tench, Peter Martin too had been following closely the daily transcripts of evidence from the Commission hearings. 'Mr Martin said both he and his clients were becoming alarmed at the nature of the evidence being produced before me by Air New Zealand. He then ventured upon the delicate task of endeavouring to find out whether I agreed with him.'[17]

Mahon was instantly fascinated by the game being played here. He sensed immediately that a golden opportunity had fallen into his hands in the Lloyds of London coffee shop.

He was pleased to be able to help Peter Martin out. In fact, with the Air New Zealand defences of altitude and navigation crumbling badly at the Royal Commission, with the airline evidence looking absurd to everyone including the news media — those members of which were still able to follow it — Mahon had already warned the Air New Zealand counsel that not only he but everyone else was finding the airline's evidence not credible. The view was developing, he had told Air New Zealand counsel David Williams, that the stories being told by the airline witnesses were 'concocted' to conceal the real facts.

'I therefore had no hesitation in expressing the same doubts to Mr Martin,' Mahon writes, then '. . . I was, of course, aware of what it was that Mr Martin wanted to know. He wanted to know whether his own anxiety as to the evidence being produced before me was shared by me. He now knew the answer.'[18]

However, as he had with David Williams, Mahon was careful to assure Martin that all the evidence had yet to be heard. He was required to keep an open mind. His years in courtrooms had taught him never to make his mind up until all the evidence had been heard. You never knew if some dramatic confirmation that 16,000 feet really was the minimum safe altitude might appear. After all, said Mahon to Martin, 'Air New Zealand documents were popping up here and there at the hearing like rabbits out of a hat, though mostly because of the industry of counsel for the passengers' consortium, counsel for the Airline Pilots' Association and counsel assisting the commission.'[19]

Martin knew exactly what Mahon was saying. Then he shared his greatest fear, that the Air New Zealand evidence was so destroyed that Mahon would have to find against the airline, and he wanted Mahon to know 'that Lloyds had played no part in the concocting of these false explanations',[20] and that Lloyds would resent it deeply if Mahon were to make such a determination. He said that in New Zealand, before the start of the Royal Commission hearings, he had made it clear to Air New Zealand that Lloyds were prepared to wear substantial claims, so Lloyds, he said, 'had no possible motive for being involved in the type of evidence which I had been listening to. He asked that I should bear this carefully in mind.'[21]

In fact, Mahon already knew that Lloyds had set aside $50 million for compensation claims. It would not be nearly enough should Air New Zealand be found grossly negligent unless things were settled out of court.

Then, to Mahon and Baragwanath, Peter Martin savaged Air New Zealand's management. He said he had left sole control of the inquiry in Air New Zealand's hands and this had been a great mistake. Martin then 'used a particularly vituperative epithet with regard to Mr Davis. He said it had been a great mistake to leave the presentation of the case solely within the control of Air New Zealand management.'[22]

I have found myself wondering what that vituperative epithet was. With some knowledge of the swearing habits of Englishmen at that time, I think he would be most likely have described Morrie Davis as a twat.

But Mahon was warming to Peter Martin. Like Tench, Mahon observed, Martin knew his job, he knew aviation law and aviation insurance. Then Martin, like Tench, made a pointed observation.[23] He told Mahon of the trap that airlines tend to walk into when there is a serious accident involving loss of life and a public inquiry is set up. Martin said that the first thing an airline does is to hire the best lawyers available. Of course, said Martin, that is a natural thing to do.

> Unfortunately, so Mr Martin went on to say, the counsel so selected were always successful trial counsel, and they tended to see every such an inquiry as a court case. Their whole careers had been bound up with the concept that success at the Bar depended upon winning cases. Airline counsel in such situations always tried to 'win the case' for their clients. The fact that the hearing was an inquiry to ascertain the true facts very seldom crossed their minds. They only saw it as a courtroom battle between one side and another.[24]

This was, of course, exactly what was happening back in Auckland. Mahon had noticed it right at the start. Air New Zealand counsel were treating the Royal Commission not as an inquiry but as a trial, with the airline as the defendant. They were revealing nothing. They had come to the inquiry to blow smoke. Well, it was unravelling badly. The coordinate change had been fatal to the aircraft. Everyone knew it.

Again, that attitude was 'highly regrettable', said Peter Martin. The lawyers should rather advise their airline that they've cocked up and that they should admit it and wear responsibility. Failure to do so generally meant that, after the evidential ins and outs had been explored publicly, the airline's fraud would be exposed and the airline would not only have killed people and destroyed an expensive aircraft, but may well also have lost its reputation and have to endure a judicial finding of credibility against it.

'In other words,' Mahon said, 'he was telling me what Mr Tench had told me. If there had been a blunder then the airline or the manufacturer should admit it at the outset. By doing so, it enhanced its own reputation

Mahon family

The iconic photograph of Peter Mahon taken in 1984 for the publication of his *Verdict on Erebus*. Margarita took Peter, already ill, to a 'broken down' photographic studio in New Regent Street, Christchurch. The session was not going well when Margarita told Peter to look up and suddenly they had their shot.

Bob Thomson

Bob Thomson

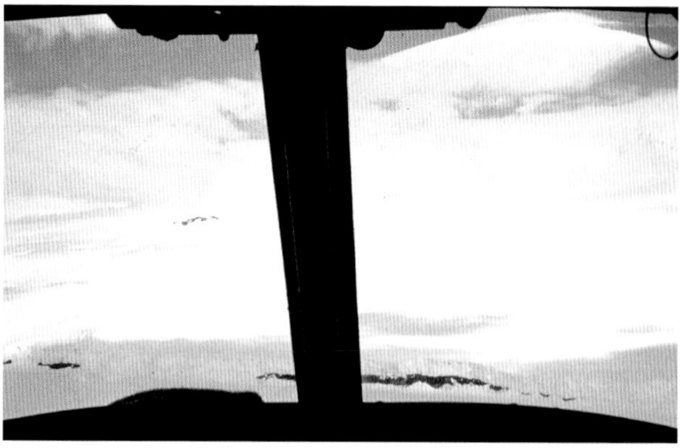

Bob Thomson

Whiteout. This extraordinary series of photographs was taken at 30-second intervals by the DSIR's Antarctica Director, Bob Thomson, from Mahon's helicopter as they approached Mt Erebus on the same flight path as the DC-10, almost a year to the day after the accident. In a minute, the mountain has disappeared.

Gordon Vette

LEFT: Chief Inspector of Air Accidents Ron Chippindale on the ice.

BELOW: Air New Zealand's Chief Executive, Morrie Davis (left) and chief pilot, Captain Ian Gemmell.

New Zealand Herald

Stuart Macfarlane

```
                CENTRE LANDING GEAR IS EXTENDED FOR TAKE OFF
OPS FLASH
NZN NZAA-NZCH RT NO       /       CAPT DALZIELL      RADIO LOG
06/11/79-1900Z  TRK.T  W/V  G/S  DIST ZEET FUELRM STN
N82  TE 901/07  TRK.H DDVVV FL   ZATA ZETA RQFUEL GMT

NZAA  AUCKLAND                                   .  FREQ P
3700.6S17446.9E                   S/H ....  101.4       S

NP    NEWPLMTH  193.6       400   123   21
3900.2S17410.9E 174.3       CLB   .... ....   XX.X

NS    NELSON    199.3 23037 448   146   22    .
4117.8S17308.0E 179.3       FL31  .... ....   91.3

RY    MT MARY   216.2 24037 444   208   28    .
4408.2S17016.8E 195.2       FL31  .... ....   86.5

NV    INVRCRGL  211.8 27037 457   163   21    .
4624.8S16819.1E 189.2       FL31  .... ....   83.1

AUKIS AKLND IS  198.4 29078 478   271   34    .
5042.0S16610.0E 173.4       FL29  .... ....   77.5

55S   55S       185.7 29098 497   259   32    .
5500.0S16527.2E 156.2       FL29  .... ....   72.5

60S   60S       185.7 31060 504   302   36    .
6000.0S16431.1E 150.2       FL33  .... ....   66.8

BLYIS BALENYIS  185.7 31053 504   407   48    .
6645.0S16300.0E 349.5       FL31  .... ....   59.6

CPHLT C HALLET  155.8 31063 532   367   41    .
7220.0S17013.0E 322.4       FL31  .... ....   53.6

MCMDO MCMURDO   188.9 34054 517   337   40    .
7753.0S16448.0E 357.4       FL35  .... ....   47.9

CPHLT C HALLET  008.9 34054 425   337   47    .
7220.0S17013.0E 177.4       FL33  .... ....   41.5

70S   70S       358.8 33060 420   139   20    .
7000.0S17003.6E 168.9       FL33  .... ....   38.8

65S   65S       358.8 31068 425   300,  42    .
6500.0S16946.6E 168.7       FL33  .... ....   33.2
```

Fig. 15. McMurdo Sound flight plan; copies handed out at briefing.

A copy of the 7 November 1979 flight plan on which Captain Collins and First Officer Greg Cassin were briefed on 9 November, three weeks before the fatal flight. The crucial coordinates are those of the destination waypoint, McMurdo, given as 164 degrees 48 minutes. This flight plan had taken Captain Dalziell straight down the centre of McMurdo Sound.

```
ZKNZP ON GATE 2. CLG DOWN FOR DEPARTURE.
OPS FLASH
NZP NZAA-NZCH RT NO      /       CAPT COLLINS      RADIO LOG
27/11/79-1900Z  TRK.T  W/V  G/S  DIST ZEET FUELRM STN
M82  TE 901/28  TRK.M DDVVV FL   ZATA ZETA RQFUEL GMT

NZAA  AUCKLAND                             .  FREQ P
3700.6S17446.9E                 S/H ....  100.9      S

NP    NEWPLMTH  193.6        425   123   20
3900.2S17410.9E 174.3        CLB  .... ....   XX.X

NS    NELSON    199.3 30027 486   146   21      .
4117.8S17308.0E 179.3        FL31 .... ....   91.0

RY    MT MARY   216.2 31027 481   208   26      .
4408.2S17016.8E 195.2        FL31 .... ....   86.5

NV    INVRCRGL  211.8 31029 485   163   20      .
4624.8S16819.1E 189.2        FL31 .... ....   83.3

AUKIS AKLND IS  198.4 32029 495   271   33      .
5042.0S16610.0E 173.4        FL29 .... ....   77.9

55S   55S       185.7 31033 498   259   31      .
5500.0S16527.2E 156.2        FL29 .... ....   72.9

60S   60S       185.7 30034 487   302   37      .
6000.0S16431.1E 150.2        FL33 .... ....   66.9

BLYIS BALENYIS  185.7 29026 481   407   51      .
6645.0S16300.0E 349.5        FL31 .... ....   59.3

CPHLT C HALLET  155.8 29021 490   367   45      .
7220.0S17013.0E 322.4        FL31 .... ....   52.8

MCMDO MCMURDO   188.5 24015 463   336   43      .
7752.7S16658.0E 357.0        FL35 .... ....   46.5

CPHLT C HALLET  008.5 24015 483   336   42      .
7220.0S17013.0E 177.0        FL33 .... ....   40.8

70S   70S       358.8 29024 465   139   18      .
7000.0S17003.6E 168.9        FL33 .... ....   38.4

65S   65S       358.8 29024 465   300   39      .
6500.0S16946.6E 168.7        FL33 .... ....   33.3
```

Fig. 43. The Mt Erebus flight plan handed out immediately before the flight.

Stuart Macfarlane

The flight plan issued to Captain Collins the morning of the flight. The destination waypoint has overnight become 166 degrees 58 minutes east, a change of over 2 degrees, setting him on a course straight to Mount Erebus. Note 'OPS FLASH' — second line from the top — where the course change should have been notified.

Stuart Macfarlane

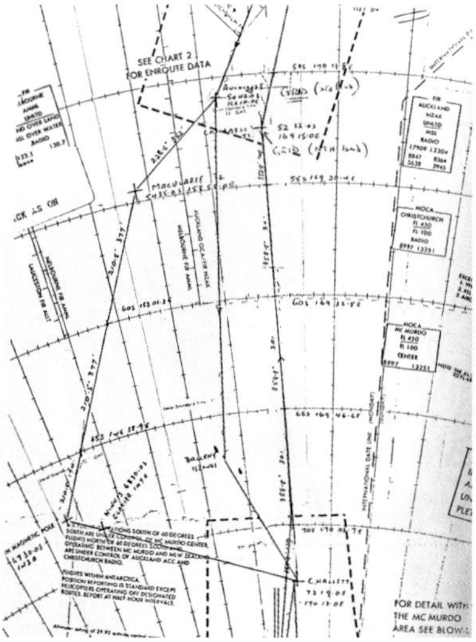

Exhibit 164: a track and distance diagram that Mahon believed was issued to the Antarctic pilots in 1978 and 1979. It takes the aircraft down the middle of McMurdo Sound.

US GNC 21

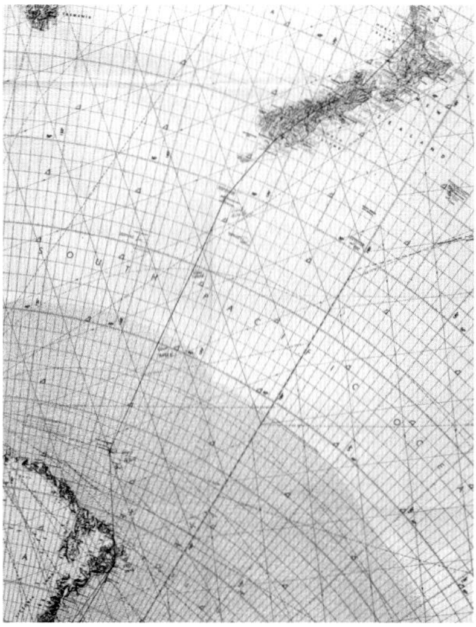

A copy of the big American chart, US GNC21N; which Kathryn and Elizabeth Collins saw their father working on the night before the flight.

Squire Speedy

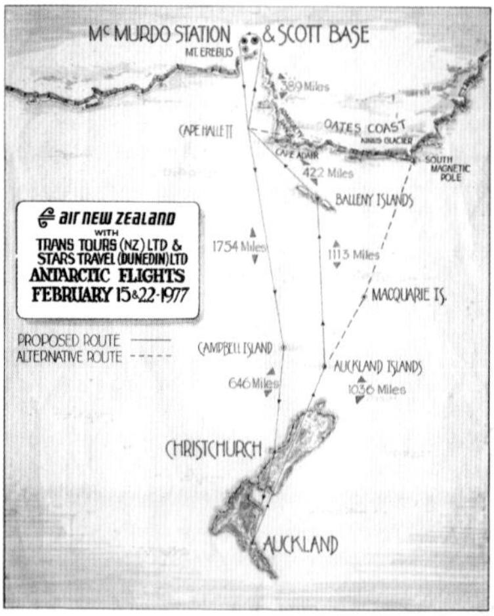

The map issued to passengers on the first Antarctic flight. Even then, the map appears to take the aircraft down the centre of McMurdo Sound, with Mount Erebus well out to the left.

NZMS 135

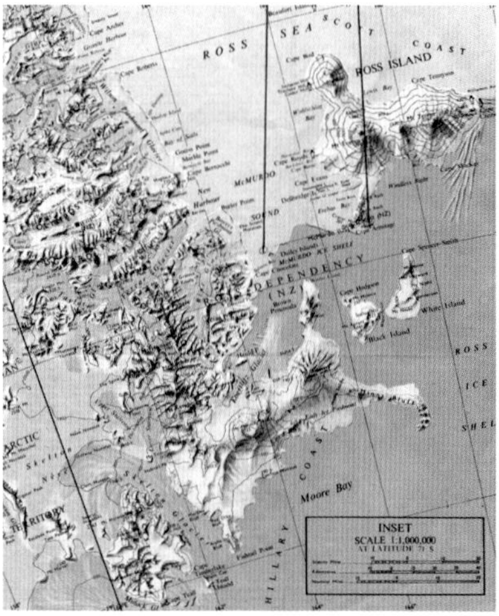

A copy of Collins's smaller chart, NZMS 135. In this illustration, the red line shows the course he believed he was following and on which he had been briefed. The green line shows his actual course.

New Zealand Herald

Paul Davison QC, who represented both the pilots and Maria Collins at the Royal Commission.

New Zealand Herald

David Baragwanath, Counsel Assisting the Commission. Later Justice Sir David Baragwanath.

New Zealand Herald

The aviation expert, Prime Minister Rob Muldoon in his office with his aeroplanes, 1982.

Ross Land

Margarita Mahon photographed in May, 2011.

Antarctica New Zealand/Sam Shepherd

Pip Collins arrives at McMurdo Base in November 2009 for the 30th anniversary of the Erebus disaster.

New Zealand Herald

At the service to commemorate the 30th anniversary of the disaster. From left, Maria, Kathryn, Pip and Elizabeth. Between Maria and Kathryn is Tonci Farac, whose partner, Sue Marinovic, was a cabin attendant on the fatal flight.

and incurred the sympathy of all people associated with the consequences of the disaster.'[25]

Better, therefore, to admit the blunder, apologise, wear the compensation claims and move on with a clean slate. It was advice Mahon would repeat to Air New Zealand on the very last page of his report, written specifically perhaps for his former friend, the trial lawyer Lloyd Brown QC, the senior counsel for Air New Zealand. The airline should have laid its cards on the table, said Mahon. They did not. The pilots were left by the airline to wear the blame.

Mahon said he sat on the aircraft on the way back to New Zealand after his meeting with these two remarkable men, Tench and Martin, and gave thought particularly to Peter Martin. Mahon knew Martin would pass on to Air New Zealand what he thought of the Air New Zealand evidence. Martin had a sense of impending catastrophe and just wanted to get a heads-up from the judge. Mahon was happy to oblige because he wanted Air New Zealand's counsel to be made to understand that the evidence being presented was working against the airline.

He wanted Air New Zealand to understand once and for all that he was not biased, but the evidence was not stacking up. He did this out of a sense of fairness, the same fairness that made him tell the judge in chambers at the Parker-Hulme trial many years before that his opponent, the counsel for defence, must be allowed to use the defence of insanity for the two girls or he, Mahon, would withdraw from the case.

Shrewd Mahon was also hoping, he said, that Peter Martin didn't really think Mahon had believed him when he said that he had left the case entirely in Air New Zealand's hands. Insurers, said Mahon, 'monitor very closely indeed every stage of the inquiry and this was one of their legal rights created by the contract of insurance'.[26]

This was another aspect of Peter Mahon. He had handled many difficult and detailed commercial and taxation cases in New Zealand courts by the time he was appointed to the bench. Mahon even wondered if Peter Martin was supplied in advance with copies of evidence the airline was about to present. If he disapproved, Mahon had no doubt Martin would strike it out. 'It was Lloyds who would have to pay in the end, not Air New Zealand. He would without doubt have studied and approved the nature of the case which the airline was proposing to advance and he would have been quite right in giving his approval.[27]

What Mahon was saying was that Lloyds might have run the entire Air New Zealand defence. He had no doubt Lloyds played a big part. Martin might have been impressive, knowledgeable and charming but he wasn't playing Mahon with an entirely straight bat. But then, quite a few were not.

Martin, Mahon thought, knew that the Air New Zealand case had broken down irredeemably. He knew there was no hope. Martin met Mahon to confirm he was right. Having confirmed it, he simply did not want Lloyds to be associated with yet another disaster, the fate of the airline at the Royal Commission.

The report was released in April 1981. All hell broke loose, as Mahon predicted to his son. The Court of Appeal eviscerated Mahon. Mahon resigned the bench. Hearts broke. The storm died. And in late January 1983, from out of nowhere, Peter Martin made another dramatic appearance.

He did so in the form of a letter leaked from an insurance company and published in newspapers round New Zealand. The letter was from Peter Martin in London to Lloyds insurance brokers round the world, including those in Auckland, and was sent shortly after Mahon met Martin in the Lloyds Coffee House.

Martin had acted precisely as Mahon predicted and passed on to Lloyds brokers everywhere Mahon's gloomy opinion of the Air New Zealand evidence being presented to the Royal Commission and the danger now facing the airline in terms of what Mahon was likely to find.

Peter Martin acknowledged in the now public letter: 'It cannot be said that, from Air New Zealand's point of view, the evidence which has been brought out at the Royal Commission has been satisfactory. There have obviously been various "political" and personal differences and difficulties which have resulted in a rather grimmer picture being presented to the Royal Commission than was anticipated.'

Martin told his brokers that some weeks before his writing this letter, Justice Mahon was in the UK and by a 'lucky coincidence' Martin was introduced to Justice Mahon and Mr Baragwanath and was able to have 'a brief, without prejudice' discussion with them. It was not, of course, 'without prejudice', meaning off the record. Baragwanath had made that clear to Martin, that a Royal Commissioner may use in his report anything anyone tells him.

Then Martin wrote:

> That 'without prejudice' discussion revealed some anxiety on the part of the court about the way evidence had been presented and might be presented in the future.
>
> As a result there has been further discussion of the whole matter between [the lawyers for Lloyds in Auckland and the lawyers for Air New Zealand in Auckland], and there has been some considerable modification of certain proposals for evidence which have resulted in a far better impression of Air New Zealand having been given during recent days than previously.
>
> The evidence of Mr Davis, the Chief Executive of Air New Zealand, is still to be given and it is very much to be hoped that he will come up to proof and not be damaged by hostile cross-examination.[28]

What the letter showed — and no one ever denied either its validity or its meaning — was that Mahon had warned Air New Zealand not just through one of its lawyers in the privacy of chambers, but through its insurers as well, that their case was not good and was not being believed — his implication being that his findings might have to be very bad for the airline. 'I had deliberately warned the airline, through its insurers, that the altitude and navigation evidence [the 16,000 feet MSA and the coordinate change], in my opinion at that time, was false evidence given in concert and the airline had immediately acted in response to that warning.'[29]

With the release of Martin's letter, anyone who scoffed when Mahon spoke of a conspiracy to lie was now silent. When it came to the top former Air New Zealand people, Mahon writes, 'all their protestations about the terms of my report ceased. Even the Prime Minister was silent.'[30]

Mahon was writing in 1984, two years after the Court of Appeal minority judgement of Woodhouse and McMullin accused him of abusing natural justice in not letting the Air New Zealand executives know that he was going to accuse them of conspiracy to perjure.

Airline executives would not acknowledge this at the Court of Appeal, of course, but Mahon had given the airline a very direct warning, which they had heard clearly.

25

The Girls Meet the Judge

Always tell the truth. That way you don't have to remember what you said.

— Mark Twain

From May 1980, when Chippindale's report was released to universal dismay at the astonishingly foolish actions of the skylarking, low-flying DC-10 pilots, Maria Collins and her two older girls lived with the official opinion that Jim Collins was to blame for his own and 256 other deaths when his DC-10 struck the slopes of Erebus.

Through the second half of 1980, Justice Mahon's Royal Commission ground interminably and painfully on, with the entire world trying to get to the bottom of what had caused this incomprehensible air disaster.

It was a mystery, the entire thing. The evidence was baffling and impossible to understand. And, complicating it all was what was known of the caution and thoroughness of the pilot. Even senior figures in the airline who had chosen to accuse him of 13 different varieties of pilot error spoke highly of his reputation and abilities as an airman.

Every day she could, Maria Collins went to the hearings and watched and listened. 'I wanted to hear what was said as it came out, not read about it later in a newspaper. I expected the inquiry wouldn't last long. The papers were full of "pilot error" from the Chippindale Report and I thought the inquiry would be a waste of time. Paul Davison urged me to be patient.'

Maria describes watching the 'clear difference' develop between the route the executive captains described and the route the line captains described. Finally, there was a delicious moment when Peter Mahon intervened, asking why a sightseeing flight would go over an active volcano where nothing could be seen by the passengers when there was a route down McMurdo Sound, free of obstructions where the passengers could see what they paid for.

Davison, for his part, would make his name at the inquiry with some brilliantly lucid and revealing cross-examinations. It was he, really, who exposed the Navigation Section errors that sent the aircraft to its doom, in his savage cross-examination of the hapless Chief Navigator, Brian Hewitt — who had made the original navigational 'error', which he then 'corrected' early in the morning of the fatal flight. Maria says Davison 'minced' Brian Hewitt in the cross-examination quoted earlier. 'My heart began to beat faster with vindictive indignation.' No one could blame her.

And of course, there was Justice Peter Mahon himself, the judge with a deep understanding of men and the psychology of corporate entities, the lay-person who understood the critical importance of the radical changes in the way modern jet airliners were navigated. Computers navigated aeroplanes eight miles high, day and night, across the continents and the seas. What was put into the computers, therefore, had to be right. Error could not be countenanced.

In the days after the accident, Maria told several people, including Jim's friend Captain Ross Gordon, that Jim had been working at the dining room table with charts and plotting equipment the night before he flew to Antarctica and had done so for a couple of hours. She had not paid much attention, however. Maria didn't pay a lot of attention to aviation things. She knew Jim was excited about the challenge of the Antarctic flight and what splendours all on the aircraft would see below them, but that was the extent of it. If he was excited about his flight, she was happy for him. That was how their marriage worked.

One of the universal criticisms, one even accepted by the architect of the Antarctic flights, an area of negligence even identified by Ron Chippindale, was Air New Zealand's failure to print topographical charts for the pilots, with the flight plan drawn on them.

If Captain Collins had been given such a chart when he arrived at Flight Despatch he would, upon opening it, have seen that his flight path was to take him across the summit of Mount Erebus. He would have asked some immediate and serious questions because this flight plan was at considerable odds with the course upon which he had been briefed three weeks before. There would have been no accident. All 257 souls would have returned safely to New Zealand.

One of the great questions to emerge at the Royal Commission was whether Jim Collins plotted the McMurdo flight path upon which he had been briefed on 9 November, three weeks before his Antarctic flight, on his own topographical map or maps. To have done so accorded with what was said of the man. He prepared, he was cautious, he was methodical, he thought ahead.

Mahon believed it was beyond doubt that Jim Collins had not only obtained a topographical map of the McMurdo/Ross Sea but that he had plotted his course upon it.

One of the ways, in fact, in which Jim Collins lives on, is through his daughter Elizabeth's belief in the value of planning. Elizabeth Collins is a serious planner and organiser. In autobiographical notes she wrote when she began her MBA at Otago University, she wrote from the perspective of being 13 years old in anticipation of her fourteenth birthday party picnic. She was planning it. Well, it had to be planned, of course. It would be simple, but planned nevertheless. And what she could already see happening, she wrote, was the little girls would delay things. Pip and Didi were too young. They would be disorganised. They would slow everyone down. Things would fall behind schedule.

There are two parts for us to explore in the matter of whether Jim Collins plotted his McMurdo Sound course on maps. The first is the testimony of his two older daughters, Kathryn and Elizabeth, who saw him working on his maps the night before the flight and testified so on oath.

The second is the attitude of Chippindale to the map evidence. There is his disgraceful doubting of the girls' evidence as worthless and false. And there is his dishonest denial of any knowledge that Jim Collins had a significant topographical chart on the flight deck of TE901 as he flew south.

We must start by going back to what Chippindale wrote in his report at paragraph 2.5 regarding whether the crew had been deceived by the change in the coordinates. We know that, unbelievably, he found they had not been.

But here is what he wrote. 'In the case of this crew [the fated crew] no evidence was found to suggest that they had been mislead [sic] by this error in the flight plan shown to them at the briefing.'

Meaning, Collins and Cassin had not been deceived by being briefed on 9 November with the printout of the actual digitised flight plan used two days previously by Captain Dalziel — one of whose passengers was Captain Wilson, the very man conducting the briefing. Several copies of

Dalziel's flight plan were handed out. Captain Wilson said he thought all were collected at the end of the briefing.

But Jim Collins appears to have taken his home and used it to plot the course on his topographical map. Jim Collins had every reason to believe that the flight plan on the day of the flight would replicate that plan on which he had been briefed. The absence of any adherence by the airline to the Civil Aviation stipulation that no pilot should command an Antarctic flight without at least one flight to Antarctica increased exponentially the need for the integrity of the RCU briefing to be sacrosanct. In other words, where you were briefed to go was where the flight plan would direct the aircraft to go. That was a golden rule of commercial aviation.

We can deduce that Jim Collins took a copy of the printout home because in the first days after the accident, Captain Ross Gordon was telephoned by Captain Dave Eden, Director of Flight Operations. Eden wanted to know whether Ross Gordon had found a flight plan amongst Captain Collins's personal papers. One of those handed out was obviously missing. Mahon was told this by Maria Collins in February 1981 and recorded it in a note. Mahon checked with Ross Gordon. Gordon told Mahon that there was no flight plan or any other material relevant to the flight.

Of course, Jim Collins had the McMurdo Sound flight plan. He had taken it with him in the black flying bag in which he carried his flying requirements, his paperwork, his charts, his navigational aids and instruments, the bag he told his girls was his 'brain bag'. His brain bag was his office, his HQ.

No such flight plan was ever found. If it was, it was never declared and never made its way to the Chief Inspector. But Chippindale was clever. 'No evidence' was found to indicate the crew had been deceived by the change in the coordinates, he wrote in his report.[1]

'It turned out, not unnaturally, that he [the Chief Inspector] did not really mean what he had said,' Mahon wrote. 'He agreed, in the course of his evidence . . . that in his opinion the crew had a misconception as to where their flight path was taking them in relation to Ross Island.'[2] What he really meant, apparently, was that there was no documentary evidence that Collins had plotted the 'old' flight path on a map or that he was seriously committed to the Dailey Islands destination waypoint.

In fact, Maria had told friends that Jim Collins had been working on his maps the night before the flight. His children would affirm this at the Royal Commission.

Chippindale said in evidence that no one at the briefing saw Collins write any notes indicating 'a track to the incorrect destination or a note of the incorrect coordinates'.[3] By 'incorrect' Chippindale is speaking of the McMurdo Sound route. In fact, Erebus researcher, the indomitable Stuart Macfarlane, explained that it might not have been possible for anyone except Greg Cassin to have seen Jim Collins writing. And Greg Cassin was deceased. Captain Wilson, the briefing officer, from the front of the classroom might have seen Collins writing, but he most certainly wasn't going to say so.

Maria told the Commission that Captain Collins owned a copy of a limited edition New Zealand atlas. In fact, it was not the limited edition. It was the standard hard-cover edition which cost about $35. Maria's parents had given it to him as a gift a couple of years before. Maria and the girls will tell you that Jim Collins loved his maps and charts. It was not disputed by anyone that Collins took the atlas with him to the 9 November briefing. Pages 184 and 185 displayed a couple of useful maps for the Antarctic pilots. The pilots being briefed gathered round as Collins showed the atlas pages. It was agreed that he was examining closely these two pages while holding a copy of the printed flight plan.[4]

His mind was already working it out at the briefing. He would see the longitudes on the flight plan and would be comparing them with the longitudes on the maps and the atlas pages, especially the longitude straight down the middle of McMurdo Sound.

He would not be thinking for a minute that he was being sent over the top of an active, seething, steam-belching volcano because that would be daft and, cautious no-risks man that he was, he would certainly have said so.

Maria said Jim Collins worked at his maps on the dining room table from about 8 o'clock on the Tuesday night until about 10 o'clock. She said it was not uncommon for him to do so, especially before flying a new route and sometimes, she noted, if he hadn't flown a certain route for a while. He would bring himself up to speed.

But Kathryn, who had been studying for Thursday's General Science School Certificate examination, and Elizabeth were still up, and they began to talk to their father about his flight to Antarctica next day. Kathryn told the Commission that her father had been working 'with a large chart of the Antarctica/Ross Sea region'.[5] Then he opened up the New Zealand atlas. He then said the scale of that was too small to show her much. So he grabbed a larger map 'which was not the one that he had been working on when I interrupted him'.[6]

From this we know that Jim Collins had at least two topographical maps. The second map was very large, too big for the table, so he opened it out on the living room floor.

I asked Kathryn how she was so certain always that the accident could not have been her father's fault. Her reply was very simple. 'I knew my father. He was such an articulate, clear-thinking, well-organised, sensible person and especially with his approach to flight planning.'

Holmes: 'Let me say this. I'm intelligent and eloquent and trained and methodical in my work and I still fuck up.'

Kathryn: 'He told me the route he was going to take and it didn't add up to where the plane ended up. It wasn't where he said he was going. That's why I couldn't understand.'

H: 'Why he was over there . . .?'

Kathryn: 'Why he was over there when he never mentioned he was flying anywhere near that.'

H: 'Had he said Erebus to you at any stage?'

Kathryn: 'No, no.'

H: 'Had you ever heard of Erebus?'

Kathryn: 'No. I remember the Dry Valleys, the coast of Victoria Land, the Williams Field ice runway, the McMurdo Sound approach. He didn't mention Mount Erebus because I would have remembered it. It was unusual terrain. Mount Erebus is 13,000 feet high or something, the height of Mount Cook.'

Kathryn said her father told her he would fly to the left of the Victoria Land coast on the way down so people on the right-hand side of the aircraft would see it and then fly back the same way, so that passengers on the left could then view Victoria Land.

Elizabeth asked her father if he was going to land on the ice. He answered in the negative. He told Elizabeth that the aircraft would be going down McMurdo Sound and would keep 'fairly close to this bumpy lot' — meaning, obviously, the eastern coast of Victoria Land. Elizabeth then went away. But she did notice what a large map it was, laid out there on the floor.

Both girls were careful in the testimony they gave under oath to Paul Davison in affidavits constructed in his office before they went to meet the judge. Mahon noted the integrity of the testimony. No rash claims were made.

There was no gilding of the lily. These were the Collinses. They were honest. As Maria said, it never occurred to her that anyone would lie to a judge.

Elizabeth: 'Dad was studying the maps and charts of the Antarctic and, yeah, I was pretty impressed from a distance that he was being studious, you know, he wasn't a dad who sat and watched telly for the hell of it, he was actually doing something in a planning capacity and I was wondering what it was, what he was doing.'

Holmes: 'There were big charts?'

Elizabeth: 'He was working from a small . . . from a map on the table, and then when Kathryn and I approached him and asked him what he was doing, he then undid the larger map and spread them onto the living room floor and we went down on the floor with him so he could show us what he was planning to do. There was a book, an atlas he had been looking at.'

H: 'How many maps? You say he had a small map . . .?'

Elizabeth: 'Well, he had a . . . there was an atlas he'd been looking at. And when Kathryn and I interrupted him and asked him what he was doing, he went on to open the big maps and lay them out on the floor so we could see.'

H: 'Had you known before this that he was going to Antarctica the next day?'

Elizabeth: 'Don't think so.'

H: 'Did you recognise what he was looking at was Antarctica?'

Elizabeth: 'Yeah, when he explained it. But I think what I had difficulty understanding to start with was the perspective in relation to New Zealand, because we were looking at it upside down.'

H: 'Yes.'

Elizabeth: 'And also the colour scheme on the map with the Ross Ice Shelf being green, I couldn't understand how an ice shelf, why an ice shelf would be painted green and mountains in pink and it took a few minutes to understand what the key was.'

But Elizabeth didn't want to ask too much. Dad was renowned for his lectures. 'You'd ask him a simple question, we'd get a lengthy answer, which was always very descriptive and explanatory and factual and informative, but sometimes a bit tedious if all we wanted to do was watch something on telly.'

Elizabeth: 'Kathryn asked him, I think, or I asked him, whether he was planning to land on the ice and I felt a bit dumb because he said it was thick ice but not thick enough for them to land on. Kathryn and I have difficulty remembering correctly who said what, because often I ask the intelligent questions and Kathryn likes to take the credit for it, you know, it goes both ways.'

I asked how long she and her sister were on the floor with their father and his map. She replied that perhaps it was 20 minutes or more.

H: 'During that time, did the name, can you remember if the name Erebus was mentioned?'

Elizabeth: 'No.'

H: 'Had you heard of the mountain Erebus before your father went on his flight?'

Elizabeth: 'No. My geographical knowledge was zero, really.'

H: 'Well, nobody had heard of Erebus.'

Elizabeth: 'Yeah. I've heard it quite a few times since.'

H: 'Yes.'

Elizabeth: 'Yeah.'

H: 'So when it came to the bumpy ground he said he was going to stay close to it?'

Elizabeth: '[He said] "Bumpy lot".'

Jim Collins was telling his daughters he would fly well clear of the coast of Victoria Land with its spectacular peaks and glaciers, that great mountainous spine from northern Victoria Land stretching south to infinity beyond.

The elder Collins girls were no strangers to the Royal Commission. They had gone to watch several times after school. Kathryn, on the days when she and her mother would be briefed by Paul Davison that he would be examining a witness on important evidence, might take a break from school to be at the hearing and watch it unfold. This was Maria being honest with the girls, allowing them to be involved in the process as the fate of their father's name was decided.

Mahon intrigued Elizabeth. To the 15-year-old, 'He was quite a grandfatherly looking chap but obviously a man of great importance sitting on the bench all by himself. He was on the highest bench in the Commission room. Yeah, it was fascinating to see him seemingly fall asleep then actually vocalise a really crystal clear phrase to sum up what he'd just heard from a witness, be it truth or untruth. Just incredible. Incredible brain.'

Kathryn said: 'At times you'd sit there and [you'd] think he wasn't there. He was just a very good listener and he let the lawyers question the witnesses or cross-examine the witnesses and then he'd come in with his . . . he came and went, in and out of the presence of the court, if you know what I mean

. . . He'd sit here with his eyes down, almost like he was asleep, like an owl in a tree or on a perch, then he'd go, "but surely Mr So and So" . . . and I thought he was asleep. You could tell people thought he was asleep but he was listening intently.'

It is poignant to hear from both Kathryn and Elizabeth, 17 and 15 respectively at the time they went to read their affidavits to Justice Mahon, that neither girl really understood where their evidence fitted into the whole sad, confusing affair. Kathryn said that by the time they had sworn their affidavits, 'probably by that stage we knew it would help [Dad's] case'. Elizabeth said she had no idea whether her evidence was going to help her father or dob him in.

Which is a credit to their mother. She wanted them just to tell the truth.

So they went to see Mahon. He decided not to put them on the stand. Elizabeth described going to see him in his chambers. 'There was, you know, antique furniture, and he was surprisingly low key. He was grandfatherly. He was warm, he was friendly. He was disarming. He was quite jovial. He was very nice and very unpompous and unthreatening, trying to put us at ease. We were two young teenagers at the time, so he was very affirming.'

Holmes: 'Did he invite you to sit down?'

Elizabeth: 'Yes. Oh, we were very obedient. We were getting to see the great Justice Mahon.'

Kathryn described going into the room. 'It was like being in the presence of a wise old owl. He had this presence. He had a deep voice. He was quite dry, he was very kind.'

I suggest his reputation had him as a very austere character. Kathryn believes it was a screen. She found him warm. 'I think he was still austere [during the meeting] but he was quiet and kind. He wasn't the same judge we saw in the courtroom. I think he showed us empathy. I think that he was kind to us. He made us feel less . . . it was probably less frightening than being in court in a public inquiry situation.'

Justice Mahon, father of three, would have seen the pain in the eyes of Kathryn and Elizabeth Collins. They had lost their father so suddenly, so violently, so far away, only to endure the subsequent humiliation of seeing him blamed for the entire catastrophe in the official air accident report written by a narrow-minded man who, the more his evidence and conclusions were challenged, became ever more defensive.

Kathryn's and Elizabeth's evidence was going to be hugely important. If it were to be shown that Jim Collins had plotted a route down the centre of McMurdo Sound on charts the night before the flight — 'and he was a qualified navigator'[7] — then he would have done so from the digitised flight plan he took with him from the briefing. And from what he understood from the flight plan and the briefing his route would have taken him down the centre of McMurdo Sound. And his certainty as to where he was being sent would explain why he so conscientiously returned the aircraft to Nav Track, the track in his computer, after each of his descending orbits. Both orbits took him no further south than when he began his descent and the second orbit took him safely back to the north whence he had come. So the credibility and the evidence of his daughters was about to matter hugely.

On the stand, Maria kept it concise. Jim had been working on his maps till about 10 o'clock the night before the flight. Other pilots at the 9 November briefing saw Jim with his atlas. On 14 December 1979, a fortnight after the accident, Chippindale came to see her — she told the inquiry — wanting to see Jim's atlas. Maria said she noticed that it was no longer on its shelf. A general search of the house revealed it was not there. Jim had taken it with him. Maria told Chippindale that others in the neighbourhood might have a copy and she could send out to borrow one. No, no. Chippindale was insistent. He wanted to see Jim Collins's copy of the atlas.

The atlas, we now know, was later found in the cockpit wreckage area by the mountaineer, John Stanton. He handed it in.

It was never seen again.

Maria told the court Jim Collins, an inveterate note taker, had a diary. She never saw the diary again. He also had a black ring binder. When she last saw it, it contained its usual sheaf of blank pages. The cover of the ring binder was returned to her but all the pages, she told the court, were missing.

Then came the girls.

Sensing their vulnerability, Mahon did not want to subject them to the witness stand.[8] Nevertheless, once he read their evidence, he knew how important it was. Counsel for the airline and for Civil Aviation and for the Chief Inspector might want to cross-examine them and he would have to offer them up if counsel insisted.

> I decided to interview the two girls in my room. They were alert, obviously of high intelligence, and to all outward appearances, quite composed. I went carefully through their

> affidavits with them and checked the contents line by line. I could not help but observe that the affidavits had been most scrupulously drafted. Neither girl said that she had actually watched her father as he laid off any leg of the flight track from one point to another and drew the respective lines on a map or on his atlas. All they said was that they had seen him working, with 'a ruler or some measuring equipment', on a large chart of the Antarctic Ross Sea Region.[9]

Mahon said he asked Baragwanath and Harrison to check with all counsel to see if any wanted to cross-examine the girls. All counsel had the girls' affidavits, of course. 'I made it clear that the two girls were quite willing to appear if necessary. But all counsel replied that they did not require the girls to give oral evidence.'

Mahon says he understood that the Chief Inspector was also happy not to have the girls cross-examined but, curiously, he also said that he heard that from neither Chippindale nor his counsel.[10] This would come up later on as a matter of particular grievance to the Chief Inspector. There was no way, of course, that Chippindale would have gone near the girls. They were grieving girls telling the truth. It was obvious.

The expressed lack of a need by any counsel at the Royal Commission to cross-examine Kathryn or Elizabeth Collins was a dramatic and formative moment at the Royal Commission. Wrote Mahon: 'This meant that all counsel at the inquiry conceded the fact that Captain Collins had been plotting the flight track to McMurdo on a map or maps on the night of 27 November.'[11]

What is disgraceful, however, is that Ron Chippindale knew that Jim Collins had been plotting on a map or maps the night before his departure. Maria had told him. He made no mention of this in his report. Mahon noted that under cross-examination at the inquiry, 'He had agreed that this information had been known to him . . . He had replied by saying that this information was not "evidence" as he understood that term.'

Mahon wrote that Chippindale had a 'simplistic' idea of evidence. For Chippindale, evidence had to be a document, something on paper, apparently.[12]

What Chippindale was doing of course, was carrying on the cover-up. The powerful idea that Collins had been plotting his course for the next day completely ruined Chippindale's absurd position that the crew was not deceived by the coordinate change. Apparently for the rigid, military Chippindale, something was evidence only if it was a document, rather than something a decent, honest person might tell him. Maria and Kathryn Carter had told Chippindale about Jim Collins working on charts with plotting instruments and he put no store by it at all. He did not mention it in his accident report at all. It was a cruel disgrace.

He seemed, publicly at least, to believe everything that Air New Zealand management told him. This is something that Paul Davison so objected to.

'I think he was a rather narrow-minded individual. He was very, very focused on aviation and what the regulatory requirements were. And he had not conducted anything like an adequate investigation of people. He took statements or he got other people to take statements . . . of their accounts of events. And he acted on them. But he didn't penetrate beyond what was presented to him so he, in my view, his major failing was that he didn't really conduct an investigator's investigation. He was very good on the technical, but he wasn't very good on what people did, what they understood or what they knew.'

Mahon, on the other hand, was a born investigator. Should he get a whiff of dishonesty he was on the trail. His was a mind that had not only a command of labyrinthine detail but of subterfuge as well. Said Davison, with a huge, shrewd grin: 'He loved it. He had a great ability to look past what people said.'

Not only did Chippindale put no store on the Collins girls' evidence, he went significantly further. He claimed that Jim Collins had no topographical map or maps of his own on the flight deck to Antarctica. This was another lie from the Chief Inspector. What has emerged since those passionate, disputatious days of the Royal Commission is that not only did Chippindale know Collins had been plotting on charts the night before the flight but he knew also that Collins had his own chart on board the flight.

'His way of dealing with this inconvenient knowledge was to leave it all out of his report and even out of his testimony,' said Stuart Macfarlane in a study he made of the matter of the maps.

When counsel for Maria Collins, Paul Davison, heard the girls' evidence, he and Gordon Vette made attempts to identify which chart or charts Jim Collins had been working on. What maps or charts had he acquired upon which to do his own plotting? Elizabeth said in evidence, and she had repeated it to the judge, that the chart was so big her father had to lay it out on the floor and the sea and the ice were green and the land was pink or purple. What's more, the map he opened up on the floor had not been the one on which he was working, Elizabeth said. So there were two.

But Chippindale already knew by the time he was writing his report that Collins had this same large chart on the flight deck with him on his journey south. And here is how.

As the DC-10 approached Cook Strait on its way south, the spare first officer on the flight, Graham Lucas, came onto the flight deck and called the Nelson airport control tower on the radio. Chippindale had the transcript, it emerged later.

Lucas: 'Nelson tower . . . New Zealand 901.'

NS Tower: 'New Zealand 901 . . . Nelson.'

Lucas: 'I wonder if you could get in touch with Peter Tait over in Helicopters [New Zealand Ltd] and could you . . . I wonder if you could find out what his frequency is?'

NS Tower: 'Roger. Stand by.'

Air traffic control rings Helicopters New Zealand.

NS Tower: 'New Zealand 901. Peter will be waiting for you on 122.7.'

Lucas: '122.7. Thank you very much.'

Chippindale had transcripts of all radio communications between TE901 and New Zealand stations. This conversation between the DC-10 and Nelson Tower must have intrigued him. He arranged therefore for the Nelson police to go round and obtain a sworn statement from Peter Tait on 12 December 1979. Peter Tait was a helicopter pilot friend of First Officer Lucas with flying experience in Antarctica. Tait's statement is a revelation.

Peter Tait confirmed to the police that a message was sent to him that the DC-10 wanted to speak to him. Tait said:

> I spoke to Graham LUCAS. For starters he identified that they were en route to the Antarctic and at that point about 100 miles North of NELSON. I recall asking him how long the trip would take. He indicated approximately 5½ hours flight time on the outward leg, and a similar time back to Christchurch. There was some comment about the passengers already getting into the food and liquid refreshments.
>
> I think at this point I asked him if he had received a

> map which he had requested from me about a week earlier. I had sent the map up to him by regular airmail. This was an Aeronautical Global Navigation Chart. From memory I think the number of the chart was 21. (Twenty One)
>
> About four months previously, I borrowed a book of Hughes Tables [marine and aeronautical navigation tables] from Graham LUCAS. When he rang me approximately a week prior to the 28th November, he asked me if a navigational chart of the Antarctic area belonging to him was inside the book. It was not and I then offered to loan him a map. The map was of North Victoria Land. This was the map which I sent up to him. We discussed the map for a short time and he told me that it was suitable for his requirements.

Obviously, Lucas had lent the chart to Jim Collins, his captain for the Antarctic flight. We know that Lucas had been diligent in his preparation for the flight because he and Jim Collins had paid a visit to Operation Deep Freeze for a briefing a month before, a visit confirmed by Chippindale, according to ALPA investigator First Officer Peter Rhodes.[13]

Constable Parfitt of Nelson police then added on the signed statement that Peter Tait had later 'phoned to confirm No. of map as follows. GNC21N Addition [sic] 6'.

There were at least three references to a rustling of paper in the last minutes of the flight and behind the pilots there seemed to be a good discussion between Mulgrew and the two flight engineers comparing what they were seeing on the chart with what they were seeing outside the windows. Brooks at one point, a couple of minutes before impact, says, 'Didn't want to block the window too completely with it.'

GNC21N is a huge chart, the kind you would need to lay out on a floor in order to show your children. It is an American chart, well over a metre long. The sea and the ice are green and the land is purple-orange. This was the large chart Elizabeth saw Jim Collins working on. Chippindale identified the chart, therefore, and identified its provenance, but said nothing about it.

Gordon Vette took chart after chart to Elizabeth. None could she identify. Well after the Royal Commission, Stuart Macfarlane heard about a chart that might fit the bill from, of all people, Justice Mahon. Mahon had called the RNZAF and they identified it immediately as GNC21N. Mahon said he believed Bob Thomson in Christchurch had a copy. Thomson sent it to Macfarlane. Macfarlane took it round to Elizabeth. She identified it positively.

Reading Baragwanath at the Commission of Inquiry attempting to get Chippindale to own up to his knowledge of the radio transmission between Graham Lucas and Peter Tait, and to the statement Tait had given, is to watch the pulling of teeth. I could print it here, but the reader would find it incomprehensible gobbledegook.

Later, after the Court of Appeal and the Privy Council, and after Mahon had walked away from the bench, Chippindale unleashed his attack on Mahon in his lengthy press release denouncing the many mistakes made by Mahon. The government allowed him to do so, of course — anything to finally discredit the findings of Mahon.

In it Chippindale writes, oddly:

> Again, during my investigation I was unable to locate any map supply location with maps readily available which had provided maps for Capt. Collins. Although available in Los Angeles by prior order, they were not readily available over the counter and the Air New Zealand briefing officer had to resort to a photostat copy of a map for his RCU briefings. Therefore, from whence [sic] came his large map?[14]

This is quite disingenuous.

Chippindale's statement, 'available in Los Angeles by prior order', indicates he knew the name of the chart and that it was an American one, GNC21N. What is quite despicable in his statement is the implication Elizabeth Collins perjured herself. But how in heaven's name would young Elizabeth Collins, at 15, know about a large map her father had to lay on the floor, a map with a green sea and purple land, if she had not seen her father explaining it to her?

But there were two maps. Elizabeth made this clear at the Royal Commission. There was the large chart he opened on the floor and the one he was working on when she approached him.

Indeed, after Cape Hallett, Jim Collins was going to need a more McMurdo-specific chart. Chippindale knew the identity of this map too. And he implied it was so hard to get — the RCU briefing officer had to resort to a photostat copy, he said — that Collins couldn't possibly have obtained a copy.

That was nonsense. The chart was a New Zealand Lands and Survey chart, NZMS135, out of print now, but easily available at the time. It was a closer up view of the Ross Island/McMurdo area. As Antarctic researcher Stuart Macfarlane said:

> It was on public sale and available to anyone. I found it easy to buy a copy. Whatever reasons Air New Zealand had for not obtaining a copy, whether they were incompetent or a couldn't-care-less attitude, non-availability was not a reason. Captain Wilson, the briefing officer, could have obtained one, at any time, a few blocks up Queen Street from Air New Zealand House, as I in fact did.[15]

Elizabeth identified that one too, but this time to Gordon Vette.

Jim Collins had plotted his course from the flight plan he was shown on maps he had acquired.

Chippindale knew all about it. And he covered this up too.

26

The Report is Released

A good and faithful judge prefers the honourable to the expedient.
— Horace

The Royal Commission of Mr Justice Mahon began its hearings on 7 July 1980. The Commission sat for 75 days. It heard from 52 witnesses. They produced their evidence and were then examined and further cross-examined.

Justice Mahon and David Baragwanath, counsel assisting the commission, travelled, as we have seen to the United States, Canada, the United Kingdom and Antarctica to gather more evidence. The case seemed deeply complicated. If the accident had been caused, as the airline implied, and as the Chief Inspector of Air Accidents stated, by pilot error, then the pilots had acted egregiously.

Mahon started to see that he was being lied to by Air New Zealand's senior or management witnesses. He sent word, through counsel for the airline, David Williams, that the airline evidence was not being believed. Not only did he not believe it but no one else did either, he told Williams. He sent word, as we have seen, through the airline's international insurers, that the evidence was not stacking up and that he was aware he was being lied to in concert. Still the airline never yielded. The airline never acknowledged fault or blame for the catastrophe in any way. Never once. Not to this day.

In the final submissions before the hearings were completed, Paul Davison delivered a moving oration that burned with the anger of a young man who believed in justice.

> The release of the [Chippindale] accident report containing such damning comments about Captain Collins, in the face of requests that it be withheld until the sitting of the commission, for whatever reason, was not justifiable. Its effect was to promote in the public's mind the cause of the crash as pilot error. The damage that this did is immeasurable. The heart-wrenching suffering it caused the Collins family cannot be measured or erased ...
>
> For their part, Air New Zealand simply ditched a captain and crew that had served them so well over a long number of years. Are the stakes too high to expect open self-appraisal and impartiality rather than self serving defensiveness?
>
> CAD [Civil Aviation] resorted to suggesting that the captain, crewmembers, and Mr Mulgrew (five in all) were simultaneously subjected to some mental or physical disorder which would account for their actions ...
>
> CAD promoted the theory of 'out of character actions' of the pilot to explain the accident.
>
> All they were doing was unmercifully attacking those least able to defend, in order to divert attention from themselves.
>
> These tactics have failed, and it is in the province of Air New Zealand and CAD that the real causes of the accident occurred ...
>
> The vast number of errors and omissions perpetrated by those in CAD and Air New Zealand [about 231 of them, according to Stuart Macfarlane in *The Erebus Papers*, pages 329–340], the misconceptions, the lack of organisation within Air New Zealand, all contributed to the contemporaneous co-existent conspiracy of circumstances which trapped and deceived Captain Collins and his crew. The deception could not have been designed to be more total or absolute as that which led to this accident ...
>
> There is no blameworthiness which can attach to Captain Collins, or his crew, for their conduct on this ill-fated flight.[1]

Mahon was supposed to report to the Governor General by 31 October 1980. In the end, he needed two time extensions. When closing submissions had been heard, he had 3083 pages of evidence to go through, 284 exhibits to think about and 368 pages of the most lengthy, detailed closing submissions from counsel representing the various interested parties, Air New Zealand, Civil Aviation, the consortium of passengers, the Air Line Pilots' Association, the estates of the pilots and the Ministry of Transport.

That done, Mahon went home and in the quiet study of the house in Upland Road, Remuera, began to write his *Report of the Royal Commission to Inquire into the Crash on Mount Erebus, Antarctica of a DC10 Aircraft Operated by Air New Zealand Limited, 1981*. No one knew what he was going to find.

Mahon's son, Sam, has at his own house now the table on which Mahon wrote his exhaustive, groundbreaking and historic analysis of the accident. Sam remembers Mahon sitting at this table 'hour after hour, tracking his pen across the white sheets, a cigarette poised in his left hand, reading glasses half way down his nose, composing a novel which would grasp the public's imagination like a fist'.[2]

Mahon submitted his report to the Governor General on 16 April 1981. It went off to Government Print where he never doubted, according to his wife, Margarita, that Muldoon had his spies. It was published on 27 April 1981.

Now, we have to remember, Robert Muldoon was the most dictatorial, authoritarian, vindictive, ruthless and brutal prime minister this country had ever known. No one stood up to Muldoon. We forget the fear of God he put into anyone who challenged him. It was an extraordinary feeling to experience and I only felt the remains of it in the odd television interview with him in his twilight. At his peak, his face would set like granite and you never knew where he was going to hit you from.

Muldoon was not only the well-established, powerful Prime Minister, however. He was also the powerful keeper of the country's finances, the Finance Minister. And he loved Air New Zealand. He could see the damage Erebus had done to the airline and he could count the hundreds of millions of dollars in claims upon both the company and upon the country should Air New Zealand and/or Civil Aviation be found, through their negligence or through any act or omission, liable for the destruction of the aircraft and all who were on board. The airline could not be found liable. It was as simple as that.

Justice Mahon knew all this, of course. He knew the game. He had litigated countless commercial cases as a barrister and Crown Prosecutor over many years in Christchurch. He knew what a dollar meant to people.

Mahon knew who, and what, he was about to take on. He was about to come up against the might of the political establishment. He knew that. He must have. He knew what it was to go against Muldoon. He knew the decision that Muldoon wanted and he knew that because of the determination and speed with which the government had published the Chippindale Report, which so damaged the pilots, just days before the hearings of the Royal Commission began.

Peter Mahon burned with a sense of justice. In his last years, well after the Royal Commission and after he became very ill, Mahon became friendly with Paul Davison QC, whom Mahon had come to admire over the long months of the Royal Commission.

'We shared something. We shared a belief in what was right and certainly in this case,' Davison says. 'I think from his point of view he saw in me some of the same aspects that he probably had as a young lawyer making his way. But we shared a belief that there had been an intent to pull the wool over his eyes and that we both knew the real picture. And that drew us together.'

Sam Mahon, in one of the loveliest moments in the book about his father, tells of himself and Mahon out duck shooting in the cool of an April autumn evening in 1981, the Sunday night before the release of his report, and Mahon saying — with the wind swirling around him the smoke of the cigarette he had just lit — 'All hell's going to break loose tomorrow.'

Peter Mahon, knowing the stakes — and he loved calculating odds — was about to speak truth to power.

The effect of the release of what became famous as the Mahon Report was seismic.

At paragraph 39:

> Captain Collins is dead. His own account of what he had done can never be told. But there was evidence adduced before the Commission which made it certain that on the night of 27 November he had plotted the flight path from Cape Hallett to McMurdo, using the destination coordinates which he had noticed 18 days before. But apart from that, there was the incontrovertible evidence that as the aircraft levelled out on its final approach to the mountain, Captain Collins had been careful to arm the nav track. He could not possibly have done this unless he was certain as to where the nav track would lead him, and he must therefore have been quite satisfied that

> the nav track would take him down the centre of McMurdo Sound, with flat terrain extending for many miles both to the left and right and ahead.

At paragraph 392:

> ... I am able to reach a decision as to whether or not there was a single cause of the disaster. In my opinion there was. The dominant cause of the disaster was the act of the airline in changing the computer track of the aircraft without telling the aircrew. That blend of act and omission acquires its status as the 'dominant' cause because it was the one factor which continued to operate from the time before the aircraft left New Zealand until the time when it struck the slopes of Mt Erebus. It is clear that this dominant factor would still not have resulted in disaster had it not been for the coincidental occurrence of the whiteout phenomenon. But the conditions of visual illusion existing in Lewis Bay would have had no effect on Flight TE901 had the nav track of the aircraft not been changed, for it was only the alteration to the nav track which brought the aircraft into Lewis Bay instead of McMurdo Sound.

Then the immortal paragraph 393:

> In my opinion, therefore, the single dominant and effective cause of the disaster was the mistake made by those airline officials who programmed the aircraft to fly directly at Mt Erebus and omitted to tell the aircrew. That mistake is directly attributable, not so much to the persons who made it, but to the incompetent administrative airline procedures which made the mistake possible.

At paragraph 394:

> In my opinion, neither Captain Collins or First Officer Cassin nor the flight engineers made any error which contributed to the disaster and were not responsible for its occurrence.

Mahon was appalled by the entire approach taken by the airline to the Antarctic flights. He found routing an aircraft above an active volcano whose steam cloud climbs thousands of feet into the air 'indefensible'.[3] The minimum safe altitudes were unrealistic and hopeless for sightseeing, which was why they were immediately departed from by the pilots after mid-1977 with a nod and a wink from the company.[4] The United States Navy at McMurdo was never consulted about the flight path, the approach or the altitudes.[5] The RNZAF, with its many years of experience in flying round Antarctica, was never consulted on what crews should be told about Antarctic weather.[6] The airline knew that both the US Navy and the RNZAF had a policy that no airman should command a flight on his first flight to Antarctica but Air New Zealand abandoned this practice in mid-1977.[7]

What's more, said Mahon, directing an aircraft over Erebus while it descended to flight level 160 was madness in regard to radio communication. Radar was only operative in line of sight. So was VHF radio. HF radio in Antarctica is notoriously subject to disruption from weather and atmospheric conditions. Mahon worked out that an aircraft approaching Erebus at 16,000 feet would suffer radar and radio blackout contact with McMurdo for 20 to 30 miles until it arrived over the summit of the mountain.[8]

What's more, the agreement between the airline and Civil Aviation for the let-down procedure from 16,000 feet to 6000 feet over McMurdo base 'was regarded by the Americans, when they found out about it after the disaster, as quite impracticable'. The MacCentre supervisor described it as 'absurd'.[9]

Civil Aviation had committed 'a serious breach of its duty' by failing to monitor if Air New Zealand was complying with the requirement that all pilots on command should have undertaken at least one supervised flight to Antarctica before making the journey as a commander.[10] On the Antarctic flights of 1978 and 1979, no captain had been previously to the ice.

He believed Civil Aviation had committed 'a breach of statutory obligation' by not ensuring that the pilots were issued with a topographical map with the flight path printed on it. This was a 'major omission'.[11]

Mahon had taken the trouble to fly to the ice. He was struck by 'the complete lack of similarity between the actual terrain and its appearance upon a topographical map, and that only a previous flight to Antarctica could educate the pilot-in-command as to the physical and meteorological features of the region'.[12] Then he made a crucial point.

> But a previous flight under supervision would have almost certainly resulted in Captain Collins noting the distinctive feature of Beaufort Island which would have been apparent as the only identifiable island in the area . . . Had Captain Collins seen Beaufort Island previously, and identified it on the fatal flight, he would certainly have realised that his nav track had been changed.[13]

But Mahon was by no means finished. He wrote a chapter called 'THE STANCE ADOPTED BY THE AIRLINE BEFORE THE COMMISSION OF INQUIRY'.[14] In it he said he had no doubt that the Chief Executive, right after the accident, 'adopted the fixed position that the flight crew was alone to blame, and that the administrative and operational systems of the airline were nowhere at fault'. And he had no doubt that that attitude dictated the stance taken at the inquiry by all of the senior management witnesses. In *Verdict on Erebus*, Mahon clarified this point. He said he did not think that Morrie Davis was the 'person responsible for the planning of the altitude and navigation and evidence'.[15]

But the destruction of documents was hair-raising. New Zealanders didn't do this. This was not our way. When word of it got out, it did the company terrible damage. When Davis appeared at the Royal Commission — 'subdued, highly co-operative and apprehensive' — he was asked at considerable length about the destruction of 'surplus documents'.[16]

'Surplus documents.' The trouble for Davis was that Mahon had heard the very same expression used in two other air disasters, both involving McDonnell Douglas DC-10s. The same instruction, to destroy 'surplus documents' in order to conceal information, had been given after the Windsor Incident of 1972, involving pilots losing control of a DC-10, and after the Chicago American Airlines DC-10 crash in May 1979. Documents detrimental to McDonnell Douglas and American Airlines disappeared.[17] It's possible Davis's friends at McDonnell Douglas had offered him what they thought was helpful advice.

But Morrie Davis, Mahon believed, simply led the culture that prevailed in the airline's attitude to the Royal Commission. He formed the 'fixed opinion that the flight crew was alone to blame, and the administrative and operational systems of the airline were nowhere at fault. I have been forced to the opinion that such an attitude, emanating from this very able but evidently autocratic chief executive, controlled the ultimate course adopted by the witnesses called on behalf of the airline.'[18]

However, in *Verdict on Erebus*, Mahon appeared to moderate this view when he said, 'I could not possibly envisage Mr Davis taking an active part in the preparation of all the technical evidence which formed the basis of the airline's case as to altitude and navigation procedures . . . I believed I could not fairly nominate him as an active party to the plan of deception.'[19] And in this sentence, you have to read Mahon between the lines again.

He is telling us exactly who did.

During his research for the docu-drama *Erebus: The Aftermath* back in the mid-1980s, when Mahon was very ill, Greg McGee spent a lot of time with him. His voice was very weak, said McGee.

He was sitting opposite Mahon one day at the Mahons' house in Brighton Road, Parnell. Mahon suddenly said, 'The orchestrator was Des Dalgety,'[20] a director of the board of Air New Zealand and Muldoon's personal lawyer.

'A directive on strategy from Muldoon through Des Dalgety to Air New Zealand made a lot of sense,' wrote Greg McGee in 'Dancing on the Coffins of the Dead', about his Erebus experience, 'as did a reverse flow of technical information from somewhere in the airline's operational command about the tactics necessary to execute that directive'.[21]

And it was clear to Mahon who that person was.

In the end, how did senior people not know the flights were heading down McMurdo Sound for 14 months? How could they not know that crews were taking their DC-10s down anywhere between 1500 feet and 4000 feet? There had been so much publicity, including a brochure to nearly every household in New Zealand. There had been people describing the flights on radio talkback. And no one senior knew? Why did Captain Simpson, at the same briefing as Captain Collins and First Officer Cassin, say that after hearing Captain Johnson's evidence on what he said at the briefing that he, Simpson, felt he must have been at another briefing entirely?

There was one single, cynical and original part to the cover-up. The airline did not disclose publicly that the navigational coordinates had been changed at the last minute and that the pilots had not been told.

Well, the airline had adopted the course it had. It had turned out exactly as Bill Tench had predicted to Mahon in London months before. It had all come apart. Mahon concluded that Morrie Davis had told senior aircrew that the Royal Commission didn't matter and that the government stood behind management. Therefore, 'they [management] must have thought that with the government behind them that they were immune from any criticism'.[22] They had badly underestimated the integrity and the courage of Peter Mahon.

And as Tench said, the airline had simply adopted the stance taken not uncommonly by other airlines and aircraft manufacturers overseas, and cross-examination by clever and determined counsel had picked the deception apart. In *Verdict on Erebus* Mahon wrote, 'But whereas the "cover-up" tactics in other major disasters had been skilful and sophisticated, one could hardly say the same about the present case. The tactics employed had been unintelligent and obtuse . . .'[23]

In the end, Mahon's view was Tench's view. The airline should have laid its cards on the table right at the start. There might have been severe financial penalty, but 'the whole inquiry would probably have been over in three or four weeks and would have terminated in the airline's being complimented for its frank disclosure of all the facts'.[24]

Mahon told Lloyd Brown, after Brown and he fell out, that his job had been to represent 257 dead men and women. But to the powers that be, it was never about the deceased. It was about circling the wagons and saving the airline and its reputation.[25]

Way back, straight after he was appointed Commissioner, Mahon had received a most interesting phone call from someone he merely describes as highly placed in government in Wellington. He does not say whom. 'By reason of his particular employment,' said Mahon, '[the caller] was familiar in detail with the contents of the Chief Inspector's interim report, and with the general circumstances of the whole matter, and in particular with what he said were "profound differences of opinion" about the Chief Inspector's interim conclusions'.[26]

This man went on to tell Mahon that the 'essential questions' were not going to be technical. The inquiry would simply come down to which and whose evidence the Commissioner was going to believe. 'I was going to be faced with some vital questions of credibility . . .'[27] And indeed, that is entirely the way it turned out. In the end, it wasn't technical. It was about who you believed.

Mahon believed the Antarctic pilots. He did not believe the executive pilots. There was plenty of evidence. But what it came down to was credibility. He told us in *Verdict on Erebus* that if he was going to exonerate the pilots, he was also going to have to tell the airline witnesses why they were not believed, or Mr Davis and his men would simply turn round and thump him. He had to make it clear why he had rejected the airline evidence about navigation and altitude.

Thus Mahon wrote on page 150 of the accident report the famous paragraph 377, which reverberated through the nation and in aviation circles round the world and which ultimately gave his enemies the chance to destroy him.

> No judicial officer ever wishes to be compelled to say that he has listened to evidence which is false. He always prefers to say, as I hope the hundreds of judgements which I have written will illustrate, that he cannot accept the relevant explanation, or that he prefers a contrary version set out in the evidence.
>
> But in this case, the palpably false sections of evidence which I heard could not have been the result of mistake, or faulty recollection. They originated, I am compelled to say, in a predetermined plan of deception. They were very clearly part of an attempt to conceal a series of disastrous administrative blunders and so, in regard to the particular items of evidence to which I have referred, I am forced reluctantly to say that I have had to listen to an orchestrated litany of lies.

Seismic.

Judges did not talk or write like this. But this judge had the whole accident sorted. This judge could write elegantly and this report was, in the main, eminently readable. Some of it, it has to be said, is very difficult reading indeed because of Mahon's mastery of the technicalities of flight and navigation and his understanding of the importance of the development of the AINS. But its conclusion was simple.

What happened to the pilots was diabolically so. The DC-10 flew by the AINS. You trusted it completely, with your life. The crew had been cruelly deceived by the change in route, had been trying to do their best for their customers and had been finished off by the weather. Without the change in coordinates, there would not have been an accident and I would not be writing these words over 30 years later. Despite the deaths of 257 people, the airline had tried to deny its own administrative dysfunctionalism and to blame the pilots. Mahon had taken on the mighty powers and had chalked one up for the little man.

Jim Collins had been too conscientious. His diligence, his belief in the importance of planning, had made him plot his briefed course on a chart. It had cemented his mindset about where they were headed on 28 November 1979.

It was the only story in the land. Muldoon was furious. Sir Don McKinnon, who was in the National Party caucus at the time, told me that he remembered Muldoon saying angrily, 'We should have appointed more than one judge instead of just the one running off on his own.'

Air New Zealand management was stunned. They were knocked for six. The newspaper headlines made it clear. Davis and the management team locked themselves away inside Air New Zealand House. The *Auckland Star* headline of 28 April 1981 read: 'RANKS CLOSE AS REPORT IS REJECTED'. How Air New Zealand felt it had any right to reject the findings of a Royal Commission is anyone's guess.

But it was entirely expected, such was the arrogance of the old Air New Zealand. An hour after the Mahon Report was released 'a shaken' Morrie Davis and Air New Zealand Chairman Bill Mace appeared before reporters. Davis declared that his professional competence and his integrity had come under attack in the report. 'The attack is totally indefensible. I reject entirely any allegations that my performance of duties, giving of evidence or relationship to the giving of evidence by others, was in any way inadequate or improper.'

He got up to leave the room. Reporters, as they do, when a man is wounded, shouted random questions. Davis didn't answer. He turned to a television crew member and barked, 'Clean this room up before you go.'

Mr Ron Chippindale, reported the *Star*, was unavailable for comment. His officer said he was in the United Kingdom and he would not be back until July. This would have been, no doubt, one of his important trips on the taxpayer to the northern hemisphere summer. A day later, he was found in Bedford. He was aware of the Mahon findings, he said, but he would be sticking to his own findings. It was ignorant of Chippindale. It was outrageous. It was also foolish. Most New Zealanders who thought about it could see the inexorable logic of Mahon's findings. But so it always was with Chippindale. Only Chippindale was right.

Mahon had hit the airline in its pocket. Because of what he saw as the airline's intractable attitude towards the Royal Commission, he directed Air

New Zealand to pay $150,000 towards the public cost of the Commission. He wrote with a tone of sad resignation on the final page of the exhaustive 167 pages of the accident report, in the appendix:

> In an inquiry of this kind, an airline can either place all its cards on the table at the outset, or it can adopt an adversary stance. In the present case, the latter course was decided upon. The management of the airline instructed its counsel to deny every allegation of fault, and to counter-attack by ascribing total culpability to the aircrew, against whom there were alleged no less than 13 separate varieties of pilot error. All those allegations, in my opinion, were without foundation. Apart from that, there were material elements of information in the possession of the airline which were originally not disclosed, omissions for which counsel for the airline were in no way responsible, and which successively came to light at different stages of the Inquiry when the hearings had been going on for weeks, in some cases for months . . .
>
> So it was not a question of the airline putting all its cards on the table. The cards were produced reluctantly, and at long intervals and I have little doubt that there are one or two which still lie hidden in the pack.

So Air New Zealand would pay a price for the failure and reluctance to disclose. The reader will have noted Mahon's gesture to Air New Zealand's counsel, his now estranged friend Lloyd Brown QC. It did no good. The friendship was over. Mahon would never see Brown again. He reached out to Brown with an invitation to lunch. Brown refused. Mahon never forgave him.

There was an Air New Zealand board meeting lasting four hours. Then Mace, the Chairman, and Deputy Chairman — and Muldoon's lawyer — Des Dalgety flew to Wellington to confer with Prime Minister Muldoon. Arriving back in Auckland they announced that the company would seek a review of the Mahon Report in the High Court.

Muldoon was playing a subtle double game. He was questioning the integrity and the quality of the Air New Zealand board publicly on the one hand while, on the other, it seems unlikely that Air New Zealand would have been able to seek and commit the funds to a High Court review without the prime ministerial nod. The review would be 'in the area of staff integrity,' company chairman Mace told the *New Zealand Herald* on 29 April.

On 30 April, a stern editorial in the same newspaper made it clear what Air New Zealand should do. The company's directors, for the sake of the airline's reputation, should accept what the judge had emphatically discovered, accept it, admit its mistakes and make the changes necessary.

Two hundred and fifty-seven people had died. A brilliant jurist had discovered why. The airline still blamed pilot error. But what really mattered, it seemed, was Morrie Davis's reputation. The airline was now prepared, with the approval of Davis's mate, Robert Muldoon, to spend public money on a High Court review of the report in order to counter Mahon's claim that there had been an 'orchestrated litany of lies', that senior people in the airline had acted in concert to perjure.

Muldoon then declared that there had been no litany of lies. He had been advised thus and he was satisfied there had been no such thing. Mahon went public. Judges never do. The Prime Minister's faith in his advisers could be 'sadly misplaced', he warned. Who had advised the Prime Minister? Des Dalgety, said Muldoon, and Lloyd Brown QC; men 'who would not tell lies'. Muldoon said he could find nothing in the report that showed there had been an orchestrated plan to perjure. He would not be reading the transcripts of evidence. Asked whether his advisers perhaps had a vested interest, given their connection with Air New Zealand, Muldoon was not prepared to argue. End of the matter.

What did Mahon mean by a conspiracy to perjure? Did it have a beginning, as the Privy Council would later ask pointedly? Did senior people actually sit down and decide to perjure? In other words, was it a formal conspiracy, was there a moment when it began, or was decided on, or agreed?

Or was it just unspoken company loyalty about an occurrence that remained too horrific to admit to? Whatever it was, there were a good number of fellows singing in harmony from the same page, defying what was not only common sense but emerging more and more as nonsense. Everyone could see it. That's what Arthur Cooper told Morrie Davis when he requested their meeting to warn him of the damage the inquiry was doing the airline. It looked as if, Arthur said, the executive pilots were singing from the same hymn book.

Mahon explained his thinking nowhere better than in his previously mentioned speech to the Australian aviation lawyers in August 1982.

> When disaster befalls a company, or any other corporate entity, or a department of state, there almost invariably commences a process of seeking a scapegoat for the occurrence. Each person with some apparent responsibility will seek to shed the burden and place it elsewhere. But most significant of all, the corporate or departmental entity will seek to place responsibility upon a person or persons, so as to exonerate the management and to keep untarnished the image of the corporate or departmental employer and in many cases a group of employees will have been induced, by corporate loyalty, by managerial suggestion, and possibly by fear of managerial retributive action or discrimination in the future, to combine together to tell a false or misleading tale.
>
> This aspect of corporate testimony is so well known in litigation as to require little comment, and in the case of major aircraft disasters it is a process which has been adopted on many occasions . . . And in a massive air disaster there is always a ready-made target of responsibility, and that is the aircrew. In most cases they will have perished, and the manufacturer or operator of the aircraft can attempt to fix responsibility, in cases where it does not in fact exist, on men who cannot reply.[28]

On 4 May 1981, Morrie Davis quit as Chief Executive of Air New Zealand. The board 'reluctantly accepted Mr Davis's personal sacrifice'. It was all about Morrie. 'In doing so,' Davis said, 'I would hope that attacks against Air New Zealand and the many people in it who are suffering at this time will diminish.'

Muldoon supported his friend. 'In essence he [Davis] has said "I think now that I've retired some of you will get off my back." Well, I can only echo those sentiments.' Morrie Davis went home to Epsom and, as a police investigation got under way, waited for a knock on his door.

Meanwhile, Air New Zealand named the group of executive pilots who had been grounded since the release of the report. They were Captains Dave Eden, Ian Gemmell, Ross Johnson, Maynard Hawkins, Bruce Crosbie, Peter Grundy and J. P. Wilson. Two of these executive pilots had been due to fly the airline's first Boeing 747 to New Zealand from Seattle. Those on restricted duties in the Navigation Section included Brian Hewitt and Keith Amies.

By mid-July Air New Zealand was facing $69 million in claims from the families of 100 deceased passengers. Further parties were expected to join the 100, taking claims for compensation to $80 million, reported the *New Zealand Herald*.

So it was off to the High Court for Air New Zealand and for Morrison Ritchie Davis and Ian Harding Gemmell. Air New Zealand — Davis and Gemmell — appealed to the High Court to conduct a judicial review of paragraph 377, the litany of lies paragraph in which Mahon is asserting an Air New Zealand management conspiracy to perjure.

The men wanted it to go straight to the Court of Appeal. The Court of Appeal obliged.

27

The Courts Thump Mahon

All his usual perfidies were observed with scrupulous technique.
— Winston Churchill

Well, what the Privy Council said was that while they all sang the same song, they sang it as soloists not as a choir.
— *Impact Erebus*, the DVD, Gordon Vette

Five judges heard the review of the Mahon Report at the Court of Appeal. They were Richardson, Cooke, Somers, Woodhouse and McMullin. The latter two, Woodhouse and McMullin, should not have been there and the Chief Justice should have insisted upon it, given the immense sensitivity of the issues.

Owen Woodhouse's daughter worked in the public relations section of Air New Zealand. Duncan McMullin's son flew as a pilot for Air New Zealand. This surely made his presence on the bench questionable. They had, after all, hired his son. And he had another possible conflict. The junior counsel for Air New Zealand at the Commission was Richard McGrane, Kathryn Collins's erstwhile driving instructor. Mahon knew McGrane had been close to the McMullin family during the Royal Commission.

In a letter to one of his great supporters, Justice Laurie Greig in Wellington, written days after his resignation from the High Court in late January 1982, Mahon noted that Air New Zealand's law firm, Russell McVeagh, knew a week before the Court of Appeal judgement was released — just on Christmas — that the court was coming down with a 3:2 split decision. In other words, Air New Zealand knew.

> I . . . made my mind up that if Woodhouse announced there were no grounds for my credibility findings, as I understood he would, then I would take that as a vote of no confidence and hand in my portfolio. This decision was reinforced when I read in the paper a fortnight ago that Owen's daughter was in the PR department at head office [at Air New Zealand]. I knew about the McMullin connection [with Air New Zealand] and had objected to his participation, not on my own behalf but on behalf of the pilots. The pilots were anxious about McGrane [junior counsel for Air New Zealand at the Royal Commission] spending nearly every weekend with the McMullins before and during the inquiry, knowing that McGrane had briefed the evidence which I disbelieved. But the objection was overruled, McMullin insisting that he had every right to sit. If I had known the Woodhouse connection I would have objected to both of them.
>
> . . . Also, I observe that nearly every one of their evidential conclusions is wrong.[1]

McMullin's view of these events is quite different. In his *A Lawyer's Tale*, he says Mahon knew well that he, McMullin, had a son who was an Air New Zealand pilot. 'Moreover,' says McMullin, 'before the hearing the question of my sitting was discussed with Cooke J, the acting President. Mahon said that he had no personal objection to my sitting and the matter was left on the basis that if any party had any objection to the constitution of the Court for the hearing, he could say so.'

All of which still begs the question of why a man with a son who flew for Air New Zealand could still think it proper for him to sit in appeal on one of the most sensitive cases in New Zealand history.

In an even tougher letter written to Sir Brian Todd, of the Todd Corporation, after the Court of Appeal, Mahon wrote of Woodhouse:

> His own omniscience, aided by a remarkable intuition to which he frequently alludes, told him the aircraft had been flying in cloud and the crew did not know where they were. On the very last day of the appeal hearing he posed a rhetorical question: 'How could the crew have flown directly into the mountain

> when it was right there in front of them?' At this juncture, counsel for the Attorney General despondently sat down.
>
> As for McMullin, his position was graphically revealed in *Truth*. The young lawyer [McGrane] who briefed the . . . evidence [given by the airline witnesses] was virtually living at the McMullin residence both before and during the inquiry, and McMullin's insistence on sitting on the case, despite objection by the Pilots' Association, is almost unbelievable. And those are the two judges who attacked me in a manner described by the Auckland Law Society president as 'vindictive.' It was the content of their joint judgement which decided me to resign. Their judgement is nothing more than a disguised approbation of the Chippindale Report, and in reality reflects the attitude of the management of Air New Zealand, each such opinion being quite outside their jurisdiction.[2]

Neither man ever expressed any doubts about sitting. It is reminiscent of the scandal involving Justice Bill Wilson in 2010, who would not resign from the Supreme Court of New Zealand despite having failed fully to disclose a connection at a trial in 2007.

Let us be clear about what exactly the Court of Appeal decided.

The Commissioner's findings as to the causes of the Erebus disaster were not challenged and the Court of Appeal did not touch them, although, to the lay reader, Woodhouse and McMullin appear to make it clear they would dearly like to have been able to. What the Commissioner found to have occurred was left alone.

But the court was unanimous that Mahon had committed a breach of natural justice in his Royal Commission report in paragraph 377 when he spoke of 'a predetermined plan of deception' and 'an orchestrated litany of lies'.

That, indeed, was the clear decision of the majority. In other words, 'Peter, old chap, paragraph 377 is out of order, but we sense your frustration, outrage and indignation, we admire that intricate work you did and we were not there in front of those witnesses to watch you pulling teeth. So we'll let paragraph 377 stand but we'll quash the punitive costs of $150,000 against Air New Zealand for their holding the inquiry up and dragging it out.'

The court found that the Royal Commissioner had no powers to make any finding of guilt in respect of any crime. The majority held that even though Mahon was a judge of the High Court he was, in this capacity at least, a Royal Commissioner and his declaration of a conspiracy to perjure . . .

> . . . is scarcely distinguishable in the public mind from condemnation by a Court of law. Yet it is completely without the safeguards of rights to trial by jury and appeal. In other words by mere implication any Commission of Inquiry, whatever its membership, would have authority publicly to condemn a group of citizens of a major crime without the safeguards that invariably go with express powers of condemnation.[3]

So the court held that the Commissioner went too far in 'convicting' the Air New Zealand Management of a conspiracy to perjure.

But Woodhouse and McMullin went further. They attempted to take Mahon apart. The Commissioner had no real evidence that Morrie Davis determined that 'no word of this incredible [navigational] blunder was to become publicly known'.[4] One wonders why else Davis would have ordered the collection of any relevant documents and the wholesale document shredding that took place in the days after the accident. Woodhouse and McMullin then quibbled about the words 'relevant' and 'irrelevant' in terms of destruction of the documents,[5] as if any shredding of documents at Air New Zealand at that time could even remotely have been acceptable.

And while Woodhouse and McMullin declared that they could and would have nothing to say about what the Royal Commission found as to the causes of the disaster, they had a go at reinstating Chippindale anyway. They suggested he had reached the same conclusions as to cause as the Commissioner.[6] This was most certainly incorrect. And if Chippindale did so, why did he not say so? They formed their belief from an exchange between Mahon and Chippindale at the inquiry. Mahon suggested to Chippindale that surely Captain Collins must have thought he was flying down McMurdo for him to continue on his flight path. Chippindale replied, 'It is my belief that this could be the only possible reason for him to continue.'[7] Woodhouse and McMullin were wrong. Despite his answer at the inquiry, Chippindale held on to pilot error forever.

And while the ultimate causes of the Erebus accident comprise a very simple combination of factors, the road to their discovery was tortuous. Mahon never found out when the conspiracy started, but he assumed that while Davis did not put the nuts and bolts of the technical information together, he was most certainly the cultural leader. Mahon had to put it together. He had to work out what didn't add up.

A reading of the transcripts shows the frustrations of all who were trying to find out the truth. The airline persisted week after week with the assertion of the 16,000-foot altitude requirement until past Erebus and with the assertion that no one in management knew that for 14 months the DC-10s, despite the publication of article after article, were programmed down McMurdo Sound. Of course they were lying. And they were all saying the same thing. Mahon decided that could not be a coincidence. And, of course, the management witnesses volunteered nothing.

But the Cooke judgement accepted that, while there may have been a bit of lying to the Commission, to then assert it was a conspiracy to perjure added a 'further and sinister dimension' to things. This would be a 'major crime'. And really, you have to warn a man you are going to write that he was part of a conspiracy to perjure at an inquiry into the deaths of 257 people in an aviation accident.

It was too hard for New Zealanders then, even Court of Appeal judges perhaps, to accept that such 'major crime' had been effected by a few senior people at Air New Zealand. Never mind that Mahon had watched 75 days of torture. Never mind that it took 10 weeks before Captain John Wilson, the briefing officer, admitted that pilots were permitted to descend below 6000 feet with the permission of McMurdo Air Traffic Control.

But in the dissenting Woodhouse judgement, everything Mahon said and did was wrong. Everything he claimed had happened had not. Or there was doubt about it. Everything he claimed was proven he had not. Everything he claimed was obvious — such as being lied to in the face of overwhelming evidence to the contrary — was not at all. Mahon claimed that Air New Zealand tried at all times to ascribe blame to the pilots. In fact, he says, they came up with 13 ways in which Collins had been negligent. Not so, claimed the Woodhouse judgement. Look at Lloyd Brown's final submission, which the Woodhouse judgement claimed had been exemplary in not attributing blame to any specific quarter.

Brown, breaking off from the written submission, in a brilliant oratorical at the Royal Commission, had said:

> By now, it should be apparent to the smallest mind that the company has not espoused, and does not espouse, a proposition

> that the accident can be attributed to a sole cause, let alone a sole cause of pilot error. If . . . there emerges or is implicit a criticism of the company's flight crew, that criticism has been moderate, informed and responsible.[8]

Mahon was appalled by Brown's claim:

> Counsel [for the airline] were very careful not to say explicitly that the aircrew alone was to blame, but on the thesis which they were putting to me then no one could have been blameworthy except the aircrew. In other words, the position of the airline had not changed one iota through the course of this long hearing. The fact that their case had irretrievably collapsed was simply disregarded.[9]

But to Woodhouse and McMullin, Brown's oratorical apparently negated Mahon's statement in the report that 'the management of the airline instructed its counsel to deny every allegation of fault, to counter-attack by ascribing total culpability to the aircrew'.[10]

Mahon said that, no doubt, because it was true. And when the two pilots went to see Morrie Davis to warn them the case was going appallingly for the airline, he told them the crew were totally culpable.

Lloyd Brown also told the Commission in his final submission that the airline 'had come to the Inquiry in order to see that all relevant facts were revealed to the Royal Commission'.[11] Mahon's comment on that is lethal. 'This was certainly an astonishing submission.' Mahon railed about the lack of documentation and the reluctance with which any had been produced, and how so many documents had not been produced at all.

There is another reason for Lloyd Brown's moderation in the final submission. It is contained in the letter of Mr Martin of Lloyds in London and is a result of the information the airline received through him after his meeting with Mahon — a meeting in which Mahon had seized the opportunity to warn the airline through Martin, its insurer, that its case was going badly, that its evidence was being disbelieved and that a finding as such might have to be made. The insurers and the airline had met in Los Angeles to doctor the preparation of the final submission.[12]

In late 2009 I was called one evening by Sir Duncan McMullin. He asked me to address his Probus Club on the matter of pure methamphetamine with which my family has had some unfortunate business in the past few years. I readily agreed. For some reason, perhaps only because I had been thinking about the idea, I suggested it might be time for someone to re-examine Erebus in order to achieve an official exoneration of Jim Collins. Instantly, sharply, he replied — and I shall never forget the tone and the metric balance of the phrasing — 'Collins is redeemable, Mahon is not.' That was that.

The day came and I spoke at his function. He was charming, warm and courteous and took me to his home for lunch. I felt this was half hospitality and half to check me out. We avoided the elephant in the room. Some comments came up as I prepared to leave. I had no doubt he actually believes Mahon got it wrong, that Chippindale got it right. Then he gave me a copy of a little book he wrote which was published by the Auckland District Law Society, *A Lawyer's Tale*, the story of his life and career. It is clear that he regards Collins as being responsible for the accident.

I mentioned this to Paul Davison QC.

'Well, all I would say is that a closer examination of the evidence would suggest that was not a justifiable conclusion. It was Jim Collins's conscientiousness which unseated him in the end. It wasn't a failure to respond to all of the aviation aids that he had. It was his adherence to them that led him to find himself in this insidious position where he believed he was going to be safe by adhering to his Nav Track and, looking ahead, of course, he was seeing what he expected to see and that's what happened.'

Davison regards the Court of Appeal minority decision as 'a somewhat academic analysis that didn't sit easily with the factual events that took place at the hearing'; in other words, with what they had all seen and heard. Davison believes senior airline management who denied knowing about the coordinate change in 1978, and who denied knowing about the low altitudes the DC-10s were flying at, had to appreciate, from the questions asked and the challenges mounted against them at the Commission, that it was likely that they were not being believed and that clearly their credibility and reliability were very much in issue.

The *Auckland Star* journalist John Macdonald wrote at the time that the Court of Appeal should have sat day after long day at the Royal Commission and watched the teeth being pulled.

This is why Mahon went through two channels to warn the airline. He worried that if he gave the warning in open court he would be accused of bias.

It all came down to whether or not the airline should have known it wasn't being believed; whether or not its management's evidence was all too similar; and whether or not Mahon should have warned the management in open court that they were not being believed. Could that see him accused of being biased? Were the very credible back channel warnings enough?

In the end, 10 superior court judges, the Court of Appeal and the Privy Council, decided he should have given warning that they were not going to be believed. The Court of Appeal also found that a Royal Commissioner could not convict a group of people of conspiracy to perjure without their having the safeguard of a jury.

While the Court of Appeal judgement said Mahon exceeded his terms of reference and breached natural justice, the long Woodhouse judgement, in Mahon's view, seriously undermined his ability to judge the credibility of witnesses, one of the most important functions of a judge. A judge has to know when he or she is being taken for a fool. That is why judges look down from the bench like owls. This is why the magistrate was always called 'the Beak'.

So the Court of Appeal delivered its verdict on 22 December 1981, just before Christmas, timed so as to be noticed and then to disappear in the general haze of the festive season. On the day the ruling was handed down, Peter and Margarita Mahon were headed to Christchurch for their holidays.

The Court of Appeal was a media sensation. The public perception was that Mahon had been overturned, his findings negated. He had been seriously damaged. He had been criticised by the entire Court of Appeal and savaged by two of them. Margarita Mahon spoke of the media being camped on their lawn as they packed up for Christchurch.

'[Justice] Speight came round, saw what was happening and said, "Oh, Peter, you don't need this." Peter said, "Well, there it is." Then when we got south he got to know a bit more about it all, he came to me and said, "I've just rung Davison [the Chief Justice] and I'll be tendering my resignation." And I said, "Oh, Peter do you think that's wise?" and he said, "Well, I can't continue on the bench because if I hear a case, give a verdict and it goes to the Court of Appeal and either of those two judges are sitting on it, how will the lawyers know they're getting a totally unbiased result?"'

Margarita said judges and lawyers were shocked by the whole affair. Judges understood how the Court of Appeal minority judgement had ruined Mahon as a judge. Mahon was good friends with Ted, Sir Edmund Somers, one of the Court of Appeal judges.

'We didn't get to see him again. He was very sad about the whole affair. I met up with Ted once. I went to a dinner at Government House in Wellington and the various judges were there and they were all so welcoming and "lovely to see you again" and so forth. Ted was good. Louise [Somers] has tried very hard not to tell me, if you know what I mean, but she has indicated it was all wrong. She has certainly told me that Ted had no time for Woodhouse at all on the Court of Appeal.

'Peter could live with the Court of Appeal judgement,' Margarita told me. 'He said the judgement the three gave, "You can live with that." They weren't right but you live with it and just go on, but these two men, they were really castigating him for not knowing what he was doing and couldn't tell when people were lying.' It is the families of the dead she really feels for.

'Those people got clarification [from the Royal Commission] of what happened down there, they were so grateful for it and it all became lost, didn't it? It all became lost because of those wretched two men, really. None of this should've happened. Peter did the job to the best of his ability, he handed the report to the Governor General and that was the end of his part in it. The Governor General hands the report to the Prime Minister for it to be discussed in Parliament, finish. None of this "after-shock" should have happened at all. I shouldn't be in the position I'm in today. Nothing like this should have happened.'

Holmes: 'What do you mean the position you're in today. You should be better provided for, you mean?'

Margarita: 'Yes. Not everything is about money but still, it could be easier. It could be easier. I've never asked for much in my life. Not ever. When I married Peter there were no expectations. In those days when you got married if you could pay for a little flat, then you did.'

When Peter Mahon resigned he was not yet eligible for a judge's pension. Jim McLay, the Attorney General, arranged for a small pension. Margarita told me that when Peter, delighted — everyone who knew him says he didn't care about money — told Margarita the amount, she replied, appalled, 'Peter, how are we going to live on that?'

When Peter Mahon died, Margarita was 58 and ineligible for national super. She then received only a part of his small pension. 'Two people knew about this . . . Jim McLay and Jim Anderton. Jim Anderton was hot about this. Jim McLay jumped in and tried to have an adjustment made for my pension. Geoffrey Palmer was Attorney General. McLay said Palmer could have made the adjustment himself. "But," he said, "I'll have to put this to Cabinet." And, on the day it happened to go to Cabinet, he was overseas so he couldn't be seen to have anything to do with it. It was rejected.'

So late January 1982, a month after the Court of Appeal report was handed down, Mahon decided that he and Margarita would shift back to Christchurch. Margarita says she knew that was a mistake. She found out about the move from remarks Peter made in a newspaper. But something else had happened to this conservative legal family. Peter was suddenly famous. The country was in love with him. Margarita says women always loved him. She said: 'I was aware of his general exhaustion which was not so much to do with what the Court of Appeal had done but it was about becoming a star overnight and you didn't intend to. It's exhausting, utterly exhausting. The public were so overwhelmingly wonderful.'

H: 'The public loved him?'

Margarita: 'They did, but you know, it can be exhausting.'

Was moving back to Christchurch running away? 'I think he just wanted to run somewhere and write his book [*Verdict on Erebus*] and prepare for the Privy Council. When you can't go to the dairy without someone saying, "I hope you don't mind, but . . .".'

Mahon was fleeing the fame. He was the popular hero — at that time, probably the most admired man in New Zealand. The public sensed something special in him, some love of justice, a very brainy man who had worked out something very difficult and shocking, who had worked out why that DC-10 had crashed and had stood up to liars and bullies. And the country was pretty much sick of being run by a bully.

Suddenly, at the end of January 1982, Peter Martin's letter was leaked to the press. There it was, proof that Air New Zealand was doctoring its evidence to protect itself, and proof that Mahon had warned Air New Zealand that its evidence was not being believed. The airline was furious. Its new, pugnacious, blustering chairman, the Tauranga trucking contractor Bob Owens, was making all kinds of threats, vowing to flush the leaker out. It was all huff, puff and bluff.

And down in Christchurch, Mahon got sick. Margarita made him go to the doctor. He came home. 'He said, "You haven't asked me about going to the doctor." I said, "No, I haven't, did you go?" "Oh yes, I went. I want you to sit down for a moment. I have heart failure," and I said, "Oh yes?" and he said, "I'm going on bed rest for two weeks and see how I get on." It wasn't getting any better so they put him in Princess Margaret Hospital. The doctor said he'll go into such and such a ward as opposed to the heart ward.'

This was to protect Mahon from publicity.

H: 'So that was always going to be a problem? The heart?'

Margarita: 'Forever.'

H: 'Then we get a tumour in the sinus.'

Margarita: 'Yes, at the same time as he received a telegram to say that he'd been given this award in Canada by the international pilots. At that moment he said, "My gum is very sore," and he was having a bit of a problem. He's had dentures for years but you couldn't really tell. I asked him a bit about it and I said, "When we get to Auckland we'd better go and see about this" and he said, "I think it's just my dentures need adjusting".'

They were moving back to Auckland. On examination it was discovered that it was cancer in the sinus, which had made its way down into the gum. With Mahon's heart condition, no operation was possible. Doctors recommended radiotherapy.

'When I went to see him at Greenlane — they were just wonderful. They thought the world of him — and he told me about the radiotherapy — you see he wouldn't talk about anything, I could only get what he offered — so he told me about it and I said, "What have you decided?" and he said, "Well, it's worth a go, I don't want to talk about it any more." When he went off to the toilet I saw that there was some printed material there and I picked it up and read it. If there was radiotherapy to the head, it often passed through the mouth and what could happen in that event and how much the mouth had to be cared for. I didn't tell him that I'd read it. I didn't say anything.'

Normally, the doctors would have transferred Mahon from Greenlane, the heart hospital, as it were, to Auckland, home of the Oncology Department. The doctor came and sat with Margarita.

Margarita is sitting in her living room talking to me on a Saturday afternoon. She fixes up a cassette player and starts playing Mahon's interview with Sharon Crosbie. I ask her to turn it off. I cannot stand Crosbie's voice. Margarita says, 'Everywhere we went, everywhere, after the Court of Appeal, there was so much respect. So much respect for Peter.'

Mahon's old friend John Burn, in an obituary published in *The Press*, remembers being in a restaurant with him round this time. The two of them made their way through their meal. The waiter came over and told them there would be no charge, that another customer had fixed up Justice Mahon's bill.

So the doctor sat and talked with Margarita.

Margarita: 'They could transfer him to Auckland and he'd be right next to Oncology. He talked with me about it and then he said, "But I won't do it, Mrs Mahon. This is his home".'

H: 'Greenlane?'

Margarita: 'They were wonderful. I said, "I'm relieved to hear you say that." He said, "He can start his treatment from here." I could've picked him up in the car and taken him over for treatment, but no, he was going in the ambulance with all the other people. Even the ambulance driver got in touch with me to say how much he enjoyed those journeys. Peter would get in and sit beside him and they'd talk about cricket and the football or whatever, over to Oncology and back again.'

The mouth had to be kept moisturised. Mahon's radiotherapy appears to have been excessive. The mouth became a terrible problem, dry and uncomfortable.

'He had frightful trouble with the mouth, in that all our mouths have lots of germs in them, and if there are lesions of any sort, the germs jump in. An amazing man in the dental department, Alan Coster, had to try and control all of that. It was all very painful.'

Margarita became the nurse. Mahon had lesions in the mouth 'just from the treatment. I used to stand with him while he did it all. The mind was active and it had to keep active. He had to give up lecturing at the university and on his last day there . . . I think he went from the hospital to do his last lecture. Janet went just to sit in the back of the room and make sure that he had the glass of water there and so on. At the end, the students stood up and gave him an ovation. He loved going to the university. You can see how hard it was for her because she was studying and working and what not.

'Anyhow, we did all this going back and forth and then the mouth would come right for him to have more treatment but after each treatment he'd get in the car and he'd say, "Take me to the TAB, Mother." He was supposed to go straight home to rest, so we'd go to the one in Newmarket where he knew the lady and he'd put a few bets on. I'd go out and get all the racing papers for him. It was keeping the papers going. He'd do his study and I'd sit in the car and wait for him. I never knew if the lady was going to come out and say, "He's dropped dead" or not.'

John Burn believed he had an arrangement with a woman at the TAB by which she not only placed his bets but provided him with a cigarette or two.

'He'd come out of the TAB and we'd go home and he'd have a rest,' says Margarita. 'All the time, I was having to find food that wouldn't sting his mouth and what didn't sting it one day would sting it the next. I'd have to give him stuff to anaesthetise it and then I'd have to dream up something else that I thought wouldn't sting the mouth. He sat down and wrote the short story, *The Sniper*, just to keep the brain going . . .

'I was allowing him to think he was doing everything on his own and he was the master . . . but he could only do it if I was thinking 20 steps ahead. That was how we operated. It took about three months, with the doctor, me and Peter working at his mouth 24 hours a day and we got it right. We got it right. Saliva was there, everything. We changed our car in the midst of this and he'd told Coster. Now, these people never took a minute off their work, but Coster and his nurse and another person said, "We're coming with you down to the carpark to see your new car." At the funeral when we were walking out, I couldn't believe it, there was Coster and his nurse. They never took time off. He was the same sort of person as Peter. He was passionate about his work.'

In mid-1983, Mahon's appeal against the Court of Appeal was heard at the Privy Council in London, a court that once presided over the lives of a quarter of the world's people. Mahon was too ill to travel. Margarita went on his behalf. Lord Diplock, the senior Law Lord, presided. The courtroom, on the corner of Downing Street and Whitehall, was packed, uncomfortably so, every day. The case was said, by one of the staff, to a *New Zealand Herald* correspondent, to be the most heavily attended since an Australian banking case in 1948. It is hard to know how a banking case could pack a courtroom, but Mr Pickersell, who had been on the staff of the Privy Council for 35 years, assured the *New Zealand Herald* that 'what I do not know about this place no one will ever know'. The Law Lords were said, during the Erebus hearing, to disappear sometimes behind the mountains of literature generated by the case.

At one point, Lord Diplock wondered if 'litany' had a different meaning in New Zealand to what it had in England. He said, 'I think it means a prayer.' Robert Alexander, representing Air New Zealand, suggested helpfully, 'I think it undoubtedly means a prayer.' Lord Scarman helped out. He said it meant a service with the congregation taking part.

In late October the Privy Council delivered the final blow to Mahon. The Council 'reluctantly' upheld the Court of Appeal decision.[13] They found against him in law. He had no right in his warrant to impose a $150,000 fine to punish the airline for its management staff stalling through the inquiry and telling lies. He had no right to convict of a crime.

It is a strange judgement.

The Privy Council said Mahon had probative material that he had been lied to by management witnesses but their lies were 'an understandable human weakness . . . that they should shrink from acknowledging, even to themselves, that something that they had done or failed to do might have been a cause of so horrendous a disaster'.[14] On the altitude evidence: 'Their Lordships accept unreservedly that the Judge was entitled to take the view, that upon this particular matter, the evidence given by several of the executive pilots at the inquiry was false.'[15] Again, on the altitude evidence: 'If, in seeking to support the case put by Air New Zealand that this minimum altitude should have been strictly maintained by the crew of the fatal flight, those witnesses whom the Judge disbelieved on this issue were, as their Lordships must accept, being untruthful, they were also being singularly naïve,' such was 'the mass of evidence of flights down McMurdo Sound at low altitudes and the publicity given to them . . .'[16]

Despite this, Mahon's 'orchestrated litany of lies' simply could not be proven, apparently. 'There had been no material of any probative value on which to base a finding that a pre-determined plan of deception ever existed.'[17] This despite their Lordships' acceptance that they had not been there through the long 75 days weighing the evidence and hearing the witnesses in person, as Mahon had.

Stuart Macfarlane, the Erebus researcher, says that in the end, if what the airline witnesses said was true, then the airline made 54 mistakes concerning the flight path of the airliner and 177 mistakes regarding altitude. It wasn't possible for a commercial airline to make that many mistakes. Therefore, the airline was lying. But it didn't matter. He knew before Mahon took his case to London that Mahon would fail at the Privy Council. He would fail not on causation, but on law. The Privy Council would find that he breached natural justice.

Margarita says that she knew that going to the Privy Council, like moving back to Christchurch, was a bad idea.

The public misinterpretation of the Privy Council was exactly what happened.

The Privy Council did not remotely challenge Mahon's causation findings. In fact, Lord Diplock made it clear that the Law Lords marvelled at Mahon's report. When it came to Mahon's findings, the Privy Council actually ratified them. They said Mahon's greatest handicap had been the pressure of time. And they could understand the indignation that built within him as he put the report together and came to realise 'the appalling blunders and deficiencies' of the airline's executive staff. 'Their Lordships can well understand the growing indignation of the Judge when, after completing the hearings and for the purpose of preparing his Report, he brought them together in his own mind and reflected upon them.'[18] But . . .

> In relation to the three matters which were principally canvassed in this appeal [destruction of documents, altitude and navigation] and upon which he based his findings that there had been a pre-determined plan to deceive the Royal Commission and a conspiracy to commit perjury at its hearings, their Lordships have very reluctantly felt compelled to hold that . . . the Judge failed to adhere to those rules of natural justice that are appropriate to an inquiry of the kind he was conducting and that . . . it was not open to him to make the finding that he did in paragraph 377 of his report.[19]

They would also have appreciated Mahon's turn of phrase, his rare literary gifts. They would have thought the phrases very neatly constructed: 'A predetermined plan to deceive . . . an orchestrated litany of lies.' That is why they spoke humorously about the meaning of 'litany'.

As Sam Mahon wrote in the book about his father, the phrases are perfect iambic pentameter, the invention of Chaucer, whose rhythm is said to be that of the human heart. 'Da daa da daa da daa da daa.' And no army of lawyers and judges could ever destroy or undo them. You could go to the highest court in the Commonwealth and you could never destroy them. The words floated free forever in the world and in the minds of New Zealanders who knew that Mahon was the good guy. Such is the power of poetry.

The Privy Council agreed completely that the pilots were not to blame. There was no negligence. Mahon had proven Chippindale wrong. Captain Collins had been briefed on the McMurdo Sound route three weeks before the flight, he had noted the destination waypoint coordinates and his family had seen him working on his charts the night before he took off for the ice. He had explained the flight to his daughters. He received MacCentre's clearance to descend. The Lordships said, 'That on completing this descent he switched back to nav track is incapable of being reconciled with any other explanation than that he was relying upon the line he had himself plotted on the flight track on which he had been briefed.'[20] Mahon 'makes an overwhelming case' that the aircraft was in whiteout when it crashed'.[21] And there was nothing on the CVR 'capable of throwing any doubt upon the confident belief of all members of the crew' that the aircraft was headed straight down the middle of McMurdo Sound.[22]

Then Diplock said that the Law Lords had . . .

> . . . occasion to read and to re-read with close attention before, during and since the hearing of the appeal all 167 printed pages of the Royal Commission Report. Having done so, they would desire to place on record their tribute to the brilliant and painstaking investigative work undertaken by the Judge . . . in the course of hearings which lasted for 75 days and other investigations that he or counsel assisting him undertook in addition to the public hearings.[23]

They praised Mahon's courtesy and patience. In other words, they knew what he'd been up against.

So, despite so brilliantly determining the cause of the disaster, despite the wall of obduracy put up against him, Mahon was to be taken down. Mahon wasn't fooled. He understood. The Privy Council were having a bob each way. Their Lordships knew that a few people had lied to Mahon. Their Lordships said they knew that a few people had lied to Mahon but it was all right for them to do so. One could excuse people who might be blamed for such a horrendous disaster trying to avoid taking responsibility.

It was appalling.

What's more, there had been no orchestrated litany of lies. As Mahon put it much later, 'What the Privy Council said was that while everyone sang the same song, they sang it as soloists, not as a choir.'

In the end, despite it all, they found against him. In the end, while 10 superior court judges were bothered by the natural justice aspect of the Mahon Report, they, nevertheless, gave the impression of being more concerned with the reputations and sensitivities of those alive whose actions or omissions caused the disaster than with the rights of the 257 deceased. The Establishment had seen itself right.

Their Lordships, with a certain exquisite fatuousness, concluded their judgement with a plea for 'all parties to let bygones be bygones so far as the aftermath of the Mount Erebus disaster is concerned'.

Two hundred and fifty-seven people had died through administrative bungles.

The Privy Council finished by patronising Mahon. 'There were what in retrospect can be recognised as having been faults or mistakes at the inquiry but which . . . appear to their Lordships for the most part to have been the manifestations of human fallibility that are easy to understand and excuse.'[24]

Greg McGee summed up the Privy Council thus by having Mahon explain to Margarita, in his brilliant *Erebus: the Aftermath*:

> The Privy Council is simply saying: one, that my analysis of the cause of the accident is brilliant and correct; two, that my analysis of the cause of the accident is incorrect, in so far as I give any weight to executive knowledge of low flying; three, that the Air New Zealand executives might well have been lying about their knowledge of low flying; four, that that doesn't matter because their Lordships don't consider low flying had anything to do with the disaster; and five, that because at the time they lied, the executives thought low flying *was* a cause of the disaster, it was quite understandable for them to want to lie.[25]

In the end, it was all about a few lines of a comprehensive 167-page report now universally acknowledged to be years ahead of its time in terms of its approach to accident inquiry. Perhaps, as John Blumsky put it: 'Mahon got so furious that this gentle, quiet, determined, steely, brilliant legal mind blew its stack.'

Probably if Mahon had simply said he did not believe witnesses A, B and C, he would have been left alone. His answer to that in *Verdict on Erebus* was that the airline and Civil Aviation would simply have said he was wrong. They would immediately have attacked him.

He wanted to knock them for six in no uncertain terms. Which he did.

After which, they set out to destroy him. Which they did.

28

Farewell Mr Mahon

Live as if you were to die tomorrow, Learn as if you were to live forever.

— Mohandas Gandhi

That was late 1983, the end of October. Peter Mahon was a very sick man. His heart was terribly weak. He was back in Christchurch. Men with whom he had been friends all his life turned their backs on him. Justice Sir Clinton Roper, Clint, whom Mahon had befriended during the war and looked after on the journey home to New Zealand — Roper sick in the head, Mahon protecting him all the way — turned away when Mahon came across him one day walking in the Cashmere Hills. Betrayal, says Sam Mahon, is more dependable than friendship.

Mahon was a proud man. And he was broken. As doors closed on him, he started writing. The family noticed a new vigour, a new life, a new surge in him. Did he sit there each morning, as he had hour after hour in Auckland when writing his accident report, fountain pen in one hand skating across the pages, cigarette forgotten in the left? He wrote *Verdict on Erebus*, Sam Mahon tells us, in three months. It must have poured out of him. You cannot get much better writing than the final two paragraphs.

> By a navigational error for which the aircrew was not responsible, and about which they were uninformed, an aircraft had flown not into McMurdo Sound but into Lewis Bay, and there the elements of nature had so combined, at a fatal coincidence of time and place, to translate an administrative

> blunder in Auckland into an awesome disaster in Antarctica.
>
> Much has been written and said about the weather hazards of Antarctica, and how they combine to create a spectacular but hostile terrain, but for my purposes the most definitive illustration of these hidden perils was the wreckage which lay on the mountainside, showing how the forces of nature, if given the chance, can sometimes defeat the flawless technology of man. For the ultimate key to the tragedy lay here, in the white silence of Lewis Bay, the place to which the airliner had been unerringly guided by its micro-electronic navigation system, only to be destroyed, in clear air and without warning, by a malevolent trick of the polar light.[1]

Margarita watched her husband carefully.

It was many years since he had come courting, with his strange reserve. Once he made to kiss her as he took her to her front door. She was having none of that. She knew he was serious about her when one day he presented her with a page on which was neatly typed some lines from T. S. Eliot's 'The Love Song of J. Alfred Prufrock'.

> And indeed there will be time
> To wonder, 'Do I dare?' and 'Do I dare?'
> Time to turn back and descend the stair,
> With a bald spot in the middle of my hair —
> [They will say: 'His hair is growing thin!']

She liked that about him. He was a reader. He sent her poetry. Her father was a keen reader.

'I suppose they always say that girls look for their fathers and I suppose there was an element of my father there . . . the appreciation of language, reading and the wit. I think I married the sense of humour . . . which is not a good idea.

'And I'm reading this and I'm thinking why did he give me that to read? I'm desperately trying not to take any notice and I was about to go down to Dunedin for a couple of months to stay with my parents prior to going to Australia. All the bookings were made and everything. Then one evening he came to visit. As I walked him to the gate he said, "I want to tell you that I would like to marry you but there are certain conditions." Just like that. I said, "What are they, Peter?" He said, "You've planned to go to Australia. Nothing must interfere with that. I might very well say, we can go another time, but you don't know in this life and I wouldn't want to have the responsibility for your not going. I believe that it's a good idea. New Zealand is still relatively isolated and it's good for people to go and see something outside of New Zealand."'

And indeed, she did go. She went as she had planned, to Australia for three months.

Mahon continued there at the gate that evening, as Margarita tells it: '"I will marry you in your church," and I said, "How will your father feel about that?"'

Mahon was Catholic. Margarita was Church of England.

Holmes: 'So that was the second condition?'

Margarita: 'Yes. And if we had any children they would be brought up in whatever faith I decided on. It was all like that.'

H: 'So what did you say?'

Margarita: 'It was a bit of a shock, really. He said, "Oh well, go away and think about it." I had a number of weeks to think about it. I wasn't sure.'

H: 'Did he say, "I love you?"'

Margarita: 'No.'

H: 'Did you?'

Margarita: 'No.'

H: 'Did you say that to each other before you got married?'

Margarita: 'No.'

H: 'Perhaps people didn't then.'

Margarita: 'I said to him once, and this was long before Prince Charles, "You've never actually said 'I love you'," and he said, "Well, whatever that means".'

H: 'Did he ever say it?'

Margarita: 'I don't think so. I don't think he said he loved anybody, really.'

H: 'In all the years?'

Margarita: 'I don't think so.'

H: 'Did you fall in love with him?'

Margarita: 'What happened was, something developed that was, I suppose, a meeting of minds and an affinity, a certain warmth when I was with him. I don't know. It was something that grew.'

I look across at Margarita. I listen to her voice, her way of telling a story, her subtlety. I think about her obvious organisation, the way she has searched Mahon's files for a document for me, handing it to me, chatting on, saying nothing about the document, my having to realise its importance and relevance myself. At 82 years old she is elegant, dignified and charming. She has a wicked sense of humour. I can see why Peter Mahon married Margarita Smith.

Another thing he liked about Margarita was that her family had some nice horses. Mahon loved his horses.

H: 'Sam says in his book that some of us were almost orphans of the war because parts of our fathers never came home. Tom Scott's way of putting it is that we grew up in the shadow of the war. I certainly feel both those things. How did the war affect Peter, do you think? I know you didn't know him before the war . . .'

Margarita: 'He was a bit given to saying, "It doesn't matter." After a while and as the children began to grow, I said to him, "Peter, you can't go on saying nothing matters because things do matter, particularly with your children growing up — things will matter." And he didn't answer me but he never said it again. When he died, next morning I woke up and looked across the room and there was a picture hanging there and I thought, it doesn't matter that that's there. And I realised that was a result of the war.'

H: 'That particular thing is not important?'

Margarita: 'After he died, it was about three weeks after, I was so busy, I picked up a duster to dust a table and that's when I shrieked with tears because I realised that I had only ever hung a picture or dusted a table hoping that it would be agreeable to his eye. That's why when I woke up and looked across and saw the picture, I thought, "It doesn't matter." Funny isn't it? What a fool I was to go to all that trouble!'

H: 'What was that about? Crying when you went to dust the table?'

Margarita: 'It was that I'd never cried.'

Margarita's was a life lived for her husband and her children. She says that each time she made plans to branch out, something would destroy those plans. Back in Christchurch after the Royal Commission, she set about getting her real estate licence in order to sell property. Then Peter got sick and they moved back to Auckland.

Mahon finished his book. The famous stern, black and white photograph on the back cover of the original edition Margarita arranged. Mahon was very ill. She took him into Christchurch, to a broken-down-looking upstairs photographic studio that had seen better times in Colombo Street. The man took many photographs. Peter had no energy. Finally, at one point, his eyes looked up at Margarita as the camera clicked. They had their photograph.

Verdict on Erebus sold out in a week and went straight to a second print run. In 1985 it won the supreme publishing award for non-fiction in New Zealand. The book was really Mahon's answer to the Court of Appeal, although not once in the book is the Court of Appeal mentioned. Not once. But he answers the court in the book when he spells out his reasons for what became the inflammatory language, one of which was that he knew that the board of Air New Zealand had no idea of the extent to which the case presented by the airline at the Royal Commission had collapsed.

But it is more than that. When he wrote and published his accident report, he did so under full judicial privilege and protections bestowed a royal commissioner. He was, in any case, a Justice of the High Court.

In fact, in the *Law Quarterly Review* in July 1987, Dunedin legal academic Andrew Beck argued that the Court of Appeal hearing was really the trial of a High Court judge for defamation. It was the closest the Air New Zealand executives could get to a defamation proceeding.

But by the time he wrote *Verdict on Erebus*, he was a private man again, Mr Mahon. He had no protection from defamation. Yet in *Verdict on Erebus* he repeats the conspiracy allegations word for word. No one ever sued him. No one came forward. That, ultimately, demonstrated the courage of Peter Mahon, and that of his publisher, the firm aptly named Collins. But then, to help him out, Mahon had a way of speaking between the lines.

It is the custom for retiring judges to be knighted. Mahon received no honour for his life's work, for his dedication to the law and for his achievement in the Erebus investigation. Probably, after the deep offence he caused Muldoon and his public spat with the prime minister, no one expected any honour to come from there. But midway through 1984, a Labour government came to power.

Late in 1984, 48 prominent and eminent New Zealanders made the case to David Lange for a knighthood for Peter Mahon. Orchestrating the support were a Wellington judge by the name of Kearney and the current Governor General Sir Anand Satyanand. Ted Thomas, now Sir Edmund, then president of the Auckland Law Society, described Mahon's service on the Erebus inquiry as 'outstanding . . . His conclusions have about them an inexorable logic . . . yet without his objectivity, determination and perception it must be doubtful whether the true causes of the accident would have been revealed.'

Richard Sutton, Dean of the Otago University Faculty of Law, spoke of Mahon's 'numerous scholarly judgments' which were 'models of lucid writing and profound research' which 'display a deep understanding of the development of the law over the preceding century'. Sutton described Mahon's handling of the technical side of the evidence in the Erebus inquiry as 'a remarkable piece of analysis, showing to the full his ability to come to grips with expert evidence'.

Mahon's friend Justice Sir Graham Speight wrote that Mahon 'has I feel raised the image of the Judiciary in the public eye by his courage and his outspoken attitude at a time when lesser (or perhaps more discreet) men would have remained subdued ... he has for many years through his friendly contacts with the younger people in the law, become the idol of the students and the new practitioners, demonstrating a humanity and an understanding of realities which more conservative lawyers sometimes lack.'

Sir Anand Satyanand, at the time a District Court Judge, wrote that three aspects of Mahon stood out for him: 'First, a laconic and mercurial brilliance, in both writing and speech, not often observed in this country. Secondly, a judicial presence which was encouraging to the lawyer and litigant ... Thirdly and finally he is as events have proved, a person of bravery and principle.'

The Solicitor General wrote in support. There are letters of support from Roger Maclaren, Paul Davison and David Baragwanath, all speaking of Mahon with infinite respect and admiration. The only two journalists to cover the Commission from start to finish, Radio New Zealand's Carmel Friedlander and the *Auckland Star*'s John Macdonald, wrote in support. Macdonald wrote:

> I recall especially, during the course of the inquiry, Mr Justice Mahon's exhaustive efforts to seek out the truth from witnesses who were often secretive and hostile, his ability to test experts, such as master navigators, to the very foundations of their knowledge and the revelations this questioning uncovered. I also recall the extent of these inquiries; for instance, his double checking of evidence already submitted by the accident investigator. In returning to the sources, including American manufacturers, Mr Justice Mahon was able to provide new and vital clues to the inquiry.

Macdonald spoke of his dismay at the attempts by some to malign Mahon subsequent to the inquiry.

Carmel Friedlander sat through every day and saw the entire exhibition Mahon had to watch. She wrote that:

> It is a truism to say that truth can hurt. In a way, he became as much a victim of the Erebus disaster as those who died in the crash. His honesty would not allow him to stray from the truth for the sake of a popular verdict . . . At a time when many turned away from him, he still clung to the truth . . . My admiration for him is boundless. And I say this professionally as well as personally. His fortitude and perseverance on behalf of his fellow men, his courage and his honesty have all been well proven.

Friedlander noticed something else too, the respect men showed him in Antarctica, by both the Americans and the New Zealanders. This was the respect which caused the Australian aircrew to invite him onto the flight deck in order to demonstrate whiteout.

Former Attorney General, Martin Finlay QC, joined the call to Lange. So did the present Chief Justice, Sian Elias. She wrote: 'I have always been of the view that the judge's early retirement from judicial office was not only a personal tragedy but an incalculable loss for the Bench.' She praised his great concern for civil liberties. She spoke of his courage. She described him as an extraordinary judge.

John Burrows, Professor of Law at Canterbury, and Bernard Brown, Associate Professor of Law at Auckland University, also sent letters.

Throughout the entirety of the 48 letters are recurring themes. The writers praise Mahon's brilliance as a judge, his lucidity, his writing, his clarity of thought, his courage, his grasp of the finest detail, his thoroughness and his commitment to fairness, honesty and the truth. Baragwanath reminded Lange of Mahon's service in Italy as a frontline infantryman. The petitioners spoke of Mahon's qualities as a man, his courtesy, his decency to younger members starting out in the profession of law and his wit and his humour. When the petitions for a knighthood failed, Sir Anand had the letters bound and sent to Margarita.

The years went by. Sam Mahon wondered at the role of Sir Geoffrey

Palmer. Palmer's premiership, which lasted a year, was a singular political failure. Palmer, the law professor, the academic, simply could not connect with people. For a long period after his political career was over, Palmer, in an inept piece of broadcasting judgement, was given a weekly slot on National Radio to discuss constitutional matters. They were not discussions, as such. They were blustering, sesquipedalian verbosity from a man who appeared to be a know-it-all of the first order.

Geoffrey Palmer's mentor, his legal hero, was Sir Owen Woodhouse. Woodhouse was already a judge when, on a trip to the University of Chicago, during the preparation of his report on accident compensation, he met a very smart young New Zealand postgraduate law student. They got on famously and fell for each other immediately. Later, when Woodhouse was invited by the Australian Prime Minister to write a report on Australian accident compensation, he invited Palmer to go with him as his assistant. This became a very close relationship.

When, in late December 1981, the five Court of Appeal judges all agreed that, in alleging a conspiracy to deceive the Commission, Mahon had overstepped the mark and gone beyond his powers, Palmer agreed. Palmer, like the judges, of course, had not had to witness the performances that played out at the Commission. Instead, when Mahon, probably unwisely, criticised the judges in public — knowing that his career was over — Palmer became his huffiest, most pompous self. In his notes at the time, Palmer wrote that he felt the judge had been 'unjudicial in the extreme. He has shown partiality, lack of balance and acted in a political way. If I were the Attorney-General I would accept his resignation because I have no confidence in his ability to impartially dispense justice anymore.'[2]

This was Palmer, out of touch not only with what the people thought but what some of the best legal minds in the land thought, which was that the report had been a brilliant pioneering analysis of an accident. Nowhere does Palmer seem to give that any thought at all. His biographer, Raymond Richards, does not tell us if Palmer even read Mahon's accident report.

In late January 1982, when Mahon resigned as a judge, Woodhouse was in Kansas.[3] Palmer kept him informed of developments.

'Palmer spent several hours reading the evidence that was placed before the Court of Appeal,' writes Richards, 'and became convinced that the most persuasive analysis of the issues was contained in the judgement of McMullin and Woodhouse.

'He could see no cover-up by Air New Zealand, which had made available to Chippindale the material about the flight computer.' This was Palmer's naivety. Of course Air New Zealand had told Chippindale about the coordinate change. They did so because it was too big to keep quiet, too big for him not to find out. But this was a very elaborate deception being undertaken. The coordinates were 'correct'. Collins was too low. And the company had no knowledge of flight below 6000 feet. Chippindale bought it. And deliberately found the coordinate change to be irrelevant.

Palmer said in a press statement that he thought Air New Zealand and the pilot were equally to blame for the accident.[4] It was an ignorant assessment. As if, with respect, Palmer would know after 'several hours' reading the Court of Appeal documents the causes of the accident. Richards went on to describe the Privy Council judgement dismissing Mahon's appeal as 'damning'. It was no such thing.

Thirty years on, it is Mahon's report that is remembered. It is Mahon's analysis that is recognised internationally, not the judgements of McMullin and Woodhouse.

Sam Mahon did an incredible thing. In exploring his father's life while writing his memoir, *My Father's Shadow*, he visited the Law Commission in Wellington where he knocked on Palmer's door.

'Did you get my letter?' he asked Palmer.

A week earlier, he said, he had written to Palmer asking him why an honour had been denied his father. After all, said Sam, his father had stood up to Muldoon. The Mahon Report is now praised internationally. Sam's inquiries had already told him that it was Palmer who blocked such an honour. Word was that Woodhouse would have resigned if Mahon had received a gong.

Palmer said he had received Sam's letter. Sam said, 'Do you think you might find time to reply?'

Palmer replied, 'Well, I've only had it two or three days.'

Sam wrote:

> It was not an answer. We both knew that. We sat in silence for a moment. 'Is there anything you can tell me now?' I asked.
>
> A few empty seconds followed during which his smile disappeared, his eyes dulled and his face assumed the personality of cardboard.

> 'I've had to take advice from the Cabinet Office,' Palmer growled.
>
> We stared at each other for what seemed a long time. Perhaps as long as it takes to press the butt against the shoulder, feel the curve of oiled walnut against the cheek and take a careful lead on an incoming duck. I smiled. 'Right then,' I said, getting to my feet. 'I should go.' And I left him to his work, sitting in the same chair once occupied by his mentor, Sir Owen Woodhouse.[5]

But in the *Dominion Post* of 2 February 2008, Sam Mahon found this: 'Sir Geoffrey Palmer who was Minister of Justice and Deputy Prime Minister at the time, seemed particularly disdainful to the idea of knighting Justice Mahon and remains so to this day. "Justice Mahon was a very eminent New Zealander and he did a lot of good things, but [the Erebus Report] wasn't one of them," Sir Geoffrey said caustically.'

By August 1986, Margarita knew the end was near. Peter Mahon was simply running out of life.

His close friend Justice Graham Speight went to see Mahon one afternoon. 'How are you, friend?' Mahon, in his bed, replied, 'I nightly pitch my moving tent a day's march nearer home.'

Margarita said: 'He never talked about the possibility of dying. I knew that in the condition he was in he could just fall down dead. We just dealt with every day. And on the Saturday, a golfing friend of his, who had become a very good friend, Stuart Naismith, called round to watch the football with him and Janet had called in for some particular reason.

'Janet said, "I've got to hurry away, Dad, I've got to get into these books." He said, "All right, dear." I can still see him going to the door with her and Janet starting down the wee path and she turned round and said, "I won't see you tomorrow because I've got to get my head down to it," and he said, "All right, dear," and that was that.'

On the Sunday Peter and Margarita drove the car to the North Shore, to Bayswater, to see a friend who made them laugh. 'We came home and he was tired. I said, "Well, you're going to bed early, I don't think I'll light the fire." He said, "No." Then I said, "Yes, I will, you love to see a fire." The wood and everything wasn't on hand but I decided to light the fire and I did that and that was good. Then I said, "I've got to be off to bed because we've got to be away early in the morning to go to the appointment."

'He'd been in bed for a while and I went in to see that he had his water and his tablets and I was thinking, "I'm tired, I want to go off to sleep," but he had to pass through my room to go to the toilet so on the way back I was reading something and he said, "I think it's a little warmer tonight," and I knew he was longing for the spring and I said, "Well, if you say so, that must be right." Then as I was putting my book down and turning out the lights, I thought, "I should just go and make sure, oh stop being stupid, stop being stupid," so I didn't. Those were our last words.

'When I got up in the middle of the night to make a cup of tea and I looked in the fridge and I'd left him little soft sandwiches and things because he used to get up and make a drink and have something soft to eat, and I thought, "Oh, he hasn't been up tonight, oh, well, perhaps that's good." On my way back I put my cup down on the table and I just sort of peeped into his room in the darkness and it was very still. I quietly crept forward because I didn't want to wake him. So I went a wee bit closer and I said, "Peter?" and I knew it wouldn't take much to disturb him. "Peter?" Nothing. "Peter, are you all right?" Nothing. So I put my hand under his arm and nothing. When I took my hand away, I thought, "He's gone".'

It was 11 August 1986. Peter Mahon was 63.

'I didn't turn on the light, or do anything. I thought, "Nobody tells you what to do." I didn't know. We'd never talked [about it]. Nothing. This was about 4 o'clock in the morning. I was just standing there, looking out the window. I didn't know what to do. I didn't want to ring the doctor but I didn't know what to do but I did ring his GP. He said, "It's all right, Mrs Mahon, I'll come," and he came straight away and I saw him close the eyes. I was just numb. My head was like concrete.

'He sat down for a while and he said, "Now, you'll have to think about his funeral," and I said, "Well, there'll just be the children and myself and his sisters might want to come, we'll just do it quietly like that." He said, "Mrs Mahon, I have to tell you that it will have to be a public funeral," and I said, "I just wanted it to be us." He said, "Well, you think about it, but I have to say that to you."

'Then I thought, "My God, I've got to go and tell Janet." On the Saturday I'd gone into the kitchen and left them together because there was a great rapport between them that I'd never seen before and I was so delighted, but having to go and tell Janet that he'd gone was the hardest thing in the world.

I said, "Janet, your father died this morning, but don't stop what you're doing, you just keep . . ." She said, "Mum, what are you saying?" And I said, "Well, it's happened, he's gone, you must keep going. I'm all right, I'm perfectly alright . . ."

'Then I rang Stuart Naismith. I said, "Joan, would you tell Stuart?" And straightaway he yelled out, "Tell Margarita it has to be a public funeral".'

Now the letters started arriving, letters deeply moved at the death of a courageous judge. From London came this, immediately after Mahon's death:

> Dear Mrs Mahon,
>
> When in Jamaica for the Commonwealth Law Conference I heard from George Barton [Mahon's great friend] of the most sad death of your husband. I can understand only too well how difficult the last years must have been for both of you. It is now three years since the Mt Erebus appeal was heard in the Privy Council but I avidly remember meeting you one lunchtime on the steps of the court and your remembering that the tragedy of that disaster unfolded indefinitely in personal terms for those who had become involved.
>
> And so it must have been for your husband. He had such a fine reputation as a judge and man and his report on the way in which the accident happened was a masterly analysis. But he became clouded by the controversy over what happened afterwards.
>
> I hope that your husband — who has many admirers — will be remembered for his great service to the law long after these events cease to be of consuming interest. May you remember these achievements and treasure them. At our meeting in strange circumstances I admired beyond telling how you were through the whole appeal. And how you were prepared even to engage in conversation with counsel who had the job of presenting the opposing case.
>
> I hope very much that down the years you will get great satisfaction from all you did for your husband, from his achievements and from what you did together.
>
> Yours sincerely,
> Robert Alexander

Robert, Lord Alexander of Weedon, was the London barrister who represented Air New Zealand at the Privy Council.

And there was this:

> Dear Margarita,
>
> For me the saddest thing arising from Erebus was the loss of Peter's friendship when the fates drove us onto opposing paths. Now I am even more saddened by the news of his death. Despite everything and in all sincerity I send my deepest sympathy to you and the children.
>
> Yours,
> Lloyd Brown

Peter Mahon's doctor was right. It had to be a public funeral. The Holy Trinity Cathedral in Parnell was packed.

From all walks of life they came, the highest to the humblest in the land, to pay their last respects to the judge who was never frightened to speak the truth to power.

29

Journey to the Ice

We don't receive wisdom; we must discover it for ourselves after a journey no one can take for us or spare us.

— Marcel Proust

There's rosemary, that's for remembrance. Pray you, Love, remember.

— William Shakespeare, *Hamlet*, Act 4, Scene 5

The years pass. In 2002, Elizabeth Collins graduated as MBA through Otago University. In the past decade she has worked at Parliament and in the corporate sector. She has remained dedicated to animal welfare. Elizabeth loves her animals, right from the time of the two kittens brought round for the children after the Erebus disaster, Romeo and Juliet, which gave her such joy in those dark days.

Kathryn Carter still misses her father desperately and recalls him vividly. She remembers a dry wit, flashing eyes and an infectious laugh. She remembers that he wore a tea towel on his chest if he ate a meal wearing his uniform. 'If we drove him to the airport at night . . . usually in our pyjamas, past our bedtime as a treat . . . he'd tell us how important it was for us to be good and help Maria and not fight about things but just get on and get the jobs done that had to be done.'

She remembers the treats he brought home from the exotic locations he flew to. 'He'd bring me leather shoes, slip-ons in maroon with gold buckles from Hong Kong and jewelled Asian-style jandals. He bought our shoes from drawings he made of our feet. We had to stand on paper while he drew round our feet, tickling us with his pen.'

If Maria and Jim held a dinner party the children had to bid everyone goodnight. Kathryn remembers how 'all the adults would admire how polite we were and how charming and they would laugh with us, with our shining faces and clean hair and we felt so proud of ourselves.

'In the morning there would be a "goodies" selection from the night before of chocolates, raisins and nuts, encouraging us to stay in bed and listen to the Request Session on the radio which Maria had placed there.'

Elizabeth recalls how right from the start, when the children were young, Jim and Maria Collins took time away every now and then, time away from the children, for their own mental health and their marriage.

Kathryn: 'Sometimes in the daytime we had to be quiet because he had come in from a long flight and was asleep. I remember the alarm being set so that Dad was woken after a few hours' sleep but not too much. I remember creeping in to see him against the sunlit blackout curtains billowing in the breeze while he slept. Sometimes we hadn't seen him for ages, and I can remember looking at him and thinking that even though he was asleep, he was present, and with us, and he was back and he was ours, and that soon we'd be able to talk when he woke up.'

One morning in May 2010, I saw an email from Kathryn. It was timed at 12.01 a.m. It was very reflective.

> The day he didn't come back was terrible, indescribable, horrifying in its bleakness, its possibilities of nothing, no way through, no way out. We had to take some bits of ourselves that were left and reassemble a vestige of something in order to go on somehow. When Dad was blamed for causing the death of 256 others, it was like another death, a re-killing, a re-assassination of him for us, a scene of possible guilt for the deaths of the crew and the passengers on the ice, in the cold, in a faraway place. What were we to do? Who would or could help us? Thank God for Maria.

Yes, many years have passed since the Erebus disaster.

Many anniversaries have come and gone.

In August 1999, at Maria's request, Transport Minister Maurice Williamson, the man who saw the shredding going on under Morrie Davis's orders, tabled the Mahon Report in the House. Williamson describes the achievement as his proudest moment in politics. The international status of the report, however, in relation to the Chippindale Report, remains unclear. Both appear to be held at the ICAO in equal status. This is an absurd situation. Certainly, since Mahon, air accident inspectors round the world have to consider events preceding any air accident, including administrative mistakes or omissions.

In November 2009, Air New Zealand planned to honour the thirtieth anniversary of the dark day with a big get-together of the families of the deceased. And there was to be a flight to the ice. The Collinses were invited to send a family member to McMurdo.

Maria had no desire to go. 'I don't need to look for Jim by saying X marks the spot down there. We had to make a decision and because I wasn't kind enough to say, "It's going to be me therefore there's going to be no discussion," I said [to the girls], "It's going to be one of you." I had actually made up my mind who I thought should go and then she decided that she couldn't do it. And so we had to make another decision. And so I went through the remaining three possibilities and Adrienne said that she wasn't fussed either way, she really wasn't. So, therefore, there were only two possibilities. And the way I made up my mind on that was that if the unthinkable were to happen again, Kathryn would leave behind a husband and four children if she were to go. So, I thought, it's got to be Pip. And that's how Pip got to go.'

Kathryn desperately wanted to see where her father died. But her eldest daughter had NCEA exams and Kathryn knew she ought to be in Auckland for her. Then her father came to her in a dream. It was a night in which five doors slammed unaccountably in the house. 'Look after the living, Kathryn. You look after the living.'

So it was Pip. Bachelor of Arts with First Class Honours in French from Otago, straight into the Ministry of Foreign Affairs as a diplomat, with service in Wellington, Canberra and Paris. She did eight years with Foreign Affairs, then worked in Australia for a couple of years. Since 2004 she has occupied a senior position at PricewaterhouseCoopers.

But before she flies to the ice, we must go back a little, to 2007.

In March 2007, on a Tuesday, Pip was in Auckland tooling round on the Internet. She saw there was to be a ceremony at Parliament on the Thursday to award medals to the New Zealanders and Americans who helped in all phases of the Erebus body recovery and identification. This was the New Zealand Special Service Medal (Erebus). She rang Police Headquarters.

They said she was welcome to come down. Pip hoped Inspector Greg Gilpin would be there. She knew of him. She knew he had been on the mountain early on in the body recovery. She wanted to go. To find, possibly, more pieces of the puzzle.

'What I've realised is that every time a big anniversary [of Erebus] comes around you start talking about it and it's like you enter this realm which is Erebus. And it's quite a draining place to be. It's as if you have to go there but when you start coming out of it again, and there's not so much media attention and people stop talking about it, you always felt a sense of relief that you can return to a sense of normality and you're out of that zone. Talking about it doesn't come cheap.'

Pip took a taxi from Wellington airport to Parliament. She was early so she bought a paper and repaired across the road to a small cafe. 'And I opened the paper and on page three or five there was a picture of a guy who'd come from the States to receive his medal. And I suddenly got the sense that this was going to be a bigger ceremony than I'd expected it to be. I really hadn't given it any thought other than that I wanted to go. It began to dawn on me that this was the first time I'd been to an Erebus ceremony on my own, as the only member of my family, and I wondered if I was going to have to deal with the media.'

In the Grand Hall she got a frightful shock. She saw a tall, erect, white-haired military-looking type. She knew immediately who he was. She reeled back into the corridor.

'I walked out and tried to call Mum. When I couldn't get hold of her I rang Kathryn and I just said, "My God, this is crazy, I've just seen Ron Chippindale." All I want to do is actually figure out how I handle this situation.

'Shit, what do I do? What do I say? What if I'm introduced to him? Do I try and meet his eyes. But the other thing was, the other thing that struck me was like, what is he doing here? I thought this was about the police, about the mortuary staff and the people who were involved in the recovery, what is Ron Chippindale doing here? That was my phone call to Kathryn.'

The answer was that this was Wellington and Ron Chippindale was the great, unbowed retired Chief Inspector of Air Accidents and he was, after all, on the mountain. Who was going to deny him?

Pip went back into the room. A group of women from Police Headquarters beckoned her over and she joined them. 'I didn't know anybody there. And

I asked one of them whether she knew Greg Gilpin and she did and she pointed him out. And lo and behold, there is this cop walking past and she introduced us and Greg just looked at me and he grabbed my hand and he just held it. He shook my hand but just kept on holding it.'

Inspector Greg Gilpin had wanted to meet the family of Captain Jim Collins for nearly 30 years.

'And he said, "I found your father on the mountain." And he said, he was . . . and this was all in the first couple of moments . . . he said, "and he was lying like he was propped up on his elbows, on his forearms and he was just looking down the mountain". And by this stage the room was really full and there were people buzzing round and it was like it was just the two of us at this thing. And I said, I mean, it sounds ridiculous now, I suppose, I said "Well, what do you mean propped up? Was he like this?" And he was like, "No, no, not like that".'

Pip said that in those first, crowded, breathless moments she wanted to know exactly how her father was when he was found frozen, in his short-sleeved, summer uniform shirt, the four stripes on the shoulders. And in this moment with Inspector Greg Gilpin she had something of what she went for.

Greg Gilpin went off to get his medal. At some stage a retired Air New Zealand DC-10 pilot, meaning it kindly no doubt, asked Pip if she wanted to meet Chippindale. It seems an extraordinarily gauche thing for such a man to have asked. She was curt. 'No thanks.'

She said it was a refusal not because she didn't feel she could cope: 'It was something that was very, it was like a deep . . . primeval is maybe too strong a word . . . it was a "I do not want to meet him".'

Next thing, the ceremony was over. Then it was a whirl and Pip was centre stage. 'And that's not a place I'm comfortable being in.' She met Annette King, the Police Minister. Greg Gilpin tried to get to talk to her again and he introduced Inspector Stu Leighton who was on the mountain with him — at the time, a 22-year-old constable.

'I remember standing talking to them on the side of the room where Chippindale had been, and I had these two uniformed policemen, who had this knowledge of what had been, what had gone on, and that's when I felt the sense of being completely safe and looked after. And invulnerable, in a way.'

Then the *Dominion Post* reporter wanted to talk to her. There were photos and downstairs Greg Gilpin was waiting for her. It was all a flurry, a rush of people and it was back off to the airport. But Greg Gilpin, at last, had met one of Jim Collins's daughters and had told her how her father was found, how he looked, that he was found intact and that in his opinion, the family could have viewed him upon the return of his body to Auckland.

Something had been nourished deep in the soul of Philippa Collins.

And she had proven to herself and to her mother that she could handle an Erebus ceremony on her own, a public appearance as a daughter of Captain Jim Collins. Maria smiles now at how amazed she was by Pip's attendance at the medal ceremony and how she conducted herself.

Then it was November 2009 and she was off to Antarctica where the cameras were waiting.

The night before they left, Pip and the five other family members of the deceased who were going on the trip had dinner together. A couple of them told her independently of each other that they did not blame her father for the Erebus disaster. 'It was special. I mean, hearing it from them gave a greater sense of Dad's vindication.'

All the way through the journey to the ice, Pip took emotional comfort from being one of a group who had shared the tragedy of 30 years before.

'Well, at least I'm one of six. So, I'm not the only one who's going through something emotional here. But even by their saying that . . . that they didn't hold Dad to blame . . . I then started to feel different again, because I was the captain's daughter. And that permeated the whole trip, the sameness and the difference, the sameness of the experience of grief and the difference coming from all the baggage that went with the inquiry and everything else that followed it. We were together and apart.'

On the way in, the American Globemaster approached Victoria Land as Jim Collins once had so long ago. Pip was taken up to the cockpit, this at the instigation, she thinks, of Captain Dave Morgan, Air New Zealand's chief pilot.

'I was the first person taken up. I was treated incredibly well. I was introduced to the captain and I just stood there and there was this incredible panorama like you could never imagine. It was like this vast white meringue that just went on and on and on and there were whole valleys of white with mountain peaks. As far as the eye could see. It was totally amazing and I was completely beside myself.

'This is Antarctica and this is what the crew would have seen as they were flying down. And what took me completely by surprise was that for a moment I felt like I was looking through Dad's eyes and I was seeing and experiencing something that he'd never been able to tell us about.'

The crew on the Globemaster flight deck were Americans, in their thirties. Pip was in her thirties. 'They were lovely, they were great guys. They had no idea what had hit them. They had this woman up there who was just, you know, weeping, trying to take videos and photos and weeping . . .'

I asked Pip Collins if she was thinking thoughts like, 'I'm coming to see you, Dad.'

'I felt, I felt . . . it was like this. It was like being in a parallel universe where you felt you could touch the other side. That's how it felt. And I couldn't say that to anybody on the plane because they didn't feel it the same because their relatives weren't up there [on the flight deck of the DC-10]. Their view would have been different. The only person I told it to was Mum that night when I phoned from Scott Base. And Mum said that [what I was feeling] was the experience Dad had that had been locked up inside him. And she understood it.'

They landed. The door opened. Pip Collins stepped out into a starkly brilliant blue and white Antarctic day. Someone said, 'There's Erebus.'

'And it was just there, right there in front of us as we walked. And it's this sort of innocuous-looking bump with smoke coming out of it. And it looked, it was just beautiful, the whole scene was just surreal in the sense that it was this beautifully clear day, you know, bright blue sky, sunshine, sparkling snow but this mountain was right there. And that was it.'

Next day, Pip and the camera crew — the ubiquitous camera crew — boarded a New Zealand helicopter for the trip across the saddle between Mount Bird and Mount Erebus to the crash site.

'And I'm thinking, the site must be way over somewhere and all of a sudden the site is there and they've pointed down to the cross that's been erected on the slope where the crash actually occurred. And it's an incredibly gentle slope. I mean, it doesn't even look like it's even a slope. There were the shadow of a few clouds on it but it was otherwise completely pristine. We went down very low, trying to land, but the pilot suddenly said, "It's just too windy".'

That was the closest Pip got to standing on the ground on which her father's aircraft crashed and disintegrated.

And on the ice, she was to have another dramatic experience. Shortly after they first landed at McMurdo, someone took a photograph of Pip with Erebus behind her in the distance. And Erebus was clearly visible.

'And then a couple of days later I took some photos in the same place and the weather is not quite as clear but it was still a nice day and you could see that everything was exactly the same in the photo as in the first one — except that Erebus has just vanished. And I remember asking our chopper pilot, "Well, where's Erebus?" And he said, "That's whiteout".'

I ask if it frightened her. 'No. It reassured me.'

She was on the phone to her mother and her sisters time and again. The Scott Base speakers announced constantly, 'Pip Collins, you've got a call.' Pip was experiencing Antarctica for all of them.

But she had dearly wanted to land, to stand at the site that had claimed her father and so many others. She had with her a small vial of sand from the beach at Matapouri Bay in Northland, the beach upon which she and her sisters had played with their mother and father summer after golden summer when life was perfect or, as Maria puts it, 'when we were just normal'.

Kathryn got Pip the sand. Kathryn asked the local tribal elders at Matapouri Bay if she might take a little from the beach so that Pip could take it with her to Antarctica. At an intimate ceremony the kaumatua blessed the sand, saying that it was going from one sacred place to another.

On Pip's last morning on the ice, she and a friend whose father also died on the DC-10, climbed Observation Hill, the hill between Scott and McMurdo Bases. She had kept the vial on her at all times. She hurried up the hill to be alone for some moments. She came close to the great cross erected for Captain Scott. She went to the highest point of the hill.

'I took it out and I just sprinkled it there, and a lot of the sand was picked up by the wind. And I thought of Matapouri and I thought of the ice and the snow and I thought of Dad and I just . . . I don't know. I had a sense of these two really different places somehow coming together. And I felt that was the most appropriate place to put it. The sand just dissolved into the wind.'

Pip was invited onto the flight deck for the take-off and the climb-out for the flight back to New Zealand. The American pilot had been in Christchurch for some days and he'd seen the publicity the trip to the ice was getting in New Zealand. He knew exactly who Pip was. He was a polar pilot himself. He flew for Alaska Airways. He knew whiteout.

And as the aircraft climbed to the north, straight up the middle of McMurdo Sound, Pip looked constantly out to the right at Erebus. She stared at it until the great mountain withdrew behind the aircraft and was gone.

She thought about her sisters. As they all do, always. They are all, always, thinking about each other. 'I mean, we rely on each other, possibly more so than other families.'

Pip's partner flies Airbus A330s and A340s in the left-hand seat for Cathay Pacific. He is a captain. He is the man she wants to spend the rest of her life with. This year she gave birth to their baby girl. She doesn't think this would have happened if she had not gone to Antarctica.

The sister with whom Pip is closest is Adrienne, the other of the two younger girls. The girls who were little when Jim Collins died.

'She's my best friend. Mum and Adrienne and I used to go on holidays together. Mum enrolled us in looking out for the next train stop or looking at the timetable or whatever it was. So we're all playing a part in making the trip work. We knew there was this big piece missing there and we had to try and make it easier for her.

'That's how I felt, anyway. And Adrienne and I have always got on well. It wasn't like we had to put our differences behind us and make this work. So we could go on holiday and have a pretty event-free time. And I think, if you talk to Kathryn, Kathryn would say that while Mum had a lot of stresses on, she didn't take them out on Adrienne and me. So we were quite protected from the big picture stuff that was going on; we were too young to understand anyway.'

And she thinks about her father: 'You know, there have been moments over the years when I've felt really angry about what I missed out on, in terms of not ever getting to know him really as a person. I can only rely on what other people have talked about, and my own memories of him as a father, but even they're fairly patchy. And I wonder what he would think of me now. When I graduated with first class honours, well, of course, I know he would have been proud but you don't get his reaction. When I had the posting in Paris at the Embassy and Mum came to see me every year, it was great, but wouldn't it have been fantastic if Dad could have seen and experienced this too?'

They have all survived, scarred but undamaged, as Maria Collins likes to say. 'Yes,' says Pip, 'we've survived and we are people like Mum and her parents, the role models who got us through, including those friends who also survived the Holocaust and helped us. So this crappy thing happened but we also were given the best possible way of surviving it. We were given the tools to survive it. I think for anyone who's been through a death or who has knowledge of grief, you have a greater understanding of the relativity of things. So when that other stuff is going on you have a scale in your own head about actually how important or not something is.'

Kathryn, too, yearns for her father at key moments in her own children's lives. Maria said that when she and Kathryn went to some school function in 2010, for example, when Kathryn's eldest daughter received a scholar award, 'Kathryn said, "Jim would have been so proud, he'd have loved to come to this." Each time, when each of the grandchildren was born Kathryn would say, "Jim would have been so proud." And then we'd fantasise about what it would have been like.'

Maria was very proud of how her third daughter handled herself in Antarctica for the thirtieth anniversary commemorations of the disaster. She was watching Pip closely on the Antarctic trip.

'Pip underrates herself a little bit. She always looked at herself as this sort of insignificant younger sister, number three, down the pecking order. And the brilliance and the loveliness of her really was made manifest when she went to Erebus. I mean, she looked stunning, she did. And she's very confident now, Pip. She's not flamboyant, she's not beautiful like Kathryn for all to see. She's not, "Right, we'll do this and then we'll do that," as Elizabeth is. Pip can work out how something works and if all of a sudden there's a crisis, then you'll know about her. Pip goes along very quietly. There are no dramas like there could be with Kathryn and Elizabeth. But when Pip's had enough, oh boy, then she explodes. But it takes a lot to make her explode.'

And Adrienne. Still waters run deep, says Maria of Didi.

At the end of her seventh form year, Didi wrote a story called 'Kingdom in the Sky' that was published in the school magazine. A little girl, Emma, went to a funeral for someone unnamed, obviously close. It was raining, just like it always rains on the important occasions, thought Emma. There were flowers, there was a cemetery and they came home.

The story is about adults talking above her and down to her, as if she understood nothing. Whoever dies goes to a kingdom in the sky, she had been told. She knew what the man meant. He meant heaven.

> Voices upstairs recited the same pity lines. The smell of flowers made her feel ill. Plonking herself on her bed tummy-down, she sighed deeply to herself. Emma lifted her head and looked imploringly at the sky. She laid her head back on the pillow and felt a single fat tear slip silently down her cheek. Outside it had stopped raining.

Adrienne was six when her father was killed. For months afterwards, she slept in Maria's bed every night, to make sure Maria stayed alive.

Adrienne wrote to me: 'I had a fear for a number of years that Mum would die too. Every time she went out I'd say to her, "Don't die," which I would abbreviate to "Don't." She'd reply, with a laugh, "Oh don't worry, I won't." Poor Mum, having a kid put a guilt trip on you like that every time you left the bloody house.

'I always loved Air New Zealand as a kid, thought flying and hostesses were so glamorous. I wanted to be one. The hostesses would ask if I wanted to hand out the sweets. I hated doing that. I was so shy. When we went on long car trips Dad would always make me a little bed in the back of the station wagon for me and I think for Pip too. With my favourite blanket.

'At the tenth anniversary of the crash [November 1989], we had a remembrance service at a little church. Pip was on holiday in Melbourne with Elizabeth. There was a sprig of rosemary stuck to the front of the programme with the quote about remembrance, from Hamlet: *There's rosemary, that's for remembrance. Pray you, Love, remember*. It was a crappy day. I was sitting next to Kathryn. I was 16 now and I remember thinking there must be a leak in the roof because I could feel water falling on me. Then I realised it was Kathryn's tears.'

Two years after her father died, Kathryn sat Bursary examinations. She scored 96 per cent in both English and Art History.

A year after her husband was killed, after the Royal Commission of inquiry had reported, Maria attended an Air New Zealand function. Morrie Davis greeted her. Quietly he suggested, 'Let's let bygones be bygones.' Maria replied, 'Never.'

Pip's flight from Antarctica, ending her epic emotional journey to the ice, landed in Christchurch. She asked Lou Sanson, head of Antarctica New Zealand, if a certain fish shop still existed. He confirmed it did. Pip said she had business there.

Maria drove out to meet Pip at Auckland Airport. As Pip came out to the car, she held up a white plastic bag.

'Blue cod,' she said, with her sudden wide smile. 'I've got the blue cod.'

It is a Friday evening. I've called round to Kathryn and Luke's for a drink. Maria is there. The house is a flurry of activity. Kathryn's eldest, aged 17, is running late for a pre-ball party. This is the end of the world. Her daughter has all the beauty of youth. Dad wants a picture. So does Maria. Photos are taken. I'm sitting at the dining room table. Kathryn is standing to my left. I look up at her. Her smile is radiant. Her eyes are sparkling sapphire.

Kathryn is looking after the living.

Epilogue

Erebus is what Margarita's son Tim calls her 'unwarranted burden'.

A few days before the memorial services to commemorate the thirtieth anniversary of the Erebus disaster, in November 2009, Margarita Mahon took a phone call from Hawke's Bay, from a man who lost two relatives in the crash. He wanted to tell her, he said, how much the Commissioner's report had meant to him and how much it had relieved his grieving. It gave reason to what happened.

Margarita found herself thinking about the call. She went and retrieved the letters that came in from round the country and round the world from loved ones of the deceased, thanking the judge for the clarity he gave to it all, for explaining what had happened, thanking him for the comfort he brought.

Margarita doesn't do the Erebus ceremonies. But she found herself thinking about the call from Hawke's Bay. At 81 years old, she drove to the Waikumete Cemetery for the memorial service to be held in the Erebus Memorial Garden. It is here that the bodies and body parts of those 44 passengers who could not be identified are buried in a mass grave.

She intended, she says, to stand with those who still mourn.

'It was an afternoon of sun and showers with puffs of cloud being blown across a blue sky. This garden is a peaceful place with a central marble column bearing the names of crew and passengers resting there, and identifying the countries involved. I placed some flowers at the base of the memorial and moved into the crowd.'

Suddenly, a tall young man appeared and asked her if she had a seat. She said she was quite happy to stand. '"You will have a seat," he insisted, and he guided me to a seating area. And he said, "I feel most honoured to give you my seat." I noticed it was one set aside for Members of Parliament. Recognition of my presence then brought about many handshakes and good wishes.'

At 3 p.m. the service started. There was a prayer.

'A young lady stepped forward to lead us in the New Zealand national anthem. Her strong voice encompassed us as the rain fell gently. The sun came out for the speeches. In silence, the names of those buried at the cemetery were read out, followed by the laying of wreaths by representatives from the Waitakere Council, the New Zealand Government, Air New Zealand, the New Zealand Police and the Consulates of Australia, Canada, France, Japan and the United States. Family and friends were invited to lay tributes in front of the memorial. From a large wicker basket of long-stemmed white roses little children joined men and women of varying ages in laying these roses in remembrance. Thirty years on there were still tears.

'There was a minute's silence to remember the deceased. As the service closed, the sun reappeared. The beautiful flowers, the damp bushes and the moving clouds became a poignant backdrop for the strong unaccompanied voice singing "Amazing Grace". As I drove away from the ceremony, I felt the warmth of the expressed gratitude to Peter spanning more than 28 years.'

In 2009, Margarita was invited to accept, on behalf of Peter, the Jim Collins Memorial Award, now a major international aviation medal, during a conference of the Federation of International Airline Pilots in Auckland.

Kathryn Carter was asked to make the presentation.

As Margarita Mahon approached the stage, 500 international airline pilots from around the world gave her — and Peter Mahon — a prolonged standing ovation.

It might have seemed to Margarita at that moment that the applause might never end.

Notes

Chapter 3: It Got Too Hard

1. McGee, 2008
2. *Aircraft Accident Report*, para. 3.37
3. Royal Commission transcript, p. 211
4. Royal Commission, para. 71
5. Royal Commission, para. 393

Chapter 4: McMurdo

1. Macfarlane, p. 270
2. Vette & Macdonald, p. 119
3. ibid., p. 226
4. ibid.
5. Hickson, p. 87

Chapter 6: Alan Dorday Works it Out

1. Macfarlane, p. 287
2. ibid.
3. ibid., p. 288
4. ibid.
5. ibid.
6. ibid., p. 289
7. Royal Commission, para. 360

Chapter 8: The Ring Binder

1. Macfarlane, p. 155
2. Royal Commission, para. 227
3. ibid., para. 240
4. ibid., para. 241
5. ibid., para. 240
6. Royal Commission transcript, p. 1138 (T1138), as quoted in Vette & Macdonald, p. 305
7. Mahon's memo recording his meeting with Maria Collins, February 1981
8. Royal Commission, para. 259
9. T1808
10. T1784
11. Burgess Report, August 2008, p. 3
12. Royal Commission, para. 354
13. Burgess Report, p. 4
14. P. Mahon, 1984, pp. 142–3
15. Burgess Report, p. 8
16. ibid., conclusion 5
17. ibid., conclusion 13

Chapter 9: The Trials of John Blumsky

1. Hickson, p. 103

Chapter 10: The Centrality of Chippindale

1. P. Mahon, 1984, p. 63
2. *Aircraft Accident Report*, para. 1.17.46–1.17.58 and Royal Commission, para. 165
3. *Aircraft Accident Report*, 1.17.48
4. ibid., 1.17.46
5. ibid., 1.17.47
6. P. Mahon, 1984, p. 42
7. ibid.
8. *Aircraft Accident Report*, para. 3.37
9. Hickson, p. 211
10. ibid., p. 221
11. Royal Commission transcript, p. 242 (T242)
12. Chippindale press release, pp. 6–8
13. T211
14. Royal Commission, para. 71
15. T242 as quoted in Vette & Macdonald, Notes on Text, p. 308
16. T1713
17. Vette & Macdonald, Notes on Text, p. 308
18. Royal Commission Exhibit 38
19. Macfarlane, p. 477
20. Vette & Macdonald, p. 119
21. Chippindale press release, p. 8
22. Royal Commission, para. 289(d)
23. ibid., para. 33
24. *Aircraft Accident Report*, para. 1.7.2c

25. P. Mahon, 1984, p. 61
26. ibid., pp. 61–2
27. *North and South*, November 1989, p. 78
28. Chippindale press release, p. 2
29. ibid., p. 19
30. Vette & Macdonald, p. 301
31. ibid., Notes on Text
32. Macfarlane, p. 39

Chapter 11: What Chippindale Said and Why He Was Wrong

1. Vette & Macdonald, Notes on Text, p. 315, Exhibit 55
2. ibid., Exhibit 58
3. Royal Commission, para. 151
4. *Aircraft Accident Report*, para. 3.36
5. Royal Commission transcript, p. 75 (T75)
6. T306
7. T309
8. Vette & Macdonald, Notes on Text, p. 342
9. ibid., pp. 341–2
10. T186
11. T309
12. T186
13. T306
14. T75
15. T189
16. Macfarlane, p. 340
17. ibid., p. 39
18. Royal Commission, para. 256
19. ibid., para. 196
20. ibid., para. 334(1)
21. ibid., para. 334(2)
22. ibid., para. 334(2)
23. ibid., para. 335

Chapter 12: Chippindale and the Cockpit Transcript

1. *New Zealand Herald*, 1 December 2004
2. Royal Commission, para. 102
3. ibid., para. 103
4. ibid., para. 103–6
5. ibid., para. 108
6. *Aircraft Accident Report*, para. 3.24
7. Vette & Macdonald, p. 256
8. ibid., Notes on Text, p. 343
9. Royal Commission, para. 118
10. Chippindale press release, p. 9
11. Royal Commission, para. 121
12. Vette & Macdonald, p. 149
13. Memorandum of the Royal Commissioner [to counsel] as to Evidence and Information Obtained Overseas. Vette & Macdonald, p. 287
14. Royal Commission, para. 198
15. ibid., para. 289(f)

Chapter 13: Enter Justice Peter Mahon

1. P. Mahon, 1984, p. 35
2. *Coleman v Myers* (1977) 2 NZLR 225
3. S. Mahon, Introduction
4. Macfarlane, p. 35
5. ibid., p. 39
6. Royal Commission, para. 377
7. S. Mahon, p. 130
8. Macfarlane, p. 36
9. P. Mahon, 1984, p. 43
10. ibid., p. 44
11. P. Mahon, 1984, p. 38
12. ibid.
13. Royal Commission, para. 78–97

Chapter 14: Mahon Begins to Wonder

1. P. Mahon, 1984, p. 239
2. ibid.
3. Macfarlane, p. 323
4. P. Mahon, 1984, p. 75
5. ibid., p. 76
6. Macfarlane, p. 161
7. P. Mahon, 1984, p. 78
8. ibid., p. 79
9. ibid., p. 89
10. ibid., p. 81
11. ibid., p. 84
12. ibid., p. 223
13. ibid., p. 251
14. ibid., p. 85
15. ibid.
16. ibid., p. 223

17. ibid., p. 86
18. ibid.
19. ibid., p. 87
20. ibid., p. 88
21. ibid.

Chapter 15: Captain Keesing Shows Up

1. P. Mahon, 1984, p. 127
2. ibid., p. 130
3. ibid.
4. ibid.
5. ibid.
6. ibid., p. 131
7. Vette & Macdonald, p. 96
8. Macfarlane, p. 212
9. ibid., p. 227
10. ibid., p. 213
11. P. Mahon, 1984, p. 119
12. Macfarlane, p. 214
13. P. Mahon, 1984, p. 118
14. ibid.
15. Royal Commission para. 289(k)
16. ibid.
17. P. Mahon, 1984, p. 118
18. Vette & Macdonald, Foreword
19. P. Mahon, 1984, p. 121
20. ibid.
21. ibid.
22. Royal Commission transcript, p. 1687
23. P. Mahon, 1984, p. 119

Chapter 16: Mahon in Wonderland

1. Vette & Macdonald, p. 207
2. Royal Commission, para. 40(b)
3. ibid.
4. ibid., para. 229
5. *Weekend Star*, 1 January 1980
6. *Auckland Star*, 26 February 1980
7. Royal Commission, para. 289(g)
8. ibid.
9. ibid.
10. Royal Commission, para. 381
11. Vette & Macdonald, Epilogue, p. 197
12. ibid., p. 198
13. S. Mahon, p. 16
14. ibid., p. 85

Chapter 17: The 'Mistake' is Corrected

1. Royal Commission, para. 239
2. ibid., para. 240
3. ibid., para. 241
4. Vette & Macdonald, p. 253
5. Royal Commission, para. 240
6. Royal Commission transcript, p. 1680
7. Vette & Macdonald, p. 227
8. Macfarlane, p. 243
9. ibid.
10. ibid., p. 252
11. ibid.
12. Royal Commission, para. 243
13. Gabriel's brief of evidence, Macfarlane, p. 232
14. Macfarlane, p. 261
15. Royal Commission, para. 243
16. Vette & Macdonald, pp. 204–5
17. Royal Commission, para. 244
18. ibid., para. 245(b)
19. ibid., para. 255(d)
20. ibid., para. 247
21. ibid., para. 250
22. P. Mahon, 1984, p. 141
23. Royal Commission, para. 255(f)

Chapter 21: What Gemmell Knew and Oldfield Did Not

1. Royal Commission, para. 48
2. T1806/8 as quoted in Macfarlane, pp. 295–7
3. Conversation, Paul Davison/David Greenwood
4. Macfarlane, p. 298
5. ibid.
6. Royal Commission transcript, p. 1858 (T1858)
7. T1852
8. Royal Commission, para. 362
9. ibid., para. 54
10. T1875

11. Royal Commission, para. 341
12. ibid., para. 44–5
13. McGee, pp. 256–7
14. Royal Commission, para. 48
15. ibid.
16. ibid.
17. ibid.
18. T1962
19. T1963/4
20. Hickson, pp. 199–200
21. T1791
22. T1797
23. ibid.
24. T1812
25. T1827/8
26. T1833/4

Chapter 22: Gordon Vette Shows Up

1. Vette & Macdonald, p. 168
2. ibid., p. 169
3. P. Mahon, 1984, p. 152
4. Royal Commission, para. 40(a)
5. ibid., para. 165
6. Macfarlane, pp. 113–4
7. Royal Commission, para. 168
8. Macfarlane, p. 117
9. ibid., p. 115
10. Vette & Macdonald, p. 171
11. ibid.
12. ibid., p. 173
13. P. Mahon, 1984, p. 153
14. ibid., p. 154
15. Royal Commission transcript, p. 1803
16. P. Mahon, 1984, pp. 193–4
17. ibid., p. 199
18. ibid., pp. 198–201
19. Royal Commission, para. 289(i)

Chapter 23: The Malevolent Trick of the Polar Light

1. Royal Commission, para. 277
2. ibid., para. 279
3. P. Mahon, 1984, p. 206
4. ibid., p. 207
5. Royal Commission, para. 175–98
6. ibid., para. 172
7. P. Mahon, 1984, p. 159
8. ibid., p. 160
9. ibid., p. 162
10. ibid., p. 207
11. ibid., p. 207–8
12. ibid., p. 208
13. ibid.
14. Royal Commission, para. 284–7
15. P. Mahon, 1984, p. 209
16. Royal Commission, para. 177/180/181
17. P. Mahon, 1984, p. 209
18. Royal Commission, para. 284
19. ibid., para. 288

Chapter 24: The Wise Mr Tench and the Clever Mr Martin

1. P. Mahon, 1984, p. 142
2. ibid., p. 143
3. ibid., p. 148
4. ibid.
5. ibid., p. 149
6. ibid.
7. ibid., p. 166
8. ibid.
9. ibid.
10. ibid., p. 169
11. ibid., p. 170
12. ibid., p. 180
13. ibid., p. 183
14. ibid.
15. ibid., p. 184
16. ibid.
17. ibid., p. 186
18. ibid., pp. 186–7
19. ibid., p. 187
20. ibid., p. 188
21. ibid.
22. ibid.
23. ibid., p. 189
24. ibid.
25. ibid.
26. ibid., p. 190
27. ibid.
28. ibid., p. 253

29. ibid., pp. 253–4
30. ibid., p. 254

Chapter 25: The Girls Meet the Judge

1. *Aircraft Accident Report*, para. 2.5
2. Royal Commission, para. 258
3. Royal Commission transcript, p. 242
4. Royal Commission, para. 259
5. ibid., para. 260
6. ibid.
7. P. Mahon, 1984, p. 213
8. ibid., p. 215
9. ibid., pp. 215–6
10. ibid., p. 217
11. ibid.
12. ibid., p. 213
13. Email to Paul Davison, 5 December 2009
14. Chippindale press release, pp. 7–8
15. Macfarlane, p. 336

Chapter 26: The Report is Released

1. Macfarlane, pp. 497–9
2. S. Mahon, p. 37
3. Royal Commission, para. 147(a)
4. ibid., para. 148
5. ibid., para. 149(b)/(c)
6. ibid., para. 149(d)
7. ibid., para 149(f)
8. ibid., para. 149(g)
9. ibid., para. 149(h)
10. ibid., para. 381(c)
11. ibid., para. 381(a)
12. ibid., para. 381(c)
13. ibid.
14. ibid., para. 373
15. P. Mahon, 1984, p. 247
16. ibid., p. 227
17. ibid., p. 228
18. Royal Commission, para. 373
19. P. Mahon, 1984, pp. 247–8
20. McGee, p. 244
21. ibid.
22. P. Mahon, 1984, p. 251
23. ibid.
24. ibid.
25. McGee, p. 248
26. P. Mahon, 1984, p. 35
27. ibid.
28. Macfarlane, p. 40

Chapter 27: The Courts Thump Mahon

1. Papers of Margarita Mahon
2. ibid.
3. Cooke Judgement, Court of Appeal, *Re Erebus Royal Commission; Air New Zealand Ltd v Mahon (No 2)* [1981] 1 NZLR 618
4. Royal Commission, para. 45
5. NZLR, p. 638 (see n. 3)
6. NZLR, p. 649
7. ibid.
8. L. Brown, Final submission, Royal Commission
9. P. Mahon, 1984, p. 237
10. Royal Commission, Appendix, p. 167
11. P. Mahon, 1984, p. 237
12. New Zealand publication of the full letter, *NZ Herald*, 29 January 1982
13. Privy Council, *Re Erebus Royal Commission; Air New Zealand v Mahon* [1983] NZLR 662
14. NZLR, p. 686 (see n. 13)
15. NZLR, p. 674
16. NZLR, p. 674
17. NZLR, p. 662
18. NZLR, p. 685
19. NZLR, p. 685
20. NZLR, p. 684
21. NZLR, p. 675
22. NZLR, p. 685
23. NZLR, p. 665
24. NZLR, p. 687
25. McGee, p. 253

Chapter 28: Farewell Mr Mahon

1. P. Mahon, 1984, p. 295
2. Richards, p. 123
3. ibid., pp. 123–4
4. ibid., p. 124
5. S. Mahon, 2008, p. 189

Bibliography

Aircraft Accident Report No. 79-139, Air New Zealand McDonnell Douglas DC10-30 ZK-NZP, Ross Island, Antarctica, 28 November 1979, Office of Air Accidents, Ministry of Transport, Wellington, 1981.

Beaty, David. *The Naked Pilot: The Human Factor in Aircraft Accidents*, Airlife Publishing, 1995.

Chippindale, R. *Comments on the report of the Royal Commission to inquire into the accident involving an Air New Zealand DC-10 aircraft in Antarctica on 28 November 1979*, Office of Air Accidents Investigation, Wellington, 1982.

Cooke Judgement, Court of Appeal, *Re Erebus Royal Commission, Air New Zealand Ltd v Mahon* [1981] 1 NZLR 618

Hickson, Ken. *Flight 901 to Erebus*, Whitcoulls, Christchurch, 1980.

Macfarlane, Stuart, ed. *The Erebus Papers*, Avon Press, Auckland, 1991.

McGee, Greg. *Tall Tales (Some True)*. Penguin Books, Auckland, 2008. ('Memoirs of an Unlikely Writer: Dancing on the Coffins of the Dead', Chapter 14)

McMullin, Duncan. *A Lawyer's Tale*, Auckland District Law Society, Auckland, 2008.

Mahon, Peter. *Verdict on Erebus*. Collins, Auckland, 1984.

Mahon, Peter. *Dear Sam . . .*, Fontana/Collins, Auckland, 1985.

Mahon, Sam. *My Father's Shadow: a Portrait of Justice Peter Mahon*. Longacre, Dunedin, 2008.

Privy Council, *Re Erebus Royal Commission; Air New Zealand v Mahon* [1983] NZLR.

Richards, Raymond. *Palmer: The Parliamentary Years*, Canterbury University Press, Christchurch, 2010.

Royal Commission. *Report of the Royal Commission to Inquire into the Crash on Mount Erebus, Antarctica, of a DC10 Aircraft Operated by Air New Zealand Limited*, Government Printer, Wellington, 1981.

Shackleton, Ernest. *South: the Endurance Expedition*, Penguin, London, 1999. (Originally published as *South: the Story of Shackleton's Last Expedition 1914–1917*, W. Heinemann, London, 1919.)

Vette, Gordon & Macdonald, John. *Impact Erebus* (Foreword by Hon P. T. Mahon QC), Hodder & Stoughton, Auckland, 1983.

Woodhouse Judgment, Court of Appeal, Re Erebus Royal Commission; Air New Zealand Ltd. v Mahon (No 2) [1981] 1 NZLR.

The interviews by the author with Maria Collins, Kathryn Carter and Elizabeth, Pip and Adrienne Collins and Margarita Mahon were conducted in the winter of 2010.

Index